TRAIL OF MIRACLES

TRAIL OF MIRACLES

STORIES FROM A PILGRIMAGE
IN NORTHEAST BRAZIL

Candace Slater

University of California Press / Berkeley / Los Angeles / London

University of California Press
Berkeley and Los Angeles, California

University of California Press, Ltd.
London, England

© 1986 by
The Regents of the University of California

Library of Congress Cataloging in Publication Data

Slater, Candace.
  Trail of miracles.

  Bibliography: p.
  Includes index.
  1. Batista, Cícero Romão, 1844–1934—Legends.
2. Christian pilgrims and pilgrimages—Brazil—Juazeiro
do Norte. 3. Juazeiro do Norte (Brazil)—Religious life
and customs. 4. Story-telling—Brazil—Juazeiro do Norte.
I. Title.
BX4705.B25317S53 1986 248.4′63′098131 84–16236
ISBN 0–520–05306–0

Printed in the United States of America

1 2 3 4 5 6 7 8 9

For my father,
whose heart went out to
the people of Brazil

Oh que caminho tão longe, cheio de atravessia.
Saí no frio da noite, levei sol do meiodia.

Oh what a distant road, full of crossings!
I set out in the cold of night,
I endured the midday sun.

Northeast Brazilian
pilgrim song

Contents

Acknowledgments

This study was made possible through the financial support of the John Simon Guggenheim Foundation, which also provided a generous publication subvention. The American Philosophical Society of Philadelphia and the National Endowment for the Humanities supplied supplementary grants. I am grateful as well to the Tinker Foundation and the Fulbright Commission for sponsoring previous fieldwork in Northeast Brazil.

I owe much of what I learned about the Padre Cícero stories to Francisca Inácio da Costa, in whose home in the Rua do Horto I lived for seven months. I am equally grateful to Anne Dumoulin and Therezinha Stella Guimarães, researchers and pastoral workers. I would like to thank the other members of their congregation, as well as Padre Murilo de Sá Barreto, Padre José Alves de Oliveira, Padre Antonio Elias Cedraz of the Salesian Archives, and author Dona Amália Xavier de Oliveira, for their assistance in Juazeiro do Norte. Dom Miguel Fenelon Câmara and Dona Maria Ivanilde dos Santos aided me in Maceió; Frei Lucas Dolle and Antonio Mourão Cavalcante facilitated my research in Canindé. I also benefited from contact with Riolando Azzi and Rubém César Fernandes, in Rio de Janeiro, and Ralph della Cava, who was in Fortaleza during part of my stay in the Northeast. I am grateful as well for the hospitality of Luis and Mariza Velho and their daughters in Rio de Janeiro, of Lucíola Halliday in Recife, and of Emília Pedreira in Fortaleza.

A multidisciplinary conference, "Pilgrimage: The Human Experience," which was held in Pittsburgh during May of 1981, raised questions that helped guide my research. I thank the conference's organizer, E. Alan Morinis, and the leader of the Latin American section, N. Ross Crumrine. I have other, longstanding debts to Elizabeth Kirk, who awakened my interest in medieval literary forms when I was an undergraduate at Brown University; to Morton Gorden and the late Daniel Lerner for their introduction to the social sciences during a year of study in a half-dozen Asian and European countries through the International Honors Program; and to the late J. Edward Dirks who, as vicechancellor for the humanities at the University of California, Santa Cruz, encouraged my interdisciplinary interests at a critical moment in my academic life.

The first draft of this book took shape at the Stanford University Center for Latin American Studies, whose then-director John Wirth was particularly helpful to me when I was a graduate student. In California, I had the inspiration and encouragement of Samuel G. Armistead, Alan Dundes, James Fernandez, Bernard Siegel, and, especially, Peter Brown, who forced me to rethink the basic premise of a "life." Back in Philadelphia, my friends and colleagues Dan Ben-Amos, Sylvia Brown, Lee Cassanelli, Nancy Farriss, Daniel Hirschberg, and Gerald Prince helped me through various revisions. Doris Kretschmer, Jane-Ellen Long, and Mary Renaud of the University of California Press played a significant role in seeing this book into print. Very special thanks go to David Staebler for his skilled professional printing of the photographs I took in Brazil, and to Professor Benjamin W. Woodbridge, Jr., for his knowledge and his most painstaking editorial assistance.

My parents, Frank and Adelaide Nielsen Slater, helped me unstintingly in the preparation of this manuscript. Agnes C. Robinson and her family provided added support. Special thanks are due my husband, Paul Zingg, for his patience during repeated separations and his good humor throughout the long months in which the manuscript took shape.

My biggest debt is to the storytellers whom I met in Juazeiro. In the course of writing, I have often thought back upon a group of pilgrims from João Alfredo, Pernambuco, who, after spending several hours one night exchanging tales of Padre Cícero, invited me to return the next morning before they set out for home. When I arrived at the makeshift hotel in which they had been staying, however, the group was nowhere to be seen. The owner of the house explained that the driver of their truck had advanced the hour of their departure, then handed me a crumpled envelope which the travelers had left for me. It contained several tattered bills plus an assortment of coins, and "To help pay for the airplane" was laboriously lettered across the front. I have tried my best to make this book worthy of these individuals' generosity. I thank them and all those who shared their stories with me.

Introduction

> And if the story which I am about to tell you is not a
> miracle, then there are no miracles left in the world today.
>
> Pilgrim from Paraíba

"Juazeiro do Norte?" exclaim educated Brazilians in Rio de Janeiro or São Paulo if one tells them one's destination. "You mean that you are headed for 'my Padrinho's' Juazeiro!" They are talking about a city that has become synonymous with a major pilgrimage in honor of Padre Cícero Romão Batista, a Roman Catholic priest who died in 1934. Their lighthearted tone and perhaps assumed Northeastern accent imply that they do not count themselves among the priest's followers. If, however, the conversation turns to Padre Cícero or Juazeiro, their interest is clear. The pilgrimage, which draws a million visitors yearly, is not the largest in this, the world's biggest Catholic nation.[1] Nevertheless, it is the one that most fascinates and baffles the non-believer.

This perplexity is not hard to understand. Juazeiro is unique not only in Brazil but also in the modern world. Almost a century old, it is the

---

1. Brazil has over 131 million people. It is the world's sixth largest country in terms both of size and of population.

The biggest pilgrimages in Brazil, all located in or near major urban centers, are Nossa Senhora de Nazaré or the Círio in Belém do Pará, Nosso Senhor do Bonfim in Itapagipe (Salvador), Bahia, and Nossa Senhora Aparecida not far from the city of São Paulo. Other pilgrimages, more or less comparable in scope to Juazeiro, are São Francisco das Chagas in Canindé, Ceará, and Bom Jesus da Lapa on the São Francisco River in Bahia. Bom Jesus de Pirapora in the state of São Paulo is another major center. For a list of studies on Brazilian pilgrimages see Pedro A. Ribeiro de Oliveira, "Expressões religiosas populares e liturgia." Recent studies of note that are not on Oliveira's list are Isidoro Maria da Silva Alves, "O carnaval devoto": Um estudo sobre a Festa de Nazaré em Belém; Rubém César Fernandes, Os cavaleiros do Bom Jesus: Uma introdução às religiões populares; Maria Cecília França, Pequenos centros de devoção paulistas de função religiosa; and Therezinha Stella Guimarães, "Os jovens de Juazeiro do Norte e sua devoção ao Padre Cícero." Two important doctoral dissertations are Therezinha Stella Guimarães, "Etude psychologique de la fonction d'un Saint dans le catholicisme populaire," and Pierre Sanchis, "Arraial—la fête d'un peuple," which has been translated into Portuguese in revised book form as Arraial: A festa de um povo.

only Christian pilgrimage of its magnitude in honor of a non-saint.[2] There have been and continue to be numerous local "holy men" like Padre Cícero among Hispanic populations.[3] Don Pedrito Jaramillo in southern Texas, Cura Brochero near Córdoba in Argentina, and Fray Leopoldo de Alpandeire in southern Spain are only a few of many twentieth-century heirs to a broader Mediterranean tradition that has roots in antiquity.[4] None of these figures, however, has managed to generate as large a following as that of the priest of Juazeiro. Padre Cícero has become a symbol of a way of life, a social class, and a region comprising nine states and more than 35 million people. The devotion to him is presently spreading into the industrial south as Northeasterners migrate in search of better-paying jobs. To say, however, that one is a follower of the priest is still tantamount to declaring, "I am poor, I subscribe at least in name to a series of traditional values, and I am a Northeast Brazilian."

This study constitutes a literary ethnography.[5] It is narrower in scope than more conventional ethnographies because I did not set out to describe a culture or representative aspect of a culture. I began and ended with a group of stories—technically, legends—which happened to prove inseparable from a larger social frame. I did not try to enrich a textual

2. There are presently over a thousand Christian pilgrimages in the world that draw more than one thousand people yearly. The great majority of these, however, are in honor of officially recognized saints. For an overview see Victor Turner and Edith Turner, *Image and Pilgrimage in Christian Culture.*

3. Present-day miracle workers are not limited to Hispanic populations. One of the better-known of these holy figures is Padre Pio of Pietrelcina (1887–1968) in southern Italy. See Malachy Carroll and Pol de Leon Albaret's laudatory *Three Studies in Simplicity: Padre Pio, Martin de Porres, Benedict the Black.*

For another useful parallel see Issachar Ben-Ami, "Folk Veneration of Saints among the Moroccan Jews (Tradition: Continuity and Change. The Case of the Holy Man, Rabbi David u-Moshe)."

4. For a discussion of don Pedrito Jaramillo (who was a *curandero* or medicine man rather than a priest), see Octavio Ignacio Romano V., "Charismatic Medicine, Folk-Healing, and Folk-Sainthood." An uncritical biography of Fray Leopoldo is Angel de León's *Mendigo por Dios: Vida de Fray Leopoldo de Alpandeire.* I am grateful to my colleague José Regueiro for information regarding Cura Brochero. For an introduction to the Mediterranean holy man of whom Padre Cícero is surely a latter-day descendant see Peter Brown, "The Rise and Function of the Holy Man in Late Antiquity," in Brown, *Society and the Holy in Late Antiquity.* See also Brown, "The Saint as Exemplar in Late Antiquity," and David Lenz Tiede, *The Charismatic Figure as Miracle Worker.* The reader may also wish to consult Stephen Wilson, ed., *Saints and their Cults: Studies in Religious Sociology, Folklore and History,* which includes an excellent bibliography (pp. 309–417).

5. After deciding on this description I was pleased to discover R. Howard Bloch's *Etymologies and Genealogies: A Literary Anthropology of the French Middle Ages.* The introduction (pp. 1–29) discusses some of the problems faced by both anthropologists and literary scholars in attempting to interpret another culture.

analysis by introducing supplementary cultural material or to illustrate cultural propositions through literary means. Instead, I attempted to see a group of stories (or perhaps the stories insisted that I see them) as an expression of individuals who define themselves largely in terms of interpersonal obligations. Although all human beings are necessarily part of a larger cultural matrix, a sizable number of Northeast Brazilians still find themselves enmeshed in a rigid hierarchy of the sort most commonly associated with the Middle Ages. It is therefore almost impossible to speak of the Padre Cícero stories without reference to the community upon which they draw and into which they feed.

The pitfalls inherent in any ethnography are present in this study.[6] Just as each storyteller creates a slightly different Padre Cícero through the ordering and selection of multiple elements, so by choosing to stress certain aspects of their narratives and not others, I have in a sense helped to fashion the tales I relate. Then, too, in the same way that these individuals' circumstances are reflected in their accounts of miraculous actions, my own identity is apparent in the questions I do, and in those I do not, pose. I hope, however, that while this discussion reveals my empathetic blind spots as well as the limitations of my fieldwork, it also possesses some of the advantages of an ethnography. Chief among these are an openness to varied oral and written sources, a willingness to watch and listen, and a conscious vulnerability.

There are many reasons to be interested in the stories people tell about Padre Cícero. First, they constitute extraordinary social documents. The faith in "my" (never "our") Padrinho or "Godfather" serves as a confirmation of a highly personalistic patron–dependent system, which has managed to survive in fragmented form into the present. These stories show that in spite of dramatic changes in the Northeast over the last few decades, the past continues to exert a powerful hold.

Because of their association with a pilgrimage over which the ecclesiastical establishment exerts minimal control, the tales are reflections of regional as well as universal folk beliefs. Although the secular clergy and monastic orders are strong today in Juazeiro, longstanding hostility to Padre Cícero has limited the church's involvement with his followers. As a result, these tales reflect the Northeastern poor with unusually little contamination from other sources.

---

6. For an analysis of some of the problems inherent in ethnographical description see James Clifford, "On Ethnographic Authority," and Vincent Crapanzano, "On the Writing of Ethnography." A helpful overview of past and present ethnographical approaches is George Marcus and Dick Cushman's "Ethnographies as Texts." See also James A. Boon, *Other Tribes, Other Scribes: Symbolic Anthropology in the Comparative Study of Cultures.*

The stories are equally important as a special form of artistic creation. The great majority of the miracles attributed to the priest recall others dating back many centuries. A knowledge of hagiography therefore enriches understanding of these contemporary narratives, while they in turn shed invaluable light on their forebears. The miracle tales and saints' lives that have come down to us are the written work of educated compilers or, in the case of shrine books, literate notaries. Although a Jacobus de Voragine or a Caesarius of Heisterbach must have drawn heavily on oral traditions, they were individuals with a particular ideological formation as well as a narrative style. The Padre Cícero narratives therefore offer a means of distinguishing the living voices often hidden beneath the surface of much older, printed texts.

At the same time, the tales provide a dramatic illustration of the resilience of all symbolic forms. By focusing on differences and then similarities between stories told by residents and by pilgrims to Juazeiro, this study underscores the ability of a literary genre to adapt to continually shifting demands.

Even though not all citizens of Padre Cícero's adopted city believe in his thaumaturgic powers, perhaps as many as three-quarters do. I will therefore use the term *resident* to mean *resident believer* unless otherwise indicated. The outward sign of these people's faith is a rosary with a medal of Padre Cícero and Our Lady of Sorrows, which they wear about the neck.[7] Some individuals wear two rosaries, to assure their salvation in the event that they should die with one set of the beads in hand. Many residents insist that they are the real *romeiros* or pilgrims. ("A *romeiro* is someone who suffers in order to live in Juazeiro," they frequently declare.) I have nevertheless reserved this term for visitors who attribute their presence in the city to a desire to pay homage to Padre Cícero.

Comparison of pilgrims' and residents' versions of the best-known stories reveals two separate, if interrelated, processes. While most residents engage in systematic privatization, presenting even the most familiar tales as memories, a sizable number of pilgrims lean toward the construction of a communally meaningful master legend, which I will call a *life*.[8] Because, however, both groups are interested above all in the

---

7. The wearing of the rosary, but not the addition of a medal with his image, was encouraged by Padre Cícero. The priest's public demonstrations of loyalty to Our Lady of Sorrows, patron saint of Juazeiro, fits the larger pattern of Marian devotion characteristic of the second half of the nineteenth century.

8. I will use "life" throughout this study to indicate a more-or-less standard oral biography of Padre Cícero. I have chosen the term because it suggests the literary genre of the saint's life without implying that the priest has any official canonical standing.

creation of a Padre Cícero who can help them as individuals in the present, these dissimilar approaches should not obscure the miracle corpus's underlying unity.

The body of this book is divided into three sections, followed by a conclusion. The first part summarizes the history of Padre Cícero's Juazeiro and identifies the storytellers and the conditions for storytelling. The second provides a general introduction to tales told by residents and pilgrims. Here, in order to make a sprawling narrative corpus more manageable, I have concentrated on the twenty stories most frequently recounted by each of the two groups, summarizing a number of similarities as well as differences between them.

The third part of the study offers specific examples of the division between residents and pilgrims. In order to assure a common point of departure, I have chosen three tales that deal directly with a specific historical personage or event—the Revolution of 1913–14; the supposed confrontation between Padre Cícero and his political advisor, Dr. Floro; and the alleged transformation of a communion wafer into blood in 1889. As these narratives reveal a progression from relative similarity to marked opposition between the two groups of storytellers, they document successive stages in the shaping of a "life."

The conclusion looks at the best-known stories in relationship to the miracle corpus as a whole. It reemphasizes the extent to which dissimilarities between residents and pilgrims can be seen both as separate steps in an evolutionary process and as two essentially comparable ways of achieving the same goal. This section also reaffirms the fundamental ambiguity of Padre Cícero as a literary figure. Appendix A, containing a numerical breakdown of the storytellers with whom I spoke in Juazeiro, follows. Appendix B gives the Portuguese originals of the miracle texts that appear, in my English translation, in the body of this study.

In choosing *Trail of Miracles* as the title of this study, I had more than one motive. The name first came to me when I was attempting to describe to an American friend the neighborhood in which I had lived in Juazeiro. The Rua do Horto (the "Horto," or "Orchard," is meant to suggest the Garden of Gethsemane) is literally a street. This term, however, suggests an urban quality foreign to this two-mile stretch of rudimentary houses on the outskirts of a backlands city of 130,000 people. The Rua do Horto winds upward to an enormous statue of Padre Cícero. This expanded goat path along which the priest used to ride on a small white horse led by a helper is now obligatory passage for pilgrims to Juazeiro. Although the three rickety buses constituting the Good Saviour

Transport Company have recently begun to brave the incline, pedestrians and donkeys still dominate this thoroughfare. Paved in cobblestone at the bottom, toward the top the Rua do Horto becomes a sandy stretch of increasingly poorer houses lacking electricity and running water.

The word *trail* also refers to the first roads to Juazeiro. Many older residents and visitors to the city can remember journeying for as long as a month along the parched cattle trails that were the precursors to today's highways. In order to mark the way for others these early pilgrims, who often traveled by moonlight to escape the sun's heat, cut crosses into trees at strategic intersections. Today trucks and buses speed through an interior once the province of cowmen and bandits, but the memory of the past lives on in the Padre Cícero tales.

Often, it is not today's storytellers who made their way on foot to Juazeiro but parents and grandparents whose adventures the storytellers recall with pride. Their stories are therefore not only celebrations of the priest but expressions of what poet Carlos Drummond de Andrade calls *a idéia da família viajando através do sangue,* "the idea of the family traveling through the blood."[9] "My father gave [*not* told] me this tale," the teller may explain, thereby emphasizing the stories' almost material reality.

Then, too, this title is meant to recall *Grande sertão: Veredas (Great Interior: Trails),* a novel most critics consider to be the preeminent work of twentieth-century fiction in the Portuguese language.[10] Its extremely erudite author, João Guimarães Rosa, grew up among individuals much like the farmers, washerwomen, and itinerant peddlers who appear in the pages of this study. His success in transforming their language and customs into a work with universal meaning emphasizes the contribution men and women with no formal education have made to Brazilian literature.

Finally, the trail is the seeming infinity of narratives that focus on Padre Cícero. The word suggests the tales' ability to move the teller in either a straight line or a circle toward an end which then comes to serve as a new beginning. Because the story of the priest is also the story of his followers, this line is marked by countless bifurcations.

In carrying out this study of the Padre Cícero stories I have drawn heavily on the work of not only literary scholars but also historians,

9. Carlos Drummond de Andrade, "Retrato de Família."

10. The English translation is *The Devil to Pay in the Backlands,* trans. James L. Taylor and Harriet de Onís. For a discussion of Guimarães Rosa's use of language see Nei Leandro de Castro's *Universo e vocabulário do 'Grande sertão.'* See also Teresinha Souto Ward, *Oralidade em "Grande sertão: Veredas."*

anthropologists, folklorists, and students of folk religion. Above all, I have relied on on-site investigation in Northeast Brazil. Because this discussion is based primarily on tape-recorded stories, it is essential to say something about how they were collected. I should begin by pointing out that while I spent a total of only seven months in Juazeiro, I have been doing research in the Brazilian Northeast for approximately ten years. Many of my observations are therefore grounded in past experiences and readings. I would not have been able to understand the highly colloquial language of the stories, let alone attempt to analyze their potential relationship to the tellers' lives, without this backlog of experience and information.

During the time I spent in Juazeiro, I taped the stories of 250 residents and 500 pilgrims. Although the number of pilgrims is double that of residents, I devoted approximately the same amount of time to each. This book draws on well over 150 hours of narration, from which I made a selective transcription of just under 2,100 typewritten pages. Given the background noises and peculiarities of speech which make a toothless storyteller's Portuguese difficult even for a native speaker, I decided to transcribe the tales myself. The work took many months and was often frustrating because no matter how hard I tried, I regularly heard what people "should" say rather than what they did say. I would often play back the tape only to discover that their words were quite different from those I had just transferred to paper.

This process, nonetheless, had benefits quite apart from giving me confidence in the accuracy of the texts. First, it obliged me to relive the recording process in a slow, methodical manner and to listen two and three times to each speaker. In transcribing I discovered much that had escaped me when I was busy worrying about whether my tape recorder needed new batteries or whether a potential storyteller was going to wander off before the current speaker had finished. Second, transcription brought home to me the consistency with which people impose a series of preestablished patterns on a given body of narrative material. If I, who was consciously struggling to reproduce what I was hearing, could still end up with the grammatical constructions I had learned in a classroom rather than those the storytellers were employing, how could these persons not motivated to identify their habitual way of thinking or speaking fail to leave their mark upon these tales?[11]

My first trip to Juazeiro in April of 1978 grew out of a study of the

11. For documentation of how preconceived patterns shape visual as well as verbal responses see Judith Mara Gutman, *Through Indian Eyes,* which examines differences between Indian and Western uses of the camera.

Northeast Brazilian stories-in-verse called *literatura de cordel*.[12] I went to Juazeiro, a principal publication and distribution center for these booklets, to interview a number of printers and poets. When I asked about their stories of Padre Cícero, they informed me that almost all of these were verse "translations" of tales that they had heard from others. Curious about the relationship between the oral and written versions, I began talking to the storytellers to whom the poets referred me. These persons were usually friends, relatives, or next-door neighbors.

At the same time, my hosts, Anne Dumoulin and Therezinha Stella Guimarães, introduced me to a number of residents of the Rua do Horto. Among them was Francisca Inácio da Costa, a young woman who had moved with her family to São Paulo at the age of thirteen. Recently returned to Rua do Horto, where she hoped to devote herself to handicrafts, Francisca had bought the small house—located only three doors down from the house of her aunt, Josefa André Gonçalves—where she had been born. Both she and Dona Zefinha presented me to other residents of the neighborhood.[13]

One of these individuals was a woman called Dona Maria dos Benditos after the *benditos* or hymns of praise she writes for a living. Because Francisca thought that Dona Maria also sold *cordel* stories, one windless afternoon we climbed up the long hill to her house. When we arrived, we found a lame, cross-eyed woman plaiting straw for hats on the floor of a house that smelled of urine and old fish. When she said she knew nothing about *cordel* or *cordel* poets, I wondered why I had ever left my apartment with a sea breeze in Recife to come to Juazeiro. Only because I was too hot and tired to walk back down the hill, I sat and listened while Francisca tried to coax the woman into singing one of the hymns she hears in dreams and upon waking dictates to a semi-literate daughter. Finally Dona Maria agreed to sing a few verses into the tape recorder that I grudgingly produced. She then proceeded to intone the praises of Our Lady of Pleasures in a voice not quite like any other I have ever heard. After hailing the Virgin Mary as the white star of a new morning, she went on to thank Padre Cícero for the overwhelming happiness he had bestowed upon her. When Dona Maria finished, Francisca expressed appreciation, the tape recorder clicked off, and we walked back down the hill. But I could not forget Dona Maria. From what depths, I wondered,

12. Candace Slater, *Stories on a String: The Brazilian "Literatura de Cordel."*

13. "Dona" is the polite title for a woman; "Seu" (an abbreviated, colloquial form of "Senhor"), for a man. The title "Doutor" or "Doctor" is reserved for males of high social status, but "Dona" may be used for women of all social classes. These titles are normally used with a first name. Zefinha is the diminutive form of Josefa.

had that remarkable voice come? Why, in a city dedicated to Our Lady of Sorrows, would a person sing the praises of Our Lady of Pleasures?[14] And what was the unbounded happiness for which this penniless woman was thanking Padre Cícero? These unanswered questions were a major factor in my decision to return to Juazeiro.

During the summer of 1981, Francisca took me into her home in the Rua do Horto. She did so again for four months in the fall of 1982. Her hospitality gave me a certain degree of built-in acceptance. At the same time that people considered her different because she has lived and studied in São Paulo, her aunt's status as a respected member of the community makes her an insider. Francisca regularly drew my attention to or explained points that I had misunderstood or missed. I also owe her a debt of gratitude for making me feel free to express confusion or surprise. I could go home after recording miracles all day and exclaim, "You won't believe this!" without worrying that Francisca would think me hypocritical or transmit my astonishment to others. I could also play back for clarification any portion of a story which I had not understood.

My neighbors in the Rua do Horto proved to be excellent teachers. Although initially wary of a foreigner, they began little by little to include me in their conversations. At first we talked about their children, how to tell one kind of mango from another, or the best way of treating a particularly stubborn cough. After a while, however, they began to tell me stories, many of which focused on Padre Cícero.

To call my extended talks with the people whom I came to know "interviews" suggests a degree of formality they did not possess. Most of my "informants" were people I had happened to see sitting on the sidewalk or in the front room of their houses, which remain wide open to the street during the day. Once one person started speaking, passersby inevitably joined the conversation—not one of the storytelling sessions was limited to the individual and myself. More often than not, the teller would speak directly to the persons who had begun to gather and who regularly interrupted to ask questions or to comment. Sometimes the "audience" would consist only of one or two other persons, but there were often as many as a dozen individuals present. Children in particular would ask my destination so that they could tag along to hear the stories.

These on-the-spot recordings complemented sessions in the home of Josefa André Gonçalves. Dona Zefinha's house, perched on a sudden rise

14. Prazeres ("Pleasures") is the name of a neighborhood in the Pernambucan capital of Recife. "Our Lady of Pleasures" is therefore a local name for the Virgin Mary. Dona Maria, however, believes that the Virgin's seven sorrows must be balanced by seven pleasures which she enumerates in one of her *benditos*.

along the hill, receives a breeze which other houses do not share. Her neighbors therefore spend many hours in her company, plaiting straw hats, shelling beans, or extracting cotton from the pod while she irons an endless pile of clothes to earn her weekly income of just under three dollars. At night, the same people reappear to resume their labors, exchanging stories and bits of gossip to which I listened with great interest.

I also spent large amounts of time sitting on the sidewalk beside Mariano Ferreira da Silva. Now in his eighties, Seu Mariano no longer works in the fields but spends his days beneath a dusty shade tree. From time to time a pilgrim drops a coin into his outstretched guava-jelly tin. A gifted storyteller, he is invariably surrounded by eager listeners as soon as he starts recounting his adventures as a young pilgrim bound for Juazeiro.

When Seu Mariano was occupied, I could count on my next-door neighbor, Manuel Roberto, to tell me about the days when he traveled through the surrounding hills selling the pungent oil of the pequi nut (prized for the distinctive flavor it gives to an otherwise dry and largely tasteless mixture of rice and beans). And if Seu Manuel were busy, there were always Cosma Cícera da Conceição and her husband, Casimiro Antônio Bezerra, caretakers of a local chapel who also sell coffee, bananas, and homemade coconut bars beneath an adjoining canvas awning.[15] Over time, Dona "Corma" became my trusted collaborator, or perhaps accomplice, coaxing unsuspecting customers who had taken refuge from the sun beneath the tattered cloth to reminisce aloud about Padre Cícero. With a wink in my direction, she would proceed to ask the questions she had heard me ask so often. "Did your grandparents know my Padrinho Cícero?" "Do you own or rent your farmland?" "Now is it true that my Padrinho will always punish an unbeliever?"

Local storytellers who did not live in the Rua do Horto might be friends or acquaintances of the four *cordel* poets whom I had gotten to know during my first trip to Juazeiro. Others were persons whom I met during the course of my work in the rustic hotels, called *ranchos,* where most pilgrims stay. They were often the owners of these establishments or employees such as guards or cooks. They were also vendors of the sort who regularly enter the *ranchos* to sell texts of pilgrim songs, home-brewed medicines, aluminum spoons, saints' pictures, or cheap earrings to the people lodged there. Often these individuals would pause to hear a pilgrim tell a story, then interject a tale or observation of their own. A

15. Dona Corma's full name is Cosma Cícera da Conceição de Bezerra. She, however, like a number of other Brazilian women, customarily uses just her maiden name.

few were gifted storytellers who got so caught up in their presentations that the spoons or earrings were quickly forgotten.

Over time, I got to know a small number of persons outside the Rua do Horto quite well. The *cordel* poet Manuel Caboclo e Silva spent whole mornings recalling his own encounters with Padre Cícero as he worked on the figures for his yearly astrological almanac. Maria Selvina da Silva and I had at least a dozen conversations about television soap operas, the proper length of dress sleeves (she finds anything above the elbow suspect), and the end of the world. Dona Selvina's friend Luzia Maria das Neves told stories about her maternal grandmother, who was a slave during the days of the Empire, and sang some of the loveliest ballads I have ever heard. For the most part, however, it is the people of the Rua do Horto whom I came to know best and whose voices dominate the hours of recording.

I do not mean to imply by this generally positive description of my own relationship with the tellers that these are poor but happy people who while away the time exchanging stories. Almost all of their lives have not simply been touched, but have been marred and splintered, by continued hardship. My next-door neighbor, for instance, a forty-four-year-old woman, had lost thirteen of eighteen children during or shortly after birth. The young woman across the street had lost eleven out of twelve. My next-door neighbor's father, a sixty-eight-year-old man who still gets up to work in the fields at 4:30 every morning, began to spit blood one day when I was living in the Rua do Horto. He went twice to see a state-paid medical assistant who was too busy each time to see him. The trips, however, were so taxing as to increase the flow of blood to the point where it threatened to choke him. When I asked if he ought not to see a private doctor, he explained that the last time that he had scraped together the money for such a visit, "the man prescribed a medicine that would have cost more than I now earn in a year."

Death is a constant presence in Juazeiro. The very first day I set foot in the city I found myself attending an all-night vigil for a young girl who had died hours before. I still remember a bouquet of white paper flowers inserted between hands so gnarled by work that they could have belonged to her great-grandmother. In the year between my first and second longer stays in Juazeiro, six of the people who had told me stories died. It is therefore not surprising that many residents of the Rua do Horto keep a supply of the candles used in the last rites of the Catholic Church ready to slip into a sick person's hand.

My relationship with visitors to Juazeiro was necessarily different. Because most pilgrims stay in the city only one or two days, it is impossible to get to know them well. People tend to have a full schedule of visits to various landmarks, and little time or energy is left for telling stories. Moreover, many are understandably fearful of strangers.

By volunteering for the daily 6 A.M. shift in the parish-run information center which serves pilgrims to Juazeiro, I was able to meet a number of the pilgrim organizers, or *fretantes*. In the process of taking down their names and addresses for an ongoing file I often managed to strike up a conversation that led to an invitation to meet other members of the group.[16] I would then set a time to appear at the *rancho*, where the organizer introduced me to the pilgrims in his or her group. As they had already met me, people were usually considerably more expansive than on those occasions when I showed up without an introduction.

I also met a number of storytellers at the end of a special meeting held for pilgrims by the parish on most weekday afternoons. At this time, Anne Dumoulin would tell people that she had a friend who had come all the way from North America to hear stories about Padre Cícero. As a result, once the meeting was over, there were usually ten to fifty people crowding around me. Some were eager to tell stories; others were equally eager to listen. On most of these occasions I was able to record for about an hour, taking care to note the lodgings of persons willing to continue talking at another time. I would then appear at these individuals' *ranchos* immediately following the regularly scheduled evening mass or just after lunchtime the next day, the two periods in which pilgrims are most apt to be unoccupied.

Recording conditions in the *ranchos* were never optimal. The main section of most of these "hotels" is nothing more than a long hall marked by a series of pegs on which pilgrims hang the brightly colored, cocoon-like hammocks in which many Northeast Brazilians sleep.[17] Often small rooms line both sides of the corridor. These rooms, usually windowless to make construction cheaper, serve as an invitation to Juazeiro's ubiquitous thieves. Toward the back of the *rancho*—which, depending on its size, may lodge anywhere from fifty to six hundred people at a time—there is a kitchen area with one or more wood-burning stoves. Beyond this is a courtyard in which stand a faucet or series of faucets, a latrine or toilet, and a single shower stall.

16. The addresses of the pilgrims are collected for parish mailings. The location of the *rancho* where each group is staying in Juazeiro is also noted, in order to aid the sizable number of persons who get lost during the course of their stay in the city.

17. These hammocks not only take little space and are easy to transport but also are much cooler than beds because the air can enter from beneath. The custom of sleeping in hammocks was borrowed by the Portuguese colonists from the Tupi Indians. See Luís da Câmara Cascudo, *Rede de dormir: Uma pesquisa etnográfica*.

The fact that people are constantly walking through the *rancho* complicated my attempts to tape the Padre Cícero stories. Congregating in
one of the small rooms off the hallway cut down on the traffic but the
heat quickly became so intense that the door had to be opened and more
pilgrims crowded in. Often so many people wanted to hear and tell stories that there was no choice but to group in the kitchen, which was not
only hot but extremely noisy. My recordings are therefore full of children's screams, the slow fizz of frying oil, the drip of showerbaths, the
whine or buzz of insects, and the varied drone of a long procession of
vendors. From time to time I can also distinguish tantalizing bits and
pieces of background conversations, church bells, the squeak of bats,
snatches of imported rock music, the syncopated fall of grains of rice in
a straw sieve, and the insistent wheezing of one of the donkeys that
sometimes bed down in the *rancho* beside their owners. Every once in a
while I would sit with pilgrims on the steps of the church of Our Lady
of Sorrows, which even in the darkness remain warm with the day's sun.
A number of storytellers found this space too public, however, and the
group would usually retire to a *rancho*. We would then remain until the
clanking of the guard's keys brought the session to a halt.[18]

As with residents, the conversations I recorded among pilgrims were
almost never limited to a single individual. On many occasions one or
two storytellers would dominate a session while a shifting string of
people drifted in and out. It was not uncommon, however, for a dozen
or more individuals to exchange stories, cutting each other off from time
to time with an indignant "Now it's my turn—you've said enough!"
Occasionally a family would spirit me away into their room, calling in
friends and relatives to add to the store of tales. Once in a while a *fretante*
would assemble all the group members he or she could find, urging each
to tell a story. ("Come on, João, tell us something about my Padrinho.
Everybody knows how much you love to talk!")

Many pilgrims told me only one or two stories before disappearing
into the night. As a result, their names do not evoke a face. And yet,
despite the relatively short time we spent together, other persons are impossible to forget. There was, for instance, the visitor who shared with
me the tales she had heard as a child from a beloved grandmother. As the
hours wore on, the old woman named Dindinha seemed to emerge from
the shadows to take her place beside us. And I can still hear the cackling
of the four old men from Flores, Pernambuco, who told me the most

---

18. The *ranchos* are locked from the outside at ten or eleven o'clock at night in order to
keep out thieves and to prevent latecomers from waking the others. The guard theoretically
remains at the door throughout the night. In practice, he often vanishes, making the *rancho*
a potential firetrap.

ribald miracle stories I have ever heard. The tale I remember best concerns four men ("No, no, not us, ma'am!") who argue all the way from their home town to Juazeiro about which one is responsible for the baby of a woman with whom all have slept. When they arrive, Padre Cícero asks if they want to see a miracle. Their enthusiastic response leads him to summon the mother and the child, who, he announces, has not one but four fathers. He then directs each of the friends to treat the baby as his own.[19]

I can also visualize the middle-aged woman who pressed my hand along her shin bone to let me feel the bumps that resulted from improper healing after a furious childhood beating. When another pilgrim asked if she felt anger toward the father who "had gone crazy when he lost his job and couldn't get another," she shook her head. No, she said, all she felt was gratitude toward the priest whom she credits with saving her life. Occasionally an individual who was semi-literate would write to me after returning home to a farm with a name such as Wide Horizon or Lion's Paw. A few enclosed tattered photographs "so that you'll always remember the woman from Bonito who told you the story of how my Padrinho opened that great door in Rome."

The fact that I met large numbers of people for whom the pilgrimage holds a deep significance does not mean that many do not make the journey out of curiosity or boredom. The existence of mixed motives, however, does not obviate most visitors' faith in Padre Cícero. Then, too, what starts as a vacation or a commercial venture may end quite differently.

Both pilgrims and residents were usually willing to talk to me. Because malnutrition, overwork, and a relentless sun age them so quickly, I struck them as very young. When they asked what I did back home, I told them I was a *professora,* a word that encompasses everything from kindergarten teachers to college professors. I did not mention the word *university* or *research,* largely because no one would have believed me. In my rubber sandals, my increasingly sun-bleached dresses designed to cover knees as well as shoulders, and my straw hat anchored with a stringy ribbon, I neither looked nor felt much like a visiting scholar. At the same time that my presentation of myself constitutes a decided simplification, there is no doubt that storytellers regularly resorted to comparable simplifications in an attempt to make their own lives intelligible to someone so obviously different from them.

19. Although the point of this story is highly moralistic, the supporting details were less than puritanical. Rubém César Fernandes indicates in his *Os cavaleiros do Bom Jesus* that this sort of joking and explicit reference to sexual matters is an important part of the all-male pilgrimage to Bom Jesus de Pirapora; see especially pp. 36–40.

Most people asked few questions about what I was doing in Juazeiro. It was usually enough for them that I was interested in Padre Cícero. Visitors' apparent lack of concern for a stranger's motivation was largely a result of their own intense involvement in the pilgrimage. Not only do their thoughts and feelings often lead them to look inward but the varied emotions many experience also intensify the need to communicate. As a result, they talk at length, cry easily, and are quick to form personal relationships that would normally be much longer in the making. The fact that Padre Cícero allegedly prophesied a time in which foreigners would seek out "holy Juazeiro" may have made an otherwise potentially disturbing presence comprehensible to many.[20]

Residents, particularly those who live in the Rua do Horto, often assumed that I was Francisca's sister. Her long sojourn in São Paulo seemed to explain my accent, for citizens of Juazeiro consider that those from São Paulo talk in a "foreign" manner. Local storytellers tended, however, to ask a few more questions than pilgrims. Most did not find it odd that I should want to come to Juazeiro—after all, they themselves cared enough to move there. Nonetheless, they were usually distressed to discover that I was married. Because most Northeast Brazilians would not permit their wives to travel alone even to visit family members in a neighboring city, they could not understand how I could have traveled alone to a foreign country where I had no relatives to serve as chaperones. My husband made my neighbors feel that my journey had his approval—and that I myself was worthy of their confidence—by copying out letters that I periodically wrote for him in Portuguese. In these he thanked the people of the Rua do Horto profusely for their consideration and asked them to continue keeping such a watchful eye on me. The people who received these letters—complete with oversized postcards of the Liberty Bell—did not let me forget them. Whenever they thought I ate too little or worked too hard, they inevitably quoted to me the words I myself had written. "What will we ever say to Paulo José if something happens?" they demanded with a hint of pride. "You know, he expressly asked us to take care of you!"

For the purposes of this study it was helpful to be a woman. First, my sex assured me a certain degree of trust. "I wouldn't tell Saint Peter

20. Padre Cícero is credited with a large number of prophecies, many of which had previously been ascribed to other Northeastern holy men. A printed, verse illustration of a series of practically interchangeable prophecies is Rodolfo Coelho Cavalcante, "O sonho do Padre Cícero Romão Batista." Other prophecies attributed to the priest are considerably less common. When I first arrived in Juazeiro, for instance, people inquired if some of my friends back home did not have a single eye in the middle of the forehead. Later I learned that Padre Cícero had allegedly prophesied a time in which one-eyed persons from a foreign land would visit this part of the backlands.

the things that I am telling you," an old woman once confided. It would have been difficult, if not impossible, for a man to walk in and strike up a conversation with people in a *rancho*. The women would have melted away and the men would immediately have demanded to know who he was and what he wanted. As females in general, however, are regarded as insignificant and therefore not threatening, I enjoyed a somewhat ironic advantage. Then too, since most Northeastern men feel obliged to ignore females when other males are present, I was able to listen as men talked to one another. Some men spoke to me directly because of my elevated social status as an educated foreigner. Many, however, sought to direct the conversation at another man.

And yet, despite this show of male superiority, the poor of both sexes are subjected to repeated humiliation. I still remember the afternoon when I found myself trapped along with a group of people from the Rua do Horto in a bus that broke down a block after it pulled out of the city's central square. Although the windows would not open and the bus was soon like an oven, the driver would not let the passengers leave until he consulted his boss. He therefore locked the door, returning almost forty minutes later with the owner, who announced that we could either pay the full fare to Crato—the intended destination—or get down on our stomachs to crawl under the metal "butterfly" or turnstile. Many of my neighbors therefore started crawling. The owner and the driver must have assumed that I was simply another passenger. Therefore when I said in a loud voice, "But it is you who should pay us for what we have gone through," not only the two men but also many of the riders looked at me incredulously.

My own ambivalence about Padre Cícero made incidents such as these particularly disturbing. It was impossible to remain unmoved by my neighbors' poverty. Especially at the beginning, I found it hard to see beyond the more escapist aspects of people's faith in the priest. I also worried about whether I was providing positive reinforcement for these very aspects by expressing interest in the miracle stories.

Another difficulty of working in Juazeiro was the ease with which I found myself jumping to conclusions. Once the initial strangeness had worn off, I often caught myself acting on assumptions based on my own (admittedly somewhat distant) Christian upbringing. Time and again I would suddenly realize that a fundamental concept, such as the Trinity, meant something quite different to my neighbors than it meant to me.

Then too, I could not escape a certain unpleasant sense of myself as a voyeur. Much as I wanted to comprehend what storytellers were experiencing, many times I felt acutely like the outsider I never ceased to be. It is difficult to know how to respond when an individual in the midst of an emotional experience asks with shining eyes, "And do you understand what I am saying?" If one says "no," the look of hurt quickly translates into silence. If one says "yes," one is betraying both the person and oneself. My own solution was to say, "I'm not sure, but please tell me more." Sometimes this tactic worked, sometimes it did not.

I chose not to offer money to the persons who told me the miracle stories. This was not only because I was not taking them away from other, wage-earning activities—the usual rationale for payment—but was also because I would have found it impossible to put a price on their narratives. Accustomed to having nothing, many individuals seemed pleased to find themselves in the unexpected role of donor. In fact, an occasional pilgrim would attempt to pay *me* for listening to him or her. I gave the children candy and I handed out the seashells my husband and I had gathered on a New Jersey beach for the storytellers. Because many of them live in the drought-stricken backlands and have never seen an ocean, these tokens of the distant Atlantic had a special significance for them. Although I tried to help the most needy in the Rua do Horto I always did so through a third person who agreed not to reveal the source of aid.

In retrospect I realize that part of my overall success with both groups of storytellers lay in my readiness to sit on the floor. I adopted this custom early in my research because I needed to get my unobtrusive but not particularly powerful tape recorder as close as possible to the speaker's mouth. Also, as there were few chairs and I was usually hot and weary, I simply sat wherever and whenever I could.

Northeasterners almost never sit on the ground in the presence of a stranger, because it is a declaration of inferiority.[21] As my mind was on the task at hand, however, I never stopped to think about the statement I might be making until an old man impulsively confided that he had initially resolved to tell me nothing. "You never know about a stranger, and why would a woman be here all alone?" he explained. The man had changed his mind, however, when I sat on my heels beside his hammock, "because then I knew that you *really* wanted to hear the miracles of my Padrinho." When I reflected on his remark I remembered how embarrassed people in the Rua do Horto would get when they did not have a seat to offer a visitor and to what lengths they went in order to keep a

21. Men are even less apt than women to sit on the floor. In a well-known pan-Hispanic ballad of the warrior maiden ("Doncella guerrera" or "Donzela guerreira"), one test of a would-be soldier's sexual identity involves a choice between sitting on a chair or on the floor *(Os homens procuraram cadeiras altas, as donzelas é no chão)*.

guest's possessions off the floor. I recalled how lodgers in the *ranchos* would send a child scurrying for a stool on which I could sit and their expressions of concern when I nonchalantly brushed the dirt from my clothes. Then, too, I thought of a pilgrim song that asserts that Padre Cícero's word "never fell upon the ground for the world to trample." Thus while I cannot claim anything but good fortune in the matter, my habit of sitting beside or beneath storytellers as they sat in chairs or hammocks appears to have made a difference in the way they responded.

I had hoped to participate in a number of pilgrimages as part of the recording process. I did take part in one fourteen-hour journey in a crowded bus from Juazeiro to the shrine city of Canindé.[22] This trip almost became my last when the headlights failed at two o'clock in the morning and the bus veered toward a cliff. Although the driver appeared determined to go on as if nothing were the matter, the passengers screamed in unison until he decided to halt. He then proceeded to find a place to string his hammock, but the others either had to sleep doubled up in a crowded bus or stretch out on the ground. Faced with these options, a number of individuals proceeded to tell miracle stories until dawn, making me the only happy person in the group. After this trip, however, I felt forced to forego more of these time-consuming journeys in the interest of collecting the widest possible variety of stories within Juazeiro.

Although I was most interested in hearing people's versions of the best-known miracles, I always began by urging them to recount whichever incidents came to mind. I did try to steer the tellers toward the more familiar stories, which provide a useful basis for comparison, by expressing a particular interest in Padre Cícero's life. If a person insisted on describing a cure that had occurred six months ago, I did not stop him or her. Once this narrative was finished, however, I would attempt to bring the conversation back to the days when the priest was still alive. Only after people appeared to have exhausted their supply of stories did I begin to probe for additional tales.

My questions were purposely vague. I might ask, for instance, how Padre Cícero helped his followers, or if anyone actually knew a person he had helped or punished. If this line of inquiry proved fruitless, I might say something like, "Someone told me a story the other day about a girl who turned into a dog but then someone else said that it was a snake—

22. Canindé, located some two hours from the state capital of Fortaleza, is devoted to São Francisco das Chagas, Saint Francis of the Wounds—a reference to the stigmata of Saint Francis of Assisi.

or maybe it was a horse. Now I don't know what to think. Can you tell me which it was?" The oblique approach was almost always more successful than asking point-blank about the girl who had turned into a dog. If people suspected that I was familiar with a tale they did not want to tell it, "because a story is no good if you have already heard it." Even more, they worried that I might want to compare their version to another that I considered "right."

In spite of the fact that I tried my best to encourage people to recount stories about Padre Cícero, it was the tellers themselves who dominated these sessions. They were often capable of talking for hours among themselves, occasionally even forgetting that I happened to be present. "Are you still here?" people would sometimes ask in surprise after several hours of animated conversation. "I thought you'd gone home a long time ago."

I do not mean to suggest that my presence did not have an influence on the storytellers. The fact of having an outsider in their midst made them considerably more careful than they might otherwise have been about what they said. Then, too, my presence spurred them to clarify points they would not have bothered to explain to their peers. By and large, though, the fact that these individuals were almost always speaking to others like themselves as well as to me is obvious in the more or less private exchanges that regularly crop up in the middle of these narratives. "Do you remember the Pereira family, Seu Domingo?" the speaker may ask. "Well, it was the uncle of João Pereira who knew that man who turned into a frog. Not José Pereira, but João. Remember? The one whose wife had a crippled hand?"

In Northeast Brazil, names, like possessions, are jealously protected by their owners. Poor people's refusal to divulge their names and their practice of hiding behind an alias often create problems for census-takers and social workers. This behavior stems from the belief that knowledge of the name represents a form of power over the individual to whom it belongs.

Because I knew about this sensitivity from previous research, I initially refrained from asking pilgrims to identify themselves. Instead, I inquired about their place of residence, their age, marital status, and occupation, and the number of trips they had made to Juazeiro. When, however, one man asked if he could say his name into my tape recorder, I realized that these people had already committed themselves by sharing something so personal as their faith in Padre Cícero. I therefore began to ask for names as well as the other information at the end of each tale.

Sometimes the tellers hesitated but they almost always decided of their own accord to identify themselves. ("That is what my Padrinho would have wanted," an initially timid woman explained.)

Because the number of storytellers with whom I spoke is very small compared to the hundreds of thousands of Padre Cícero's followers, this study is necessarily an approximation.[23] In writing, I have often thought of a fifty-two-year-old pilgrim named Maria Lira de Araújo, who came to Juazeiro from the state of Sergipe with various other members of her family for All Soul's Day, the biggest pilgrimage of the year. As befits her name (*lira* means "lyre"), Maria Lira, although illiterate, is a poet. In the course of an extended conversation one evening, she recited to me numerous poems and hymns she had composed in honor of Padre Cícero. At the same time, she traced on a piece of white cloth and then carefully colored the shape of a bird who she asserted was the Holy Spirit. Because an enormous mass in memory of Padre Cícero was to be held the next morning, Maria Lira wanted a flag she could raise above the crowd. "You're crazy to do this," her older brother told her when he joined us. "Who's going to notice a scrap of bedsheet among so many people?" "I don't care," Maria Lira told him. "You say what you want, but I'm going to wave my banner all the same."

By dawn the next day, crowds of residents and pilgrims had already filled all the streets leading to the chapel of Perpetual Help, where Padre Cícero lies buried. When I climbed to the belfry with a television reporter, we found ourselves looking out over a seemingly endless swarm of people. The reporter, who had come from Rio de Janeiro for the filming, estimated that there must be more than a quarter of a million persons. As I stood watching the multitude below us I thought, "How can I possibly write anything about Padre Cícero? There are far too many of his followers to talk about them as a group." Just at that moment, however, a hint of white appeared against the morning sky. I leaned out of the window as far as I could and, sure enough, Maria Lira's banner was fluttering above the left center of the tightly packed church square.

23. Given the enormity of both the storytelling population and the actual narrative corpus, one would face difficult questions regarding closure even in a much larger sample. Moreover, while more statistically accurate studies would provide invaluable background information, it is not certain how much light they might shed on more qualitative problems involving textual variation among individuals as well as subgroups. Clifford Geertz addresses this primary issue of "representativeness" in ethnographical research in the introduction to his *The Interpretation of Culture: Selected Essays.*

It would be awkward to insist at each turn of this discussion that I have asked the limited number of persons whom I met in Juazeiro to speak for a necessarily heterogeneous community of storytellers. All my observations are based on a part that I hope, but cannot guarantee, is representative of a much larger whole. I have staked this book upon Maria Lira's banner. She would be pleased to think that someone saw it.

PART ONE

THE LARGER CONTEXT

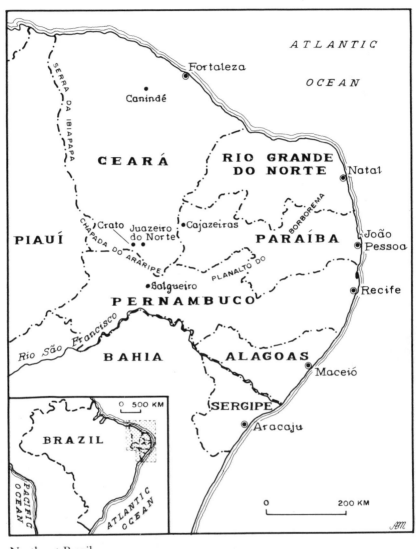

Northeast Brazil.

1.

Historical Background

Padre Cícero's greatest miracle? I think that it is Juazeiro.
Because where there was once nothing he made a whole
city grow.

                            Resident of Juazeiro

Juazeiro do Norte sits almost exactly in the middle of the Northeast
Brazilian backlands, an apt location for a city that Padre Cícero's
followers insist on calling "the center of the world." The interior's longstanding marginality, however, gives this label a certain irony. Although
the Northeast accounts for about a third of the Brazilian population, it
remains one of the poorest and most technologically backward areas of
the country.

Because the miracle stories are so closely tied to this region, a brief
look at Northeast Brazilian history will be useful. This chapter examines
the rise of Padre Cícero's Juazeiro from several different angles in order
to provide a sense of that larger world of which these tales are a part.[1]

Background to the Northeast

The 1494 Treaty of Tordesillas, in which Pope Alexander VI divided the
New World between Spain and Portugal, gave the Spanish kings exten-

1. For a general introduction to Brazilian history see E. Bradford Burns, *A History of Brazil*, and Rollie E. Poppino, *Brazil: The Land and the People*. Poppino's book includes a useful
bibliographical essay (pp. 338–352) and a chronological summary of major political events.
A brief but useful introduction to Brazil is Richard Morse's "Some Themes of Brazilian
History." A socioeconomic introduction to the Northeast is available in Manuel Correia de
Andrade, *A terra e o homem no nordeste*. A detailed listing of works on the region published
before 1970 is *Nordeste brasileiro: Catálogo da exposição*. For studies published after 1930 see
listings under "Northeast" in Robert M. Levine, *Brazil: An Annotated Bibliography for Social
Historians*.

sive gold and silver deposits. Portugal, however, discovered little more than dyewood (the *pau brasil* that gave Brazil its name) and a huge expanse of fertile land. Therefore, unlike Spanish adventure hunters who were often able to return home after making their fortunes, the Portuguese were apt to stay in their new country.

Colonists, however, were understandably slow to penetrate the vast *sertão* or Northeastern backlands, a periodically drought-ridden area larger than France and Germany combined. Tupi Indians therefore remained the region's principal inhabitants during the first century after Cabral discovered Brazil in 1500. Then, little by little, an increasing number of cowmen began to join the missionaries, outlaws, and runaway African slaves who had already begun moving inland along dry riverbeds. As coastal lands once reserved for pasture became absorbed into the plantation economy, ranchers had no choice but to drive more deeply into the interior.

The Dutch presence in the Northeast (1630–54) slowed formal settlement of the backlands, but the guerrilla fighters who opposed the invaders frequently took refuge there. After the Netherlands' defeat, many of the guerrillas stayed in the region. Generally, when colonial authorities discovered that a sufficiently large number of squatters had moved into a given area, they presented the land in question to a powerful cattleman. These grants, called *sesmarias,* might be as small as ten or as large as two hundred square leagues. In return for legal title to the land, the recipient theoretically enforced the dictates of the Portuguese monarch. Owing to the distances involved and the difficulties in communication, however, these rural chiefs known as *coronéis* made almost all decisions on their own. Bands of hired gunmen called *jagunços* enforced their employers' will. Even when Napoleon's invasion forced the Portuguese emperor to take up residence in Brazil for the thirteen years betwen 1808 and 1821, the distance between the Crown and its supposed lieutenants remained as great as ever. When Pedro I declared Brazil an independent empire in 1822, the backlands were still a violent, sparsely settled region.

Changes in imperial land policy during the second quarter of the nineteenth century contributed to an increase in the interior's population.[2] By 1850, most inhabitants were subsistence farmers. Usually descendants of unions between Portuguese colonists and African slaves or Tupi Indians, almost all were poor and illiterate.

---

2. See Manuel Diégues Júnior, *População e propriedade da terra no Brasil,* for documentation of changes in land tenure patterns affecting Northeast Brazil.

Some of these subsistence farmers owned a small plot of earth, but most rented land from a powerful *coronel*. In some parts of the Northeast this patron-dependent system was originally intended to foster the integration of large numbers of ambulatory workers into a stable social framework. As urban demand for agricultural products grew and new taxes were levied by state governments, the arrangement became an economic necessity.[3]

Although the specific rights and duties of subsistence farmers varied, tenants were usually obliged to hand over from a quarter to a half of their harvest. They were supposed to vote as their patron directed and, should the need arise, to defend the owner's interests as part of a makeshift army. Some were required to furnish a certain number of days of unpaid labor each week.

In return the renter received the right to farm. Those tenants called *moradores* (*morar* means "to live" or "to dwell") were also given the use of a house; *rendeiros*, who did not require the landlord's housing, had somewhat fewer responsibilities. Both groups were dependent on the patron for their land and thus their survival.

Born of economic considerations, this patron-dependent system was sanctioned by "a set of general propositions about submissiveness to authority and obligation to meet debts which are reinforced by ideas from a variety of domains, above all the religious."[4] The unwritten one-to-one contracts binding landowners and tenants theoretically offered protection in return for deference. Given the insecurity born of drought, bandits, and warring *coronéis*, most landless farmers had little choice but to accept the patron as counselor, judge, and guardian of public morals as well as employer.[5]

3. For insight into the social as well as economic transformations in the land tenure system see Billy Jaynes Chandler, *The Feitosas and the Sertão of Inhamuns: The History of a Family and a Community in Northeast Brazil, 1700–1930*. Although remnants of this system are still very much in evidence, the Northeast has undergone significant modifications in social and economic structure. For a discussion of these see Kempton E. Webb, *The Changing Face of Northeast Brazil;* Shepard Forman, *The Brazilian Peasantry;* Lia Freitas Garcia Fukui, *Sertão e bairro rural;* and Tamás Szmrecsányi and Oriowaldo Queda, eds., *Vida rural e mudança.*

4. Forman, *The Brazilian Peasantry,* p. 76. For detailed discussions of the Northeastern land tenure system see, in addition to Forman, Allen Johnson, *Sharecroppers of the Sertão;* and Bertram Hutchinson, "The Patron-Dependent Relationship in Brazil: A Preliminary Examination." Simon Mitchell, ed., *The Logic of Poverty: The Stagnation of North East Brazil,* offers a series of essays focusing on continuing problems.

5. This sort of patron-client or patron-dependent network based on a series of vertical asymmetric dyads is in no way limited to Northeast Brazil. For correlative material see Peter Blau, *Exchange and Power in Social Life;* George M. Foster, "The Dyadic Contract: A Model for the Social Structure of a Mexican Peasant Village"; John Duncan Powell, "Peasant Society and Clientelist Politics"; and Eric R. Wolf, "Kinship, Friendship and Patron-

Because of its relative abundance of water and fertile soil, the Cariri Valley, where Juazeiro do Norte is located, attracted sizable numbers of ranch and plantation owners. These in turn employed many small farmers.[6] (*Cariri* is the name of a local Indian tribe as well as the indigenous term for a type of thorny vegetation characteristic of the backlands. A *juazeiro* is a kind of drought-resistant tree.) The valley's strategic location, in southeastern Ceará not far from the borders of Paraíba and Pernambuco, gave it economic importance. By the middle of the nineteenth century its largest settlement, Crato, was a major food and cotton producer and a principal distribution center for European imports channeled through the port of Recife. The most populous city in the Northeast and the capital of Pernambuco, Recife was far more important to the Cariri's economy during this period than was Fortaleza, the capital of Ceará. Even today, residents of the Cariri are said to "talk like Pernambucans," an indication of lingering cultural as well as commercial ties.

A drought in 1845 hurt the lucrative sugar business, but the industry made a comeback in the 1850s. Economic development intensified in the 1860s with the rise in exports to Europe of cotton when the Civil War cut off United States trade to Europe. By the time Padre Cícero assumed responsibility for the lone chapel in Juazeiro in 1872, an increasingly prosperous Cariri was clamoring for a proportionate share of state revenues. Aware of the benefits modernization was bringing to the coast in the form of better roads and increased health and educational facilities, a backlands elite composed of landowners, merchants, and clerics struggled to attract the state capital's attention.

The Brazilian Church

The first missionaries in Brazil were Jesuits eager to convert the native Indian population.[7] To this end they founded schools and developed new methods of religious education, soon becoming the single largest order

Client Relationships in Complex Societies." See also James C. Scott's "Patron-Client Politics and Political Change in Southeast Asia," and his "The Erosion of Patron-Client Bonds and Social Change in Rural Southeast Asia."

6. For a summary of the history of the Cariri Valley see Joaquim Alves, "O Vale do Cariri."

7. There is an extensive bibliography on the history of the Catholic Church in Brazil. I have drawn heavily in this section upon Thales de Azevedo, *O catolicismo no Brasil;* Roger Bastide, "Religion and the Church in Brazil"; and Thomas C. Bruneau, *The Political Transformation of the Brazilian Catholic Church,* especially pp. 11–37. For additional bibliography see Bruneau, *Political Transformation,* pp. 253–264. A number of more recent articles are listed in Levine, *Brazil,* pp. 252–259.

in Brazil. When the Portuguese crown, increasingly unhappy about the group's direct ties to Rome, expelled the Jesuits from both Brazil and Portugal in 1759, their absence was duly noted.[8]

The Brazilian clergy remained weak throughout the rest of the eighteenth and nineteenth centuries. As in Portugal, where the Crown used papal bulls issued after conquests in Africa as the basis for its domination of all religious institutions, the colonial church functioned as an arm of the civil bureaucracy. The Portuguese monarch not only nominated bishops and collected tithes but also paid the salaries of parish priests.

Throughout the period between 1500 and 1822, only a handful of clerics served the interior. Difficulties in communication and transportation, coupled with a chronic lack of funds for salaries, meant that most communities had little or no contact with the official church. As a result, their inhabitants—almost all nominally Catholic—came to rely heavily if not exclusively on a series of folk practices designed to ward off evil spirits believed responsible for sickness and bad weather. The cult of the saints, home altars, and *promessas,* or vows to saints, often served as substitutes for formal religious activity.[9] Backlands residents also turned to a wide variety of messianic movements (described later in this chapter).

During the second half of the nineteenth century, growing anticlericalism in Europe led Pope Pius IX to attack not only the *philosophes* who had spearheaded the French Revolution but also socialists, communists, and liberal capitalists.[10] The beatification and subsequent canonization of Jean Baptiste Marie Vianney, the Curé d'Ars (1786–1859) and Giovanni Bosco (1815–88) reflect the church's desire to reaffirm the continued vitality of traditional Christian values in an increasingly secular world.[11] Both men came from the provinces rather than big cities, were given to

8. For an overview of the Jesuits in Brazil see (Pe.) Serafim Leite, *Summa Histórica da Companhia de Jesus no Brasil.* The same author has written a ten-volume history.

9. The bibliography on folk and popular Catholicism within Brazil is large and growing. For an introduction see Riolando Azzi, *O catolicismo popular no Brasil: Aspectos históricos,* and Bernardino Leers, *Catolicismo popular e mundo rural: Um ensaio pastoral.* For further listings see Pedro A. Ribeiro de Oliveira, "Expressões religiosas populares e liturgia." The journals *Revista Eclesiástica Brasileira, Cadernos do ISER,* and *Religião e Sociedade* regularly publish articles on the subject.

10. For a summary of key events in nineteenth-century Church history see Paul Droulers, "Roman Catholicism."

11. Vianney and Bosco were extremely important to Padre Cícero, who seems to have looked to them as models for his own spiritual life. Examination of the mass of uncritical writing on the two men reveals a series of common patterns (prophetic dreams, supposed cures, ascetic practices). For an introduction to Vianney and Bosco see the respective entries in the *New Catholic Encyclopedia:* (Bosco) vol. 3, pp. 714–715, and (Vianney) vol. 14, pp. 636–637.

ascetic practices and extraordinary visions, and acquired considerable fame as champions of the poor. The long lists of miracles included in their official canonization proceedings make clear that an enthusiasm for the supernatural was in no way confined to the Brazilian lower classes.

The Ultramontanist movement that emerged in Europe during this period sought to eradicate regional peculiarities the church had tolerated as long as heads of states had also been willing to pose as defenders of the faith. Religious authorities accordingly began to place new stress on formal training of a national clergy as well as on revamping and centralizing ecclesiastical institutions.

In Ceará, this concerted push toward "romanization" resulted in the naming of the state's first bishop, Dom Luís Antonio dos Santos, a native of Rio de Janeiro.[12] Dom Luís actively encouraged the founding of a new seminary run by French Lazarist fathers in Fortaleza in 1864. This institution was intended to increase both the number and quality of native-born clergy in the interior, where priests' often dubious behavior had severely tarnished the church's image.

The new bishop's job could not have been easy. Not only did he have to cope with centuries of neglect but he also, like his fellow bishops, found himself caught between Pedro II's determination to maintain the church as a dependent arm of the bureaucracy and Rome's growing insistence on the supremacy of canon over civil law.

Not all clerics succeeded in maintaining this delicate balance. In line with the Vatican's new militancy in regard to religious matters, Dom Vital Maria Gonçalves de Oliveira, the new bishop of Olinda, ordered members of the clergy to take no part in a commemorative mass scheduled by a Masonic lodge in 1872. In so doing he touched off a church-state confrontation known as the Imperial Religious Question.[13]

Even priests had joined the Masonry during the Brazilian independence movement, but Rome's growing hostility toward the organization as an agent of anticlericalism prompted the bishop's action.[14] When his National Council of State sided with the lodge, Pedro ordered Dom Vital and another bishop who had joined him to comply, imprisoning them

12. The concept of *romanization* is Bastide's but the term is Ralph della Cava's. See the latter's *Miracle at Joaseiro*, pp. 20–24. Joaseiro is an older spelling of Juazeiro.

13. For a discussion of the Imperial Religious Question see J. Lloyd Mecham, *Church and State in Latin America: A History of Politico-Ecclesiastical Relations*, pp. 316–321. Some historians believe that Pedro's opposition to the church contributed to his later downfall: see George Boehrer, "The Church and the Overthrow of the Brazilian Monarchy."

14. A history of the Masons in Brazil is available in (S.) Mary Crescentia Thornton, *The Church and Freemasonry in Brazil, 1872–1875.*

for three years upon their refusal. This action on the part of a nominally Catholic head of state shocked and troubled religious leaders.

At the same time that these events were occurring, Dom Luís found himself head to head with the powerful Northeastern folk religion, in the guise of a zealous native-born missionary known as Padre Mestre Ibiapina.[15] Born in 1807, the lawyer José Antonio Pereira Ibiapina entered the priesthood at the age of forty-seven. Eight years later, in 1862, the outbreak of a virulent cholera epidemic prompted him to ask authorities for permission to preach in the backlands near the city of Sobral. There people began to venerate him as a holy man, and he went on to establish an unofficial religious sisterhood called a Casa de Caridade or "Charity House." Because Dom Luís had not authorized Ibiapina to found what amounted to a canonically unapproved order, he demanded that the missionary leave the diocese. Ibiapina obeyed but soon began establishing a series of similar Charity Houses in cities throughout the interior. These Houses served as de facto convents for women called *beatas* who were often, though not always, from the lower classes.[16] They also functioned as orphanages, centers for the production of cheap textiles, and schools for daughters of the local elite.

As wealthy landowners and merchants frequently contributed to the Charity Houses' construction and upkeep, Dom Luís hesitated to mount a frontal attack. He did, however, finally call a halt to all missionary work in the interior in 1869. This decision was largely a response to a series of newspaper accounts in which the journalist José Joaquim Teles Marrocos enthusiastically described a number of Ibiapina's allegedly miraculous cures. Three years later, when the bishop came to Crato to break ground for a minor seminary, he demanded and obtained authority over the valley's four Charity Houses, thereby forcing Ibiapina to leave the Cariri for good.

The bishop's quarrel with the missionary underscores much larger tensions between nationalistic and universalizing factions within the Brazilian church. In seeking to tighten its control over popular religious practice in the Northeast, Rome ran up against the centuries-old tradition of the charismatic healer. Moreover, although not all native-born priests approved of Ibiapina, many resented what they perceived to be the ar-

15. For more about Ibiapina see Celso Mariz, *Ibiapina, um apóstolo do nordeste*.

16. For a discussion of the *beatas* in and around Juazeiro see Renato Dantas, *As beatas do Cariri e de Juazeiro*. The medieval *beguines,* who have certain parallels to the *beatas,* are discussed in Ernest W. McDonnell, *The Beguines and Beghards in Medieval Culture.* For the *beatos* or male counterpart of the *beatas,* see Antônio Xavier de Oliveira, *Beatos e cangaceiros.* The *beatos* did not form communities but were otherwise quite similar.

bitrary imposition of foreign standards on domestic realities, seeing the pope's sudden insistence on religious orthodoxy as unrealistic in the long-neglected backlands. This larger conflict between regionally minded and more Rome-oriented segments of the Northeastern clergy provides the backdrop for the "miracles" of Juazeiro.

Padre Cícero and Juazeiro

Cícero Romão Batista was born in 1844 to Joaquim Romão and Joaquina Vicência Romana in the city of Crato.[17] His father, a modest shopkeeper, died in the cholera epidemic of 1862 which prompted Ibiapina's first mission. Joaquim Romão's death seemed to dash his son's hopes of entering the priesthood. The young Cícero, however, responded with one of the many prophetic dreams that were to come to him at moments of crisis. When he told his wealthy godfather, Antonio Luis Alves Pequeno II, about this apparent confirmation of his vocation, the man agreed to send him to the seminary that had just opened its doors in Fortaleza.

Official records indicate that the young man's teachers found him headstrong and that some voiced doubts about the wisdom of his ordination.[18] Nevertheless, around the time of Dom Luís's visit to the Cariri

17. There is a long bibliography regarding Padre Cícero and Juazeiro. The single best discussion of both is unquestionably della Cava's *Miracle at Joaseiro,* upon which I have drawn extensively for historical documentation both in this chapter and throughout this book. For a summary of book-length studies of the priest see Ildefonso Silveira, "Estado atual da pesquisa sobre o Padre Cícero." Among the more important of these works, most of which are blatantly partisan, are Otacílio Anselmo e Silva, *Padre Cícero—Mito e realidade;* Floro Bartolomeu da Costa, *Joaseiro e o Padre Cícero: Depoimentos para a história;* Manoel Dinis, *Mistérios do Joazeiro: História completa de Pe. Cícero Romão Batista do Joazeiro do Ceará;* Rui Facó, *Cangaceiros e fanáticos: Gênese e lutas;* Neri Feitosa, *Eu defendo o Padre Cícero;* Manuel Bergström Lourenço Filho, *Joaseiro do Padre Cícero (Scenas e quadros do fanatismo do nordeste);* Manuel Macedo, *Joazeiro em foco;* Nertan Macedo, *O padre e a beata;* Helvídio Martins Maia, *Pretensos milagres em Juazeiro;* Edmar Morel, *Padre Cícero, o santo do Juazeiro;* Amália Xavier de Oliveira, *O Padre Cícero que eu conheci: Verdadeira história de Juazeiro do Norte;* Irineu Pinheiro, *Efemérides do Cariri;* Tristão Romero, *Vida completa do Padre Cícero Romão Batista (Anchieta do século XX);* and Azarias Sobreira, *O patriarca do Juazeiro.*

18. The exact notation in reference to Padre Cícero in the official seminary notebook, dated August 8, 1867, is: "Il a été dit qu'il ne méritait pas l'ordination parce que, depuis longtemps il ne se confesse pas ni communie, et qu'il est peu régulier; qu'il a beaucoup d'idées confuses, qu'il a beaucoup de Foi dans sa propre raison; la 1e raison est d'autant plus grave qui'il est employé au seminaire. Pour cela il a été dit que, s'il continuait ainsi, il ne pourrait plus remplir cet office en raison du scandale qu'il donnait, et que néanmoins on le laisserait libre pour les deux ordres afin de ne pas désaccréditer les professeurs choisis." Although if considered in isolation this comment casts doubt on Padre Cícero's character, a look at the Lazarist fathers' opinions of other students confirms their rigid expectations of a future priest. Any student who did not devote himself wholeheartedly to public displays of piety appears to have incurred their displeasure. I am grateful to Anne Dumoulin for allowing me to see the original.

Valley in 1872, Padre Cícero returned to Crato as a full-fledged priest. Shortly afterward, he accepted an invitation to celebrate a mass in what was then the small chapel of Our Lady of Sorrows in Juazeiro, a hamlet that was looking for a priest. Bent on a teaching career, the young cleric had no intention of remaining until, that night, he had one of his fateful visions. In his dream, Christ directed him to care for the Northeastern poor. When the priest awoke the next morning he had made his decision. Not long after, he moved to Juazeiro with two unmarried sisters and his mother.

Padre Cícero quickly proved himself to be unlike the preceding permanent priest, rumored to have fathered numerous children. From 1872 onward, the cleric appears to have dedicated himself unstintingly to the welfare of his parishioners. Although it was church practice at the time to charge for religious services, Padre Cícero refused payment. Walking from farm to farm, he provided both spiritual counsel and practical advice. The drought of 1877–80—a calamity which resulted in the death or emigration of over 300,000 persons, a third of the total population of the state—spurred him to redouble his pastoral efforts.[19] The priest succeeded in finding places in the Cariri for many of the refugees to work and farm and in obtaining government support for the most needy. In the process he enhanced his reputation as a friend of the poor.

The following decade saw far-reaching social changes. Slavery was abolished in 1888; the Empire fell and a secular republic was proclaimed in 1889. Earlier in that year, the prospect of a new drought led residents of the interior to embark on a series of novenas and vigils in which Padre Cícero played a major role. On the first Friday in March of 1889, the priest prepared to celebrate the monthly mass in honor of the Sacred Heart of Jesus. As several of the women had already taken part in a special all-night service, he decided to offer them communion so that they could go home to rest. The first recipient was the *beata* Maria de Araújo, an unmarried, illiterate, twenty-eight-year-old mulatto laundress.

Before that fateful morning, Maria de Araújo had not commanded any sort of special attention. When, however, Padre Cícero placed the communion wafer upon her tongue on this occasion, the host allegedly grew red with blood, and a fragment fell from her mouth to the floor. Padre Cícero picked up this fragment with an altar towel, later placing both objects in a glass urn for safekeeping. This receptacle was removed in 1892 to Crato because the city was the seat of the larger administrative

19. For a discussion of the drought see Roger Lee Cunniff, "The Great Drought: Northeastern Brazil, 1877–1880." See also Anthony Hall's more general *Drought and Irrigation in Northeast Brazil*.

district to which Juazeiro belonged at that time. The transformation reportedly recurred on every Wednesday and Friday until Easter, and then daily until the Feast of Christ's Ascension, forty days later.

During this period Padre Cícero, evidently uncertain about the event's significance, did not report it to anyone. Other members of the clergy were not as discreet. One of these was Monsignor Francisco Monteiro, a longtime friend and distant relative who was the rector of the new Crato seminary. On July 7, the feast day of the Precious Blood, the rector led approximately 3,000 persons from Crato to Juazeiro, where he publicly identified the stains on a handful of altar linens as the blood of Christ.

Friends' and peers' enthusiastic confidence in the "miracle" seems to have affected Padre Cícero. The separation of church and state within the new republic may also have disposed the priest to conclude that the host had indeed been transformed into the blood of Christ. The official report reached the bishop in January of 1890, some two months after the military coup that overthrew the Empire.[20]

Dom Joaquim José Vieira, who had replaced Dom Luís in 1883, had already learned of the reputed miracle through a newspaper account. The author of the account was the same José Marrocos who had outraged the bishop's predecessor two decades earlier by heralding the missionary Ibiapina's allegedly miraculous cures. Dom Joaquim's dismay at hints of a Second Coming may reflect his fears about the reaction of a superstitious populace to the event. He also appears to have interpreted Padre Cícero's delay in contacting him as an affront to his authority. Accordingly, the bishop placed the burden of proof entirely upon the priest. Forbidding him to make any public declaration about the events until the church had reached a verdict, Dom Joaquim dispatched an official Commission of Inquiry to Juazeiro in 1891.

The two priests who constituted this commission were the bishop's trusted colleagues. He was therefore astounded when they, perhaps in response to the fervor of the moment, affirmed the supernatural nature of the event. Unable or unwilling to accept their findings, Dom Joaquim sent a second panel to Juazeiro in 1892, and this panel indeed failed to find any evidence of divine intervention in the events of 1889.

This second commission also reported the theft of the stained hosts and linens from the Crato altar. (The urn containing them was to turn up among the personal effects of José Marrocos at his death in 1910.) The

20. The alleged appearance of the blood at a moment of intense social stress has parallels in the rise of Marian apparitions in similar moments of tension: for other examples see William A. Christian, Jr., *Apparitions in Late Medieval and Renaissance Spain.*

disappearance of the evidence confirmed for the bishop his suspicions that Padre Cícero was either an active participant in a hoax or else the pawn of others with dubious intentions. He therefore suspended the priest from preaching, hearing confession, and counseling the faithful.

Dom Joaquim's actions diminished Padre Cícero's early support among the upper classes and the clergy, most of whom renounced, under episcopal pressure, their initial belief in the alleged transformation. Official disapproval did nothing, however, to discourage the often penniless pilgrims who began arriving in Juazeiro soon after the "miracle" became public knowledge. Many of these individuals came from the states of Alagoas and Pernambuco, to which, as already mentioned, the Cariri Valley had close economic ties. The disruptive activities of outlaws in the eastern portions of these states may have further encouraged their residents to seek refuge in Juazeiro. A relative abundance of jobs and somewhat more favorable land-tenure conditions than in the coastal sugar plantations probably provided added incentives.[21]

A series of exchanges between Padre Cícero and the bishop as well as between the bishop and the pope occurred between 1892 and 1894. At the end of this period the Roman Inquisition stunned the priest's followers by denouncing the alleged transformation. Not long afterward, Dom Joaquim summoned Padre Cícero and four of his supporters to Fortaleza, where he ordered them to submit to the decree. In 1897, he insisted that the priest leave Juazeiro, leading Padre Cícero to move temporarily to nearby Salgueiro, Pernambuco.

Convinced of the justice of his cause, the priest left Brazil for Rome a year later in the company of José Lobo, the chief organizer of Juazeiro's powerful religious brotherhoods. Although Pope Leo XIII did not recognize the "miracle" or restore Padre Cícero's orders, he did absolve him of censures resulting from previous decrees. He also granted the priest provisional permission to celebrate mass, thus placing any future change in his clerical standing directly in Rome's hands.

The lack of further concessions is not hard to understand. First, the alleged transformation raised a series of disturbing theological questions not apparent to most of Padre Cícero's followers. Then, too, the pope could not have simply ignored the findings of the second Commission of Inquiry. Bent on uniting Catholics against a multitude of enemies, he must have perceived the threat posed by the "miracle" to an already fragile ecclesiastical structure. There is no indication that the pope himself

---

21. Even today, one of the principal motives for moving to Juazeiro from the coastal region is to escape the *usina* or sugar factory: as many as a third of the residents of the Rua do Horto were formerly employees of the sugar industry.

considered the events of 1889 to be in any way extraordinary, but even if he had, it would have been politically disastrous for him to have over-ridden Dom Joaquim. Moreover, given the pope's explicit interest in maintaining satisfactory relations with all established governments, he would have been most reluctant to antagonize a new and therefore extremely sensitive republic.

Considering the problems that the events of 1889 posed for ecclesiastical authorities, Padre Cícero's trip must be deemed a success. Some persons of the period suggested that the mass stipends contributed by many thousands of pilgrims to Juazeiro had influenced Leo XIII's reaction to his case.[22] It is equally possible that the pope sought to cool a potential schism within the Brazilian church by handling Padre Cícero and his followers with moderation. In any case, although his audience with the pontiff failed to effect any real change in the priest's standing, it enhanced his prestige among his followers, most of whom grasped little more than the fact that he had actually been to Rome.

Northeasterners' newfound faith in Padre Cícero's miraculous abilities had profound economic and political ramifications. As growing numbers of believers continued to gravitate toward Juazeiro, the once tiny hamlet began to dwarf its neighbors. Padre Cícero's increasing involvement in practical affairs was an inevitable result of this expansion.

The priest had already revealed a certain capacity for administration by finding jobs for the newcomers in the manufacture of handicrafts and in farming. Successful in persuading the state and federal government to establish schools and health-care facilities, he introduced rudimentary notions of hygiene and nutrition among the poor. At the same time, Padre Cícero was able to make a number of sound investments with the money donated to him by followers. Even his detractors usually concede that the profits from these did not go into his own pocket but were placed at the service of the needy.

Padre Cícero had less talent for direct political dealings. Perhaps because he had grown up in a social system characterized by confrontation rather than compromise, he had little conception of how to balance opposing forces to his advantage. He initially managed to avoid taking sides in local disputes, but as Juazeiro grew this neutral stance became increasingly difficult to maintain.

The arrival in Juazeiro in 1908 of Dr. Floro Bartolomeu da Costa, a politically astute physician, signals the priest's official entry into the sec-

22. For the figures see della Cava, *Miracle at Joaseiro,* pp. 78–80. A summary of Padre Cícero's activities in Rome appears in Amália Xavier de Oliveira, *Dados que marcam a vida do Padre Cícero Romão Batista,* pp. 20–23.

ular arena.[23] For the moment it is enough to note that Floro was one of the middle-class power-seekers typical of that period between 1894 and 1914 called the Old Republic. Known as *bacharéis* ("university graduates"), these individuals sought to increase their influence by serving as advisors to representatives of a faltering but still powerful old-style oligarchy.

Because of his immense appeal among the poor, the priest soon assumed a leading role in state as well as regional affairs. Although he did not have political ambitions, he became the first mayor of Juazeiro in 1911 and third vice-president of the state of Ceará, a largely honorific title, in 1912. A new governor, Franco Rabelo, turned on Juazeiro not long afterward in an armed confrontation that has become known as the Revolution of 1913–14. At Floro's urging, Padre Cícero succeeded in mobilizing his followers, who soundly defeated the state militia when it attacked the city. Not long after this victory, a new governor assumed power and promoted the priest to first vice-president. Floro went on to the state legislature, later representing the Cariri in the national assembly.

Despite this increasing involvement in political matters, throughout the almost half-century following the "miracle" of 1889 Padre Cícero appears to have been primarily interested in—if not obsessed with—the restitution of his priestly orders. Relations between him and the church had improved to the point of the reinstatement in 1916 of his right to say mass, but this privilege was again revoked in 1920.[24]

Floro's death in 1926 signaled the beginning of Padre Cícero's political decline. The priest, however, continued to receive multitudes of pilgrims until his death eight years later. Toward the end of his life, his household staff and a number of merchants eager to exploit ingenuous visitors to Juazeiro exerted increasing control over the infirm old man. These individuals often refused pilgrims access to the priest unless they bought one or another religious article as a ticket of admission. Some pilgrims spent every penny intended for food and lodging in an ultimately fruitless effort to obtain Padre Cícero's blessing. Not infrequently, people who had walked for weeks to reach Juazeiro stood weeping at the door the merchants callously slammed in their faces.

The priest, however, had the final say in the disposition of his property, leaving the bulk of his wealth to the Salesian Order. Padre Cícero's

23. For more about Floro see Chapter VI.

24. Della Cava, *Miracle at Joaseiro,* pp. 184–186, notes that Rome sent an order for Padre Cícero's excommunication to Fortaleza in June of 1916. It was pragmatically ignored by the new bishop, Dom Quintino Rodrigues e Silva de Oliveira, who must have been well aware of the upheaval its implementation would have caused.

choice of the Salesians confirms his admiration for Dom Bosco. The Order's close ties to a papacy Padre Cícero may have hoped would vindicate his memory are another possible motive for his selection.[25]

During the priest's lifetime, Northeastern priests, acting in most cases on directives from their superiors, attempted to stamp out the pilgrimage to Juazeiro. They regularly denied the sacraments to anyone who refused to assert his or her disbelief in the alleged transformation. They also destroyed rosaries bearing medals of Padre Cícero and refused to baptize children with the name Cícero or Cícera. In response to this systematic repression, many Northeasterners stopped going to confession. They crossed state lines to search for a sympathetic priest who would give a child the name they had chosen, and they hid the forbidden rosary under layers of clothing if they went to church.

Padre Cícero's death did not end the tensions between Juazeiro and the Roman Catholic hierarchy. Several of the clerics who served the city after 1934 had considerable difficulties with the populace. In 1935, for example, twelve self-styled guards expelled Padre Juvenal Colares Maia from the church of Our Lady of Sorrows. Considering the priest to be one of the communist enemies against whom the former vicar, Padre Pedro Esmeraldo, had warned, they refused to open the doors to him on command. Ten soldiers then fired on the guards still in the sanctuary, killing six. Padre Juvenal's replacement, Padre Joviniano Barreto, was assassinated in 1950; his successor, Padre José Lima, who was more tolerant of popular sentiment, fared considerably better.

Larger changes within the Roman Catholic Church have enabled Padre Lima's successor, Padre Murilo de Sá Barreto, to widen and intensify the parish's involvement with pilgrims to Juazeiro.[26] The Puebla Latin American Bishops' Conference of 1979, for instance, made a positive if cautious statement regarding pilgrimages and similar unofficial expressions of faith.[27] In line with this pronouncement, the pastoral staff of Our Lady of Sorrows has increased its efforts to accommodate the priest's followers by stressing Padre Cícero's loyalty to fundamental

25. Della Cava, *Miracle at Joaseiro*, p. 206.

26. For a detailed discussion of recent developments within the Brazilian Roman Catholic Church see Bruneau's *Political Transformation* and his *The Church in Brazil: The Politics of Religion.* See also Ralph della Cava, "Catholicism and Society in Twentieth-Century Brazil."

27. The Puebla conference defined popular religion as "not only the object of evangelization but also . . . an active form through which the people continually evangelize themselves." The full proceedings of the conference are available in *Evangelização no presente e no futuro da América Latina. Conclusões da III^a Conferência Geral do Episcopado Latino-Americano, Puebla de los Angeles, México 7–1 a 13–2 de 1979.*

Christian principles as well as his practical attempts to better the life of his followers.

A number of other priests and representatives of various religious orders in Juazeiro have not, however, followed suit. The Capuchins and Salesians offer masses that are heavily attended by pilgrims, and the Capuchins house numerous visitors to Juazeiro, but many representatives of these orders are clearly uncomfortable about the pilgrimage.

This continuing coolness toward Padre Cícero is not lost on his followers. Although the Igreja Católica Apostólica Brasileira (Brazilian Apostolic Catholic Church), a breakaway faction of the Roman Catholic Church, declared him a saint in 1973, most pilgrims are aware of the priest's lack of official standing.[28] "He has not yet been 'colonized' [canonized]," one woman explained to me. Her remark underscores the lack of church participation in the pilgrimages to Juazeiro. In Canindé, for instance, fifty priests from all over the Northeast minister round the clock to visitors who pour in to honor Saint Francis during major feast days, but no such effort is made to serve those who journey to the Cariri on similar occasions.

Padre Cícero and His Followers

The highly partisan nature of most of the existing documentation makes it difficult to speak with any certainty about the early followers who looked to Padre Cícero for guidance. Some critics have accused the priest of encouraging uneducated pilgrims' faith in his thaumaturgic powers.[29] Aside from his avowed belief in the alleged transformation, however, there is no concrete evidence to link him to any extraordinary event.

The existence of early printed editions of some of the miracle stories suggests that Padre Cícero must have had some idea of what people were saying about him.[30] Because Northeasterners fully expect a saint to deny his or her sanctity, they would have seized upon any disavowal of his own powers by Padre Cícero as added proof of his privileged spiritual status. The existence of such stories therefore tells us little about the priest's presentation or perception of himself.

28. Some of the priest's followers see this alternative canonization as a victory for the priest. A verse (*cordel*) commemoration of the event by Antônio Batista Romão, "A Igreja Brasileira canonizou em Brasília o Padre Cícero Romão," is reproduced in Paulo Machado, *O Padre Cícero e a literatura de cordel: Fenomenologia da devoção ao Padre Cícero*, pp. 38–41.

29. See, for example, Antônio Gomes de Araújo's virulent "Apostolado do Embuste."

30. A number of the stories told today are summarized in Dinis's *Mistérios do Joazeiro*, published in 1935. There are also several printed (*cordel*) versions that date back to the 1920s.

One of the few direct indications we have of Padre Cícero takes the form of a hundred or so letters, many in his own handwriting. These are kept in archives maintained by the Salesian Order, by the Bishopric of Crato, and by the parish of Our Lady of Sorrows.[31] Addressed primarily to family members, friends, and colleagues, they span some fifty years. Because their author was clearly aware of the eyes riveted on him, the letters have a public as much as a personal quality. They attest above all else to Padre Cícero's deep identification with Juazeiro and his bitter incomprehension of the church's treatment of him and his followers.

The author of these letters is involved in every facet of life in his adopted city. He is the undisputed head not only of his own family but also of the extended household that is Juazeiro. As such, he feels compelled to oversee and comment on every detail of daily life. Have those four lots of manioc on the São Pedro hillside been harvested? Are Dona Leopoldina's daughters getting enough to eat? Was a certain sum of money duly deposited to the London and River Plate Bank a week ago last Monday? Has the herbal remedy he prescribed in his last letter begun to take effect? Could his sister send a half-dozen tins of candied wine-palm and some choice pineapple to a couple who received him graciously in Salgueiro?

Like a proper chief of a Northeast Brazilian family, the priest insists on counseling those in his charge. One can practically see him shaking a patriarchal finger at his sister for her lack of caution in safeguarding of material possessions.[32] He is equally blunt with two young men who are thinking about leaving school. Pointing out that he has made "no small sacrifice" to provide them with an education, he asserts that it is their duty, not their privilege, to become "men of good character and useful citizens."[33] He urges a fellow priest who has taken a mistress to send the woman and their child to Juazeiro. In this way, the two will lack nothing and his friend will then be able to begin a new life.[34]

An apparent pragmatist when it comes to spiritual as well as to ma-

31. I am grateful to Therezinha Stella Guimarães and Anne Dumoulin for access to photocopies of the majority of these letters, as well as for allowing me to read a manuscript version of their *O Padre Cícero por ele mesmo*. For a guide to the Salesian Archives see Antenor de Andrade Silva, *Os arquivos do Padre Cícero*.

32. In a letter to his sister Angélica dated October 24, 1897, Padre Cícero chides her for not keeping the household keys on her person at all times: see Letter 11, Packet 12, Salesian Archives.

33. The letter, dated June 9, 1933, is addressed to "Godofredo and Alfredo." It is Letter 60 in Packet 36, Salesian Archives.

34. Letter 17, dated July 18, 1918, addressed to a "Padre Lúcio" in Packet 25, Salesian Archives.

terial matters, the priest speaks enthusiastically of "the high number of
holy results" obtained during the first, golden days of the pilgrimage to
Juazeiro.[35] He also rails at finding himself treated "like a common criminal" by the bishop, whom he considers to be stricken by an "infamous
delusion which only a miracle" would dispel.[36] Over and over he demands how he, who "has spent his whole life seeking the salvation of
others," could find himself repaid in such sorry coin.[37] "Only the devil
himself," he asserts on more than one occasion, could have led church
officials to believe the accusations leveled by "scores of enemies."[38]

Padre Cícero's incomprehension of the bishop's initial coolness and
his eventual mounting anger and frustration indicate a singular insensi-
tivity to Dom Luís's difficult situation. At the same time, there is no
denying the priest's feeling for the downtrodden, who speak for themselves in other letters preserved in the Salesian archives. Grim testimony
to economic conditions that still prevail in many parts of the Northeast,
these letters written during the first decades of the century provide a
valuable insight into the lives of Padre Cícero's followers. Less self-
conscious than those composed by the priest, they document their authors' overwhelming need as well as their faith.

The misspellings and non-standard grammatical constructions that
are the rule rather than the exception in the letters to Padre Cícero point
to their authors' lack of formal education.[39] In many cases, the individual
probably dictated to one of the barely literate "secretaries" who used to
serve unschooled clients in open-air fairs. A number of letters are written
on an immediately recognizable cheap blue paper folded over to form an
envelope. Something in these turn-of-the-century "mailgrams" has
caused the ink in many cases to acquire a curious translucence.

A number of key words reappear throughout the letters sent by
people from all over the Northeast. These include *remédio* ("cure"), *es-
mola* ("alms") and *recurso* ("financial resources"), *sossego* ("relief, "com-

35. Letter 37, dated October 23, 1914, addressed to Padre Augusto Constantino, in Packet
36, Salesian Archives.

36. Letter 10, dated October 20, 1897, addressed to Padre Cícero's mother and his sister
Angélica, in Packet 12, Salesian Archives.

37. Letter 8 (no date), in Packet 36, Salesian Archives.

38. In a letter addressed to a fellow cleric, Padre Soter (Letter 4, dated March 28, 1912, in
Packet 34, Salesian Archives), Padre Cícero speaks of the bishop's actions as "unconsciously
diabolic." "May God convert them," he says in regard to Dom Joaquim and Padre Quintino, "because the demon deceives them."

39. A minority of letters were written by well-educated persons: some are admirers; others
write to ask the priest to recommend potential employees. The overwhelming majority,
however, come from the poor. A small number are reproduced in Silva, *Os arquivos,*

fort"), *conselho* ("counsel"), *amparo* or *proteção* ("protection"), *garantia* ("guarantee"), and *jeito* ("way" or "way out"). The single most common term is *bença* or *bênção*, which means "blessing." Over and over, people express a longing not only for Padre Cícero's spoken or written profession of good will but also for the *act* of blessing. In the *bença* (the colloquial form of *bênção*), the social superior or older person kisses the outstretched hand of the inferior or younger person (who may kneel in his or her presence), saying, "May God bless you." It is this ritual, reenacted many times each day in neighborhoods like the Rua do Horto, to which letter-writers refer time and again. "Please accept a thousand apologies for my failure to ask your blessing [in person]," writes one man in the Araripe Mountains in 1910. "I am aware that it is a sacred duty, a strict obligation, and the greatest of joys."[40]

The writers are quick not only to ask the priest's approval but also to seek advice. "Should I marry my second cousin José, my Padrinho?" "How can I get my mother to stop drinking?" "Should I sell my cattle now or wait until the rains start?" "How can I get the father of my child to marry me? And if he refuses to do so, where would you suggest finding another man to be my husband?"

These persons may also seek a form of counsel more akin to clarification. "Is it all right to eat meat on Friday?" one man inquires anxiously. "The priest here says that I can but I will not do so until I hear from you."[41] "Is it possible to be a spiritist and a Catholic at the same time?" asks a young man worried about his own attraction to the doctrine of reincarnation.[42] A woman inquires if it is true that the world is going to end and, if so, what she and her family ought to do about it. "My Padrinho," she writes, "they say that there are going to be three days and three nights of darkness and I am very frightened because what will ever become of us if this should come to pass?"[43]

Many people ask the priest for material tokens such as a rosary, a religious medal, or simply "an object that can help me when I find myself in danger." Others request poignantly small sums of money. "Please," one woman says, "could you send me enough to buy the paper

---

pp. 78–88. As the letters by ordinary people to Padre Cícero in the Salesian Archives are not arranged in any particular order, no letter or packet numbers are provided for them.

40. "José de Hollanda Alencar. Serra do Araripe, Ceará; August 19, 1910." (The writer's name and the place heading are given exactly as they appear in the letter.)

41. Manoel Trajano de Maria. Villa de São João, September 29, 1910.

42. José Marquez da Silva. Recife, Pernambuco, November 12, 1930.

43. Helena Paiva Fontes. Riachão, October 21, 1931.

on which to write you another letter?"[44] Still others plead for rain, a baby, or a job ("Anything that feeds my sixteen children will do, my Padrinho"). They may seek remedies for ailments such as tumors, chronic headaches, insanity, tuberculosis.

One woman asks Padre Cícero to cure "a constant shiver in the heart" for which the term *anxiety* seems a weak translation.[45] Another describes seeing "hues of blue, yellow, and green, and horses, toads, and feathers" before her eyes. She then inquires if these visions are punishments for her failure to visit Juazeiro as promised. "I really would have come this year if I had only had the money," she sadly assures the priest.[46]

Some letter-writers appeal to Padre Cícero as an arbiter in seeking vindication of apparent wrongs. One writer inquires whether the slaughter of a goat on his property was really his responsibility. "I want to know for certain," he explains, "because the goat's owner, Sr. Antonio Viturino, forced me to pay without any proof of the cause of death. I would therefore like to ask you if I really owed him this money. Please tell me for the sake of the five wounds of my Lord Jesus Christ."[47]

Other individuals seek a more intimate sort of intervention on the part of the priest. One such woman begs him to rescue her son from the "*gringo* faith [Protestantism] which he embraced upon his marriage."[48] Another confides that two men are out to kill him because of a complaint he lodged against them in a district court. He cautions Padre Cícero to show his letter to no one because "I am haunted by the fear of dying at the hand of one or the other." Racked by both "a desire to leave here" and "a terrible fear which prevents me from taking any action," he begs the priest to answer him by return post.[49]

The desperation evident in this illustration permeates other letters that seek absolution for a specific wrong. In many of these, the writer has taken a lover but now seeks reunion with his or her lawful spouse. "I betrayed my husband, I traded him for another man said to be very Religious; and so I sinned," writes one woman, "but the suffering which followed our separation brought me true repentance."[50] "Please don't let my soul or that of my family be lost," pleads a man who goes on to

44. Ana Teixeira. Bom Lugar, October 11, 1902.
45. Maria Pastora Bra[n]dão Lima. Pão de Açucar, Alagoas, September 22, 1910.
46. Rita Souza.[N.p.], April 7, 1900.
47. Antonio José da Graça. Fazenda Nova, Alagoas, August 15, 1910.
48. Antonia Maria da Conceição. Santana do Ipanema, Alagoas, August 17, 1910.
49. Manoel Alves de Pessoa. Arraial, July 21, 1910.
50. Maria Cecília G. Dias. São Paulo, December 13, 1933.

describe leaving his wife and five children for "a passion which has al-most been the death of me."[51]

People's confidence in Padre Cícero's ability to help them is even clearer in those letters where the writer expresses gratitude for past as-sistance. A prostitute asks pardon for her offenses and then offers thanks for the priest's protection. "My Padrinho," she says, "I am a prostitute and as you well know I have suffered many injuries and sufferings be-cause of the way in which I make my living. I therefore ask your for-giveness for the evil that I have committed and I assure you that I have been delivered from death by knife and by revolver simply by calling on your holy name."[52]

Other letters speak hopefully of their authors' plans to visit Padre Cícero someday. "Tell me when I can come to live in Juazeiro, if it is this year or the next, my Padrinho," one woman says.[53] Another writer ob-serves that he does not have the money to make the trip in the foreseeable future but promises the priest that if he does not find his way to the city during his lifetime he will "surely do so after death."[54] One woman ends a long letter to Padre Cícero with four words in capital letters: JOAZEIRO, ESTAÇÃO DO CÉO!" ("Juazeiro, Outpost of Heaven!")[55] She then carefully underlines the phrase three times as if thereby to bring her own proposed arrival in this earthly paradise a few steps closer to reality.

The priest himself could not possibly have answered more than a few of the tremendous number of letters that reached him over the decades. His principal literate helper, the *beata* Mocinha (Joana Tertulina de Jesus) authored many of those responses routinely stamped with the priest's signature.[56] The care, however, with which many present-day pilgrims treat these "form letters" attests to the reverence with which they must have been received. Handed down from parents and grandparents, most of these notes contain nothing more than an herbal remedy for headache together with the standard injunction to pray the rosary. The people who carry these tokens of the priest in a small cloth sack around the neck of-ten touch them when they hear or speak his name. Even though the

51. Antonio José Oliveira. [N.p., n.d.]

52. Ana Maria di [de] Souza. Maceió, Alagoas, October 29, 1901.

53. Amélia Joaquina de Araújo. Maceió, Alagoas, February 26, 1901.

54. Jozé [José] Soares. Cachoeira, Alagoas, April 18, 1919.

55. Maria das Dores Alves Lima. [N.p., n.d.]

56. Orphaned at an early age, Joana Tertulina de Jesus came to Juazeiro when she was fifteen years old. Some twenty years later she became a *beata* and the powerful administra-tive head of Padre Cícero's household. Her influence faded quickly after the priest's death, and she died in poverty at the age of eighty.

words themselves have often grown illegible, these persons' sense of the man whom they believe to have been their author has remained vivid over time.

Furthermore, despite the priest's death some fifty years ago, letters addressed to Padre Cícero still arrive in Juazeiro. Usually hand-delivered by friends and relatives of people who could not make the trip, they are often tucked under the priest's pillow in the Padre Cícero Museum. Written in ballpoint pen on notebook paper, these letters echo sentiments expressed at the turn of the century. They ask the priest for help not only with serious dilemmas but also with the usual ups and downs of daily life. "I fell in love for the first time," explains a sixteen-year-old girl from Rio Grande do Norte, "and I cannot understand why it should hurt so much. Please, my Padrinho, could you make the man for whom I care fall in love with me too or could you please just make my heart the way it was before we met?"[57]

Juazeiro as a Messianic Movement

One of the most common ways scholars have looked at Padre Cícero is as a charismatic leader. Juazeiro fits the general category of a revitalization movement, which Anthony Wallace has defined as "a deliberate, organized, conscious effort by members of a society to construct a more satisfying culture."[58] The community has also been described in narrower terms as a social messianic movement. According to Maria Isaura Pereira de Queiroz, probably the best-known Brazilian writer on the subject, these manifestations are distinguished by the presence of a leader who can command his followers' trust "not because he possesses a position within the established order but because of his extraordinary personal qualities, which are proven through magic or ecstatic faculties."[59] Although found in various parts of the world and in various religions,

57. The letter was found in the street by one of my neighbors in the Rua do Horto. It is dated Caicó (Rio Grande do Norte), July 2, 1982, and signed "Your godchild Maria, who greatly esteems you." (Juazeiro's postal service usually leaves the letters addressed to Padre Cícero at the statue of the priest that stands before the chapel of Our Lady of Perpetual Help.)

58. See Anthony F. C. Wallace, "Revitalization Movements."

59. Maria Isaura Pereira de Queiroz, *O messianismo no Brasil e no mundo*, p. 5. An English-language summary of her views is available in Queiroz, "Messiahs in Brazil." Another useful overview of Brazilian messianism is René Ribeiro, "Brazilian Messianic Movements." For further listings see Alba Zaluar Guimarães, "Os movimentos 'messiânicos' brasileiros: Uma leitura." Although there is fairly ample documentation of Brazilian messianic communities, it is worth noting that most of the primary sources cited by the scholars I have noted here reveal a decided bias against these groups; the members of such

these sorts of movements have been particularly common in the rural Northeast and extreme south of Brazil.[60]

Brazilian messianic communities often, although not always, have roots in Portuguese Sebastianism. Shortly after the young King Sebastian disappeared in the battle of Alcácer-Quibir in Northern Africa in 1578, Spain annexed its neighbor. For the next sixty years, the period known as The Captivity, the Portuguese people insisted that the young king on whom they had pinned their hopes had not perished but would return to lead them to victory one day. The first colonists brought this belief with them to Brazil, where people eventually came to expect King Sebastian to reappear not in Portugal but in the New World.[61]

The best-known Brazilian Sebastianic communities are Rodeado (founded 1817) and Pedra Bonita (1838), both in Pernambuco, and Canudos, which emerged in the interior of the state of Bahia not long after the proclamation of the Republic in 1889. There have also been messianic movements not associated with the monarch, such as the Muckers (1872) and Contestado (1911), both in the heavily German extreme south of Brazil;[62] Caldeirão, which police wiped out in 1936; Pau de Colher, a Bahian settlement which met a similar fate some two years later; and Santa Brígida, also in the state of Bahia, which was founded in 1942 and which survives in attenuated form today.[63] The following greatly simplified thumbnail sketches should give a sense of the Brazilian messianic tradition.

---

communities may very well have engaged in the excesses the authors of the period describe, but the reader must take their negative bias into consideration in evaluating their accounts.

60. For useful discussions that focus on messianism in other contexts see Peter Berger, *The Sacred Canopy;* Norman Cohn, *The Pursuit of the Millennium;* Bryan Wilson, *Magic and the Millennium;* and Peter Worsley, *The Trumpet Shall Sound.*

61. For a discussion of Portuguese Sebastianism see João Lúcio de Azevedo, *A evolução do sebastianismo.*

62. For a discussion of Contestado see Bernard Siegel, "The Contestado Rebellion, 1912–1916: A Case Study in Brazilian Messianism and Regional Dynamics." See also Oswaldo R. Cabral, *João Maria: Interpretação da campanha do Contestado;* Duglas Teixeira Monteiro, *Os errantes do novo século;* Maria Isaura Pereira de Queiroz, *La guerre sainte au Brésil: Le mouvement messianique du "Contestado";* and Maurício Vinhas de Queiroz, *Messianismo e conflito social.*

M. I. P. de Queiroz summarizes the indigenous messianic tradition in *O messianismo no Brasil,* pp. 141–192. For a more ample discussion see Egon Schaden, *A mitologia heróica de tribos indígenas do Brasil.* Dinis, *Mistérios,* pp. 26–27, speaks of the belief in Padre Cícero as a reincarnation of the African Rei Congo.

63. Caldeirão was founded by José Lourenço, a *beato* associated with Padre Cícero. The leader of Pau de Colher, José Senhorinho, visited Caldeirão three times. Santa Brígida's founder, Pedro Batista, was considered by many of his followers to be the reincarnation of

RODEADO

A community in southern Pernambuco led by an ex-soldier named Silvestre José dos Santos, Rodeado managed to attract some four hundred persons. The leader built a chapel next to an "enchanted" stone, insisting that he and one other member of the community could communicate with the saint who supposedly inhabited the boulder. Santos informed his followers that King Sebastian and his army would appear in the near future, transforming the two leaders into princes and making the poor rich, the old young, and the black-skinned white. Santos delegated responsibility to twelve princes or wise men, appointed a Guardian of Women and a Guardian of Men, and formed a makeshift army. State troopers summoned by nervous neighbors later killed or arrested most members of the settlement.[64]

PEDRA BONITA

Founded by João Ferreira near Flores, Pernambuco, Pedra Bonita grew up around two tower-like boulders which the prophet proclaimed to be the gates through which King Sebastian and his court would reappear. Identifying himself as Sebastian's personal emissary and his own relatives as apostles, the leader of the community assured followers that the young monarch would make his presence known once the boulders were bathed in blood. At that time the dead were to revive, the old would become young, the black white, and the poor rich. Dogs were to be transformed into dragons that would devour greedy landowners. Convinced that bloodshed was necessary to their own redemption, on May 14, 1838, the members began to take their own lives and those of their children. The carnage went on for three days before soldiers who had been alerted to the slaughter marched on the community.[65]

Padre Cícero. The Santa Brígida group makes frequent pilgrimages to Juazeiro, and one part of the community lives in the Rua do Horto. All three movements are discussed in Queiroz, *O messianismo no Brasil*, pp. 55–79. See also Queiroz's *A dança de São Gonçalo num povoado bahiano*.

64. For a summary see René Ribeiro, "O episódio da Serra do Rodeador (1817–1820): Um movimento milenar e sebastianista." See also Benício das Chagas, "História dos acontecimentos da Pedra do Rodeador"; J. Augusto da Costa, "Expedição do Rodeador, 1–2"; Costa, "Expedição do Rodeador, 3"; and J. I. de Abreu Lima, "Combate do Rodeador ou da Pedra (1820)."

65. Descriptions of Pedra Bonita include Antônio Attico de Souza Leite's *Memória sobre o Reino Encantado na comarca de Vila Bela: Fanatismo religioso*, and his "Memória sobre a Pedra Bonita ou Reino Encantado." See also Francisco Augusto Pereira da Costa, "Folklore Pernambucano." Two important novels based on the event are José Lins do Rego, *Pedra Bonita*, and Ariano Suassuna, *A pedra do reino*.

THE MUCKERS

A community composed of German immigrants in Brazil's southernmost state of Rio Grande do Sul, the Muckers ("pious hypocrites") grew to include some thirty-four families. The leaders were João Jorge Maurer and his wife Jacobina, who was prone to trances and visions. In 1872 Jacobina Maurer proclaimed herself to be the reincarnation of Christ, singling out twelve apostles in preparation for the end of the world. Forbidding followers to attend church or to send their children to school, she pardoned debts among members and assumed the power to dissolve existing marriages. Two years later she announced that she was replacing her husband with another man and named other couples who were supposed to dissolve their marriages and take new spouses. When some refused to follow her directives violence erupted, prompting state troopers to intervene. Jacobina and a few followers escaped but soldiers eventually destroyed them in their hideout.[66]

CANUDOS

Although his father had intended Antônio Maciel, later known as Antônio Conselheiro or "the Counselor," for the priesthood, financial difficulties forced him to become a businessman. Increasingly disenchanted with both commercial matters and marriage, he became a *beato*, organizing novenas and processions, constructing chapels and cemeteries, and destroying "anti-religious" materials in large bonfires. Like many backlands holy men, he became known as a healer of the sick. After founding a settlement called Bom Jesus, which lasted some twelve years, he moved to Canudos, a former cattle ranch in northern Bahia. Renaming the site Belo Monte, he designated a number of "apostles" as his personal representatives within the community. The site was to be the future home of a King Sebastian who would lead the battle against the secular republic, which had usurped religious functions such as the registering of births and deaths and the sanctioning of marriages.

The fledgling republican government's fears that Canudos was a monarchist conspiracy resulted in four military expeditions against the community, which had grown to include some 8,000 persons. Its residents repulsed the first three attacks, but soldiers finally razed the settlement in 1897.[67]

---

66. For a discussion of the Muckers (also called Santarrões) see Leopoldo Petry, *O episódio do Ferrabrás (os Mucker)*, Ambrósio Schupp, *Os Muckers*. See also Janaína Amado, *Conflito social no Brasil: A revolta dos Mucker.*

67. There is an extensive bibliography on Canudos. The best-known description is Euclides da Cunha's *Os sertões,* translated into English by Samuel Putnam as *Revolt in the*

Most of the writers who have looked at Juazeiro as a messianic movement have emphasized the similarities between it and communities such as those described above.[68] They have noted that such settlements appear in times of acute social disorganization and intense economic hardship, which prompt poor, uneducated individuals to place unlimited trust in a charismatic leader.

Many of Padre Cícero's followers were probably much like the people who clustered about these other leaders. The letters cited earlier in this chapter indicate that they made comparable material and psychic demands on the priest. There is every indication that Padre Cícero possessed an overwhelming sense of mission and that he allowed, if not encouraged, these individuals to think of him as a sort of earthly provider. Without this sort of intense commitment he would not have remained in the Cariri. And yet, despite this fundamental similarity to other leaders, the priest was very different in some respects.

Unique Qualities of Juazeiro

Juazeiro is distinguished first and foremost by an open-endedness that results in large part from Padre Cícero's identity as a member of the clergy. Most scholars have duly noted Padre Cícero's niche within the Roman Catholic hierarchy. Ralph della Cava has done an excellent job of illustrating how Padre Cícero's priestly background made him less threatening to a backlands elite bent on increasing its participation in a unified national order. Della Cava emphasizes the extent to which the upper classes' ability to use the new settlers as a source of much-needed manpower assured the survival of Juazeiro when other such communities met a violent end.[69]

Padre Cícero's identity as a priest, however, implies much more than a loyalty to a particular institution with a vested interest in maintaining the status quo. If Juazeiro's short-term survival is undoubtedly a result of the cleric's willingness to cooperate with the local elite, its unusual longevity owes much to his personal commitment to a series of quite

Backlands. A fairly radical reassessment is Ataliba Nogueira, *Antônio Conselheiro e Canudos: Revisão histórica.* A useful discussion of Canudos' place in the popular imagination is José Calasans, *O ciclo folclórico do Bom Jesus.*

68. See Ralph della Cava, "Brazilian Messianism and National Institutions: A Reappraisal of Canudos and Joaseiro"; Duglas Teixeira Monteiro, "Confronto entre Juazeiro, Canudos e Contestado"; and Patricia Pessar, "Unmasking the Politics of Religion: The Case of Brazilian Millenarianism."

69. See della Cava, "Brazilian Messianism," and his *Miracle at Joaseiro,* pp. 81–97.

general principles. Padre Cícero appears to have taken the priestly charge to minister to all Catholics as a lifelong obligation. He also seems to have subscribed wholeheartedly to the Christian concept of earthly existence as a trial period determining salvation or damnation of the individual in an afterlife.[70]

Padre Cícero's deep sense of duty to a larger community would have kept him from limiting Juazeiro to a chosen few. Unlike other leaders who expressly sought out a geographic site removed from major cities in which to gather followers about them, the priest woke up one morning to find himself and Juazeiro the unexpected destination of a pilgrimage. Although he welcomed the persons who began to stream into the hamlet in which he had lived for almost twenty years without incident, he did nothing to exclude others who did not believe in the events of 1889. His vision of Juazeiro as a haven for "the shipwrecks of life" did not lead him to oppose those whose motives for settling in the city were purely commercial. Moreover, he does not appear to have begun acting any differently toward the powerful persons he had known since childhood. From the beginning, then, it seems that Juazeiro was deliberately a much more pluralistic community than others initiated in the countryside—Rodeado, Pedra Bonita, the Muckers, Canudos.

Far better educated and therefore open to a larger world than the other messianic leaders, Padre Cícero had no qualms about requesting material assistance for his city from a government Antônio Conselheiro rejected as "godless." Widely read for a person of his time and place, the priest did not hesitate to comment on world affairs.[71] A subscriber to a Paris news weekly, he was also concerned with technological development, expressing high hopes for advances in irrigation. His support of education contrasts with Jacobina Maurer's refusal to let her followers send their children to school.

At the same time, Padre Cícero's belief in the Christian millennium kept him from proposing a more personal sort of vision of the world.[72]

---

70. There is no doubt about Padre Cícero's commitment to the priesthood. See, for instance, the letter written in 1898 to Pope Leo XIII (Letter 14, in Packet 26, Salesian Archives) in which he describes his twenty-five years of service as a priest.

71. A glance at the titles in Padre Cícero's library confirms his wide-ranging interests. In addition to the newsweekly *L'Illustration (Journal Universel Hebdomadaire de Paris)*, there are books on architecture, artesian wells, and judicial procedures as well as copies of Horace's *Odes*, Flaubert's *Salammbô*, and La Fontaine's *Fables*. Added to these are several guidebooks to Rome, and French, Italian, English, and German dictionaries. There are also various copies of the state historical institute's annual journal. In many of these books Padre Cícero has penned his name in unexpected spaces, such as within the letter "o" of a word in the chapter heading.

72. Della Cava makes this point in *Miracle at Joaseiro*, p. 77: "Unlike the Counselor, Padre

He did not make pronouncements on the necessity of blood sacrifice
(João Ferreira), the imminent return of King Sebastian (Antônio Conselheiro, Silvestre José dos Santos), or the dissolution of existing marriages (Jacobina Maurer). Although his letters indicate his firm belief in
the end of the world as described in the biblical Book of Revelation, his
pronouncements on Christ's second coming are in no way original.
Moreover, his very general injunctions to his followers ("Don't drink,
don't steal, don't kill") set him apart from other leaders. Unlike an Antônio Conselheiro, who forbade the use of Republican arms or money,
Padre Cícero ordered residents of Juazeiro to respect all state and national
laws. While Jacobina Maurer was busy encouraging her followers to find
new spouses, Padre Cícero was urging the marriage of those persons
who had been living together out of wedlock for years.[73] Unlike a Silvestre José dos Santos who assembled a personal army, Padre Cícero
regularly exhorted his followers to refrain from violence by "voting with
their rosaries." Moreover, although Padre Cícero exhibited a continuing
interest in his followers' material well-being, there is no indication that
he presented any concrete alternative to the existing social structure.

Some of his followers, however, appear to have adopted a tighter
framework than he could or would provide. These individuals often
joined religious sects such as the Penitents or the Celestial Courts within
the city.[74] They also found their way into a series of outlying communities that retained a nominal allegiance to Juazeiro. These groups were
often headed by self-appointed *beatos* who expressed loyalty to Padre Cícero. Although most writers have portrayed these individuals as depu-
ties, it is possible to see them as loyal alternatives to, rather than direct
extensions of, the priest.

The *beato* José Lourenço, whom Padre Cícero charged with settling
the farming community of Caldeirão in the 1920s, is an excellent example of a representative of the priest who actually functioned as an autonomous leader.[75] Newcomers to Caldeirão placed their personal pos-

Cícero's cause was not social revolution, but each man's personal redemption. He was an
unwilling messiah, to whom his God had entrusted the conversion of sinners."

73. See Letter 11, October 26, 1896, in Packet 3, Crato Archives, in which the priest asks
the bishop for permission to marry an old man and the woman he had been living with for
some thirty years.

74. For a discussion of these sects and their continuation into the present see Ann Morton,
"Religion in Juazeiro (Ceará, Brazil) since the Death of Padre Cícero: A Case Study in the
Nature of Messianic Religious Activity in the Interior of Brazil."

75. For a discussion of Caldeirão see James Charnel Anderson, "The Caldeirão Movement:
A Case Study in Brazilian Messianism, 1926–1938." See also the section in M. I. P.
de Queiroz, *O messianismo no Brasil*, pp. 260–272, and the well-documented Rosemberg

sessions at the disposition of the community in return for food, clothing, and the other necessities of life. They tilled the land, which was owned communally, and were expected to participate in a full schedule of religious activities presided over by the *beato,* in whose presence they always knelt. José Lourenço, aided by two helpers, made virtually all decisions affecting the group.

As a largely self-sufficient settlement composed primarily of subsistence farmers, Caldeirão was considerably closer to the usual pattern of a Brazilian messianic community than Juazeiro. Although the settlement grew to include some 5,000 persons—mostly families from the state of Rio Grande do Norte—it was far smaller and more cohesive than Juazeiro, which had topped the 15,000 mark in 1909. Former members of the Caldeirão community consider it "more religious" than Juazeiro.[76] By this they do not mean that they spent more time praying than residents of the city, but that they followed a far more elaborate and far stricter set of rules. In Caldeirão each person had a clearly defined role to play within a strictly ordered social framework. Members were encouraged to compete against themselves and others in displaying a brand of piety demanding neither special equipment nor training. Because the community served as a forum within which even the poorest, least educated, and most insecure could theoretically excel, it attracted precisely these sorts of people. Caldeirão, however, was only one of the largest and most successful groups to operate under the umbrella of Padre Cícero's name.

The open-endedness that allowed these alternative groups to prosper is probably the key to Juazeiro's longterm survival. No measure of heterogeneity could have saved the community had local landowners perceived it as a threat to their interests. Nevertheless, Juazeiro's continued existence is as much a result of what Padre Cícero did not do as of anything he did. Free of those tightly wound social springs that usually snap when a leader dies or gradually wear out as people weary of waiting for the world to end, the city has gone on to prosper. Because a person can accept any of several sets of beliefs and still make the pilgrimage to

Cariry, "O beato José Lourenço e o Caldeirão da Santa Cruz." For a folk poet's view of José Lourenço see José Bernardo da Silva, *Santa Cruz do Deserto, Beato José Lourenço.*

76. All three of the people I knew who had lived in Caldeirão made this claim: Enrique Ferreira da Silva (born Serra de Lisgomé, Rio Grande do Norte, 1900), his wife Luzia Maria das Neves (born Lagoa de Baixo, Pernambuco, 1900), and Maria Gurgel da Silva (born Carnaúba, Rio Grande do Norte, 1916). Seu Enrique is today the guardian of José Lourenço's sepulchre in the churchyard of Our Lady of Perpetual Help. He and a small number of other followers go there every afternoon at five o'clock to pray.

Padre Cícero's adopted city, the priest continues to attract new followers throughout the Northeast.

These individuals do accept a number of general guidelines. Most, for instance, refuse to accept the death of Padre Cícero. Storytellers seldom if ever use the word "die" (*morrer*) in relation to the priest. ("He is not here," declares one man, "but my mouth will never open to speak about his 'death.'")[77] Instead, they say that the priest "moved" (*mudou-se*), "separated" (*separou-se*), or simply "left" (*saiu de*) Juazeiro, thus leaving open the possibility of his imminent return.

Few followers can agree on the details of this second coming. Some people are convinced that the priest will appear with the first ray of sun on the first day of the year 2000. Others are considerably more vague. They may claim that the world will end in flames as four angels descend with swords of light from the four points of the compass. They may also argue that the world will see a second flood. "Close your eyes and listen," they say to those around them in the Horto, where the wind among the parched leaves does sound a little like the distant sea.

The point I wish to make is that one need not believe in the apocalypse to consider oneself a follower of Padre Cícero. Some individuals flatly deny that the priest has any intention of destroying the world. "Of course my Padrinho could put an end to us if he so chose," one person observes, "but I do not believe that such destruction is his choice." There are also people who are convinced that the priest is already among them in the guise of an Italian Capuchin friar called Frei Damião.[78] Others hotly dispute these claims. ("How can one person be two people? That is ridiculous," says one.)

77. José Porfírio da Silva (P). Passira, Pernambuco, 1944. Married; canecutter. 2 pilgrimages. (September 26, 1982.) This identification and all those included in this study begin with the speaker's name. (With very few exceptions, such as Isabel, Luz, Nazaré, women's first names end in "a.") I have then noted "R" for resident or "P" for pilgrim. If the individual is a resident of Juazeiro I have given his or her birthplace and the year of birth. If the person was born outside the city, I have recorded the year in which he or she began living in Juazeiro. (Some residents may have made numerous pilgrimages before this date.) I have then given the person's marital status, his or her principal occupation (people often have several jobs), and the date of the conversation. The Portuguese terms *morador* (a landless farmer who lives in one of the landlord's houses) and *rendeiro* (a landless farmer who does not require the landlord's housing) have been retained because they are more precise than any English translation.

In the case of pilgrims, I have given the person's name and present place of residence. (This is frequently, but not always, the place of his or her birth.) I have also provided the birth date, marital status, and principal occupation for each speaker. I have then recorded the number of pilgrimages to Juazeiro (including the present one) that the person has made. The date of the conversation follows.

78. For a discussion of Frei Damião see Abdalaziz de Moura, *Frei Damião e os impasses da religião popular.*

This multiplicity of belief, which characterizes the devotion to the priest both during and after his lifetime, distinguishes Juazeiro from the movements summarized above. At the same time, the historical Padre Cícero's attachment to the city's patron saint, Our Lady of Sorrows, has undoubtedly contributed to the pilgrimage's survival by widening its appeal. The two constitute a sort of divine couple in which the priest stands for power and authority, the Virgin for compassion and a willingness to pardon as well as to intercede. As such, Juazeiro has a strong attraction for people who may have little sense of the flesh-and-blood leader who disappeared a half-century ago. "My Padrinho was a true friend of Our Lady," explains one pilgrim, "and so in honoring him we honor her as well." The fact that the medal of Padre Cícero attached to followers' rosaries always bears the image of the Virgin Mary on its reverse side emphasizes the place of Juazeiro within a larger framework of Marian devotion completely foreign to the other communities I have described.[79]

Therefore, even though Juazeiro may be seen as a revitalization movement in its most general outlines, comparison with specific communities on a point-by-point basis reveals important differences that throw into question the whole definition of messianism within Brazil. Although the hunger for a New Jerusalem pervaded and still pervades Padre Cícero's adopted city, it is not certain that the specific strictures and, in many cases, alternative structures customarily associated with such movements were ever really typical of "holy Juazeiro." This essential heterogeneity will become clearer as we turn to the miracle stories and their tellers.

79. The side of the medal bearing the image of the Virgin is always worn against the chest "in order to protect Our Lady from the eyes of the world." As a man, Padre Cícero looks outward. Unaware of this logic, some critics of the Juazeiro devotion have claimed that its adherents place the priest above the Virgin in terms of importance and respect.

II.
The Tales and the Telling

Everyone likes to hear a story about my Padrinho. And the
person who knows a story likes just as much to tell it. It is for
this reason that there are so many tales.

Pilgrim from Alagoas

I have already introduced the two groups of storytellers upon whom
this study focuses. One group consists of the residents of Juazeiro
who believe that Padre Cícero is a miracle-worker. These individuals
stand apart from other, usually wealthier and better educated inhabitants
of the city, some of whom consider the priest to be an exceptional human
being and others of whom dismiss him as a charlatan. The other group
is composed of the visitors to the city for whom I have reserved the label
pilgrims. These individuals often have multiple motives for coming to
Juazeiro, but almost all speak of the journey as a religious obligation.
The first section of this chapter identifies both groups in socioeconomic
terms. The second describes the context in which they exchange their
tales.

The people I recorded appear typical of a larger population in everything but age. Despite the fact that children are often aware of Padre
Cícero's miraculous exploits, close to two-thirds of all those who told
me stories were at least fifty years old.

Older storytellers are more apt to have had firsthand experiences of
Padre Cícero which they are eager to share. Then, too, as younger
people are accustomed to deferring to their elders, if several persons
know a given tale the oldest will almost certainly tell it: time and again a
young pilgrim or resident would launch into a narrative, only to break
off when an older individual intervened. Even when the initial storyteller

was clearly more knowledgeable, he or she would insist on letting the newcomer take command. Not infrequently, the first speaker would step back in to remind the second of parts of the tale he or she had forgotten or to help unscramble a passage that had become confused. Nonetheless, if I urged the younger person to continue, he or she almost always refused on the grounds that Joaquim or Maria or Manuel was older and therefore necessarily better suited to talk about the priest. "It's the old ones who know how to tell a story" (*São os velhos que sabem como é a história*), they often remarked.

Most tellers' relatively advanced age should not be taken as an indication of the narratives' incipient demise.[1] I was witness to the miracle tradition's vitality one particularly blistering afternoon as a group of pilgrims from the state of Paraíba yawned in the sun. No, they insisted, they had never heard a single story about Padre Cícero. Were there many tales about the priest? Well, that was news to them. Just at the moment that I was about to trudge off with my tape recorder, a nine-year-old boy took pity on me. After he had finished rattling off a stream of Padre Cícero's miracles I asked where he had managed to learn so much about the priest. "Well, he told me the story about the rancher who tried to make my Padrinho sell him winter," the boy said, pointing to one old man in a hammock who had been pretending to be asleep. "She told me about the girl who turned into a snake and went crawling off to Juazeiro," he said, pointing to a middle-aged woman who was rapidly losing the battle to look as if she were not listening. "And *everybody* knows the story of the hat that stuck to the wall without a peg," the boy asserted. The whole group burst out laughing, and the old man in the hammock began to tell a number of other stories obviously familiar to many of his fellow travelers.

There are probably many youngsters like my nine-year-old benefactor who are presently in the process of internalizing a large and varied narrative corpus. Although these young people normally remain silent, they are capable of relating miracle tales when the occasion arises. Sixty years from now, the boy may well be an old man in a hammock relating Padre Cícero's miraculous deeds to a cluster of eager children.

1. Henry Glassie's observations regarding a North Irish community are equally relevant to Northeast Brazil. "Generation after generation contains the last basket weaver and the last ballad singer," he says. "When they were young, Hugh Nolan and Michael Boyle were not noted storytellers. They would not have performed for a visiting folklorist. Their elders, George Armstrong and Hugh McGiveney, would have told the tales while the folklorist foretold the demise of the art and young Hugh and Mick cut turf and hay. But now they are the tellers": *Passing the Time in Ballymenone: Culture and History of an Ulster Community,* p. 63.

Local Storytellers

About half of the 250 residents represented in this study live in the Rua do Horto.[2] The remainder live primarily in the center of Juazeiro or on a small number of outlying farms. Almost a third of the local storytellers with whom I spoke were born in the city, but these individuals are apt to be the children of pilgrims. Most of those who were not born in Juazeiro were originally from either Pernambuco or Alagoas. Smaller percentages came from Paraíba, Rio Grande do Norte, Piauí, and Sergipe. (See map on page 24.)

Only one in five of the storytellers not born in Juazeiro has been in the city less than twenty years. A large number of the persons born in other parts of the Northeast had made the move to the Cariri as children. Others who resolved as adults to move to Juazeiro have never returned to their former home. "If people want to see me, they know where they can find me," says one man who left Pernambuco for the Rua do Horto some fifteen years ago.[3]

Although a few of the persons who live in the center of Juazeiro are noticeably better off than the others, most local storytellers belong to the same general social class. The majority whom I recorded were very poor. Only six—all of whom live in the center of the city—earn more than the minimum wage, which is not a legal requirement but an ideal that varies from state to state. In the fall of 1982, the minimum wage in Ceará was 17,000 cruzeiros a month. This represented about $90 on the official exchange but only a little more than half that on the more accurate black market.

The Rua do Horto, where I lived, is much like the other poorer neighborhoods of Juazeiro such as Pirajá, Franciscanos, Rodoviária, Rua das Flores, Rua São Damião, and Salesianos. Although it is more heavily agricultural than these other sections of the city, its inhabitants have a good deal in common with poor persons throughout the Northeast.

A little over half of the houses along the Rua do Horto are stucco over sun-baked brick. The others are often mud and sticks. Houses—which are either rented or owned outright—generally consist of one or two bedrooms, a kitchen area, and a front room for receiving friends and neighbors. Most families own one or more beds, a table, and several chairs. Others, who rely exclusively on hammocks or straw mats for

2. For a numerical breakdown of the pilgrim and resident storytellers with whom I spoke see Appendix A.
3. Casimiro Antonio Bezerra (R). Canhotinho, Pernambuco, 1910. Arrived Juazeiro 1967. Married; *rendeiro*. (September 25, 1982.)

sleeping accommodation, may have nothing but a bench or large stone on which to sit. A table in the front room, which even the poorest residents will find a scrap of lace to cover, serves as a makeshift altar. Pictures of Padre Cícero and the saints hang on the wall above it. Old photographs of the family, shot in black-and-white and then tinted to look as if they were originally taken in color, flank the saints. A donkey harness or farm implements may hang from pegs on another wall. The front of the house bears an official census number. The inhabitants will often draw a cross over the doorway with a piece of charcoal.

Most houses share a common wall with either neighbor, causing the Rua do Horto to resemble a single elongated house with many rooms. The thinness of the partition allows sound to travel easily, so most families cannot help overhearing each other's conversations.

Even those persons who do not till the fields generally get up at dawn. Since residents board up their doors and windows at night as a precaution against thieves, the heat becomes oppressive with the first rays of the sun, and the noise of radios and voices makes it almost impossible to sleep.

One private and two public telephones serve the Rua do Horto. The erratic bus line began service in 1979. Electricity became available to residents along the lower stretch of the road in 1976, but only about half the homes have indoor lighting. Although the city began supplying water on an intermittent basis in 1978, few people have storage tanks. Thus, in periods of rationing they often go without running water for as much as three days at a stretch. During this time they carry buckets to and from a muddy well located on the hillside well beyond their homes. As there is only one indoor toilet on the whole street, they depend on latrines or simply relieve themselves in their backyards.

The number of television sets in the Rua do Horto is quickly growing; between 1981 and 1982 a half-dozen new sets appeared. Most people, however, cannot afford this luxury. Transistor radios, which do not require an electrical outlet to function, are ubiquitous in Juazeiro. The most popular programs in poorer neighborhoods are religious offerings such as the Ave Maria Hour and shows featuring regional singers, called *repentistas* or *cantadores,* who improvise verses about Padre Cícero as well as other subjects.[4]

---

4. These *cantadores* have been as important as the authors of written, *cordel* verses in popularizing Padre Cícero's alleged miracles. A few of the now-classic studies on the *cantador* are Gustavo Barroso, *Ao som da viola;* Francisco das Chagas Batista, *Cantadores e poetas populares;* and José Rodrigues Carvalho, *Cancioneiro do norte.* See Candace Slater, *Stories on a String: The Brazilian "Literatura de Cordel,"* for further bibliography.

Some residents of the Rua do Horto now boast gas stoves, but charcoal, wood, or a combination of these fuels is still more common. The houses in which wood is used have an immediately recognizable incense-like smell. Refrigerators appear only in homes in which the owners sell soda or the popsicles called *dindins* to supplement their incomes. Most people, if they have the money, prefer to buy a television because they value the information and entertainment it provides. ("After all, who wants to sit there and watch a refrigerator?" one resident asked with a grin.) Moreover, the traditional diet of rice, beans, and manioc flour does not demand the use of perishable items. Residents of the Rua do Horto make intermittent purchases of meat from a passing peddler, and those with babies or small children rely on powdered milk or do without. Most people refuse to eat green vegetables, which they utilize as animal fodder, but they do eat fruit when they can get it.

The growing availability of electricity, gas stoves, television, and running water makes day-to-day existence in the Rua do Horto considerably easier and more pleasant than in the countryside from which most individuals originally came. Nevertheless they, like most Northeast Brazilians, must still struggle to obtain the necessities of life. Infant mortality remains a chronic problem. Most people are undernourished and almost all suffer from parasitic diseases transmitted through the water supply. Few residents can afford the monthly payments that would qualify them for government-sponsored medical assistance. In any case, the care provided by public clinics is often so inadequate that many persons prefer to take their chances with more traditional cures.

Government-financed schooling is now available to most children in Juazeiro, but as the teachers in many neighborhood schools are barely literate themselves the results are uninspiring. Parents often keep their offspring at home because they cannot afford the modest fees for books and school supplies. They may also claim to need the child's help with housework or in the fields. A branch of the adult literacy program known as MOBRAL serves the Rua do Horto but few older people have succeeded in learning to read or to write more than their names. "I wish I could read," says one woman wistfully, "because then I could tell from where the cars which drive past my door have come and I could imagine just how that place must be."[5]

The higher-than-average rate of unemployment within Juazeiro helps explain the steady exodus of young people to the coastal capitals of

5. Maria Antonia de Jesus (R). Garanhuns, Pernambuco, 1910. Arrived Juazeiro 1918. Married; begs for a living. (October 13, 1982.)

the Northeast and the southern industrial centers of Rio de Janeiro and São Paulo.[6] And yet, despite the fact that the people who stay complain about the difficulties of earning a living, most are still convinced that Juazeiro is a privileged place. This belief explains the steady trickle of newcomers into the Rua do Horto even in times of economic crisis. "If I am going to go hungry in any case," one recent arrival explains, "then it might as well be here."[7]

Some two thousand persons live in the Rua do Horto. The men usually engage in farming as a primary occupation. Most are *rendeiros* who rent from private landowners, to whom they normally give half their crop in payment. The small percentage who are construction workers, carpenters, ironsmiths, or employees of small factories plant vegetables in substantial backyard plots. Although some older persons receive pensions, many people in their seventies and eighties set out at daybreak for fields higher up the hillside where they cultivate sugar cane, rice, cotton, beans, corn, and manioc. ("I'd get bored otherwise, you know," many of them say.) No appreciable rainfall accumulated during the entire four-year period I worked in Juazeiro.[8] However, even in times of drought farmers plant at least part of the land in the hope that a sudden rain will allow them to harvest at least a small crop. Most individuals have little or nothing to do with downtown Juazeiro, except perhaps for the weekly open-air market or for masses in the church of Our Lady of Sorrows. Many have never been in the post office, a bank, a movie theater, or a grocery store.

Women customarily help their husbands and fathers in the fields on a part-time basis. They also cook and clean, care for numerous children, cultivate backyard gardens, and tend pigs and chickens. A few are laundresses, seamstresses, midwives, cooks, or *rezadeiras,* folk healers who rely on special prayers to cure physical and emotional disorders. Almost all the Rua do Horto's female residents also engage in some kind of handicraft such as weaving straw hats, purses, or sleeping mats. They may construct dolls from scraps of fabric, fashion the paper or cloth flowers used to decorate saints' pictures, or paint plaster-of-paris figurines of Padre Cícero and various saints.

6. The heavy influx of migrants into São Paulo has made the southern metropolis the largest "Northeastern" city in Brazil. Approximately four million persons from the Northeast are now living in the nation's biggest urban center, compared to some three million in the northern capitals of Salvador and Recife.

7. Manuel Coelho Viana (R). Souza, Paraíba, 1919. Arrived Juazeiro 1981. Single; cowman. (October 10, 1982.)

8. For a graphic description of the devastation caused by this drought, the longest in Brazilian history since 1583, see "A Tortura da Seca." The area affected by the drought is five times the size of Italy.

Because most visitors insist on walking up the Rua do Horto, virtually everyone who lives there becomes a merchant during the pilgrimage season. Food, drink, religious articles, and assorted souvenirs of Juazeiro are the most popular wares. Children scramble to earn a coin by singing pilgrim hymns. People who live next to a station of the cross rush out to scrape up the reusable wax from votive candles as soon as the pilgrims who have lit them turn their backs. On-the-spot photographers (*lambe-lambes*) compete to be the first to take a pilgrim's picture. Old women purposely attired in their most ragged black dresses sit on the curb to beg.

As in other pilgrimage centers, the relationship between residents and visitors is decidedly ambivalent. Because many of the people who live along the Rua do Horto were once pilgrims themselves, they can empathize with the visitors. In addition, the travelers represent a source of income on which residents depend for their own survival. Therefore few residents have the heart to deny a thirsty pilgrim a glass of water, although those who live in the Rua do Horto grumble a good deal about the dirt and the diseases that the visitors bring to Juazeiro. They also deride these individuals' "superstitious" beliefs, in a manner calculated to reaffirm their own superiority ("Just imagine dragging home a heap of ordinary stones to make a 'miracle' tea!").

Should the pilgrims fail—for whatever reason—to purchase a sufficient number of overpriced figurines or should they complain about the cold coffee or fly-specked cakes, normally placid residents fly into a rage. When business is good, however, they may pull up chairs for the visitors, who, although weary, are never too tired to listen to their hosts reminisce about the days when Padre Cícero paused to rest within the shade of one or another of the street's few tenacious trees.

Pilgrims and the Pilgrimage

Juazeiro is by far the largest pilgrimage center in the backlands.[9] A series of more localized shrines, such as that dedicated to Santa Quitéria at Freixeira in Pernambuco, dot the region.[10] São Francisco das Chagas in

9. For an overview of modern Christian pilgrimages see Victor Turner and Edith Turner, *Image and Pilgrimage in Christian Culture.* See also Alphonse Dupront, "Pèlerinages et lieux sacrés." Useful material on pilgrimages in the Middle Ages appears in Jonathan Sumption, *Pilgrimage: An Image of Mediaeval Religion,* and in Ronald C. Finucane, *Miracles and Pilgrims: Popular Beliefs in Medieval England.* For background regarding Portuguese pilgrimages see Pierre Sanchis, "Festa e religião popular: As romarias de Portugal," as well as his "Arraial—la fête d'un peuple." It is also worth consulting Mário Martins, *Peregrinações e livros de milagre na nossa Idade Média.*

10. Brazilian shrines fall into the same sort of hierarchical order apparent in other pilgrimage contexts, with some locations drawing more people from a wider area than others. For

Canindé and Bom Jesus da Lapa in Bahia draw crowds comparable in size to those of Juazeiro.[11] Whereas Canindé is most popular with the northernmost states of Ceará, Piauí, and Maranhão, and Bom Jesus serves the area's south and southcentral fringes (Bahia, Minas Gerais), Juazeiro draws most of its pilgrims from the Northeastern heartland.

Some of the visitors who pour into Juazeiro during the six months following the end of the winter harvest in late August are tourists attracted by the color and excitement of the pilgrimage. Most of the people who arrive in crowded trucks or chartered buses, however, are participants as well as spectators. Approximately eight out of every nine of the visitors who told me stories had been in Juazeiro at least once before. Although women are more apt than men to participate in formal religious activities back home, both sexes are well represented in the pilgrimage. And while a younger person will often cede a place to an older relative anxious to visit the city at least once in his or her lifetime, people of all ages regularly make the trip.

In terms of geographic origin, the pilgrims are much like local storytellers. The majority of those whom I recorded came from Pernambuco and Alagoas, followed by Paraíba, then Rio Grande do Norte and Piauí, with a much smaller number of individuals from Sergipe, Bahia, Maranhão, and Ceará.[12] Although almost three-quarters presently live in the countryside, it is worth reemphasizing that most residents of Juazeiro were also born in rural locations. Moreover, many of the individuals who live in neighborhoods such as the Rua do Horto remain subsistence farmers despite their technically urban status. They, like the pilgrims, have

---

a useful discussion of the relationship among local, regional, and national shrines in India see S. H. Bhardwaj, *Hindu Places of Pilgrimage in India.* See, too, S. Narayan, *Sacred Complexes of Deoghar and Rajgir.* Santa Quitéria ("Guiteria") is also honored in Spain and Gascony, where she is invoked as a protectress against mad dogs.

11. For descriptions of Bom Jesus da Lapa see Daniel Gross, "Ritual and Conformity: A Religious Pilgrimage to Northeastern Brazil"; Tim Hallinan, "Bom Jesus da Lapa: A Sertão Shrine"; Carlos A. de Medina et al., "Bom Jesus da Lapa: Uma análise sócio-religiosa"; and Ceslau Stanula, "Um lugar de romaria." In both Canindé and Bom Jesus, pilgrims congregate primarily on major feast days. In Juazeiro, however, a steady stream of visitors continues throughout the six-month pilgrimage period, which is peppered with feast days.

12. That the number of visitors from the first three states is relatively small is almost certainly due to the distance of those states from the Cariri Valley. In the case of Juazeiro's home state of Ceará, however, the very small number of pilgrims may reflect lingering bitterness about the Revolution of 1913–14, when the makeshift army that marched on Fortaleza from Juazeiro inflicted considerable damage along the way. The hostility to Padre Cícero on the part of the bishop of Ceará must also have had considerable impact on the state's residents.

little to do with the cultural, commercial, or political institutions generally associated with city life.

Some two-thirds of the non-residents who told me stories devote themselves primarily to agriculture. The men who did not work in the fields were carpenters, guards, peddlers, and factory or construction workers. A smaller number were shoemakers, fishermen, truck or bus drivers, electricians, accordian players, cowhands, barbers, and saddle makers. In addition to helping husbands or fathers in the fields, the women were laundresses, cooks, seamstresses, midwives, household servants, *rezadeiras,* and, occasionally, teachers' aides in rural communities. I met one fortune-teller, one gold-miner, one prostitute, and any number of people who engage in part-time occupations such as selling mangoes or codfish in makeshift stands outside their homes.

Visitors travel to Juazeiro from all over the Northeast, but different regions favor particular time periods. Pilgrims from Maceió, the capital of the state of Alagoas, for instance, are most apt to make the trip during the month of September.[13] Residents of the interior of Alagoas often prefer to wait until January. Visitors from Pernambuco predominate during November; the states of Paraíba and Rio Grande do Norte also make their strongest showing at this time. Pilgrims from Maranhão, Piauí, and Rio Grande do Norte often include Juazeiro on a longer journey to Canindé. These trips, called *viagens redondas* ("round" or "circular" journeys) are becoming increasingly popular. As one *fretante* explains with eminent practicality, "If you are going to spend the money to make a pilgrimage, you might as well spend a little extra and see two saints instead of one."[14]

Such trips are seldom longer than a week, and many are shorter. Pilgrims generally spend one to three days on the road in each direction and two or three days in the city proper. If they are going to visit another religious center—almost always Canindé—the trip may be several days longer. And if, as often happens, the truck or bus breaks down, the trip may be involuntarily extended.

13. The devotion to Padre Cícero in Maceió merits more study. A Padre Cícero Association in the neighborhood of Vergel has over 50,000 members. The society runs sewing classes, sponsors medical and dental services, organizes pilgrimages to Juazeiro, and has its own weekly radio program. I am grateful to Dona Ivanilde Batista dos Santos, one of the Society's founders, for introducing me to many of its members and activities. For a discussion that deals in part with followers of the priest in Alagoas see Hendricus Stephanus Maria Groenen, "Schisma zwischen Kirche und Volk: Eine praktisch-theologische Fallstudie des Volkskatholizismus in Nordostbrasilien."

14. Antônia Ferreira Batista (P). Imperatriz, Maranhao, 1926. Married; seamstress. 3 pilgrimages as *fretante.* (September 30, 1982.)

Though the journey itself is usually brief, preparation for it may go on all year. The trip organizer usually has the incentive of a free ride if the transport fills. Many individuals, however, who have made a vow or *promessa* to be an organizer expressly refuse any material reward. "The pilgrimage," insists one *fretante*, "is not a means of livelihood—it is a reflection of people's will to live" (*A romaria não é meio de vida—é o povo que quer viver*).[15] One organizer tells how he gave up a lucrative commercial sideline as the result of an admonitory dream:

1. In the past, yes, I used to do business during the pilgrimage. I took things to sell, I brought back things for the people where I live. But I don't any more. Look, one night before setting out for here, I lay down to sleep. And at a certain hour of the night, Our Lady of Sorrows appeared before me. She said, "You have made few pilgrimages to Juazeiro."
   I said, "No, I have been there twenty-three times."
   She said, "You have only been there twice."
   "How can that be?" I asked.
   "Because those two times you came alone," she said. "The other times you brought things to sell. And when you weren't bringing things, you were buying things to sell back home. Look now, take care during this pilgrimage and if someone asks you to buy something for him in Juazeiro, you bring it and give it to him for the same price that you paid. In this way you will make a 'clean' journey." So then that is what I have been doing for the past five years.
   —José Malaquides da Silva (P). Guarabira, Paraíba, 1910. Widower;
      farmer (own land). 28 trips. (October 27, 1982.)

Those *fretantes* who travel to Juazeiro regularly—often bi-weekly—are likely to conceive of the pilgrimage as a business. For most organizers, however, the trip is an annual event. Although some of these individuals may have a little more money or status than their fellow travelers, others do not stand out in any way.

Pilgrims typically scrimp and save all year for the trip to Juazeiro. Many take a second job in order to afford a seat for themselves and a son or daughter or elderly parent. In the fall of 1982, the average price of a twenty-hour truck ride was 1,500 cruzeiros, or anywhere from about four to seven dollars. Buses often cost from 3,000 to 5,000 cruzeiros, depending on the point of embarcation and the type of transport. During

15. João Emílio de Souza Lima (P). Recife, Pernambuco, 1949. Married; shoe repairman. 4 pilgrimages. (November 22, 1982.)

periods of less demand, the price falls to between 300 and 1,000 cruzeiros a night. This apparently trifling sum represents a small fortune to a person feeding a large family on less than a dollar a day. Nuclear families seldom make the trip together because most pilgrims have too many offspring to be able to afford to take them all. Usually a husband or wife takes a single son or daughter, leaving the spouse at home to tend to the others.

Unless the traveler is self-employed, he or she must arrange with the employer for time off from the job. Because few employers are eager to acquire a reputation as an enemy of Padre Cícero, they are more apt than otherwise to grant the request. Nevertheless, a pilgrim must be prepared to forego payment for the days he or she is not at work, a luxury few can easily afford.

The majority of pilgrims still get to Juazeiro in the open trucks called "parrot perches" (*pau de araras*) because of the overhead bar to which standing passengers may cling. Many pilgrims prefer these trucks to buses because they are considerably cheaper. Some states, however, such as Paraíba and Rio Grande do Norte, have outlawed the transports as dangerous. Because they routinely carry as many as 120 adults, plus numerous children wedged up against each other on a series of makeshift benches, they are top-heavy, and when they overturn, the number of deaths is usually high. As their drivers are likely to use unpaved roads full of hairpin turns and potholes in order to avoid both the police and the toll stations, accidents are common. The passengers customarily arrive bruised, sunburnt, and coated from head to foot with dust. "Your heart is *literally* in your throat the whole way to Juazeiro," one woman ruefully explains.

Conditions in pilgrimage buses are not, however, much better. Although the buses are designed to hold forty-four passengers each, I traveled with twice that number of people on my pilgrimage from Juazeiro to Canindé. Since most of the windows would not open, there was little ventilation. A series of tiny rocking chairs lined the aisle where some twenty children were seated nose to head. When the bus slammed to a halt, they all ended up in a pile at the front of the bus, from which their parents hurried to retrieve them. After the travelers, who had already made a three-day bus trip from Maranhão to Juazeiro, finally reached Canindé, many simply stretched out on the ground beneath a tree and went to sleep.

Everyone admires the small number of persons who continue to make the pilgrimage "like it was in the old days," or on foot. One older man explained that although he had passed near Juazeiro a number of times in his youth, he never visited the city because "at least the first time, a pilgrim ought to walk."[16] He had therefore waited until he was sixty-three to make the fifteen-day trek from his home to Juazeiro. For an old woman who has made the trip on foot from her home in Pernambuco every year for the past two decades, "walking to Juazeiro is the only way to get here because I can feel my heart begin to open as I walk along. I have nothing in this life except for the breath in my nostrils but if I owned a car I would leave it parked before my door."[17]

As in other cultures, the pilgrimage may serve as a form of expiation. Confidence in the possibility of paying off past misdeeds and storing up future merits helps explain visitors' willingness—even eagerness—to endure discomfort. "The pilgrimage," one man says, "is the satisfaction that the poor man feels when he finally arrives in Juazeiro, all bent out of shape and half crazy from the heat."[18] "My Padrinho Cícero looks down on us and sees us coming," says another pilgrim, "and I think that he is pleased."[19] "Who is the person," asks his companion, "who does not rush to greet a visitor from far away? Who isn't happy when a friend who lives in Paraíba or even São Paulo makes a long and difficult journey just to see him again? My Padrinho receives us so well because he knows how hard we have struggled to be here with him."[20] "I am poor but I arrive here rich in happiness," yet another traveler declares.[21]

The arrival in Juazeiro is always an occasion for celebration. "We are home!" shout the travelers, setting off a streak of firecrackers fittingly known as "tears," *lágrimas*. No matter what hour of the day or night they arrive in Juazeiro, the visitors go through a ritual composed of several stages. As the truck or bus enters the city, its passengers begin intoning hymns of praise at the top of their voices. They then circle the church of Our Lady of Sorrows three times before entering it to pray. If there is a

16. Pedro Manuel (P). Maceió, Alagoas, 1906. Widower; electrician. 11 pilgrimages. (September 25, 1982.)

17. Regina Maria de Alves (P). Águas Belas, Pernambuco, 1923. Widow; *rendeira*. 19 pilgrimages on foot, 14 by truck. (September 28, 1982.)

18. João Francisco dos Santos (P). Paulo Gomes, Piauí, 1963. Single; occupation unknown. 3 pilgrimages. (September 20, 1982.)

19. José Barbosa de Santana (P). Orobó, Pernambuco, 1907. Married; *rendeiro*. "More than 30 pilgrimages." (September 17, 1982.)

20. José Paulo Campos (P). João Alfredo, Pernambuco, 1947. Married; *morador*. 13 pilgrimages. (September 17, 1982.)

21. Claudemira Cardoso de Oliveira (P). João de Freitas, Piauí, 1936. Married; midwife. "I don't keep track of the pilgrimages that I make to Juazeiro but I have made a lot." (September 29, 1982.)

fife-and-drum band (*zabumba*), the group will follow the musicians up the aisles. Should the visitors have brought a statue of the local Virgin, she will be courteously presented to the statue of the patron saint, then left before the altar for a time so that the two Marys can converse. The whole group will then exit to the triumphant thump of drums, heading toward the *rancho* where, depending on the hour, they will either rest or sleep.

Once refreshed, the pilgrims set out to visit a series of other churches located in the center of Juazeiro. The most important of these is the chapel of Our Lady of Perpetual Help, in which Padre Cícero lies buried. Pilgrims often also pay a visit to the Salesian and Franciscan churches, to the House of Miracles (a repository for *ex-votos*, symbolizing the fulfillment of vows to saints), the Padre Cícero Museum, and the Old People's Asylum, which was once the priest's home.[22] They may then go on to make purchases in the municipal market before attending mass.

Although small in comparison to the coastal capitals, Juazeiro seems like a metropolis to many of the pilgrims who dodge cars and stare in wonder at the gleaming new Bank of Brazil. These individuals often hurry to take advantage of goods and services not found at home. "I only have my hair cut when I come to Juazeiro," says a middle-aged woman in the Good Friends Beauty Salon. "I would have it trimmed more often but where I live nobody has a steady hand and so I wait until my pilgrimage. And, to tell you the truth, I really don't mind waiting because it gives me one more thing I can look forward to all year."[23]

Before dawn the next day, the visitors usually leave the downtown area to head up the Rua do Horto several miles away. Because most believe that "the person who has not visited the Horto has not visited Juazeiro," all but the most infirm insist on making the trip. During the principal feast days the crush of visitors is so great that, viewed from a distance, the surface of the incline appears to be moving.

Although pilgrims resemble one another, minor differences in the straw hats worn as protection from the sun often set one group apart

---

22. *Ex-votos* are token payments of a successful *promessa*, or vow to a saint. If the holy figure answers a follower's request for help, he or she must oblige by rendering the stipulated payment. If the request is for a return to health, for instance, the payment may take the form of a model of the affected part of the body cast in wood, wax, or plastic. For a fuller explanation see Luís da Câmara Cascudo, *Dicionário do folclore brasileiro*, 2, pp. 480–483. For a helpful comparative perspective see also the section on votive offerings and reciprocity with saints in João de Pina Cabral, "A Peasant Worldview in Its Context: Cultural Uniformity and Differentiation in Northwestern Portugal," pp. 358–392.

23. Jovelina Maria da Conceição (P). Surubim, Pernambuco, 1927. Married; *rendeira*. 20 pilgrimages. (September 28, 1982.)

from another. One cluster of hats may come to a slight point, while others may reveal a fringed brim or a green ribbon tied beneath the chin. Then too, a particular group may elect to dress in blue, black, or brown shrouds, symbolizing one member's recovery from a near-fatal illness.

Pilgrims wending their way up the Rua do Horto often stop to light a candle at the stations of the cross. They tie blue ribbons around the statue of Christ and place crowns of wilted roses on the concrete head. Since flowers are extremely rare during the arid summer, visitors often carry large bouquets in cans of water all the way from home. At the same time that they adorn Christ, the visitors may hit Judas or Herod's soldiers with a rolled-up newspaper or slap their faces with open hands; due to years of abuse, all these statues have chipped noses and broken limbs.

Because saints' images are believed to have a special power, visitors leave fragments of shattered figurines, which they have carefully kept all year, before the stations of the cross. Pilgrims may also make small piles of stones along the road or leave stones in the forks of trees designed to "call" absent friends and relatives to Juazeiro. ("This stone is for João and this is for Antônio and this is for Catarina.")[24] Others carry a rock or brick up the Rua do Horto to leave at the site of the never-completed church that stands on the hill.[25] The pilgrims who have vowed to give to every beggar they meet in Juazeiro deposit coins in outstretched hands until their pockets are empty.

Once at the top of the hill, the pilgrims can gaze out over the Cariri Valley before scrambling up the base of the statue of Padre Cícero. The third-largest statue in the world (Rio de Janeiro's famed Corcovado is second), the nearly eighty-foot-high image was erected by city officials in 1969. The visitors pay a photographer to doctor snapshots of them to look as if the priest had placed an enormous concrete hand upon their heads. After inspecting the ruins of the church and visiting a neighboring chapel maintained by the Salesians, the pilgrims move on toward the rocky clearing known as the Holy Sepulchre, about half an hour's walk beyond the Horto.

They are besieged along the way by innumerable beggars, curers waving bunches of healing leaves, and vendors laden with printed texts of songs and stories, coffee, rosaries made of china or plastic or tiny

24. For a discussion of religious practices associated with stones see Cascudo, *Dicionário*, 2, pp. 397–403.

25. During the 1890s Padre Cícero had begun building a chapel in honor of the Sacred Heart of Jesus, in fulfillment of a vow he and three other priests had made during an earlier drought. In 1896, Dom Joaquim ordered work on the chapel halted. During his trip to Rome, however, the priest obtained blueprints for a major cathedral. When he reinitiated construction on the church after his return to Juazeiro, the bishop issued a new prohibition,

coconuts, and tobacco for the clay pipes many Northeastern women smoke. Once in the Holy Sepulchre, they attempt to squeeze under and around a series of boulders in a sort of obstacle course of faith.[26] They also try to read the "magic" letters on a rock and to insert their fingers into mysterious holes that Padre Cícero supposedly made with his bare hand. They drink and bathe their heads in a small puddle of "holy" water which collects in an outcropping.

Although visitors stream through Juazeiro during the entire pilgrimage period, a small number of feast days draw particularly large numbers of people. The most important of these are the festival of Our Lady of Sorrows (September 13–15), the celebration of *Dia dos Finados* (literally, the Day of the Dead or All Souls' Day, October 31–November 2), and the festival of *Nossa Senhora das Candeias* ("Our Lady of the Candles" or Our Lady of Light, in early February). A few major religious celebrations fall outside the regular pilgrimage season. Holy Week, Saint Joseph's Day (March 19), the festival of the Heart of Our Lady of Sorrows (May 31), and the anniversary of Padre Cícero's death on July 20 are among the best known. The single largest celebration of the year is the Dia dos Finados, which may draw as many as 350,000 pilgrims.[27]

These principal feast days also attract thousands of vendors, not only from Juazeiro but also from neighboring states. Their thatched stalls quickly turn the city into one big bazaar. Cowbells, a wide variety of plaster saints, rifles, Padre Cícero T-shirts stamped "Souvenir of Glorious Juazeiro," and hundreds of other items tempt the visitor. So do open-air restaurants, and photographers' booths in which the visitor may pose beside a life-size statue of the priest, with a live goat and a doll in a cowgirl dress for added interest. Makeshift bars vie for patrons with open-air discothèques and tents in which the prostitutes may have pledged half their earnings in advance to Our Lady of Sorrows. Once the celebration is over, truck after truck pulls away from Juazeiro, its passengers already asleep. The beggars jingle off and the miles of booths are suddenly disassembled into piles of boards and yards of cloth. What was hours earlier the commercial hub as well as spiritual mecca of the Northeastern backlands becomes an abandoned stretch of pineapple shavings and trampled paper flags.

---

and the building stopped in 1903. The priest's followers insist that from the remaining rubble a new church will one day arise.

26. Comparable practices are documented for Galicia by William A. Christian, Jr., "La religiosidad popular hoy."

27. A report from the newsweekly *Veja* puts visitors to Juazeiro on All Souls' Day of 1980 at 350,000 persons. See "Volta por cima."

Storytelling

Although residents and pilgrims are much alike in many respects, the circumstances under which they tell their stories, and thus the stories proper, are—understandably—quite different.[28] Their dissimilar relationships to the pilgrimage and varying proximity to Padre Cícero help explain this general division.

Inhabitants of the city above the age of fifty are quite likely to have had direct contact with the priest. Half the residents who told me stories claim to have at least caught a glimpse of the historical Padre Cícero. Nearly nine out of ten local storytellers cite parents or grandparents who knew him.

For those persons residing in or near Juazeiro during Padre Cícero's lifetime, contact was, at least potentially, direct and sustained. Older storytellers may recall stretching out their arms to the priest as he rode past their house on a lightstruck afternoon. "This street was his," explains one resident of the Rua do Horto, "because he always passed by here blessing the *juá* trees on either side. Sometimes he would stop along the way to pray while Zé [Joe] Beato held the little horse, white as a baby ram."[29] Other individuals were sent to Padre Cícero's house to deliver a message, a single perfect mango, or a basket full of carefully selected eggs. A number of older people attended the priest's homilies regularly for years. (Although Padre Cícero was officially prohibited from preaching, he addressed followers congregated before his house at a set hour every day.)

Even that handful of local storytellers who cannot claim any sort of contact with Padre Cícero feel a special closeness to the priest whose presence continues to permeate his adopted city. A candle burns before an image of him perched on a cash register in a fabric store. Another likeness looks down on the long loaves of fresh bread in the Portuguese Bakery. A wide white ribbon adorns his waist in a makeshift restaurant. Tinfoil flowers frame his portrait in a minuscule pharmacy. Homes may boast multiple statues of him ranging in size from several inches to seven feet. The Padre Cícero Suitcase Shop, the Padre Cícero Funerary Supply Store, and the Padre Cícero Bar and Grill are only a few of the dozens upon dozens of establishments that bear his name.

28. The act of storytelling, or the performance context, has come under increasing scrutiny from folklorists within the past two decades. For an introduction see Dan Ben-Amos and Kenneth Goldstein, eds., *Folklore: Performance and Communication*.

29. Rosalva da Conceição Lima (R). Palmeira dos Índios, Alagoas, 1920. Arrived Juazeiro 1926. Married; makes hats. (July 7, 1981.)

Newcomers to the city are usually eager to find out everything they can about Padre Cícero. "When I first arrived here," one man in the Rua do Horto says, "I spent whole days asking my neighbors to tell me stories about my Padrinho's miracles."[30] Even individuals who do not set out to learn about the priest normally absorb a good deal of information in the course of everyday conversation. The following are examples of situations in which I witnessed a tale arise in response to a specific object or situation:

Dona Zefinha finds a large toad in her backyard under the banana tree. She appears in the doorway, dangling it by one leg. Her stepmother squints at the toad and says, "Zefinha, remember how Manuel [her deceased husband, Dona Zefinha's father] used to talk about the man who turned into a toad?" The eight-year-old neighbor who had been busy pulling the cat's tail perks up her ears. "A toad?" she demands with an eager, slightly nervous giggle. "A toad, Dorinha," Dona Zefinha says firmly and proceeds to tell the story of the toad-like man her father claimed to have encountered in his travels through the backlands as a jewelry salesman. The son of a woman who said she would believe in Padre Cícero only if she gave birth to a toad, the man "bought a tiny little ring for his tiny little finger." The stepmother nods approvingly, breaking in from time to time to add a detail that Dona Zefinha has forgotten. The cat rubs against the eight-year-old's legs but she is too engrossed in the account to notice.

It is market day and the bus is crowded with enormous baskets of mangoes, oranges, and pungent coriander. A chicken scurries up and down the aisle. Wedged into their seats, the passengers mop their foreheads and start shouting for the driver, who has been flirting with the pretty owner of a makeshift refreshment stand for the past half hour. "Hell couldn't be hotter!" exclaims one young woman, and an old man shakes his finger at her. "My Padrinho always said that the fire of this earth is like water when compared to the fire of hell," he says. He proceeds to tell the story of how Padre Cícero descended into hell to save a cowman who had slipped through a crack in the earth and who then called on him for help. The young woman is not impressed, but a number of other passengers nod and murmur appreciatively as they mop their brows. The driver finally clambers over a stack of hammocks and flips the ignition key.

Seu Manuel has an injured foot that does not respond to either homemade remedies or prescription drugs. Dona Chiquinha Delmira passes by, sees the large bandage on his foot, and asks what is the matter. When Seu Manuel

30. Samuel Antônio do Nascimento (R). Murici, Alagoas, 1929. Married; farmer and landowner. (July 21, 1981.) Although the speaker has managed to amass considerable wealth over the years, he remains a resident of the Rua do Horto.

complains that nothing seems to heal the wound, she nods sympathetically. "The medicines of today are not like those of my Padrinho," she says. She then launches into a story in which a woman spends a fortune on assorted drugs and doctors until she is finally cured by Padre Cícero. "Her husband said, 'Why go to see that foolish old priest? He will only give you a glass of water,'" she explains. "So then my Padrinho filled a glass with water, just like the man said, and his wife drank it down to the last drop and suddenly she was as healthy as could be."

The light bill arrives and Dona Maria Felipe cannot believe her eyes. "How can I ever pay this?" she shouts as she rushes into a neighbor's house, the paper in her hand. The neighbor tries to calm her by telling the story of how Padre Cícero informs his followers that hard times lie ahead. A rich man responds to the priest's predictions by boasting about how much land and cattle he possesses. Padre Cícero sternly informs the braggart that his wealth is insufficient for the trials to come. A poor man exclaims in dismay that he will never survive because he has nothing to his name but a dozen children and a small wooden crucifix. Padre Cícero assures him that he, unlike his neighbor, is truly rich. Dona Maria continues to shake her head but she is no longer shouting.

These and other stories serve as a source of information, entertainment, and counsel. They allow the priest's followers to remember loved ones, justify or condemn specific actions, and console or express solidarity with those in need. At the same time, they may serve as declarations of Padre Cícero's past and present power, thereby confirming the wisdom of the individual's move to Juazeiro.

When storytellers say that Padre Cícero is not only their *padrinho* but also their *pai* or biological father, they are acknowledging him as the supreme authority in their lives. Their faith in the priest has allowed many present residents of Juazeiro to walk away from situations that appeared to offer no solution. By moving to the city they fled the danger posed by outlaws, an unhappy family situation, or a blood feud in which they found themselves embroiled against their will. Particularly for a woman, an insistence on the priest's authority remains one of the few socially acceptable means of declaring independence from a husband or domineering parent. The high number of women in Juazeiro who have left a husband in another part of the Northeast confirms the city's identity as a haven for those with marital difficulties. Abandoned wives, who would otherwise be the target of gossip or unwelcome attentions, are likely to take refuge in Juazeiro with their children. ("My Padrinho is their guardian," one resident explains.)

Female followers in the Rua do Horto may refer to the priest as both *pai* and *dono* ("owner"), a term generally reserved for a husband. (*"Você já tem dono?"*—"Do you have an owner yet?"—is a common way of asking a young woman whether she is married.) "The people who made me a prisoner in this life were my father and the creature that I married who ran off and left me with a pack of children," notes one local storyteller. "It is my Padrinho Cícero who dominates me now."[31] In this case the word "dominate" (*dominar*) does not mean to subjugate but to direct and thus to empower.

Newcomers to the city do not necessarily run from problems too big for them to handle. They may look toward a Padre Cícero whom they compare to "a green tree that gives shade on the hottest day." The miracle tales offer these people a way of confirming the priest's importance to them as individuals. "I was near death once," explains a woman, "but he placed his hand upon my forehead and saved my life."[32]

For some residents, the miracle stories are a way of remembering not only Padre Cícero but also their own first journey to Juazeiro. They may describe, as if the trip had been made yesterday, stoking the fires intended to ward off mountain lions and heating the stones to drop into the kettle of water used to brew the morning's coffee. Most persons, however, are less interested in recalling the road that led them to the city than in coping with an often trying present. As a result, they often insist that visitors fall into three "nations" or classes: pilgrims of the Virgin Mary, pilgrims of the devil, and those fair-weather pilgrims whose faith depends on the state of their stomachs. (In Portuguese, these terms are *romeiros de Nossa Senhora, romeiros do diabo,* and *romeiros do pirão. Pirão* is a dish made with manioc meal to which some sort of broth is added in order to produce a porridge-like consistency.) "The *pirão* pilgrim," asserts one man, "comes here to eat. He is only interested in getting his fill of dried codfish and beef jerky. Once his money runs out he says, 'So long, I'm leaving. This is no place to live.' The pilgrim of the devil is no better. A leaf falls and he runs away in fear. He is not like the pilgrim of the Mother of God, who digs in his heels and will not budge even if the sky falls on his head."[33]

Local storytellers proudly stress the sacrifices they or others have made to live in Juazeiro. "I have an uncle," one woman says, "who left everything—orange trees, breadfruit, a whole grove of mangoes. He

31. Maria das Dores da Silva (R). Juazeiro, 1915. Separated; laundress. (July 24, 1981.)

32. Cecília de Lima (R). Recife, 1908. Arrived Juazeiro 1915. Married; makes hats. (July 30, 1981.)

33. Manuel Roberto (R). Lagoa de Gato, Pernambuco, 1919. Arrived Juazeiro 1922. Married; *rendeiro* and pequi-oil vendor. (July 13, 1981.)

knew he was going to suffer but he came all the same."[34] "My father traveled to Juazeiro with his knapsack on his shoulder," says a man, "enduring a million trials, a million tribulations. For this reason, even though I was born in this very street I consider myself to be a pilgrim."[35]

The stories also serve to justify a sometimes difficult decision. Although the person who arrived in Juazeiro forty years ago usually takes pleasure in recalling the day of his or her arrival, the move may have meant loneliness as well as economic hardship. Some people were happy to leave their families but others did so with reluctance. The miracle stories thus offer members of a culture that stresses the importance of blood ties a way of assuring themselves that they have made the right choice.

The tales may function at the same time as a source of courage. One woman tells the story of how her father, saddened by his failure to find work in Juazeiro, prepared to return home. "And then that night," she says, "he dreamt of a tree that sprang up from the earth, then quickly flowered and bore fruit. And so when he awoke, he said to my mother, 'Let's unpack our bags, because we are going to stay.' And every time one of us would get discouraged, he would tell us about that dream my Padrinho had sent him of that flowering tree."[36]

Residents often claim that Padre Cícero instructed everyone who would settle in Juazeiro to bring "three sacks of money and then a sack of patience for when the money runs out." Some people go on to assert that stories of the priest come from the sack of patience. "They are remembrances of my Padrinho which keep us going when all else fails," one woman explains.[37]

At the same time, the tales possess value in their own right. Long after other mementos of the original journey to Juazeiro have been lost or broken, the stories endure. Over time, the familiar words assume an almost tangible quality. They are, in fact, the nearest thing to a verbal relic. For residents, storytelling is a little like fingering a holy medal that is both a symbol and a source of power. The stories affirm the continued presence of the priest, in their actual content and in the act of repetition. "The sky is seven hundred leagues above us and hell is seven hundred

34. Josefa André Gonçalves (R). Limoeiro de Anadias, Alagoas, 1916. Arrived Juazeiro 1923. Widow; irons and makes hats. (October 21, 1982.)

35. Cícero Ferreira da Silva (R). Juazeiro, 1939. Married; butcher. (August 6, 1981.)

36. Maria Inácio de Lima (R). Juazeiro, 1934. Married; housework. (July 21, 1981.)

37. Maria Rosa de Jesus (R). Matinha de Água Branca, Alagoas, 1901. Arrived Juazeiro 1940s [exact year unknown]. Separated; *rendeira*. (October 16, 1982.)

leagues beneath us," explains one local storyteller. "And so we sit here talking of my Padrinho in the center of the world."[38]

Like residents, pilgrims use the miracle tales to inform, entertain, and influence other people. For obvious reasons, however, their stories are much more closely associated with the actual journey to Juazeiro. Although half the visitors whose stories I recorded said that their parents or grandparents had known Padre Cícero as pilgrims, a mere 4 percent, as compared to 49 percent of the residents, claimed that they themselves had known the priest. Moreover, visitors' contact with Padre Cícero was usually brief at best. Then, too, as members of a larger group they were usually obliged to share their audience with the priest. Thus there was seldom opportunity for any sort of extended conversation.

This limited degree of face-to-face experience does not make Padre Cícero a less compelling presence in the minds of pilgrims who visited Juazeiro before his death. One old man remembers in nitid detail how the priest handed him a coin more than fifty years ago. "I took that coin and with it I bought two doves and then I let them disappear into the sky," the man explains. "The others in my group said that I was foolish, that I should have used the money to buy a keepsake of my Padrinho that I could carry with me. But I have no regrets and I do not think that I was foolish, because each time I see a bird fly up into heaven I think of him."[39]

Most pilgrims' lack of firsthand knowledge means that they must lean more heavily than residents on borrowed memories. An average of seven out of every ten stories told by pilgrims were originally learned from a family member, often long ago. The tales therefore serve as celebrations not only of Padre Cícero but also of the teller's relatives. "I never saw my Padrinho Cícero," says one young woman from Sergipe, "but I believe in him because of my grandparents. They told us many things, they set us in that rhythm which we continue to follow."[40] "How could I fail to be a pilgrim?" asks a man from Alagoas. "My father and my grandfather were pilgrims before me. I inherited their faith."[41] "I

38. Mariano Ferreira da Silva (R). Freixeira, Pernambuco, 1898. Arrived Juazeiro 1950. Married; begs for a living. (September 26, 1982.)

39. Francisco Ferreira de Almeida (P). São Miguel, Alagoas, 1916. [Marital status unknown]; guard. 18 pilgrimages. (October 19, 1982.)

40. Alzira de Santos Moura (P). Monte Alegre, Sergipe, 1956. Married; *rendeira*. 5 pilgrimages. (November 22, 1982.)

41. Pedro Gomes de Sá (P). Marechal Deodoro, Alagoas, 1952. Married; *morador*. 5 pilgrimages. (October 11, 1982.)

always believed the stories our parents told us," confides a woman, "but somehow being here makes them seem even truer."[42]

Pilgrims often learn some of their stories on the road to Juazeiro.[43] Particularly in the case of pilgrimage trucks, which customarily stop for meals and for the night's rest, storytelling provides a way of passing the hours. By the time they reach their destination, many travelers know as many as a dozen new tales.

A number of narratives focus on topographical formations such as rocks, trees, and springs that visitors encounter when they come to Juazeiro. The statue of Padre Cícero, his tomb, a table in the priest's former summer residence in the Horto, and the *ex-votos* in the House of Miracles also generate a number of stories. So does the image of Our Lady of Solitude, which stands in a side room of the church of Our Lady of Sorrows.

The museum run by the Salesian order in the house that Padre Cícero occupied at the time of his death is particularly popular with storytellers. A battered black felt hat said to have belonged to the priest occupies a place of honor in this high-ceilinged old structure where stucco walls dabbed with paint create the illusion of wallpaper. Pilgrims inevitably come to gaze at the narrow iron bed in which Padre Cícero is believed to have slept. With its frilly white lace coverlet, the bed seems designed more for a child than for a man whose memory still dominates the Northeast, but the people who kneel before it have clearly come to honor the all-powerful leader who gazes down at them from a portrait on the wall.

The rest of the Padre Cícero Museum is a jumble of objects that may or may not have anything to do with the priest. The dusty glass cases contain not only photographs and personal possessions of the cleric but also painted clay figures of lacemakers and cowmen, toy rocking chairs, and innumerable examples of flora and fauna from various parts of Brazil. The generally illiterate visitors logically assume that everything in the museum that bears the priest's name must have belonged to him, and they therefore tell stories relating many of these otherwise alien objects to Padre Cícero. Because it is one of the few places in Juazeiro that is almost cool, pilgrims tend to linger more than at other landmarks. As a

---

42. Maria Pureza dos Anjos (P). Campina Grande, Paraíba, 1941. Married; pineapple vendor. 2 pilgrimages. (October 21, 1982.)

43. Experiments regarding the nature of human memory reveal a propensity to recall the first and last instances of a repeated experience. Pilgrims' tendency to tell miracle stories either from their childhood or from the immediate past appears to bear this out. See Jan Vansina, "Memory and Oral Tradition."

result, the museum is an ideal place to listen to conversations about the priest.

The enormous stuffed snake that occupies the corner of one room is one of the most popular figures for anecdotes and tales. By standing off to the side as different groups arrived to press their noses against the glass case, I once recorded in less than an hour eleven completely different stories about this creature. Some people claimed the snake was a girl who mocked the priest, who then turned her into reptilian form as punishment for disrespect. Others recounted how the snake had swallowed a man to whom Padre Cícero then miraculously furnished a knife with which to cut his way out of the monster's belly. ("See that thin line there, right down its side?" one man asked three wide-eyed companions. "Well, that snake is shriveling up with age so it is harder to make out now but if you really look you can still see where that man slit the thing in two.") Still others asserted that the snake was brought to Juazeiro by a grateful rancher who had asked Padre Cícero to put an end to the monster, who was devouring his cattle one by one. ("It was in 1961. The snake weighed two hundred kilos and its mouth was still bloody from its last meal of a full-grown steer," one storyteller noted with authority.)

The stuffed birds that are the snake's neighbors also generate a wealth of stories. Because most pilgrims have never heard of taxidermy, they often think the birds have been frozen through enchantment and are still alive. They therefore talk about a future in which the return of their owner will set them warbling anew. "Each time I arrive," confides one man, "I hurry right away to the museum to see if those birds are still there. So far, they have not budged, but on the day my Padrinho returns here they will greet him with a song more beautiful than any you have ever heard."[44]

Visitors to Juazeiro also learn stories from *rancho* owners, peddlers, beggars, and pilgrims from places other than their own community. Many assume that natives of the city must know more than they do about Padre Cícero and they may therefore seek out older residents as storytellers. Pilgrim after pilgrim told me that he or she had heard one or another tale from a "108-year-old woman who has lived right here in Juazeiro all her life." I, however, was never able to locate this woman who always seemed to vanish mysteriously, minutes before my arrival. As time went on I began to wonder if she were not a composite image of the many older inhabitants of the city who regale eager listeners with

44. Francisco de Souza (P). Altos, Piauí, 1912. [Marital status unknown]; *rendeiro.* 3 pilgrimages. (September 22, 1982.)

stories. The fact that longtime residents of Juazeiro were as mystified as I about this woman reinforced my growing doubts about her physical reality.

And yet, although visitors regularly defer to natives as more knowledgeable storytellers, they nonetheless take pride in their identity as pilgrims. I once observed a group from the state of Alagoas clustered around a large, bad-tempered parrot that looked as if it would like nothing better than to bite off someone's finger. One pilgrim, however, had taken it upon himself to explain to the parrot why it had to show some manners. "You can nip others but not us because we are guests of my Padrinho Cícero," the man informed the creature, oblivious to its squawks. The bird's owner then appeared to reiterate the theme. "These are pilgrims, they are special," he said to the parrot. "Give them your foot, blow them a kiss, say something nice. They have come all the way from Alagoas to visit my Padrinho. Say 'Hello, how are you? Are you enjoying Juazeiro?' Come on now, be polite!"

No matter what their source, the miracle narratives are an integral part of the journey to a special place. They unite the travelers in an enterprise transcending differences in geography, occupation, or temperament. "A pilgrimage truck is always a family," one newcomer to Juazeiro observes. "There can be no secrets when people set out together to visit my Padrinho Cícero."[45] He goes on to tell the story of the woman in his group whose food turned "black as ash" after she refused to share it with her fellow travelers.

The stories do not always reflect the sort of fellow-feeling that has been labeled *communitas*.[46] Although persons who dislike each other may forget their differences for the moment, they are also capable of using the occasion to launch verbal attacks in the guise of miracle tales. One individual, for instance, may tell the story of how Padre Cícero hated thieves "and especially those who stole chickens from their neighbors," with a meaningful look in the direction of a person suspected of raiding another's barnyard.

Nonetheless, storytelling offers a much-needed way of sharing deeply felt experiences with both friends and strangers. Travelers to Juazeiro frequently reveal to others portions of their lives they would customarily keep secret. In so doing they reinforce the mystique surrounding the pilgrimage.

45. João Martins da Silva (P). Capela, Alagoas, 1935. Arrived Juazeiro 1980. Married; gardener and candy vendor. (July 28, 1981.)

46. The term is Victor and Edith Turner's: see *Image and Pilgrimage in Christian Culture*, pp. 250–255, for a fuller definition.

Many visitors' accounts, for instance, suggest that the decision to undertake the journey lies outside the individual's control. "My husband says I go to Juazeiro because I want to," says one woman who travels from São Paulo to Pernambuco, where she joins her father and three sisters who also make the pilgrimage each year. "That is what he says, but he is very wrong. I spend month after month washing other people's clothes in order to earn the money to come here because I must come. Really, I have no choice. Many years ago, I nearly died before I prayed to my Padrinho not to let my six small children go through life without a mother. And because my Padrinho helped me, I cannot forget that hour in which he was my only aid. My husband shrugs and says, 'So go if you wish.' He does not understand that my greatest pleasure is my greatest obligation."[47]

Pilgrims' stories also reinforce a widespread belief in the longterm benefits associated with the journey to Juazeiro. "Our Lady of Sorrows keeps a book in which she writes the name of every pilgrim who comes to see her and my Padrinho," one young woman says. "She will present this book to her son on the day of judgment."[48] When one reporter from Recife who was covering the biggest feast day of the year in Juazeiro asked a woman what she hoped to accomplish by her pilgrimage, she initially looked confused. "But you must hope to gain *something* by coming all this way," the man insisted with a certain impatience. "Yes sir, my salvation, sir," the woman then informed him.[49]

The extraordinary nature of the miracle stories is not lost on their tellers. Although it is not common for Northeastern men to cry, particularly in the presence of women and children, males as well as females may weep upon recounting a particular tale. The incident does not have to be sad for the narrator to shed tears. It may remind the individual of a dead grandmother or cherished brother, or of a critical—perhaps particularly happy—moment in his or her own life. No one looks away from the person and no one suggests that a male storyteller has done something unmanly. As a matter of fact, most of the listeners were crying along with the teller at the end of the following story.

2. Look, my Padrinho died when I was a child. I still remember the day. I was at the mill wheel in the Casa da Farinha [a communal

47. Woman, name unknown (daughter of José Barbosa de Santana) (P). São Paulo, 1936. Married; seamstress. (October 29, 1982.)

48. Maria Vilma Ferreira da Silva (P). Maceió, Alagoas, 1947. Married; handicrafts. 20 pilgrimages. (December 3, 1982.)

49. Unidentified woman from Currais Novos, Rio Grande do Norte. (November 2, 1982.)

building for grinding manioc flour] when an old man named Du, who sold bread, arrived with the news. So then I felt sad, so sad, but I said to myself, "Even though he is no longer in Juazeiro, I will go there anyway." Well, then a number of years went by, I married, I became a family man. And that is just what happened.

One day a truck full of pilgrims appeared at my door. And I said to my wife, "Do you know something? I am going to Juazeiro." And when I arrived here, I went to see his house, his bed, his picture. I knelt before his bed in that spirit of faith. So then he suddenly appeared before me. Yes. It is the absolute truth. He was there. Talking to me. And I was talking to him. We talked and talked and I told him all about my life. And even today I cannot keep from crying when I think about how my Padrinho looked at me.

—Firmino Afonso da Silva (P). Feira Nova, Pernambuco, 1915. Married; farmer (own land). "Too many trips to count," beginning 1943. (October 11, 1982.)

This account emphasizes Juazeiro's identity as a place where pilgrims may not only hear tales told by others but also actually generate their own. Once in the city, people often assign hidden meanings to events or objects to which they normally would not devote a second thought. The following speaker, for instance, attributes a near-accident, which she would almost certainly have dismissed as carelessness under other circumstances, to the priest's intervention.

3. I was up there in the Horto this morning and there was a young woman who had come to have her picture taken, dressed in one of those transparent little blouses that the girls wear today. And when I looked at her I cannot deny that I censured her in my mind. I thought, "How is it possible that this girl can be dressed like this in such a holy place?" And in that very moment I almost fell. I didn't fall only because a person close by steadied me. And so it suddenly occurred to me that I had been punished for thinking in this manner. That it was my Padrinho who had given me that little push. I mean, wasn't I offending him much more by thinking this way than that girl was in her transparent blouse?

—Helena Leda Conceição (P). Campina Grande, Paraíba, 1917. Married; housework. 26 pilgrimages. (October 30, 1982.)

Individuals not caught up in the spirit of the moment may fail to appreciate, or may misinterpret, visitors' motives. One young pilgrim describes with incredulity the inability of a group of onlookers to comprehend his actions. As Northeast Brazilian men regard themselves as innately superior to women, this man's decision to sit on the floor beside an elderly female beggar is an unusual, fully conscious expression of humility.

4. So then when we went to rest, an old lady showed up in our *rancho*. And she told us many stories about my Padrinho because she herself was from another century, you see? So I thought her stories very pretty. And when afterward she said, "I am going to church," I said, "I will go along with you, ma'am." And I gave her some money to buy bread and coffee. Then when we reached the church, she went in to pray. So I went over to where she was praying. And I began to think, "Do you know something? I am no better than her. I am just the same as her." So I went and sat beside her. On the floor. Then I saw that everyone was looking at me and I thought, "But can this be possible? They are all thinking that I want to rob her." And I was so overcome with feeling that I couldn't say a word. Because I had understood for the first time in my life that I was no better than the poorest human being. And there were those others thinking that I had my eye on the woman's money. It was something that I can't explain.

—Severino Sebastião de Melo (P). Vertentes, Pernambuco, 1959. Single; truck driver. First pilgrimage. (November 15, 1982.)

Although not every visitor to Juazeiro has the same sort of intense reaction to events and people, many do feel an exceptional urge to talk. These persons may attempt, like the young man, to translate powerful emotions into their own words. Often, however, they rely on the most familiar stories to express ideas and experiences they would otherwise find hard to share. Either way, their accounts come to serve as affirmations of "that which we always knew deep down inside ourselves but did not say until today."

PART TWO

ANALYSIS: BEST-KNOWN
MIRACLE STORIES

III.

Introduction to the
Padre Cícero Tales

And *everybody* knows the story of the hat that stuck to the
wall without a peg.

Young pilgrim from Paraíba

T he priest's followers tell a seemingly endless stream of stories
about Padre Cícero. These include tales set in the present and
recent past as well as others that take place during his lifetime. Although
the former are definitely more numerous, both sorts of narratives are
extremely important to the corpus as a whole.

Stories set after the priest's death are usually told in the first person.
As they almost always focus on the speaker or a close relative, they seldom find their way into a larger communal repertoire. These usually
very detailed accounts often deal with how Padre Cícero cures or pro-
tects the teller or how he punishes an acquaintance who does not show
proper respect. As such, they resemble stories told about the holy figures
associated with other pilgrimage centers both within and outside Brazil.[1]

---

1. For an introduction to the enormous bibliography on Christian hagiography see
the work of Hippolyte Delehaye, especially *The Legends of the Saints*, and René Aigrain,
L'Hagiographie: Ses sources, ses méthodes, son histoire. See also Sofia Boesch Gajano, ed.,
Agiografia alto medievale, especially the introduction (pp. 7–48) and bibliography (pp. 261–
302). The most extensive collection of saints' lives is the *Acta Sanctorum quotquot toto orbe*.
More accessible collections are Jacobus de Voragine, *The Golden Legend*, and Alban Butler,
Lives of the Saints. There are also a number of hagiographical dictionaries; Donald Attwater,
The Penguin Dictionary of Saints, and David Hugh Farmer, *Oxford Dictionary of Saints*, are
two of the more useful. For a discussion of the emergence of the cult of the Christian
martyrs see Peter Brown, *The Cult of the Saints: Its Rise and Function in Latin Christianity*.
Two particularly interesting studies of change in a saint's cult over time and in space are
Charles W. Jones, *Saint Nicholas of Myra, Bari and Manhattan: Biography of a Legend*, and
Jean-Claude Schmitt, *Le saint lévrier: Guinefort, guérisseur d'enfants depuis le XIIIᵉ siècle*.

Although fewer tales are set in the priest's lifetime, these incidents are more likely to be known throughout the Northeast. I will concentrate on these stories in this and subsequent chapters for several reasons. First, their range and number make the Padre Cícero tales unique. Second, at the same time that they are of special interest to the tellers, they provide the outside observer with a manageable approach to what would otherwise be a large and unwieldy assortment of tales. Finally, these accounts are essential to an understanding of the miracle stories as a whole. Not only are they many people's introduction to the priest of Juazeiro, but they also provide the model for other, more personal accounts of Padre Cícero.

The narrators may tell stories about other holy figures. Almost everyone in Juazeiro is familiar with the gold, brass, or plastic charms depicting Saint Lucy's eyes, which she chose to lose rather than deny her faith in Christ. People find it easy to remember the story of Saint Sebastian's martyrdom because of the little figure full of arrow wounds which occupies a privileged place in many homes. They may also recall bits and pieces from the lives of later, confessor saints that they have heard in sermons or learned as part of prayers or songs of praise. As stories of miraculous deeds were once a customary part of elementary textbooks, those followers with even minimal schooling are likely to have encountered them as children.[2]

These narrative fragments cannot compare, however, with the myriad episodes attributed to Padre Cícero. And although people tell a comparable number of stories about the very popular Saint Francis, these do not comprise any sort of folk canon.[3] Pilgrims to Canindé can usually repeat a few familiar incidents, but many visitors to Juazeiro know dozens, if not hundreds.

As a means of establishing a concrete basis for the comparison of residents and pilgrims that follows, I have selected twenty stories told most often by each group. (Fifteen of these tales are the same for the two groups, and five are different.) I have translated all the texts into English with a minimum of changes and additions, grouping the Portuguese originals together at the back of this book.[4] Because the tales themselves

2. Other saints whose stories are well known among Padre Cícero's followers are Benedict, George (no longer recognized by the Catholic Church but still popular among the people), Cosme and Damian, Gonzalo and Anthony. A sample of the large collection of folktales about Saint Peter appears in Osvaldo Elias Xidieh, *Narrativas pias populares.*

3. The best-known story of Saint Francis concerns his rescue of a little girl who becomes lost in a forest. A statue of the child stands in the museum dedicated to Saint Francis in Canindé, and there are various printed (*cordel*) versions of the tale.

4. See Appendix B for these texts.

are oral performances, these texts are necessarily approximations. In the presentation of their stories people often change their voices to fit the character who is ostensibly speaking. They rely heavily on gestures and, sometimes, body contact with one or more listeners. If Padre Cícero touches a child in a story, the teller may rest a hand upon the nearest person's head. Should the priest scold an unbeliever, the speaker singles out one listener at whom to shake a finger. In relating the story of the hat that stuck to the wall, he or she may grab a straw hat from someone's head and toss it up into the air, eliciting the listeners' cheers. "Then I will hang my hat here!" exclaims the teller, perhaps prompting a member of the group to stick out a finger, on which the hat remains suspended in a collective dramatization.[5]

This dramatic quality disappears in transcription. So do the changes in inflection that indicate a shift in speaker. I have therefore occasionally added a "he said" or "she told him" after bits of dialogue. I have also filled in pronouns or repeated a subject from time to time in order to make the action clearer. Although I initially bracketed these additions, I later removed the brackets because they interfered with that sense of movement so essential to the original.[6] Throughout the following texts, I have sought to keep my translation as literal as possible without becoming stilted. When faced with more than one option, I have tried to choose the English equivalent that seemed most faithful to the spirit of the Portuguese, in which rhythm is often as important as dictionary definition.

In each of the following cases, the text I have selected from many, many versions of the same story is representative in terms of plot. I have favored shorter as opposed to longer retellings of these stories simply for reasons of space. (Most accounts of well-known miracles range from one hundred to three hundred words, but others are considerably more substantial.) As there are a fairly large number of illustrations, the reader will want to form an overall impression before returning to individual stories throughout this and succeeding chapters. After the texts which appear here, I have noted a few of the more important variations not mentioned in succeeding chapters. Differences as well as similarities in style and tone should be apparent even in translation.

To be on this list, a story must be familiar to a sizable number of individuals. (Rank orderings for each group appear in Chapter IV.) Al-

5. For a useful discussion of comparable sorts of narrative interaction see Linda Dégh, *Folktales and Society: Story-Telling in a Hungarian Peasant Community.*

6. Jeff Todd Titon makes a good case against brackets and similar devices when he argues that as a transcription is always an approximation, such scrupulousness may actually represent a false loyalty to the original. See Titon, "The Life Story."

though a good deal of personal material regularly seeps into these narratives, the basic outlines of the stories are familiar to the community at large.

The action in all the tales presented here takes place during Padre Cícero's lifetime or immediately after his death. Each tale has a recognizable beginning, middle, and end. I have excluded well-known prophecies attributed to Padre Cícero, and miraculous "facts." I have also omitted those sorts of anecdotes that storytellers themselves consider to be tokens of miraculous power rather than miraculous events.[7] Descriptions of how Padre Cícero's pet vulture refused to eat meat on Fridays or of the priest's ability to pick out one or two eggs laid by a particular kind of hen from an enormous basket are good illustrations.[8] Although prayers and songs may have a narrative content, I have not considered these here, either.

The titles I have provided are based on people's own words ("Tell us the story of *the hat that stuck to the wall,* Manuel"). I have arranged the first fifteen stories in a rough chronological order beginning with Padre Cícero's birth and ending with his death. As will become clear, storytellers themselves do not necessarily present these incidents in this or any particular sequence.

Stories Told by Both Residents and Pilgrims

5. They say that Dona Quinou was the mother of my Padrinho but it was not she who gave birth to him, no. Look, shortly after he was born, her husband said, "Quinou, let the baby go on sleeping in the hammock and come with me to look for watermelon in the fields." Well now, watermelon had always been her favorite fruit. So she went with her husband—his name was Joaquim Romão—she went with him to the fields. And there they went about picking the biggest and most delicious melons.

7. A good example of an anecdote that does not qualify as a full-fledged narrative would be the statement that the famous outlaw Lampião was a follower of Padre Cícero and for this reason supposedly did not bother pilgrims headed for Juazeiro. Although the bond between Padre Cícero and Lampião is strong in the popular imagination (see *cordel* author and artist José Borges' *A vida do Padre Cícero* for intriguing pictorial representations of the two folk heroes), it has not generated a single readily recognizable story.

8. The hen, known variously as a *pinto de pescoço pelado,* a *peruana,* or a *galinha gogó de sola,* is believed to be bedeviled. The person who cuts up such a hen to cook supposedly will always find one piece fewer in the cooking pot than those he or she has put in, because the devil has claimed his due. Padre Cícero's ability to sort out the eggs laid by this hen from a large number of identical eggs confirms his ability to discern the truth that lies behind appearances.

"Eat more, Quinou."

"No," she said, "I think that the baby must be awake by now and no doubt crying for his supper." So then the two headed home. When they got near, Quinou saw a beautiful woman all in blue leaving the house with a bundle in her arms.

"Who can that woman be?" she asked her husband.

"What?" he said. "I didn't see anyone."

So then when Quinou went to look at the baby she let out a cry. "This child is not mine!" she said. "That woman must have left her little son in my baby's place."

"Stop talking nonsense, woman," her husband said. "You have eaten too much watermelon and your head is in a whirl."

"Let me look again," she said. But in that very moment the light of her eyes failed and so she could never really say for sure.

—Ana Morais de Melo (R). Natal, Rio Grande do Norte, 1952. Arrived Juazeiro 1956. Married; seamstress. (November 20, 1982.)

Observations: On occasion, the woman in blue is expressly identified as the Virgin Mary. Sometimes Quinou is actually in the house, sleeping, when the exchange occurs. A friend or the midwife may notice the beautiful woman entering or leaving the house.

6. During that time when my Padrinho Cícero was studying in Cajazeiras, the children used to hang their hats on pegs along the wall. But one day when my Padrinho arrived, he found all the pegs taken: there was no place for him to hang his hat. So then he tossed his hat up against the wall—poof!—and there it stayed. When the other children saw what he had done, they tried to do the same. You know how children are—if one of them does something, they all want to do it too. Well then, they tossed their hats up against the wall but they all just fell to the floor. Only my Padrinho's little hat stayed there without a peg. So then even when he was a little boy no bigger than Joãozinho [the speaker points to a child by this name who is among the listeners], my Padrinho Cícero was already working miracles.

   —Manoel Ferreira da Silva (R). Serra do Araripe (Crato, Ceará), 1917. Arrived Juazeiro as child. Married; repairs furniture. (July 10, 1981.)

7. There were some people who were so jealous of my Padrinho Cícero that they wanted to murder him. So then they decided to bring a "sick" man to my Padrinho Cícero in a hammock. And that man would have a fish knife in his hand and when my Padrinho

opened the folds of the hammock in order to confess him, he would plunge the knife into my Padrinho's heart. So then these people brought the man to my Padrinho's house. When they arrived there, they said, "Padrinho Cícero, we have brought you a sick man who wants you to confess him."

"I am sorry," my Padrinho said, "but no, there is nothing I can do for the dead."

"No, no," they said. "He is sick, he isn't dead."

"Well then, you take a look at him yourselves," my Padrinho said, "because that man died a while ago." And when they went to open the folds of the hammock they saw that it was true. The man was dead!

So then my Padrinho said, "Look at the big knife with which he planned to kill me." And there was that fish knife in the man's left hand.

—Quitéria Maria da Conceição (R). Freixeira, Pernambuco, 1905. Arrived Juazeiro as child. Married; farms and makes sleeping mats. (August 8, 1981.)

Observations: In the past, sick and dead people were carried in hammocks for lack of other means of transportation. The expression *Só saio daqui numa rede* ("I will leave here only in a hammock") is thus equivalent to the English "Over my dead body!" Note that the dagger (sometimes a revolver) is in the left, or unlucky, hand.

8. There was a rancher in a place by the name of Flores who did not give any credence to my Padrinho Cícero. One day when a pilgrim passed by where he lived, the rancher said to him, "Everything here is so very dry that my cattle are dying on the hoof. So then you tell your Padre Cícero that I asked him for a nickel's worth of rain." Well then, when he reached Juazeiro, the pilgrim was ashamed to tell my Padrinho.

"The messenger does not deserve to be punished for the message," my Padrinho said to him. "Don't be shy about telling me what that rancher wants."

"My Padrinho, Fulano asked you for a nickel's worth of rain."

"He wants a nickel's worth?" my Padrinho asked him. "Well, you can tell Fulano that a nickel is too much." And he gave him the change. Plink, plink, plink, plink. Four pennies in the man's palm. "Now you go back and tell the rancher that he should get ready because the rain will be arriving any minute."

So then the pilgrim went to give the rancher my Padrinho's message. "Stay and have supper with us," the rancher said. "I can't," the pilgrim told him and went running off. Well then, he had barely left there when the rain began falling hard, really hard. But only on the rancher's property, understand? So much rain fell that the man and his whole family found themselves up to their necks in water. Not even a crumb of sweet bread was left to remind him of life's sweetness.

—Alzira Sebastiana da Silva (P). Limoeiro, Pernambuco, 1919. Widow; *moradora*. Six pilgrimages. (October 14, 1982.)

Observations: The location of the ranch and the amount of money vary. So does the gravity of the rancher's fate. *Fulano* (sometimes *Fulano de Tal*) is the Portuguese equivalent of John Doe. The "nickel" in this case is really five milréis, a unit of currency no longer in circulation.

9. There was once a *beata* by the name of Maria de Araújo. I didn't know her but my aunt did and she told me the whole story. My Padrinho went to give her communion and the host turned into blood. When he placed the host upon her tongue, it took the shape of a heart. My Padrinho looked at it and said, "This is the precious blood of Our Lord Jesus Christ." So then everyone who was there in the church wept to see such a great mystery.

—Quitéria Maria Ferreira (P). Monteiro, Paraíba, 1935. Married; *rendeira*. 4 pilgrimages. (October 12, 1982.)

10. Saint Peter was the first pope. One day he locked the door of a great church in Rome and threw the key into the woods so that no one could ever open that door again. Well then, when my Padrinho went to Rome the pope said, "Padre Cícero, I have heard that you go about performing miracles. So I want you to open this door for me."

"Your Holiness," my Padrinho said, "I am a simple priest. I have no way to open that door."

"If you don't open that door I am going to send my soldiers to Juazeiro with my biggest cannon."

"All right, your Holiness. If that is what you want, then I will open it for you."

So then he spoke to the door. "May he who shut you open you," he said three times. And on the third time that he spoke, the door opened to allow my Padrinho to ascend a staircase the color of new corn.

So then the pope was sorry he had not believed in his miraculous powers. "Padre Cícero," he said, "come live with me in Rome." "Thank you very much, your Holiness," my Padrinho told him. "I thank you for your fine invitation. But my heart belongs to Juazeiro and it is there that I will stay."

—Luís Pereira dos Santos (R). Pombal, Paraíba, 1895. Arrived
    Juazeiro 1914. Married; retired. (November 1, 1982.)

11. The bishop—I think it was the bishop of Fortaleza—ran into my Padrinho Cícero one day. "I am Padre Cícero, your Excellency," my Padrinho said to him.

"Oh yes," the bishop responded. "Isn't it you who goes around working miracles? Well, I want you to cure a child who was born without the power of speech."

"I will cure him because it is you who are asking me to do so," my Padrinho told him, "but otherwise I would not."

So then he put his hand on the child's head and asked, "Boy, whose son are you?" in this way, three times.

So then the child said, "I am the son of the bishop of Ceará and the mother superior of the convent."

"So there you have it, your Excellency," my Padrinho said. And the bishop was so angry that he nearly burst. It is a story that everyone here in Juazeiro knows.

—João Quinto Sobrinho ("João do Cristo Rei") (R). Areia, Paraíba,
    1901. Arrived Juazeiro 1947. Married; cordel poet. (July 15, 1981.)

Observations: The verb used for "burst" is pipocar, which describes the noise made by popping corn. The concluding image therefore makes people laugh.

12. Right after my Padrinho Cícero "moved away" [died], there appeared a girl in the state of Alagoas who refused to wear mourning for him. She said she would sooner wear black for her dog than for a man she had never met. So then the dog died the very same day and sure enough, she went out dressed in mourning for all the world to see. But there was a little boy who spied a dog's tail hanging out from beneath her clothes. So then he started shouting and everyone stopped to stare. After that, the tail kept on growing and growing until the girl was a dog. There are people who say that she became a dog from the waist down. But there are others

who say that she became a dog, yes, a dog. I myself didn't see her
but my brother knows someone who did.

—Maria das Dores Alves de Albuquerque (R). Serra de Raiz, Pernambuco, 1920 (died 1981). Arrived Juazeiro 1953. Married; made
straw hats. (July 21, 1981.)

Observations: The story of the girl who turned into a dog is the best
known of a number of similar metamorphoses. Two other particularly
well-known transformations concern a girl who turns into a snake after
she vows she will never walk to Juazeiro (she then proceeds to crawl
there), and a young man who turns into a toad. In the latter case, the
storyteller often blames the change on the man's mother, who says she
will believe in the priest's powers only if she gives birth to a toad. There
are also somewhat less common stories about women, and occasionally
men, who turn into horses, pigs, monkeys, and burros. Sometimes, but
not always, the person regains human form after a certain number of
years.

13. A war broke out here and many soldiers came to attack Juazeiro.
So then my Padrinho Cícero assembled his followers in order to
repel them. He planted a ring of *macambira* [a form of cactus] which
encircled the city, two feet high, overnight. The soldiers could not
pass. When they started to fire their guns, the bullets did not hit
anyone but went bounding back at them. Many soldiers died but
here in Juazeiro there were only two—an old man and a boy—who
did not respect my Padrinho's word and who died on the spot.

—Manuel Messias (P). Paulo Afonso, Bahia, 1947. Married;
truckdriver. 10 pilgrimages. (November 1, 1982.)

14. One day my Padrinho was in the middle of his sermon when he
closed his eyes as if he were asleep. And so people started to go like
this [nudging gesture] and to whisper, "My Padrinho is getting to
be so old that he just drowses off this way." So then half an hour
went by, an hour, two hours, in which everyone just waited without
knowing what to do.

So then when he opened his eyes, my Padrinho said, "I was far
away in Germany stopping a very savage war. One of my followers
called upon me and I descended to earth in a cloud."

Now it so happens that there were two photographers there in
Germany who snapped a picture of my Padrinho as he descended
from the sky. Once the war was over, they went to look for him.

They searched in at least eighty countries but found no trace of him. Finally one of them said, "For goodness' sake, we still haven't been to Brazil." So then they hopped on an airplane to Rio de Janeiro.

And when they showed the picture to the people there everyone said, "Oh yes, that priest has to be the one who lives in Ceará."

Then they went to Fortaleza and the people said, "Oh yes, that priest looks a lot like the one in Juazeiro." So then they finally arrived here around three o'clock in the afternoon. Many of the people who saw them can tell you all about it.

—Sebastião Pedro da Silva (P). Currais Novos, Rio Grande do
Norte, 1942. Arrived Juazeiro 1962. Married; sells saints' pictures
in *ranchos*. (November 14, 1982.)

Observations: The war is sometimes said to be in Paraguay or in the city of Princesa in the state of Paraíba. (Brazil fought in the War of the Triple Alliance against Paraguay in 1865–70, and state forces put down an uprising in Princesa when the city declared itself an independent republic in 1930.)

15. One day when my Padrinho Cícero was celebrating mass, he suddenly closed his eyes.

"What is happening to my Padrinho?" everybody asked. He remained like that for at least half an hour without saying a word to anyone.

Then when he finally opened his eyes he said, "I have just returned from the city of Cacimbinha. A little girl who fell into a well there called on me. So I went there to help but I am back with you again."

Well now, it appears there was one man who did not accept my Padrinho's word. "How can one person be in two places at the same time? Ha, ha, ha!" He kept on making mocking comments like these. But later when he arrived home he learned that his little daughter had almost drowned in that very moment. And when his wife told him what had happened, his laughter turned to bitter tears.

—Manuel Bezerra da Costa (P). Nossa Senhora da Glória, Sergipe,
1930. Married; sells clay. 2 pilgrimages. (November 1, 1982.)

Observations: Padre Cícero may pull the drowning child out of a well, a reservoir, or the ocean. Sometimes she falls from a soapberry tree into his arms. Often, the girl's mother sees a priest rescue her daughter but when she goes to thank him he has already vanished.

16. There was a man just like myself who gathered together the people where he lived to go to Juazeiro every year. But this man had a father who did not believe in my Padrinho. "Bah, you are really crazy to waste your time in this foolish pilgrimage business," he always told his son.

Well now, one time when the man arrived in Juazeiro, my Padrinho asked him, "Where is your father? I would like to meet him."

The son said, "He stayed home, my Padrinho. He thinks that I am crazy to come here every year."

"Is that so?" my Padrinho said. And they spoke of other things. But just before the man left for home my Padrinho said, "Look, I know that you are a hunter. Could you bring me the first thing that you catch upon returning home?"

"Yes, I could, and with great pleasure," the man said.

A photograph of Padre Cícero as an old man and a picture of him supposedly descending from a cloud as in the tale of the war in Germany. These portraits are ubiquitous in Juazeiro.

So on the day after the man's return from Juazeiro, he went out with his dogs. After a little while, one of them began to bark and bark beneath a tree until the hunter climbed it. And what did he find but his own father, who had gone up there to catch one of those birds that people in these backlands like very much to eat! When the hunter saw him he said, "Father, I now see that you are the catch which my Padrinho Cícero wanted so badly. Shall we go to Juazeiro?"

Well, when the old man heard the story he could not keep from laughing. "That old priest is a wise one after all," he told his son. And from then on the two men went together without fail to see my Padrinho every year.

—Pedro Barbosa de Santana (P). Maceió, Alagoas, 1947. Married; *rendeiro*. 4 pilgrimages. (October 7, 1982.)

Observations: Some storytellers describe the ensuing trip to Juazeiro in detail, adding an incident involving the loss and restoration of the old man's gold dagger.

17. There was a doctor here, a Dr. Floro. He was a close friend of my Padrinho and one of these very important people. But he ended up fighting with my Padrinho because he wanted to be more powerful than he. This Dr. Floro was very cruel and he killed a lot of people. Finally my Padrinho could stand no more of him.

"Floro, you cannot keep on behaving in this manner," he said.

"Well, if you don't like it, then why did you make me great?" he asked.

So then my Padrinho said, "Floro, he who made you great can also make you small." And what he said was true because a few days later Dr. Floro died.

—Maria Lima da Silva (P). São Bento de Unha, Pernambuco, 1918. Widow; farmer (own land). 10 pilgrimages. (October 25, 1982.)

18. A girl set out for Juazeiro together with some other pilgrims, and when night came they all took shelter in the mountains. But the girl was so tired from walking, poor thing, that she did not awake with the light of day. So then the others left her sleeping there in the mountains where there used to be many fierce mountain lions, understand?

Some days later, the pilgrims arrived in Juazeiro. So then my Padrinho Cícero asked them, "Where is that charge I entrusted to you?"

"What charge, my Padrinho?"

"That girl whom you left sleeping in the mountains. A mountain lion devoured her but her soul arrived here before you."

So then they were all very sad and on the way back from Juazeiro they erected a cross in the road where the mountain lion had eaten that girl. The bus passed by there yesterday when we crossed the mountains and we made the driver stop so that everyone could see.

—Pedro Manuel (P). Maceió, Alagoas, 1908. Widowed; electrical
repair (automobiles). 11 pilgrimages. (September 17, 1982.)

19. When my Padrinho Cícero "separated" [died], the bishop of Crato said, "I am going to Juazeiro to take the body away from those miserable pilgrims. They are such fanatics, these people, that there is no telling what they will do if I leave the body there with them."

Well then, the bishop and his men went to the church where my Padrinho Cícero had been buried at three o'clock in the morning. He ordered his men to dig up the coffin but when they opened it they found nothing except a little black slipper with a pointed toe. So then the bishop had them close the coffin so that no one would know. But the guard whom they found snoring at the door was not really sleeping and he told the people everything he had seen and heard.

—Isidoro José dos Santos (P). Nossa Senhora da Glória, Sergipe, 1928.
Married; farmer (own land). 3 pilgrimages. (October 30, 1982.)

Observations: The object in the tomb is sometimes a mysterious book prophesying Juazeiro's glorious future, or another article of clothing such as the priest's robe. Sometimes there is nothing but a heap of rose petals or an overwhelming smell of flowers (the "odor of sanctity") when the men open the coffin.

Stories Told Primarily by Residents

20. One day when my Padrinho Cícero was building that church in the Horto some of the workers came to ask him for food. My Padrinho said to one of them, "You, Fulano, go there behind the church and bring back enough fruit for everyone." So then the men just looked at one another. Because everyone knows there is nothing behind that church.

"Are we going to eat brambles?" they asked one another in low voices. But the man went to do as my Padrinho had said. And sure enough, he found a huge expanse of oranges, bananas, coconuts, mangoes—it was almost raining those big rose-colored mangoes. So then he picked as much fruit as he could and everyone ate his fill. Well then, later on that night that man came to look for more fruit just for himself, see? He went there behind the church and looked and looked but he did not find anything. All he found was brambles. And no one ever again saw a single mango growing there.

—Florismino Alves (R). Canhotinho, Pernambuco, 1916. Arrived Juazeiro 1967. Single; odd jobs. (July 6, 1981.)

Observations: The man's wife may urge him to go back at night to look for more sugar cane or mangoes. Sometimes not just one, but all the workers go to look for fruit. As the word *horto* means "garden" or "orchard," it is fitting that the grove should be located there.

21. Manuel Germano was a poor man who had a little house here in the Rua do Horto. He was a firecracker maker and he was very well known. But one day everything blew up and he almost died, you see? So then he went to ask my Padrinho Cícero for another way of earning a living. Because he had fourteen mouths at home to feed, poor man.

"Take this money," my Padrinho said, "and use it to buy cotton." So then Manuel Germano began buying cotton. He bought and sold cotton until he had a lot of wealth. Then he went and gave half of what he had earned to my Padrinho.

"May God multiply your gift," my Padrinho told him. And God heard my Padrinho's words because Manuel Germano died a wealthy, a very wealthy man.

—Manoel Alves Vieira (R). Águas Belas, Pernambuco, 1924. Arrived Juazeiro 1954. Married; *rendeiro*. (October 24, 1982.)

22. My Padrinho Cícero was always working miracles. So Padre Monteiro said, "Padre Cícero, you are a great miracle worker."

My Padrinho said, "Thank you, Padre Monteiro, but what you say today you will deny tomorrow."

"No, no," he said, "I swear by the light of my eyes that I will never deny it."

"Then so be it," my Padrinho said.

Shortly after, the bishop came to Juazeiro. "Padre Monteiro," he said, "does Padre Cícero really work miracles like everybody says?"

"People claim that he works miracles but I have never seen him

work one," Padre Monteiro replied. And in that very instant the
day grew dark as night.
—José Dantas Filho (R). Juazeiro, 1904. Married; retired. (July 12, 1981.)

23. A man by the name of Pedro went to work in his fields in the São
Pedro Hills. One of these fearsome snakes bit him, and the man
called his family together. "Go to Juazeiro and tell my Padrinho
Cícero that I want him to confess me," he said to his brother,
"because a rattlesnake has attacked me and I will not escape death."
So then his brother rushed off to get my Padrinho and the two
hurried back to the São Pedro Hills.
   But this was in that time when the roads were very bad, and they
were only halfway there when a messenger arrived to tell them
that the man was dead. "It is no use going on, my Padrinho," he
said very sadly.
   But my Padrinho said, "I am going on, my friend."
   When they arrived at the man's house the women were cutting
the cloth for his shroud, all of them in tears. So then my Padrinho
went and said to the dead man, "Pedro, I have come to confess
you." Three times, just like that. And on the third time the man
took a deep breath and opened his eyes.
   After my Padrinho had confessed him, he asked if the man
wanted to remain on earth or go to heaven. "I want to go to heaven,
my Padrinho," he said.
   So then my Padrinho said, "All right, you have my permission to
continue your journey." And the man shut his eyes for good.
—Severino Teixeira (R). Feira de Mamanguape, Paraíba, 1923.
   Arrived Juazeiro 1932. Married; *rancho* guard. (November 22, 1982.)

Observations: Occasionally storytellers have the man return to earth instead of going to heaven.

24. Manuel Correia was the best carpenter in Juazeiro. But one day he
fell from the tower of the Horto church and broke his neck. When
my Padrinho learned that the best carpenter of all had died, he went
to see. Manuel Correia was there in a pool of blood surrounded by
a crowd of people, all crying. So then my Padrinho said, "Manuel
Correia." And again, "Manuel Correia." Then "MANUEL CORREIA!"
Just like that, three times.
   And on the third time that my Padrinho spoke, the man opened
his eyes. "What is it, my Padrinho?"

"Manuel Correia, do you want to go to heaven this very moment
or do you want to live?"
"I want to live, my Padrinho. I want to keep on working on the
Horto church."
"Then get up," my Padrinho told him. And the man climbed up
the tower again, his hammer in his hand.

—José Antonio da Silva (R). Garanhuns, Pernambuco, 1914. Arrived
   Juazeiro 1946. Widower; *rendeiro*. (July 4, 1981.)

Observations: The carpenter may explain his choice of earth over heaven
by saying that he wants to marry a girl named Manuela or wants to bring
up his children.

Stories Told Primarily by Pilgrims

25. During that time, there were still many mountain lions in the Serra
    do Araripe. So then a man went and asked my Padrinho Cícero
    for a weapon to protect him on the journey home. My Padrinho
    reached into his pocket and handed him a rosary. "Take this,
    my friend," he said. "This is the weapon that will protect you
    against all harm."
       The man took the rosary and set out on his way but he did not
    believe what my Padrinho had told him. So then when he comes
    upon another man with a good, sturdy shotgun, he asks him if he
    does not want to trade the gun for the rosary.
       "All right," he says. So then the man gave him his rosary and the
    pilgrim took the gun. He had not gone five yards when a mountain
    lion appeared. The man grabbed the shotgun but the mountain
    lion pounced before he could fire. And that was the end of a very
    foolish pilgrim.

    —João Carlos Ferreira (R). Monteiro, Paraíba, 1936. Married;
       rendeiro. 2 pilgrimages. (September 30, 1982.)

26. In my Padrinho's time there were many *mocozinhos* up in the Horto.
    [A *mocó* is a type of edible guinea pig; *mocozinho* is the diminutive.]
    They were my Padrinho's pets. They had been brought by pilgrims
    as presents to him and no one was supposed to fool with them,
    you see? But there was a man who thought he knew better than my
    Padrinho. One day when he got hungry he said, "Do you know
    something, one of those *mocozinhos* would do very well for dinner."
    So then he went and killed a *mocó* and buried its little bones so that
    nobody would know. Then he brought home the meat and roasted

it. Mmmm, what a delicious smell. But after he had eaten everything he came down with a tremendous pain. His stomach hurt so much that he sent his wife to ask my Padrinho for a cure.

So then she went and said, "My Padrinho, I have come to ask for a cure for a stomachache that has my husband crying like a baby."

So then my Padrinho said, "Tell your husband that he should dig up my *mocozinho*'s bones. He should roast and then grind them. Then he should make a tea of the powder and drink it, and the stomachache will disappear." The woman returned home and told her husband everything. And as soon as he had drunk the tea he recovered. But he could never look at a *mocozinho* again without getting that same bad feeling in his stomach.

—João Francisco dos Santos (P). Paulo Gomes, Piauí, 1963. Single; *morador*. 3 pilgrimages. (October 9, 1982.)

Observations: The protagonist may be a woman. The ailment is often a toothache. Sometimes the remedy is a tea made from the guinea pig's fur instead of his bones.

27. A pilgrim came to Juazeiro with her three small children and when the time came to leave she found herself without any money. So then she went to ask my Padrinho Cícero's help for the trip. "Take this," he said to her and handed her a penny.

"But my Padrinho, how do you want me to make such a long journey on nothing more than a penny?" And she began to cry.

"Don't you know that a little with God is a lot and a lot without God is nothing?" he said.

So then she took the penny and the four walked and walked. And wherever they arrived people gave them whatever they needed.

"If you are coming from Juazeiro you must eat with us," they said. "If it was my Padrinho who sent you, there is a place for you to string your hammock here."

So then when the woman finally arrived home the penny was still in her pocket. And I think that she ought to have kept it until the end of her life, don't you?

—Joana Pessoa da Silva (P). Rio Tinto, Paraíba, 1922. Widowed; retired seamstress. 4 pilgrimages. (October 25, 1982.)

Observations: The protagonist may be either a man or a woman, not necessarily accompanied by children. Sometimes there are two pilgrims who ask for money: one uses the penny wisely and arrives home without problems, but the other squanders it and dies upon the road.

28. There was a man who borrowed his *compadre's* little donkey in order to make his pilgrimage to Juazeiro. And when he was about to saddle the little donkey for the return home, he found the animal dead. So then he went to see my Padrinho.

"Listen carefully," my Padrinho said, "and do as I say. When you return to the *rancho,* the little donkey is going to be standing where you left him. So then saddle him and ride without stopping until you arrive home. As soon as you arrive, return the little donkey to its owner. Do you understand?"

"Yes, my Padrinho," the man said. And he went back to the *rancho,* where he found the little donkey standing. Then he put the saddle on it just as my Padrinho had said. And he rode like the wind for three nights and three days. When he finally arrived, he went right away to return the little donkey to his *compadre.*

"Thank you very much," he said. "Here is your little donkey."

"I have never seen that donkey looking so healthy," the owner said to himself. "It was so old that I thought it would have died along the way. Can it be that the air of Juazeiro is miraculous like people say?"

The next day when the owner went to feed the little donkey he found only the saddle atop a pile of bones. But there was nothing that he could do because his *compadre,* the pilgrim, brought that donkey back to him alive and well.

—Manuel Gonçalves Sobrinho (P). Espírito Santo, Rio Grande do Norte, 1924. Married; sells clay cooking pots. 2 pilgrimages. (November 16, 1982.)

Observations: Compadre is the term for the godfather of one's child; it may be used more loosely to mean "friend." Occasionally the donkey dies as the man prepares to sneak out of Juazeiro without attending mass. Padre Cícero tells him to attend mass, and when the man leaves the church the donkey revives.

29. A very poor young woman wanted to visit my Padrinho. So then one day when she saw a group of pilgrims pass before her door she said, "Wait a minute, because I am going to Juazeiro with you."

So then she quickly packed up a few things and went off after them. She was in such a hurry that she didn't even think of the hen sitting on its nest, poor little thing, and it remained there in the house without any food. Only after she arrived in Juazeiro did she remember the hen. Then when the pilgrims went to see my Padrinho he asked her, "Why this sad face? The person who travels to Juazeiro has reason to be happy."

"Forgive me, my Padrinho," said the girl. "It's just that I feel sorry for the hen that I left at home without food."

"Don't worry," my Padrinho said, "because everything is going to be all right."

Well, when the girl opened the door of her house what did she find but that hen surrounded by chicks. There were at least a dozen, each plumper and more contented than the next. "Peep, peep, peep," they had lacked for nothing.

Now who was it who gave them corn meal? Who was it that gave those chicks water to drink?

—Estaneslaus Ribeiro da Silva (P). João Alfredo, Pernambuco, 1922. Married; *rendeiro*. More than 20 pilgrimages. (September 26, 1982.)

General Characteristics of the Best-Known Tales

Although this study focuses on differences between residents' and pilgrims' versions of the best-known stories, we are clearly dealing with a common body of narrative material. In their literary antecedents, underlying structure, and guiding concept of the miraculous as well as in more obvious terms of subject matter, the two groups of storytellers are much alike. It is therefore worthwhile to discuss these essential similarities briefly.

LITERARY ANTECEDENTS

Identifying the Padre Cícero tales in terms of traditional literary categories is considerably more difficult than might at first appear. As the stories draw on multiple oral as well as written sources, they are, like many folk forms, an essentially hybrid genre.[9]

Because for them a "legend" is always a fiction, storytellers refuse to use this term for their accounts of Padre Cícero. Nevertheless, the tales are clearly legends from the scholar's point of view.[10] Set in the recent or historical past and believed to be true on some level by those by whom

9. For a discussion of problems posed by classification of folklore genres see Dan Ben-Amos, "Analytical Categories and Ethnic Genres." (Ben-Amos provides a comprehensive bibliography on pp. 249–282.)

10. The differences between outsiders' and insiders' definitions of a given literary form are the subject of Alan Dundes, "From Etic to Emic Units in the Structural Study of Folklore."

and to whom they are recounted, the stories have roots, no matter how tenuous, in one or another documentable personality or event.[11]

The sudden blindness of Padre Cícero's mother in the birth story, for instance, probably reflects the actual Joaquina Romana Batista's much later loss of sight. The tale of the hat that sticks to the wall is almost always set in the town of Cajazeiras, where Padre Cícero studied before entering the seminary in Fortaleza.

Accounts of the would-be assassin may grow out of half-forgotten memories of a real attack on the priest by five armed men, which took place in the Church of Our Lady of Sorrows in 1896.[12] The case of the church door probably has its origin in stories Padre Cícero told his followers about his trip to Rome. The priest had visited the Basilica of Saint Peter, the site of the Holy Door which is opened only in specially designated years.[13]

The supposed miracle of 1889 provided the initial impetus for the pilgrimage to Juazeiro. The tale of the Revolution or "War" of 1913–14 is based on an armed attack upon the city. The priest's descent from a cloud to halt a war in Germany may reflect Padre Cícero's frequent homilies on the horrors of World War I. Dr. Floro Bartolomeu da Costa was Padre Cícero's political advisor; Manuel Germano, a wealthy resident of the Rua do Horto after whom a present-day neighborhood school is named.

Manuel Correia and Manuel Fernandes were also residents of Juazeiro. The former's tombstone stands in the graveyard beside the

11. For discussion of definitions of a legend see Robert A. Georges, "The General Concept of Legend: Some Assumptions to be Reexamined and Reassessed," in *American Folk Legend* (the book as a whole is useful). See also Linda Dégh and Andrew Vázsonyi, *The Dialectics of the Legend,* and their "Legend and Belief"; *Handwörterbuch des deutschen Aberglaubens;* Max Lüthi, *Volksmärchen und Volkssage: Zwei Grundformen erzählender Dichtung;* Lutz Rohrich, *Sage und Märchen: Erzählforschung heute;* Helmut Rosenfeld, *Legende;* Carl-Herman Tillhagen, "Was ist eine Sage? Eine Definition und ein Vorschlag für ein europäisches Sagensystem"; and Leander Petzoldt, ed., *Vergleichende Sagenforschung.* For a comprehensive catalogue see Reidar Th. Christiansen, *The Migratory Legend, a Proposed List of Types with a Systematic Catalogue of the Norwegian Variants.* Although somewhat dated, Wayland D. Hand, "Status of European and American Legend Study," is worth consulting.

12. See Ralph della Cava, *Miracle at Joaseiro,* p. 75. For a discussion of the documentary value, or lack thereof, of legend and oral history in general see William Lynwood Montell, *The Saga of Coe Ridge: A Study in Oral History,* pp. vii–xxi.

13. The Holy Door of St. Peter's Basilica, last opened by Pope John Paul II in 1983 for the extraordinary Holy Year of Redemption, is due to be opened again in the year 2000. After opening, it is walled up with 4,000 bricks. Padre Cícero describes the staircase, which appears in numerous versions of the church door story, in a letter to his mother dated March 24, 1898 (Letter 22, in Packet 12, Salesian Archives). It is not hard to imagine how these sorts of description, which the priest seems to have repeated in his daily homilies, might serve as the basis for this miracle tale.

chapel of Our Lady of Perpetual Help. The Padre Monteiro who denies Padre Cícero's miraculous powers is almost certainly Monsignor Francisco Rodrigues Monteiro, rector of the Crato seminary. As was mentioned in Chapter I, it was he who made the first public declaration regarding the alleged transformation. Although both his repudiation of the "miracle" and his subsequent blindness are facts, he appears to have remained friends with Padre Cícero until the end of his life.[14]

The priest's early association with the municipality of São Pedro, today known as Caririaçu, helps explain why a tale should be set there. (In 1889 Padre Cícero became vicar of São Pedro as well as Juazeiro.) His success in raising the dead, in the stories of the man from São Pedro and the carpenter who falls from the Horto tower, may reflect his documented knowledge of herbal medicines and his ability to distinguish prolonged comas from death.[15] Because most of his followers lacked even rudimentary notions of hygiene, the simplest suggestions may have had a "miraculous" effect.

As for the story of the pet guinea pig, admirers often brought animals to Juazeiro for Padre Cícero's personal "zoo." Older storytellers can remember the *mocós* that used to run wild in the Horto. Then, too, the priest regularly gave pilgrims token amounts of money to aid them in their journey home. Since many persons who lived along the pilgrimage route considered it an obligation to help visitors to Juazeiro, a number of travelers were probably able to get a long way on a mere handful of coins.

The original meaning of *legend* (the Latin *legenda*) was a collection of stories about a saint. Despite the fact that the priest has no canonical standing, tales about him are much like others that deal with officially recognized holy figures. The best-known narratives have numerous analogues from the past. Although, for instance, Padre Cícero may change water to gasoline instead of to wine, the principle is the same.

The tale of the exchange of infants recalls a whole class of stories involving wondrous births. In many versions of this narrative, Dona

14. In a letter to me dated May 28, 1982, Dona Amália Xavier de Oliveira explains that Monsignor Monteiro regularly spent one or two months a year as a guest in Padre Cícero's house. "Because he was blind," she explains, "my father went to get him in Crato with a porter leading a saddled horse. They say that he [Monteiro] lost his sight after he denied those events that he had once claimed to believe. Whatever the truth of this story, it is certain that he was blind." (My translation.)

15. For documentation of Padre Cícero's curative abilities see Manoel Dinis, *Mistérios do Joazeiro: História completa de Pe. Cícero Romão Batista do Joazeiro do Ceará*, pp. 96–97. The priest appears to have relied heavily on herbal remedies and on the power of suggestion.

Quinou witnesses the same sort of signs confirming the future greatness of her child (or adopted child) as the mothers of a wide variety of Christian saints.[16]

The hat that sticks to the wall is not unlike the gloves (Saint Morant), veils (Saint Milburga), and cloaks (Saint Deicola) that medieval holy figures are reputed to have dangled from sunbeams.[17]

Would-be assassins also stalk saints such as John of Facond.[18] Many holy figures—Saint Basil, for instance—summon rain, while others (Saint Eumachus is one example) arrange for rain to fall on some and not on other properties.[19] The door Padre Cícero opens in Rome is not unlike that which flies open to allow Saint Eusebius to pass into a locked cathedral.[20] Saints Maur and Galla are two of the many medieval saints who make a mute child speak.[21]

Padre Cícero's triumph over attacking soldiers in the Revolution of 1913–14 recalls numerous other victories achieved by holy figures on the battlefield. Like Saint Ciaranus, who causes a great forest to spring up between opposing forces, he may plant a thorn or pebble that quickly burgeons into a wall of cactus or stone.[22] In some accounts, the priest also causes a smoky cloud to descend on the enemy, a tactic employed against the Persian army by Abba Jacob.[23]

The stories of the war in Germany and the child saved from drowning illustrate a bilocality common to numerous European holy figures

16. A long list of saints' stories relating to wonder children appears in C. Grant Loomis, *White Magic: An Introduction to the Folklore of Christian Legend.*

17. Morant is in William Caxton, *The Golden Legend,* 6, p. 202; Milburga in Carl Horstmann, *The Lives of Women Saints,* p. 191; Deicola in Sabine Baring-Gould, *Lives of the Saints,* 1, p. 282.

I have relied heavily on E. Cobham Brewer, *A Dictionary of Miracles;* Frederic C. Tubach, *Index Exemplorum: A Handbook of Medieval Religious Tales;* and Loomis, *White Magic,* to lead me to these examples, of which there are many, many more. For a thoughtful introduction to the saint's life as a literary genre see Alexandra Hennessey Olsen, "'De Historiis Sanctorum': A Generic Study of Hagiography." See also Régis Boyer, "An Attempt to Define the Typology of Medieval Hagiography."

18. Brewer, *Dictionary of Miracles,* p. 398.

19. For Basil see Paul Guérin, *Les petits Bollandistes: Vies des saints,* 13, p. 603. Eumachus is in ibid., 2, p. 414. Brewer gives a wide array of rainmakers: *Dictionary of Miracles,* pp. 129–130. Loomis, *White Magic,* has a section on "storms as punishment" on p. 45.

20. Brewer, *Dictionary of Miracles,* p. 442.

21. Maur (also known as Maurus) is in ibid., p. 123. Galla is in Guérin, *Les petits Bollandistes,* 2, p. 200.

22. Charles Plummer, *Miscellanea hagiographica hibernica,* p. 225.

23. Loomis, *White Magic,* cites *The Contendings of the Apostles,* p. 514. I have not seen the text. Loomis lists numerous other war-related miracles on pp. 122–123.

such as Mary Magdalene of Pazzi.[24] As Padre Cícero leaves Juazeiro to rescue a young woman in another part of the Northeast, so Saint Verulus leaves his body at Marcenay to rescue a child from a fire raging at that moment in Mussy.[25]

The girl who turns into a dog recalls the proud woman whom Saint Mochulleius turns into a goat or the vicious man whom Saint Rhipsime changes into a boar.[26] The tale recalls another medieval story, still told in Juazeiro, of how a woman, ostensibly embarrassed by her own procreative powers, tries to hide her many offspring from the Virgin Mary. When she tells the Virgin that her house is full of goats instead of children, a sudden transformation turns her lie into the truth.[27]

The account of Manuel Germano's newfound riches also has medieval antecedents. Saint Bernard of Abbeville is only one of numerous holy figures who shower riches on poor but virtuous followers.[28] The resurrection stories have parallels in the tale of Saint Severus, who revives a dead man in order to confess and absolve him, and in Saint Dominic's resurrection of a carpenter, much like Manuel Correia, who dies upon falling into a pit.[29] The penny that pays for the trip home is clearly a variation on the miracle of the unfailing purse, while Padre Cícero's resuscitation of the donkey echoes Saint George of Cappadocia's success in breathing life into a dead ox.[30]

And yet, despite their obvious debts to a centuries-old literary tradition, the Padre Cícero stories are far from identical to these. Unlike written saints' lives, they are not extended narratives in which one deed triggers another, but individual episodes that tellers do not necessarily run together. Furthermore, the similarities between these stories and their medieval forebears are sometimes superficial. Thus while the saint

24. Guérin, *Les petits Bollandistes*, 5, p. 170. A long string of other instances of bilocality is in Brewer, *Dictionary of Miracles*, pp. 470–471.

25. Brewer, *Dictionary of Miracles*, pp. 313–314.

26. Mochulleius' story is in *Analecta Bollandiana*, 17, pp. 144–145. Rhipsime is in Baring-Gould, *Lives of the Saints*, 10, p. 440. Various other sorts of punishments for insults are catalogued in Loomis, *White Magic*, pp. 98–99, 101–102.

27. E. A. Wallis Budge, *The History of the Blessed Virgin Mary and the History of the Likeness of Christ Which the Jews of Tiberias Made to Mock At: The Syriac Texts*, I, Luzac's Semitic Text and Translation Series, 4 (London: Luzac, 1889), p. 77 (I have not seen the text). This story was recounted to me by both pilgrims and residents in Juazeiro.

28. Brewer, *Dictionary of Miracles*, p. 230.

29. Brewer offers a long list of resurrections: ibid., pp. 78–87—Severus is on p. 85; Dominic on p. 81.

30. For various miracles involving increase and gifts from heaven see Loomis, *White Magic*, pp. 86–88. St. George is in Brewer, *Dictionary of Miracles*, p. 280.

who hangs his or her cloak on a sunbeam defies gravity in the same way as the priest, the motivation for this action, as well as its effect on the beholder, is really very different.

At the same time that the Padre Cícero tales draw on standard Indo-European folk motifs in the manner of traditional saints' lives, they reveal Tupi Indian and, particularly, African influences.[31] References, for instance, to *catimbó*, ₐthe sort of black magic associated with Afro-Brazilian religious cults, are very common in these stories. Padre Cícero's enemies regularly accuse him of being a sorcerer or *catimbozeiro*, because of his success in removing evil spells.[32]

The role of animals in these stories, for instance, recalls African as well as European folk tradition. In one particularly appealing variant of the birth story, for instance, the bishop of Crato sends his soldiers to Juazeiro to seek out the newborn Cícero. The men find the baby sleeping in a hammock before which kneel an alligator, a mountain lion, a snake, a parrot, and a monkey. When the animals overhear the soldiers' plans to kidnap the infant, the monkey quickly takes the lead in thwarting them. The tale is thus both a manger scene with tropical touches and a variation on African tales of the wise simian.[33]

31. Many of the Padre Cícero tales utilize motifs indexed in Stith Thompson, *Motif-Index of Folk Literature,* a standard reference tool for folklorists. The birth story, for instance, is an example of the "supernatural birth of saints" (T540.1). The would-be assassin can be seen as an illustration of "mysterious death as punishment" (Q558). The rancher who tries to buy rain might fall under both "storm as punishment" (Q552.14) and "saint controls fall of rain" (D1841.4.4). Padre Cícero's trip to Rome is an example of a door whose "lock magically opens" (F694). In the tale of the mute boy, a "saint cures a dumb person" (V221.11). The salvation of Juazeiro is an instance of a "city saved from disaster as a reward" (Q152). Padre Cícero's ability to rescue a child from drowning is a "rescue from a well" (R141). The transformation of an unbeliever into an animal is a standard punishment (Q551.3.2). There is a separate heading for the metamorphosis of a human being into a dog (Q551.3.2.7). The story of the magic grove illustrates the "miraculous blossoming and bearing of fruit" (F971). "Riches as reward" (Q111) is the theme of the Manuel Germano story. The blindness that afflicts Padre Monteiro is a common retributive measure as "punishment: man stricken blind" (Q559.2). The resurrection that climaxes the stories of the man from São Pedro and of Manuel Correia can be found in stories from other times and places as "resurrection as reward" (Q151.9). The hat that sticks to the wall recalls the sunbeam that upholds a holy man's coat. This is tale type 759b in Antti Aarne and Stith Thompson, *The Types of the Folktale.* (A tale type is an ordered sequence of two or more motifs.) For further clarification see Dan Ben-Amos, "The Concept of Motif in Folklore."

32. A good starting place in the extensive body of scholarship on Afro-Brazilian religions is Dorothy B. Porter, *Afro-Braziliana: A Working Bibliography.* For a catalogue of African tale types see May Augusta Kipple, "African Folktales with Foreign Analogues."

33. The wise monkey is a familiar figure in Brazilian as well as in African tradition. For documentation and bibliographic references for both continents see Luís da Câmara Cascudo, "Macaco" in *Dicionário do folclore brasileiro,* 2, pp. 117–119.

A small but nonetheless significant number of visitors to Juazeiro, particularly those from the states of Sergipe and Bahia as well as all the coastal capitals, frequent Afro-Brazilian religious centers or *terreiros* back home. A statue of the priest may sit on the altar along with a multitude of other Christian and non-Christian holy figures. One pilgrim sang me a long song of praise which she claimed to have learned from a spirit that possessed her after she fell into a trance in one of these Afro-Brazilian centers. According to her, the dead soul was "a priest of Itabaiana" who had opposed Padre Cícero during his lifetime. In death, his former enemy had finally recognized the power of the "saint" of Juazeiro and had composed this song as testimony to be shared with others.[34]

And yet, despite the Padre Cícero stories' debts to a larger, specifically Brazilian as well as more general Indo-European folk tradition, most storytellers react as vehemently to the term *folktale* (*história de trancoso* or simply *trancoso*) as they do to *legend*.[35] Although they accept the neutral *story* so long as it is translated *história* (a purportedly true story) and not *estória* (an overt fiction), they themselves refer to their tales of Padre Cícero as a *caso* (a "case" or "case in point"), a *passagem* ("passage," as in a selection from the Bible) or—most frequently—an *exemplo* ("example").

The term *exemplo* also applies to the medieval illustrative story known in English as the exemplum.[36] A literary form widely employed by medieval preachers to lend life to their sermons, exempla rely on a clear set of oppositions such as good and evil, divine and human, or celestial and infernal.[37] They are normally very brief tales with a mark-

34. Maria Generosa Lima Morais (P). Nossa Senhora da Glória, Sergipe, 1932. Single; seamstress. First pilgrimage. (November 1, 1982.)

35. The term *trancoso* or *história de trancoso* comes from a book of moralistic tales written by Gonçalo Fernandes Trancoso after the Lisbon plague in 1569. In the beginning of the seventeenth century the book was widely popular in the Northeast, where the first written reference to it dates to 1619. See his *Contos e histórias de proveito e exemplo*.

36. For examples of medieval Hispanic exempla see "El libro de los enxemplos" and "El libro de los gatos," both included in Pascual Gayangos, ed., *Escritores en prosa anteriores al siglo XV*, pp. 493–542, 543–569. See also John Esten Keller, *Motif-Index of Mediaeval Spanish Exempla*. For more general works on the exemplum see *Gesta Romanorum;* Joseph Albert Mosher, *The Exemplum in the Early Religious and Didactic Literature of England;* Tubach, *Index Exemplorum;* and J. Th. Welter, *L'exemplum dans la littérature religieuse et didactique du Moyen Age.*

37. Although toward the end of the thirteenth century the exemplum began to merge with other literary forms in most parts of Europe, it retained its separate indentity in the Iberian peninsula much longer: see Hilary Dansey Smith, *Preaching in the Spanish Golden Age.* The exemplum is an important part of the folk tradition not only in Brazil but also throughout Latin America. For a discussion and examples of Mexican *ejemplos* see Stanley Robe,

edly allegorical quality. Unlike the saint's life, which seeks to some extent to identify the protagonist as an individual, the exemplum makes little attempt to distinguish Saint Aphanasia from Saint Ambrose or Saint Augustine. Instead, the emphasis is on the larger moral suggested by the individual's actions.

In their focus on a single all-important protagonist, the Padre Cícero tales are quite unlike these early stories. Nevertheless, their identity as latter-day *exemplos* stresses the degree to which they are meant to show as well as tell. When I first began recording the tales, I assumed that people were employing the customary "*Ouvi contar*" ("I heard tell") in their introductions to particular miraculous actions. With time, however, I realized that a number were actually saying, "*Eu vi contar*" ("I saw tell"). Storytellers often refer to a particularly dramatic incident as *um caso muito visível* or a very "visible" case. This expression suggests the extent to which the tales are meant to dramatize a particular moral code.

UNDERLYING STRUCTURE

The exemplary, though not strictly exemplum-like, quality of the Padre Cícero stories is reflected in their narrative structure.[38] Despite their wide variety in terms of content, almost all the best-known tales reveal a small number of underlying patterns. The great majority can be seen as tests of Padre Cícero's authority.

In contrast to the martyr and later confessor saints who regularly call out to heaven for help and guidance, the priest exhibits a remarkable self-sufficiency. Whereas the *passio* or martyr's tale sees divine intervention as a reward for a human being's continuing faith in the face of persecution, the Padre Cícero stories reiterate the priest's ability to help followers and strike down detractors. As such, they may be understood as either positive or negative challenges. These two possibilities, both of which involve four basic steps, are diagrammed in Figures 1 and 2.[39] I have first

---

Mexican Tales and Legends from Los Altos, pp. 505–515. See also Ralph S. Boggs, *Index of Spanish Folktales*, and Terence L. Hansen, *The Types of the Folktale in Cuba, Puerto Rico, the Dominican Republic and Spanish South America*, particularly pp. 87–102, "Religious Tales."

38. See Charles F. Altman, "Two Types of Opposition in the Structure of Latin Saints' Lives," and Frederic C. Tubach, "Strukturanalytische Probleme: Das mittelalterliche Exemplum." Hermann Bausinger, "Exemplum und Beispiel," comments on the Tubach article.

39. In posing this sort of underlying pattern for the miracle corpus I am indebted to the works of a large number of scholars, the most obvious of which is probably Claude Lévi-Strauss's *Structural Anthropology*. For an extensive bibliography on structuralism see Bengt Hølbek, *Formal and Structural Studies of Oral Narrative: A Bibliography*. Although the limits of structuralist analysis are clear, I find it one of various useful approaches to folk literature.

Figure 1.

| Positive Challenge (Reward) | Example: The man from São Pedro |

1.
*Implicit acceptance of
Padre Cícero's authority*

| Believer follows the priest's teachings, which guarantee his or her material and spiritual welfare. | A man named Pedro lives up to his obligations as a follower of the priest by faithfully toiling in the fields to support his family. |

2.
Challenge

| Believer, faced with physical danger or attacks by enemies, calls on Padre Cícero for aid. | Bitten by a poisonous snake, the man states his desire to have Padre Cícero confess him. He dies before the priest's arrival. |

3.
Response

| Padre Cícero miraculously intervenes on his follower's behalf. | Padre Cícero refuses to turn back. He restores the dead man to life by calling his name three times. |

4.
Reaffirmation

| Padre Cícero's authority is reasserted as the follower is restored to material and spiritual well-being. | The man responds to the priest's call and makes his confession. He then closes his eyes again and "resumes his trip to heaven," presumably in a state of grace. |

---

outlined the pattern in general terms, then illustrated each with one of the stories that appear earlier in this chapter.

Not infrequently, a given story contains both positive and negative elements and thus can be read as a double challenge. In this case the tale can be diagrammed as in Figure 3. Some versions of well-known narratives may not fit easily into the general categories presented here. We will see in the next chapter that those most apt to evade the challenge framework are the birth story, the hat that stuck to the wall, the alleged transformation, and the slipper in the tomb. Although there are naturally exceptions to the rule, most versions of the best-known tales tend to fit one of the three patterns outlined above.

Figure 2.

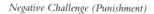

Negative Challenge (Punishment)	Example: The rancher who tried to buy rain
	1. *Implicit acceptance of* *Padre Cícero's authority*
Unbeliever does not bother the priest or his followers.	Rancher does not believe in the priest but does not provoke him.
	2. *Challenge*
Attack on Padre Cícero or a follower, in the form of verbal abuse or physical aggression.	Worried about a drought that is destroying his cattle, the rancher has a pilgrim deliver his mocking request for rain to Padre Cícero.
	3. *Response*
Padre Cícero answers this attack with ridicule, loss of property, or loss of life.	Padre Cícero promises to send the rain. The resulting storm is so severe that the rancher loses his property and/or his life.
	4. *Reaffirmation*
The unbeliever either repents or is neutralized by humiliation or death.	The rancher either repents or dies. His barren ranch remains as a symbol of the priest's power.

THE CONCEPT OF THE MIRACULOUS

The four-step challenge sequence ensures the miracle narratives' underlying unity, disposing individuals to see the most varied episodes as displays of that supernatural power known as *mistério* or "mystery." Most storytellers are not aware of—nor would they be particularly interested in—theological definitions that classify miraculous actions with regard to substance, mode, and subject. They are also by and large unconcerned with the problem of proof.[40]

---

40. According to the *New Catholic Encyclopedia,* a miracle is "an extraordinary event, perceptible to the senses, produced by God in a religious context as a sign of the supernatural." See "Miracle," *New Catholic Encyclopedia,* 9, pp. 890–894. For a more detailed discussion of miraculous actions see C. F. D. Moule, ed., *Miracles: Cambridge Studies in Their Philosophy and History.*

Figure 3.

Double Challenge (Reward and Punishment)	*Example: The young hunter's catch*

1.
*Implicit acceptance of
Padre Cícero's authority*

Believers and unbelievers alike accept the priest's authority.	Son of unbeliever goes to Juazeiro every year. His father disapproves but does nothing actively to dissuade him.

↓

2.
Challenge

a. *positive*	a. *positive*
Believer calls on Padre Cícero for aid in the face of physical danger or enemy attacks.	Son asks Padre Cícero to convert his father before the older man suffers for his disbelief.
b. *negative*	b. *negative*
Unbeliever attacks Padre Cícero or Juazeiro by mockery or through the use of force.	Father mocks son—and by extension Padre Cícero—for setting out once again for Juazeiro.

↓

3.
Response

a. *positive*	a. *positive*
Padre Cícero intervenes on the believer's behalf.	Padre Cícero sees that the son's request is granted by asking him to bring his first catch to Juazeiro. He knows that this catch will be the father.
b. *negative*	b. *negative*
Padre Cícero repels the unbeliever through force or through a punitive reduction in status.	Padre Cícero punishes the father by putting him in a humiliating position. In some versions he actually changes him into an animal.

↓

4.
Reaffirmation

All threats to believers are removed; unbelievers repent or vanish.	The father repents and goes with his son to Juazeiro. The two remain devout followers of the priest throughout the rest of their lives.

Storytellers normally reject any division between secular or scientific and religious or supernatural spheres.[41] The majority see no contradiction, for example, in the tale of Padre Cícero's "miraculous" cure of an individual through the use of a prescription drug. Because, in their view, God made all things, the sick person's recovery after ingesting a pill or receiving an injection is no less remarkable than his or her recovery through the touch of a saint's hand or the repetition of special prayers.[42]

Due in large part to this profound sense of interconnection, storytellers may speak in the same breath of "miracles" as different as the hat that stuck to the wall and the resurrection of Manuel Correia. On a more directly personal level, they are capable of describing how the priest once saved them from death by drowning, only to move on to an account of how he helped them to meet a late payment on a secondhand sewing machine. The tellers' poverty makes a missed payment on a sewing machine much more important to them than it would be to someone with more money; nevertheless, their widespread application of the word *miracle* is far less a function of inferior economic status than of their willingness to subordinate particulars to an all-inclusive whole.

Padre Cícero's punishments are as much an illustration of this unifying vision as his rewards are.[43] Like a traditional Northeast Brazilian landowner, he does not tolerate a lack of deference on the part of those less powerful than he. Since to make light of a person's word is to impugn his honor, such challenges demand physical, not simply verbal, retaliation. Accordingly, Padre Cícero destroys the property of the rancher who dares to mock him and may go so far as to take the man's life. He transforms the girl into a dog because she refuses to wear mourning at his death, and he blinds the priest who has the temerity to deny what he has seen with his own eyes.

The priest's willingness to strike down a would-be opponent may be in part a reflection of his followers' desire to retaliate for humiliations regularly visited on them. And yet, while there is no mistaking the vindictive streak that runs through a substantial number of the miracle stories, the specific offense is usually less important to the teller than the

41. The view of some present-day Northeast Brazilians is similar in some, though certainly not all, aspects to that which prevailed during the Middle Ages. For helpful background information see Benedicta Ward, *Miracles and the Medieval Mind: Theory, Record and Event, 1000–1215.*

42. See Martien Maria Groetelaars, *Milagre e religiosidade popular: Reflexões sobre pastoral missionária.* The section on miracles and science (pp. 34–49) is of particular interest.

43. For a discussion of miraculous punishments see Alba Zaluar Guimarães, "Milagre e castigo divino." See also Herbert Halpert, "Supernatural Sanctions and the Legend," and Wayland D. Hand, "Deformity, Disease and Physical Ailment as Divine Retribution."

breaking of an unwritten moral contract between a given character and the priest. As such, these narratives complement those other accounts in which Padre Cícero helps the faithful. In both cases, the tellers insist that Padre Cícero is acting in the individual's best interest. They often argue that his wrath actually helps the would-be offender. "Pardon," one storyteller explains, "is one thing and punishment is another. My Padrinho punishes in order to teach the wrongdoer so that he will not go to hell."[44]

Stories that fail to reinforce this larger framework are almost always dismissed as fictions. A tale told by one man who allegedly became bald after being swallowed by an enormous snake in the Amazon jungle serves as a case in point. The man's tongue-in-cheek claim to have lost the hair on top of his head in the process of rubbing up against the creature's ribs regularly elicits shrieks of laughter from children and appreciative grins from adults. Had, however, the teller asserted that he turned into a snake himself after proclaiming his lack of faith in Padre Cícero, people would be much more likely to accept his baldness as a lasting reminder of this punishment. As it is, the absence of a recognizable moral as well as literary pattern leads them to take his account for nothing more than an amusing fiction. When I later asked one of the listeners who laughed the hardest at this story about the girl who turns into a dog, he assumed a serious expression. "Now that business of the girl is different," he informed me. "I am sure that she did become a dog, because no one insults my Padrinho without paying a high price. There are many similar stories and so although I myself never saw her, I do not doubt that this is the truth."[45]

Few followers of the priest expect a person walking down the street to turn into a serpent or a dog before their eyes. Most agree, however, that bestial behavior has the capacity to trigger metamorphosis into animal form, that is, that the metaphor may have literal as well as symbolic truth. For them, the ordinary and extraordinary form a continuum rather than two separate categories. Once again, the issue at stake is not how a given person turned into a snake or dog or pig or monkey but whether Padre Cícero has the ability to transform people who do not behave like proper human beings into lower forms of life. "A bedeviled Christian (*um cristão endemoniado*)," insists one man, "*is* Satan. The person who refuses to obey his father and mother has no religion and so he

44. Raimundo Pedro do Nascimento (P). Currais Novos, Rio Grande do Norte, 1939. Married; peddler and lottery (*jogo do bicho*) ticket seller. 3 pilgrimages. (October 9, 1982.)
45. Pedro Araújo de Oliveira (R). Vicos, Alagoas, 1919. Arrived Juazeiro 1934. Married; carpenter. (October 10, 1982.)

becomes an animal. He has to look different because he *is* different from other people."[46]

In sum, the best-known tales are reshapings of everyday reality in accord with a small number of clearcut if not necessarily conscious rules. "A miracle," explains one storyteller, "has to be the truth. Or if it isn't the very truth, well then, it could just as well be true."[47] Although I will now proceed to concentrate on the differences between residents and pilgrims, there is no doubt that the two subscribe to a fundamentally similar vision of the world.

46. José Ferreira da Silva (R). Santa Cruz de Iguabaribe, Pernambuco, 1946. Arrived Juazeiro 1969. Married; *cordel* and *bendito* writer and vendor. (October 28, 1982.)

47. Maria Filadélfia de Souza (P). Guarabira, Paraíba, 1948. Married; laundress. 5 pilgrimages. (October 14, 1982.)

IV.

Residents' and Pilgrims' Versions of the Stories

I love to tell these stories about my Padrinho. They almost
make me feel as if I were seeing him again.
                                        Resident of Juazeiro

When we come to Juazeiro, the stories our parents told us are
no longer just their stories; they become our stories too.
                                        Pilgrims from Alagoas

D issimilarities within the most frequently told stories are, as I
have already noted, largely a reflection of the tellers' varying
proximity to Padre Cícero.[1] This chapter identifies the principal features
of residents', as opposed to pilgrims', tales. In so doing it stresses the
degree to which the best-known stories provide a privileged illustration
of the ongoing passage of personal experience into a more public master
legend or "life."

There are a good number of discrepancies between the two groups
of storytellers.[2] The most important are summarized below. I will discuss these half-dozen characteristics in detail in this chapter, drawing on
the versions of those tales we have already seen.

1. The evolution of personal reminiscences into a communally meaningful myth has been
of particular interest to oral historians. See Jan Vansina, *Oral Tradition: A Study in Historical
Methodology.* For an overview of the work of other oral historians see Joseph C. Miller, ed.,
The African Past Speaks: Essays on Oral Tradition and History. A good example of this sort of
evolution in a very different context is Fred Eggan, "From History to Myth: A Hopi Example." The reader may also wish to consult the more general *Oral History: An Interdisciplinary Anthology,* ed. David K. Dunaway and Willa K. Baum.

2. It is possible and often profitable to divide the storytellers into subgroups based on age,
sex, region, and urban versus rural character. The division between pilgrim and resident,
however, largely subsumes these other categories.

Residents	Pilgrims
High degree of personal involvement with Padre Cícero; use of memory as a literary genre.	Reduced role of personal memories of Padre Cícero.
Narrative variety.	Growing standardization; fewer miraculous episodes and less variation within these.
Concern for concrete details; sense of Padre Cícero as a physical presence.	Increasing abstraction and use of fantastic detail.
Focus on Juazeiro.	Focus on the pilgrimage and individual pilgrims.
Lack of an ordering principle, chronological or causal, between miraculous episodes (all stories seen as potentially equal).	Presence of an ordering principle, causal or chronological, for selected "historical" incidents.
Resistance to standardization on both individual and group levels.	Tendency toward development of a "life."

Residents' Versions of the Best-Known Tales

If only because many of the individuals who now live in Juazeiro were originally visitors to the city, differences between the two groups are not hard and fast. And yet, although each person has his or her own approach to a given story, residents' tales are distinguished as a group by their high degree of personal involvement and narrative variety, their concern for concrete details, their focus on Juazeiro, the lack of chronological or causal links between miraculous episodes, and a resistance to standardization.

PERSONAL INVOLVEMENT AND NARRATIVE VARIETY

The initially most striking features of residents' tales about Padre Cícero's lifetime are their number and their variety. Local storytellers can usually recount at least ten incidents, and many know considerably more. A particularly accomplished individual may relate as many as fifty different tales. One extraordinarily prolific man told me sixty-three stories in a single afternoon, then urged me to come back the next morning to hear a dozen more.

Although considerable overlap occurs between residents' stories, no

one repertoire is exactly like any other.[3] As a result, while it is not difficult to isolate the best-known stories the corpus as a whole remains decidedly open-ended. When I asked people to tell me what they knew
about the priest's life they would often say something like "Well, I certainly hope that you are planning to spend the next three weeks with
me!" When in the beginning I requested "the story of Padre Cícero's
life," many laughed. "No one knows the whole story of my Padrinho,"
one man told me. "The cases are innumerable, each one more extraordinary than the next."[4]

Those residents of Juazeiro who knew Padre Cícero as children and
young adults often have full-fledged stories of him. One woman recalls
how the priest offered her a tea biscuit she believes responsible for curing
a rash that had disfigured her since birth. Another, a man, remembers
hiding behind a pillar in the church in order to watch Padre Cícero pray.
("People said that a star came down from Heaven to talk to him," this
individual notes, "but I saw nothing, because my Padrinho must have
known that I was there.")[5]

Borrowed experiences may be almost as vivid as a person's own recollections. One woman speaks with an air of authority of her father's
attempts as a mischievous child to climb up Padre Cícero's chimney. She
has adopted the nickname of Fumaça or "Chimneysmoke," which the
priest gave him as a result of this escapade.[6]

Some memories have an air of objective reality. A storyteller may,
for instance, describe how the rooster he brings to Padre Cícero jumps
out of his arms to race around the priest's hammock, crowing and strew-
ing feathers in every direction. Although other recollections have a more
fantastic flavor, they too often take the form of personal experience stories or memorates in which the teller plays a leading role.[7] The woman

3. Residents' repertoires are not limited to miracle stories. Many individuals also tell a
variety of folktales, recite pieces of *cordel* accounts and bits of improvised *cantador* poetry,
sing *benditos,* and recount stories from the Bible—a separate study could well be made of
their versions of the latter.

4. Expedito Sebastião da Silva (R). Juazeiro, 1929. Single; *cordel* poet and typesetter. (July
5, 1981.)

5. Severino Almeida de Barbosa (R). Águas Belas, Pernambuco, 1915. Arrived Juazeiro as
child. Separated; sells aluminum spoons in *ranchos.* (November 21, 1982.)

6. Maria Antônia da Silva, a resident of Juazeiro, is also known as "Maria Fumaça."

7. The terms *memorate* and *fabulate* were introduced by Carl Wilhelm von Sydow in his
"Kategorien der Prosa-Volksdichtung" in 1934 (reprinted in his *Selected Papers on Folklore,*
pp. 60–88). There is a growing bibliography on memorates by folklore scholars. For an
overview see Linda Dégh and Andrew Vázsonyi, "The Memorate and the Proto-
Memorate"; Juha Pentikäinen, "Belief, Memorate and Legend"; Sandra K. D. Stahl, "The
Oral Personal Narrative in Its Generic Context"; Jeff Todd Titon, "The Life Story"; and

who claims to have received a visit as a child from Padre Cícero at the time when he was supposedly delivering his evening homily elsewhere is likely to describe the incident in much the same manner as the man who speaks of how the sun suddenly illumined a plate of *umbu* fruits on the priest's table.

Because of the importance of these real or imagined experiences to residents of Juazeiro, bits and pieces of the past regularly find their way into the corpus. Those individuals who knew Padre Cícero are particularly likely to use their narratives as a way of reminiscing about their own lives as well as about him. As a result, even the best-known tales may be presented in the guise of personal memories.[8]

The most obvious way to lay claim to a familiar story is to introduce oneself or a close relative as a participant. One old man, for instance, assures his neighbors in the Rua do Horto that it was he who saddled the horse on which Padre Cícero galloped off to confess the man from São Pedro. Another storyteller insists that he just happened to be strolling by the church in which Padre Cícero lay buried during the hours before dawn when the bishop and his men arrived to exhume the corpse. Still another describes how her father-in-law accompanied Manuel Germano in his visit to the priest.

30. My father-in-law was a great friend of this Manuel Germano who came to be rich. They were always together. So one day Manuel Germano decided to take a little tapioca starch to my Padrinho Cícero, and my father-in-law said, "I will go with you."

When they arrived at his house, my Padrinho Cícero put his hand on Manuel Germano's head. He said, "May God multiply your wealth, Manuel Germano," in this way, three times.

So then my father-in-law said, "My Padrinho Cícero, give me your blessing too!"

So then my Padrinho drew a deep cross with his finger upon my father-in-law's head. In order for him to accept the fact that he would die poor, get it? But Manuel Germano, no, the very next day he began to prosper. And in no time at all he was a wealthy, a very wealthy man.

—Nazaré Ferreira da Silva (P). Baixa D'Anta, Ceará, 1957. Arrived Juazeiro 1961. Married; seamstress. (July 29, 1981).

---

the special double issue of the *Journal of the Folklore Institute* devoted to the personal experience story. See also William Labov and Joshua Waletzky, "Narrative Analysis: Oral Versions of Personal Experience"; and John A. Robinson, "Personal Narratives Reconsidered."

8. For a useful discussion of point of view see Wayne C. Booth, *The Rhetoric of Fiction*, pp. 3–20, and Boris Uspenskiĭ, *A Poetics of Composition*, especially pp. 57–80.

If only because most storytellers need to believe, on some level, their own stories, this sort of direct involvement in the best-known tales is relatively rare. Residents are more likely to insert anecdotal material into, rather than tamper with, an existing narrative frame. This material may be peripheral to the story so long as there is an association between the two in the speaker's mind. Usually these recollections take the form of a momentary digression. In the following example, the teller describes her own reaction to the news of Padre Cícero's death in a way that does not conflict with the standard story line. After reminiscing about her attempts to convince her mother to let her see the priest in his coffin, she resumes her account of the empty tomb.

31. On the day my Padrinho "moved away" [died], the bishop came from Crato with his men to take the body. They arrived around midnight so that no one would see. . . . I still remember the day they buried my Padrinho, because it was so very sad. I was only six years old, you see. I asked my mother to take me with her because I wanted to see him in the coffin but she said that no, I couldn't go because I wasn't crying and only people who cried had the right to go. So then I went over to the pepper tree and I pulled off some peppers and I rubbed my eyes, like this. [The speaker demonstrates.] So then my eyes teared and smarted and I said, "Mother, I am crying now. Take me!" But she said no, that there were many people and I was too small. . . . So then only after the funeral when the people had left, the bishop came to steal the body. But he was not successful because there was nothing for him to carry off. When he opened the coffin there was only a pile of rose petals. That is, this is what people say, because I was not there to see what happened.
   —Maria Antônia da Silva (R). São José das Lavras, Ceará, 1928.
     Arrived Juazeiro as infant. Married; makes heart-shaped straw
     boxes. (July 18, 1981.)

Sometimes the speaker who embarks on this sort of tangent becomes so caught up in the details as to forget his or her original purpose. Then, too, personal material occasionally serves not only as a source of digression but also of outright contradiction. The speaker may conclude by questioning elements of a well-known story that conflict with his or her own memories of the priest.

One storyteller, for instance, ends an otherwise conventional account of the rancher who asks for rain by expressing doubts about the fate of the rancher's children. "They say that my Padrinho opened the sky until the man's cattle went floating down the river and the man himself and all his family drowned," the woman says. "That is what they say, but I did not see it and furthermore I am not sure that it is true. Because even if the man himself were very bad, would my Padrinho have let his little children meet such a terrible death?"

After pausing for a moment, the speaker goes on to recount the priest's actions after her own father was killed in cold blood. "Look," she says,

32. My father died from an assassin's bullet and for a long time we were very sad. So then finally my Padrinho Cícero called my mother to Juazeiro. "You must pardon the man who killed your husband," he told her.

"But, my Padrinho, how can I pardon the person who killed my husband and who left my children without a father?"

"You can pardon him because if you don't, your husband will go to hell along with the murderer."

And so my mother pardoned that man. And I did too. For this reason I have my doubts about this business of the rancher. I tell what others have told me but I still have my doubts, you see? Because if I heard my Padrinho say that we ought to pardon the creature who had killed my father, how then could my Padrinho take the life of those innocent children?

—Norina Sobreira Nunes (R). Bom Nome, Pernambuco, 1914.
Arrived Juazeiro 1918. Married; hatmaker. (July 14, 1981.)

In this case the woman waits until the end of the story to question its veracity, but the teller may introduce reservations or conflicting information at any point within the narrative. Some persons will not return to the original subject; others will resume the tale, concluding it in the usual way.

CONCERN FOR CONCRETE DETAILS

Direct involvement represents the most dramatic form of personalization. Residents, however, are considerably more prone to privatize a story through insistence on apparently inconsequential details. Although the identity of the fruit in the enchanted grove is not essential to the ensuing action, for instance, residents of Juazeiro are fully capable of arguing for half an hour about whether the workmen discovered oranges, mangoes, or watermelon. One individual may claim to have once encountered a man who supposedly gobbled down a section of an enchanted orange. Another may cite his mother's description of an enormous watermelon that one of the workmen—who later married her second cousin Dorinha, who has a son who is now an electrician in Recife—discovered behind the Horto church. Still another may insist she heard that the workers filled their straw hats full of mangoes from "an old man named Joaquim who lived next door to my mother when we lived in São Pedro. He had very white hair, I remember, and he never, never lied."

A listener may likewise interrupt a storyteller in midstream to embark on a detailed discussion of whether Manuel Correia's wife was named Manuela or Maria or Maria Manuela, or whether Manuel Germano originally lived in the yellow house next to the water tower or in the house with the blue door across the street from Dona Maria Furtado. Did Padre Cícero go to Rome in 1897 or 1898? Did he rescue a drowning child from a well or from the ocean, and was the child in question a little girl or a little boy?

This often overwhelming concern for concrete details makes for great variation within the best-known stories. Working within the basic outline of the tale, each person adds those distinctive touches that have become the hallmark of residents' narratives.

Precision in regard to time and place is one result of this attention to particulars. The photographers who take Padre Cícero's picture during the war in Germany, for instance, arrive in Juazeiro "at 3:00 in the afternoon." A story may take place in "the Horto" or "the hills of São Pedro," or it may unfold in "that big house on the corner of Santa Luzia Street," "there, just before the hollow where there used to be a big *juá* tree," or "along the highway to Logradouro where the road forks to the left." The speaker will often interrupt his or her own tale to describe a landmark that has since disappeared or explain a local custom no longer followed.

This specificity extends to the figure of Padre Cícero, who provides the focus for an otherwise unwieldy collection of miraculous episodes. An average of a third of the total number of sentences in residents' stories are devoted to the priest, and some tellers refer to him constantly. This Padre Cícero is often a physical as well as moral presence. Residents may, for instance, attempt to pinpoint the exact shade of the priest's eyes ("blue, darker than that scrap of paper there, but not light as the flowers in Dona Rosinha's dress").[9] They leap up to suggest Padre Cícero's way of walking, modulate their voices to approximate his way of speaking, and imitate the gestures (a tapping of his cane, a special way of pointing at a person with two fingers) that the community associates with him.

9. It is well documented that Padre Cícero had blue eyes. According to Manoel Dinis in *Mistérios do Joazeiro,* p. 7, the priest's father's family was of Portuguese descent and had come to the Cariri Valley from the state of Bahia; his maternal grandmother was a Tupi Indian.

The tellers frequently rely on action verbs as a means of reinforcing the priest's corporeal reality in these stories. The result is a protagonist who does not simply speak but who shouts and whispers, whistles, clears his throat in disbelief, and clicks his tongue. In the Manuel Correia story, for instance, the priest, who is supposedly an old man at the time of the occurrence, may saddle his horse, gallop several miles up a hill, jump off his mount, rush over to speak to the dead man, then pull him to his feet before handing him the carpenter's hammer which had dropped from his hand.

Local storytellers may also rely on the imperfect or the present tense to create or heighten a sense of immediacy. Although the great majority of miracle narratives begin in the preterite, the speaker sometimes changes tenses as the action progresses. In the following version of the priest's trip to Rome, the teller shifts from the past to the present as he becomes caught up in his own description.[10]

33. My Padrinho went to Rome and when he got there he went to see the pope.

"Padre Cícero," the pope said, "I called you here to open the door of this church which Saint Peter closed."

"I can't open that door, your Holiness," my Padrinho Cícero said, "because a priest is a soldier, a mere servant."

"You do what I tell you," the pope said, "because my army is ready to raze Juazeiro if you don't."

"All right, all right," says my Padrinho. "I will open the door if it is you who insist." So then he says, "May the hand who closed you open you!" and bangs upon the door three times. So then the door swings open and my Padrinho walks on in.

—José Antonio da Silva (R). Garanhuns, Pernambuco, 1914. Arrived Juazeiro 1946. Widower; *rendeiro*. (July 4, 1981.)

Dialogue provides residents with yet another means of affirming their proximity to Padre Cícero. Their stories are less often restatements of what happened than extended conversations held together with bits of explanation. Only two of the twenty examples provided for residents in the preceding chapter do not include exchanges between Padre Cícero and one or more of the other characters. These snatches of conversation give the stories an air not only of concreteness but also of intimacy.

Although supernatural elements appear throughout the Padre Cícero stories, the teller normally situates these within a reassuringly familiar

10. See Nessa Wolfson, "A Feature of Performed Narrative: The Conversational Historical Present," and Deborah Schiffrin, "Tense Variation in Narrative." Although the articles focus on American English, they have wider applications.

frame. The man who refers to a mysterious staircase that ascends from the church door in Rome, for instance, describes it as "the color of new corn." The woman who introduces an unusual blue fruit into the enchanted grove tale takes care to surround it with the customary mangoes and bananas. Likewise, in a well-known sequel to the birth story Padre Cícero restores his foster mother's sight for only a few hours. Humanizing touches like those in the following version of this story make extraordinary actions even easier to accept. The concluding reference to Padre Cícero's "beloved mother" is a somewhat stilted approximation of the affectionate Portuguese diminutive *māezinha* (literally, "little mother").

34. One day my Padrinho said to her, "Mother, I cannot undo what God has done. But would you like to see how pretty the Horto church is?"

"I have heard so much about that church," she said. "Let us go to see it."

So then my Padrinho took her arm and they went up the Rua do Horto together. When they arrived at the church he said, "Wait a minute, Mother, I am going to open the door." So then once they were inside, they say her eyes opened. "Look here, Mother," my Padrinho said.

"It is as lovely as people say," she told him, very content. So then they spent many hours in that church. And only when night began to fall did they finally leave.

"Are you satisfied, Mother?" my Padrinho asked her.

She said, "Yes, because I have seen so many fine things."

So then they left there and he locked the door with a key. And as soon as the last light of day touched her eyes, she went blind again. So then my Padrinho took her arm and they walked down the hill together. They went down the hill arm in arm, my Padrinho and his beloved mother.

—Marina Alves da Costa (R). Chã Morena, Pernambuco, 1923. Arrived Juazeiro 1975. Married; nurse's aide. (July 21, 1981.)

The down-to-earth quality of residents' stories facilitates their incorporation into ordinary conversation.[11] Almost no one says, "Now I am going to tell you the tale my grandmother once told me of how my

11. For a discussion of the embedding of stories in conversation see William Labov, "The Transformation of Experience in Narrative Syntax." More general discussions of the organization of stories are available in William Lynwood Montell, *The Saga of Coe Ridge: A Study in Oral History*, and in Richard Bauman and Joel Sherzer, eds., *Explorations in the Ethnography of Speaking*.

Padrinho threw his hat up against the schoolhouse wall." Instead, the person is apt to use a hat hanging from a makeshift hook in a neighbor's house as a way into the story. "When my Padrinho was a little boy he used to leave his hat on a peg upon the wall," he or she will assert with a nod in its direction. In the same manner, explicit conclusions are no more common than a formal lead-in. Once the tale is over, most tellers simply pause for a moment before going on to speak of something else.

FOCUS ON JUAZEIRO

In line with their efforts to personalize even the best-known narratives, local storytellers seek to make them relevant to Juazeiro. They are likely to favor tales that feature a resident or residents and into which they can therefore project themselves with ease.

Table 1 gives the twenty stories already outlined in the preceding chapter in descending order of the frequency with which people told them to me. It also provides the total number of tellers for each tale and the percentage of the whole that this number represents.

Because so many of the miracle narratives are common knowledge in Juazeiro, residents were often eager to talk about other, less familiar incidents. "Everybody knows that story of the hat so I am not going to repeat it," an individual might declare. "Listen, and you will hear about a miracle no one else will ever tell you." For this reason the figures in Table 1 do not reflect the number of people who knew a given tale but rather those who actually recounted it for me. The figures are nonetheless extremely useful in ascertaining the narratives' relative popularity. The slow and even fall-off between stories indicates residents' familiarity with them as a body. I have included only the twenty most popular tales; many others rank just below these in frequency of narration.[12]

A glance at Table 1 confirms the tendency of local storytellers to concentrate on situations with which they can readily identify. Both of the two most widely told tales (Manuel Correia and the man from São Pedro) involve inhabitants of the Cariri. Thus at the same time that the priest's ability to "cure" death confirms his miraculous powers, it suggests a more specific interest in those persons close at hand.

The birth episode, which ranks third among resident storytellers, makes a similar point. Although a mysterious woman "gives" the future priest to Dona Quinou, residents of Juazeiro nevertheless expect him to act like a *filho da terra* or native son. "A person's birthplace," explains one

12. I would estimate that at least a hundred stories are widely familiar among resident storytellers. Several hundred others might be considered variations on well-known themes.

Table 1. Residents' Stories by Frequency of Narration

Rank order	Story	Number of tellers (250 total)	Percentage of whole
1.	The man from São Pedro	52	20.8%
2.	Manuel Correia	51	20.4
3.	Padre Cícero's birth	47	18.8
4.	Padre Cícero opens a church door in Rome	45	18.0
5.	Padre Cícero stops a war in Germany	44	17.6
6.	The would-be assassin	43	17.2
7.	The Revolution of 1913–14	39	15.6
8.	The enchanted grove	38	15.2
9.	The hat that stuck to the wall	36	14.4
10.	The empty tomb	35	14.0
11.	Padre Cícero makes a mute boy speak	34	13.6
12.	The rancher who asked for rain	33	13.2
13/14.	The hunter's first catch	32	12.8
13/14.	Padre Cícero and Dr. Floro	32	12.8
15.	Manuel Germano	31	12.4
16.	The transformation of the host	30	12.0
17.	The girl who turned into a dog	29	11.6
18.	Padre Monteiro	28	11.2
19.	The girl eaten by a mountain lion	27	10.8
20.	Padre Cícero rescues a child from drowning	24	9.6

resident in a postscript to the story, "remains important to him because the minerals in the earth become part of his own blood. Even though my Padrinho came here directly from heaven, he grew up in this valley and so he is certain to protect it from all harm."[13]

A look further down the table reveals that the story of the war in Germany is considerably more popular than that other instance of bilocality in which a child is rescued from drowning. This preference probably reflects storytellers' interest in the grateful foreigners' arrival in Juazeiro. In much the same way, Padre Cícero's trip to Rome is almost certainly more meaningful to residents than the tale of the mute boy, because of its direct connection to Juazeiro. Although visitors often combine the two stories by locating the child behind the locked door, residents are inclined to keep these incidents separate. Often they have the priest strike a bargain with the pontiff in which the latter cedes all right to any objects inside the church. Padre Cícero then goes on to discover a likeness of the Sacred Heart of Jesus, which local storytellers identify as "the very one which you can see today in the church of Our Lady of

13. Francisco Pedro da Souza (R). Bananeiras, Paraíba, 1936. Arrived Juazeiro 1953. Married; *rendeiro*. (October 10, 1982.)

Sorrows." Although the pope then pleads with Padre Cícero to remain in Rome, the priest pointedly affirms his loyalty to Juazeiro.

The story second from the bottom of the table, that of the girl eaten by a mountain lion, offers a similar example of local storytellers' ability to alter a given body of material to fit their own needs. Unlike pilgrims, who usually allow the young traveler to perish, most residents insist that she ends up in Juazeiro. In their tales Padre Cícero usually orders the errant pilgrims to return to the spot at which they left her sleeping. They despair of finding the girl alive, but she is sitting beneath a leafy tree, a mountain lion on either side. The group brings her to Juazeiro, where she decides to stay. "Tell my family I want them to join me here," she pointedly instructs the other members of the group.

Likewise, residents' stories of the would-be assassin almost always cast a local landowner in the role of villain. The man's decision to approach Padre Cícero during the priest's daily homily means that residents of Juazeiro are witnesses to the thwarted crime. Not infrequently, the priest asks a person whom the teller may specifically identify ("It was João who used to live across from Dona Maria Fateira, remember?") to uncover the corpse in whose hand an enormous knife still gleams.

The tale of the man who asks Padre Cícero for a weapon and that of the woman who requests a coin for the journey home do not enjoy the same popularity among residents as they do among pilgrims and are thus absent from Table 1. When local storytellers do deal with these subjects, they almost always "de-pilgrimize" them. The traveler who requests the knife or gun often becomes a resident of Juazeiro worried about transporting a sack of gold belonging to his employer. In much the same way, Padre Cícero instructs the woman to whom he gives the penny how to multiply his gift to her before she returns home. When she grows rich as a result, the pilgrim decides to remain in the city. "And so," concludes one storyteller with obvious satisfaction, "she became one of us."

LACK OF AN ORDERING PRINCIPLE

Although the best-known residents' stories reveal the customary four-step challenge pattern, the tellers are unlikely to fit individual episodes into any sort of larger chronological framework. If asked which of two miraculous incidents occurred first they often have an answer, but they almost never set out to describe Padre Cícero's life from beginning to end. Local storytellers are also highly unlikely to suggest that one event triggers another. An account of the Revolution of 1913–14 may prompt an account of the war that Padre Cícero halts in Germany, but there is seldom, if ever, any direct causal relationship between the two.

The large number of stories at many residents' disposal may help explain the absence of a larger narrative scheme: the storyteller familiar with fifty miraculous incidents will understandably find it difficult to fuse these into a single story. Those persons who know only five tales, however, are no more likely to arrange these in any sort of recognizable progression.

Residents' ability to sandwich first-, second-, or third-hand reminiscences into the interstices of even the best-known stories allows them to speak of the resurrection of Manuel Correia and of Padre Cícero's trip to Rome as if both happened yesterday. The person who cannot claim to know someone who lived across the street from the carpenter's second cousin will nonetheless be able to describe the Horto church. If a teller's grandfather did not pass on to him the details of Padre Cícero's trip to Rome, then perhaps a neighbor has seen the trunk the priest took on his voyage.[14] Residence in Juazeiro normally presupposes a degree of background information and experience on which individuals do not hesitate to draw in personalizing their stories.

Memory, or the illusion of memory, is of utmost significance to local storytellers. Thus while an outside observer will immediately separate tales about historical persons and events—the *beata* Maria de Araújo or the Revolution of 1913–14, for instance—from others involving a much higher degree of fabulation, such as the girl whom the priest transforms into a dog, residents normally perceive little, if any, qualitative difference between these narratives. Asked if the cases of the *beata* and the girl whom Padre Cícero turns into a dog are not somewhat dissimilar, the teller will usually look surprised. "Of course they're different," one woman answered. "One has to do with the transformation of a host and the other has to do with the transformation of a person."[15]

Then too, most local storytellers are no more interested in questions of degree than of kind. When I asked people which of Padre Cícero's deeds struck them as most noteworthy, many simply shrugged or smiled. "But they're all important" was a common reply. Those persons who cited one or another tale were so obviously trying to please me that after a while I gave up asking.

For a number of older storytellers, the sort of ordering and selection essential to narrative construction is all but impossible. For them, Padre Cícero is much like a parent with whom their own lives are intertwined.

14. The trunk supposedly used by Padre Cícero during his trip to Rome is presently in the possession of Lucas Rodrigues Soares, who arrived in Juazeiro from Santana do Ipanema, Alagoas, in 1927. Similar mementos of the priest can be found throughout the city.

15. Emília Ludugrio Silva (R). Juazeiro 1927. Separated; seamstress. (October 24, 1982.)

Although the priest died a full fifty years ago, their memories of him remain numerous and vivid. For these individuals to formulate a "life" of Padre Cícero would require a difficult and potentially painful exteriorization and assessment of their own past. It is therefore no wonder that the best-known tales should mingle with pieces of their own experience in the random, episodic manner characteristic of personal reminiscence.[16]

Because as memories the stories have no objective value, quantity becomes all-important to the tellers. If the person who knows a hundred miracle narratives has a hundred different ways of affirming Padre Cícero's power, the one who can recount ninety-nine enjoys a less privileged relationship to the priest. For this reason, few residents will risk diminishing their store of tales by implying that one incident is of more interest than another.

Were the underlying purpose of storytelling in Juazeiro the communication of information, residents would be more prone to pre-screen and arrange their tales into a coherent whole. Most people, however, are primarily interested in establishing an individual relationship with Padre Cícero through the repetition of the greatest possible number of miraculous episodes in their own voice. Storytelling thus becomes a form of narrative circumambulation in which the tales' primary significance has little to do with content. The mere existence of the miracle stories is the ultimate source of their importance. For this reason, there is no need to create meaning through the imposition of a larger causal or chronological scheme.

RESISTANCE TO STANDARDIZATION

Local storytellers' lack of interest in fitting their accounts of Padre Cícero into any sort of larger narrative framework is repeated on the community level. "Why should everybody tell the same stories in the same way?" demands one resident of the Rua do Horto. "I do not see any purpose in hearing my neighbor tell me something I already know."[17]

Even if residents were favorable in principle to a master legend, they would almost certainly find it difficult to put theory into practice. People who cannot agree on whether the enchanted grove contains coconuts or mangoes are unlikely to reach the far more difficult consensus on which incidents should or should not be included in a "life."

Local storytellers' insistence on their own version of a given story is,

16. See Titon, "The Life Story," p. 280.
17. José Vicente Pereira (R). Juazeiro, 1938. Married; guard. (October 15, 1982.)

to be sure, less the product of inveterate individualism than of a communal agreement to disagree. In the final analysis, if privatization is a reflection of documentable proximity, it is also a literary strategy that the group as a whole has tacitly adopted. This unspoken understanding means that no one really expects another individual to accept his or her version of a given tale. Disagreements between local storytellers therefore often assume a ritualistic character. Because each person is *supposed* to insist on details, the individual who cedes to another in public often feels obliged to justify his or her behavior to anyone who will listen. "My story is really the right one," confides a man who had deferred hours earlier to another's version of the Manuel Correia story, "but Seu Pedro is getting on in years and I didn't want to hurt his feelings."[18]

Standardization is ultimately the antithesis of what most residents are seeking. The reason people come to a city plagued by an above-average rate of unemployment is that they are convinced it is unlike any other in the world. If they continue to eke out a living much as they would in any of the tiny rural communities in which most were born, they can nevertheless revel in the sense of infinite potential that distinguishes Juazeiro in the eyes of Padre Cícero's followers. "Am I the owner of this *rancho?*" demands one individual. "No, no, I own nothing. Why, I am not even the owner of my life because I may well die tomorrow. No, the owner of this *rancho* is my Padrinho Cícero. And I, I am content to live within his shadow."[19]

The fact that pilgrims threading their way up the Rua do Horto are as likely to be praying at the top of their voices at three o'clock in the morning as at any other hour confirms residents' conviction that the extraordinary is the norm. Thus while "Anything can happen" (*Tudo é possível*) is a frequent Brazilian saying, residents of Juazeiro insist that *Tudo é possível* aqui, "Anything can happen *here*." "The world passes before my door," notes one woman proudly. "The world comes to Juazeiro and I watch as it goes by."[20]

This cherished sense of possibility is in turn a function of Padre Cícero's all-pervasive presence. For individuals like the *rancho* owner cited above, Juazeiro is the shadow of a body that has temporarily disappeared. Every rock, every tree, every bend in the road recalls the priest. Talking

18. Brás Ibiapina de Farias (R). Souza, Paraíba, 1920. Arrived Juazeiro 1949. Married; construction worker. (October 24, 1982.)

19. Antônio José do Nascimento (R). Belo Jardim, Pernambuco, 1931. Arrived Juazeiro 1947. Married; *rancho* owner. (November 17, 1982.)

20. Isabel Josefa da Conceição (R). Mauriti, Ceará, 1914. Arrived Juazeiro 1936. Separated; occupation unknown. (October 19, 1982.)

to the people who live in his adopted city, one begins to feel as if his spirit hung over the entire Cariri Valley as a mist composed of millions of tiny, half-visible droplets. To accept a single account of Padre Cícero's life would be to distill these droplets into a substance which could then be bottled and set on a shelf. It would be to entertain the possibility of limits and thus to destroy that aura of imminence that local storytellers have so carefully cultivated.

Residents' stories of the priest are normally full of information about recognizable persons and events. In choosing to privatize even the best-known incidents, however, these individuals have largely rejected the sort of public definition normally associated with historical discourse. They have also eliminated all set boundaries between the past and the present. Therefore in spite of the tales' superficial documentary quality, their real purpose is to affirm the proximity of a priest who exists outside the normal confines of time and space. As such, the miracle stories are ultimately evocations rather than evaluations. "I dreamt of my Padrinho Cícero last night," explains one resident. "I saw him in the headlights of a passing car. 'Ah, my Padrinho,' I said, 'so you did not die after all!' 'Of course I didn't die,' he said. 'How could you even think that? I am here among you always until the end of time.'"[21]

Finally, it is essential to remember that Juazeiro is the only place in the Northeast where followers of Padre Cícero constitute a clear majority. There are and have always been inhabitants of the city who do not accept the priest's miraculous abilities. Because, however, these persons often have an economic interest in maintaining others' faith in him, they do not publicly challenge his powers.[22] Padre Cícero's followers therefore have little incentive to close ranks against a common enemy. As a result, instead of defining their tellers against a more heterogeneous background, the tales serve to differentiate these individuals from other persons whom they resemble. In this context they function not only as a celebration of Padre Cícero but also as a much-needed means of self-identification.

Pilgrims' Versions of the Best-Known Tales

Although differences in region, age, and sex are apparent in pilgrims' narratives, these tales as a group stand apart from those of local story-

21. José Dantas Filho (R). Juazeiro 1904. Married; retired. (July 12, 1981.)

22. Many of these non-believers are indirectly if not directly dependent on the pilgrimage trade for a living. They therefore have a vested interest in the continuation of the Padre Cícero devotion, regardless of their personal feelings about the priest.

tellers. Visitors' greater distance from Padre Cícero is reflected in their stories' increased tendency toward abstraction and fabulation, as well as their concern with the pilgrimage instead of Juazeiro. And the tellers' willingness to see connections between individual incidents signals receptivity to the notion of a master legend or "life."

REDUCED ROLE OF MEMORY AND GROWING STANDARDIZATION

Most pilgrims can describe at least one favor attributable to Padre Cícero but, lacking access to residents' seemingly endless store of personal memories, they relate fewer tales about the past. Although I spoke with twice as many visitors as residents, the latter recounted a greater variety of narratives set during the priest's life.

Pilgrims' more limited repertoires may partially reflect the circumstances under which I taped the stories. Perhaps if some individuals had been able to talk at leisure they would have told a greater number of tales.[23] As it was, I found that only a few non-residents in each group knew more than ten stories about the priest's lifetime and that the average visitor could remember only three or four. Therefore despite the impressive sum total, the numbers for individual storytellers are decidedly smaller for pilgrims than for residents.

The rank ordering in Table 2 of the most frequently told narratives reveals a sharper drop-off in terms of popularity than we saw for local storytellers. (Compare the point spread between the tales at the top and the bottom of Table 1 and Table 2.)[24] I have indicated how many people recorded each story, as well as the percentage of the sample this number represents. Once again, more people undoubtedly knew these stories than these figures might indicate. Because visitors almost always spoke with me in groups, once an individual had told a given story no one else wanted to repeat it, but this does not mean that others could not have done so had they wished.

Pilgrims differ from residents not only in their preference for certain well-known stories over others but also in their approach to the corpus as a whole. They are, first and foremost, much less insistent about the

23. In comparing pilgrims and residents I am, to be sure, comparing not only two different groups of persons but also two quite different storytelling situations. It is possible that the researcher who spent an extended period of time with pilgrims in their home community would be able to record a larger and more varied group of stories. I did find, however, that the tales I taped during a week spent in the Vergel neighborhood of Maceió were much like those I had recorded among pilgrims in Juazeiro.

24. The fact that I am dealing with twice as many visitors as residents undoubtedly affects these figures. There is no doubt, however, that pilgrims as a group know a smaller number of stories.

Table 2. *Pilgrims' Stories by Frequency of Narration*

Rank order	Story	Number of tellers (500 total)	Percentage of whole
1.	The girl eaten by a mountain lion	101	20.2%
2.	The rancher who asked for rain	87	17.4
3.	The girl who turned into a dog	82	16.4
4.	The would-be assassin	61	12.2
5.	The man who exchanged his rosary	58	11.6
6.	The hat that stuck to the wall	54	10.8
7.	The Revolution of 1913–14	53	10.6
8.	Padre Cícero rescues a child from drowning	45	9.0
9/10.	Padre Cícero stops a war in Germany	40	8.0
9/10.	The hunter's first catch	40	8.0
11.	Padre Cícero makes a mute boy speak	39	7.8
12.	Padre Cícero gives a pilgrim a penny	37	7.4
13/14.	Padre Cícero opens a church door in Rome	35	7.0
13/14.	The slipper in the tomb	35	7.0
15.	The transformation of the host	34	6.8
16/17.	Padre Cícero's birth	33	6.6
16/17.	The man who ate the guinea pig	33	6.6
18.	Padre Cícero and Dr. Floro	32	6.4
19.	Padre Cícero feeds a hen and its chicks	26	5.2
20.	Padre Cícero resuscitates a pilgrim's donkey	24	4.8

supporting details so dear to the hearts of residents. They seldom squabble, for instance, about whether Padre Cícero rescues a child from the ocean or from a well. If a listener interrupts with the observation that the man killed by a mountain lion trades his rosary for a dagger, not a rifle, most pilgrim storytellers will shrug amicably and go on with the tale. Because many visitors will simply note that the workmen in the enchanted grove found "a lot of fruit," arguments as to whether the trees were hung with oranges or mangoes are unlikely ever to arise. Should one member of the group voice a strong opinion ("My mother told me that it was mangoes"), the teller will often oblige by incorporating this detail into the narrative. "All right, then, after that man picked those mangoes," he or she will say.

Pilgrims are generally far more willing than residents to let others speak for them. This means that one or two accomplished storytellers may dominate a storytelling session. Although the members of the group may add to what these persons have to say, they will customarily defer to these "specialists." "It is João who knows all about my Padrinho's miracles," people assure me. Or, "If you want to hear about my Padrinho's life you will have to ask Maria."

Such "master tellers" clearly enjoy the status storytelling gives them.

But while they often serve as catalysts jogging the memories of others who enrich the session, they also represent a homogenizing force. Should someone express doubt about some detail, it will usually be João or Maria who renders judgment on "how it really was." These individuals may interrupt a storyteller in order to correct a supposed error or to insert a detail he or she considers important. ("Hey, you're forgetting the part where my Padrinho returns the rancher's change!")

This growing specialization or "ownership" of a symbolic property is by no means total, and most pilgrims are as likely as residents to reject modifications in certain sorts of tales. By and large, however, visitors to Juazeiro are far more disposed than residents to let a clearly gifted storyteller speak in the name of the group.

Pilgrims are more dependent not only on "specialists" who may originate or disseminate these sorts of details, but also on printed *cordel* texts. It is probably no coincidence that two of the three stories most popular among visitors—the rancher who asked for rain and the girl transformed into a dog—are readily available in pamphlet form.

Stories in verse known interchangeably as *literatura de cordel* or *folhetos* are the work of authors with little or no formal education.[25] Still printed on rustic presses in various parts of the Northeast, these booklets have served the region's poor as a primary source of information, entertainment, and moral counsel for the last century. Because many of the poet's customers were illiterate, the first vendors routinely chanted their verses in the weekly fair.[26] Attracted by this performance as well as by appealing cover illustrations, buyers would take home the tale to a literate friend or relative, who would re-perform it for the group.

Storytellers' tendency to quote at length from these printed versions confirms their importance. The widespread use of Coronel Irineu as the name for the rancher who demands rain and of Isaura for the girl whom Padre Cícero turns into a dog also points to the *cordel*'s role in the transmission of certain stories. Although the individual who employs the

25. There is an extensive bibliography on the Brazilian *literatura de cordel*. For an overview of the tradition with emphasis on recent developments see Candace Slater, *Stories on a String: The Brazilian "Literatura de Cordel."* A comprehensive bibliography is provided on pp. 275–300. For a discussion of the relationship between oral and written versions of the Padre Cícero stories see Slater, "Oral and Written Pilgrim Tales from Northeast Brazil." See also Claude L. Hulet, "Padre Cícero: Algumas Repercussões na Literatura de Cordel," in Hulet, ed., *Encruzilhadas/Crossroads: First Symposium on Portuguese Traditions, June 1–2, 1978*, 1, pp. 17–29.

26. The practice of chanting verses aloud has largely disappeared, due to changes in the traditional weekly market system. It survives in various "Northeastern" fairs in southern industrial cities. *Folheto* illustrations now include both traditional blockprints or *xilogravuras* and comic-book-like covers.

names assigned by poets to these personages need not have read the cor-responding *folheto,* there is a good chance that he or she has been in contact with someone familiar with the text.

Not all miracle tales are available in *cordel* form, and the existence of a *folheto* does not guarantee widespread acceptance among storytellers. For instance, although there is a printed version of the resurrection of the man from São Pedro, few pilgrims tell the story. A *cordel* edition of an already popular incident does, however, tend to intensify its appeal. At the same time it encourages a degree of relative standardization. Orally transmitted stories of the rancher who asked for rain (number 2 among visitors in terms of popularity) and of the unbeliever transformed into a dog (number 3) reveal considerably less variation than the tale of the girl eaten by a mountain lion (number 1), of which no *folheto* version exists. The existence of a "book" can also make some people feel more confi-dent about a story's truth. I was puzzled by the number of pilgrims who insisted that they had seen the girl transformed into a dog "in the fair where I live" until I finally realized that these persons were referring to a picture on a cover of a *cordel* pamphlet.[27]

INCREASING ABSTRACTION AND USE OF FANTASTIC DETAIL

The growing distance between pilgrims and Padre Cícero makes the priest less central to their stories. Whereas local storytellers ordinarily devote at least a third of any given narrative to him, this percentage drops to a fifth—sometimes less—in the case of pilgrims. Not infrequently a non-resident will go on for thirty sentences before mentioning Padre Cícero. Sometimes the priest appears only at the conclusion of a tale.

Details are not necessarily lacking in pilgrims' accounts. The tellers may offer lengthy descriptions of the ranch ruined by a storm or the homeward journey of the woman to whom the priest gives a penny. Nonetheless, they seldom treat the figure of Padre Cícero with the de-gree of specificity that residents do.

As a result, pilgrim storytellers are usually less successful in creating a sense of the priest as a physical being. Because statues and pictures of Padre Cícero abound, most of these individuals are quite able to describe him on request. Almost no visitor, however, refers spontaneously to the priest's eyes or hair or voice or leaps up to imitate his way of walking. When I asked residents about the size and nature of the hat Padre Cícero tossed up against the schoolhouse wall, each—true to form—had a dif-

27. The cover pictures an individual who is half girl, half dog. Although the existence of a printed version of a story increases some people's confidence in the tale's truth, others are suspicious of *cordel* authors. "It is the poet's livelihood to make ten words of one," several people told me.

ferent answer. "It was a straw hat with a little brim like this," one said with an expressive rounding of the hands. "No, no, it was a black felt hat of the sort that priests wore in the old days, only smaller," another insisted. Pilgrims seldom had this sort of concrete response. "I never really thought about it," several of them admitted. "But what does it matter?" others demanded in surprise.

At the same time that the priest begins to lose his more specific physical attributes in visitors' stories he becomes less mobile. Accordingly, the pilgrims' narratives we have seen in preceding chapters reveal an impoverished store of action verbs. Padre Cícero continues to "arrive" and "return," but he ceases the galloping, stomping, and pounding that make him such an energetic presence in residents' tales. This is not to say that visitors' stories are devoid of motion but, rather, that the priest has ceased to do the moving. Although he remains essential to the narrative, his activities are limited almost exclusively to speaking. The ubiquity of the verb "to say" suggests that, for pilgrims, he is first and foremost an authoritative voice.

In much the same vein, visitors, unlike residents, devote scant attention to when and where a particular incident occurs. Although detailed descriptions of the road to Juazeiro are common, exchanges between Padre Cícero and other personages almost always take place in an unnamed location. The priest himself thus comes to serve as setting as well as destination in many of these tales.

Lacking the background information that is common knowledge among residents, pilgrims are often tempted to reset their stories in a more fantastic universe. Instead of talking about how Padre Cícero builds a wall to protect Juazeiro from attacking soldiers during the Revolution of 1913–14, for example, they may portray him as descending from a cloud with a red rose pinned over his heart. Not content to have the priest simply open a locked door in Rome, they will speak of how he first battles a tribe of wild Indians, subdues a fire-breathing dragon, or tames a dozen fierce lions that just happen to be sitting on the doorstep of the church. Often the staircase "the color of new corn" becomes a shimmering expanse of crystal set with pearls. The baby who takes the place of Dona Quinou's own child in pilgrims' versions of the birth story may float down from heaven dressed in a tiny silver suit.[28]

Pilgrims' tendency to draw on their own imagination in the absence of more concrete details sets their stories apart from normal conversa-

28. Specialty shops in Juazeiro offer a portrait of a child, clad in a Little Lord Fauntleroy–like suit, whom they (mistakenly) insist is the young Padre Cícero. The photograph is particularly popular among pilgrims who see it as confirmation of their versions of the birth story. (A reproduction appears on page 138.)

A portrait said to be Padre Cícero as a child. The photograph is popular among pilgrims but less so among residents, who tend to doubt its authenticity.

Padre Cicero Romão Batista, aos 4 anos de idade, em 1848

tion. Unlike residents, visitors often utilize a formal narrative frame. Lead-ins such as the following call attention to the story's extraordinary nature while identifying its source.

35. I heard the tale that I am about to tell from my grandmother. She came to Juazeiro on foot every year until she could no longer walk. I used to sleep in her house, and so I heard all the stories she knew. Well then, one of the stories she always used to tell was about the girl who turned into a snake and this is how it goes. . . .
    —Carolina Pereira dos Santos (P). Recife, Pernambuco, 1941.
    Separated; laundress. 2 pilgrimages. (September 20, 1982.)

36. When my father was a boy he used to go with his parents to Juazeiro as part of one of these big pilgrimages. So then one of the pilgrims turned out to be the brother of that girl the mountain lion had gotten, you know? He told my father all about how his sister had been eaten by the mountain lion. He said that. . . .
    —Manoel do Nascimento Silva (P). Currais Novo, Rio Grande do Norte, 1939. Widowed; peddler. 11 pilgrimages. (September 24, 1982.)

37. I am going to tell you a story I heard from an old lady who is my neighbor. She lived for many years in Juazeiro and for this reason she knows many good stories. In the past, we used to wash clothes

together in the river. So then I always used to say, "Oh, Dona
Ana, tell us another story about my Padrinho Cícero." So then
once she told me this story about my Padrinho when he was a little
boy which I am going to tell you right now. Listen. . . .
—Rosa Maria Vieira de Oliveira (P). Altos, Piauí, 1937. Married;
rendeira. 3 pilgrimages. (September 27, 1982.)

Pilgrims are also more disposed than residents to conclude their stories with an explicit moral. "And so you see," the teller may say, "that
girl turned into a snake because the person who makes fun of my Padrinho is always punished." "My Padrinho saved that child from drowning," another will observe, "because he always helps the person who puts
his trust in him." This sort of formal summation not only reemphasizes
the general lesson to be learned from the specific instance but also calls
attention to the story as a special sort of discourse set apart both from
normal speech and from the normal course of life. Thus, in contrast to
residents who set out to locate the miraculous within the bounds of
everyday experience, pilgrims seek to underscore their tales' extraordinary quality.

FOCUS ON THE PILGRIMAGE AND INDIVIDUAL PILGRIMS

In the same way that local tellers insist on the role of Juazeiro in a
given story, visitors try to write the pilgrimage into their tales. Not one
of the protagonists in the three most frequently told stories (the girl devoured by a mountain lion, the rancher who asks for rain, the unbeliever
transformed into a dog) is a resident of the Cariri.

Instead, in these and other pilgrims' narratives, it is visitors to
Juazeiro who occupy a special place. The rancher who asks for rain, for
instance, relies on a pilgrim to deliver his message to the priest. The
travelers who leave a girl sleeping on a mountainside find that they must
answer to Padre Cícero. Likewise, although the story of the guinea pig
features a resident of Juazeiro, many pilgrims begin or end with a relative's description of the animals who used to run free in the Horto.
"They were my Padrinho's pets," one old man explains, "and I can remember how my father used to pack a little sack of corn meal especially
for them. When he came home from Juazeiro he always told us children
about the *mocozinhos* and we would dream of the day that we could see
them for ourselves."[29]

Although I have already noted that non-residents are generally less

29. Lívio Alves de Oliveira (P). Monteiro, Paraíba, 1911. Widower; *rendeiro*. 6 pilgrimages.
(November 19, 1982.)

interested in details than are local storytellers, they prove adamant about anything pertaining to the pilgrimage. In residents' versions of the tale of the young hunter, for instance, the initially skeptical father almost always ends his days in Juazeiro. Visitors to the city, however, take care to record the old man's return home and, thus, his continuing identity as a pilgrim. Unlike local storytellers, who refer to the tale of "Coronel Manuel Fernandes" (the father), visitors are likely to place greater emphasis on his son. "This is the story of a young hunter," they often say by way of introduction.

In a similar manner, pilgrims almost always present the would-be assassin not as a local landowner but as a visitor to Juazeiro. Accounts of Padre Cícero's rescue of a drowning girl often cast the child's father as a doubting pilgrim.

Four of the five tales told primarily by visitors to Juazeiro focus on a traveler who requests the priest's assistance. The narrative I heard most frequently from pilgrims concerns the girl devoured by a mountain lion. We have already seen that local storytellers, for whom the tale occupies second-to-last instead of first place, usually focus on the young traveler who becomes a resident of Juazeiro. When pilgrims recount the tale, they are inevitably more interested in the interaction between her and the other members of the group. Visitors' close identification with the story often results in changes that reflect the teller's circumstances. Sometimes the speaker presents the girl as a pregnant woman who cannot keep up with her fellow travelers. On other occasions she becomes an infirm old lady who develops a limp. When some members of the group complain to Padre Cícero about the woman's slowness, he points out to them that they too will be old and infirm one day. "Better to have callused feet than a hard heart," a white-haired listener may interject.

In other pilgrims' versions of this story, fear of potential injury to their own reputations leads the girl's companions to abandon her. When they reach their destination, Padre Cícero reprimands them. "I can understand your fear of gossip," he often says, "but you left a fellow traveler to be devoured by a mountain lion and so you have not acted as a pilgrim should."

Because these stories speak directly to their own situation as visitors to Juazeiro, the tellers are likely to repeat them over and over. They may go so far as to adopt the tales as a conscious model for their own behavior. "And so," says one man in concluding his account of the girl and the mountain lion, "we must always think of others when we set out upon a pilgrimage. Now João here is a donkey, but he too is a pilgrim, so I will wait to tell him my opinion of his donkey-ness until we are back home."[30]

Because of their relative distance from Padre Cícero, visitors to Juazeiro seldom attempt to sandwich personal memories of the priest into their versions of the best-known tales. These same storytellers, however, regularly incorporate recollections of some pilgrim or pilgrimage into their accounts.

Sometimes the speaker casts a friend or relative as an eyewitness. "My husband used to buy and sell things near where the rancher who asked for rain lived and he saw the house all smashed to pieces from the storm," one woman says.[31] "I never met that man who sent for rain," another comments, "but when I was ten years old my aunt made a pilgrimage to Juazeiro and she saw him weeping at my Padrinho's feet."[32] "It was the father of one of my best friends—Seu Manuel Ferreira—who took that shameless message to my Padrinho," a man asserts. "He now lives in Lagoa de Gato but in those days he lived in Brejinho. And he says that when he passed by that rancher's place on his way home from Juazeiro there was no longer so much as a blade of grass."[33]

Pilgrims, like residents, will occasionally write themselves or persons close to them into a familiar story. One man insists that his grandfather was the organizer of the group that included the young traveler eaten by a mountain lion. Another claims that he once had to run from the girl the priest had turned into a dog, when she showed up at a weekly fair. Still another asserts that the woman to whom Padre Cícero gave the miraculous penny was none other than his mother, who made her way across the sun-baked interior lands to Juazeiro during the great drought of 1915.

Because of their limited contact with Padre Cícero, visitors to Juazeiro are less likely than residents to question the truth of any tale. Simple asides, however, are fairly common in those stories that bear on the pilgrimage. A storyteller who claims that his Uncle Pedro once spent

30. Antonio Francisco da Silva (P). Limoeiro, Pernambuco, 1934. Married; farmer (own land). 11 pilgrimages. (September 27, 1982.)
31. Maria Cecília da Silva Santos (P). Surubim, Pernambuco, 1948. Married; rendeira. 12 pilgrimages. (October 15, 1982.)
32. Adélia Barbosa de Freitas (P). Boqueirão, Paraíba, 1923. Married; moradora. 8 pilgrimages. (September 14, 1982.)
33. José Antonio de Lima (P). Lagoa de Gato, Pernambuco, 1942. Single; morador. 8 pilgrimages. (November 21, 1982.)

the night at the house of the rancher who asked for rain is quite capable of going on to describe the dozen other locations where his uncle stopped along the way to Juazeiro. The woman whose brother-in-law was "so bad that they called him 'Tony Rattlesnake'" is just as likely to get caught up in a catalogue of his terrible deeds. In the process she may forget that she originally set out to tell of his supposed encounter with the would-be assassin.

Digression within the story proper is nevertheless far less common among pilgrims than among residents. Although visitors often allude to their own or relatives' experiences, they are inclined to limit these comments to explanatory prefaces or conclusions of the type that we have already seen. As a result, the body of the tale is generally freer of competing themes or tangents and the underlying challenge structure is more immediately clear.

PRESENCE OF AN ORDERING PRINCIPLE

Memories of the journey to Juazeiro and of individual travelers add color and momentum to a number of the best-known narratives. It is difficult, however, for most pilgrim storytellers to incorporate the adventures of their Uncle Pedro into an account of Padre Cícero's trip to Rome. Unlike residents, who usually personalize one incident as easily as another, they often make an implicit distinction between those tales that do and those that do not deal in some way with the journey to Juazeiro.

Even if the teller knows nothing about the specific incidents that bear upon the pilgrimage, he or she can nonetheless make a connection between these stories and his or her own experience. The individual who sets out to talk about the girl who turns into a dog, for instance, may go on to describe a woman in the city of Aroeira whom Padre Cícero recently turned into a pig or snake as punishment for doubting his continued powers. ("I didn't see her but my cousin works right next to a dance hall where she created a terrible ruckus.") The person who tells the well-known story of the would-be assassin may preface his or her account with a description of a similar attempt on the life of one of the priest's followers in the Rio Grande do Norte ("And so you see, even today . . ."). The story of the child Padre Cícero fished out of a well may prompt an account of a friend or neighbor who escaped an otherwise disastrous explosion by shouting, "Help me, my Padrinho!"

Because the narratives in our second subgroup do not bear upon the pilgrimage experience, their tellers find these stories considerably harder to relate to their own lives. The characters who people these tales—Dona Quinou, Dr. Floro, Maria de Araújo—are to most of these individuals only names. As a result, the tellers find themselves obliged to treat these incidents not as personal experience but as fact. The stories—Cícero's birth, the hat that stuck to the wall, the alleged transformation, the trip to Rome, the mute boy, the "war" of 1913–14, the confrontation with Dr. Floro, and the empty tomb—are usually briefer, more abstract, and more prone to fantastic detail than the other well-known incidents. They are also more likely to reveal causal as well as chronological links among themselves.

Considering the visitors' distance from these incidents, the increased brevity and abstraction of their accounts is hardly surprising. At the same time, these stories all reveal an unmistakable negative challenge structure. Unlike residents, who usually treat the stories of Padre Cícero's birth, of the hat that stuck to the wall, and of the empty tomb as affirmations or explanations of those miraculous powers directly evident in other tales, pilgrims are more likely to recast these tales as punishments of unbelievers.

Most local storytellers, for example, portray the relationship between Padre Cícero and his allegedly adoptive mother as one of affection. For them, Dona Quinou's blindness is a sort of divine given.[34] We have seen that the priest may temporarily restore her vision to allow her to see the Horto church, gently taking her arm when her eyes begin to cloud again. Such stories contrast markedly with others told by pilgrims, in which Quinou's loss of sight becomes a punishment. The following speaker clearly regards the birth story as a negative challenge in which Quinou (called "Janoca" here) rejects the infant Cícero and thus incurs immediate retribution.

38. People say that my Padrinho Cícero's mother gave birth to a son. And then, shortly afterward when she was sleeping, a woman all in blue arrived to ask if she did not want to exchange her child for the one she was holding in her arms. So then, still in that dream, you see, Dona Janoca said that she was not interested in any sort of trade. Then when she awoke, she went to look at her child. And she saw that he was not hers. So then she began shouting that the child was an animal, that she wanted nothing to do with this kind

---

34. At times an implicit sense of complementarity is evident in residents' stories of the blinding, in which Padre Cícero's powers as a seer or *vidente* appear linked in some manner to his mother's (or foster mother's) loss of sight.

of monster. And it was in that very moment that Dona Janoca
lost her sight.

—Rosalva Lima de Souza (P). Umbuzeiro, Paraíba, 1939. Widowed;
moradora. 6 pilgrimages. (November 20, 1982.)

The same sort of shift from an explanation to a negative challenge is
apparent in many pilgrims' versions of the hat that stuck to the wall.
Because of their desire to emphasize the innate quality of Padre Cícero's
miraculous powers, local storytellers frequently present the hat as just
one of a series of similar illustrations. Often they go on to describe how
the young priest brands a lamb with his finger or with pen and ink instead of a branding iron. They may portray him floating down a river on
a handkerchief on which he sits as if it were a raft, or plucking a star
from the sky for a toy, or constructing a miniature church from the twigs
of a lemon tree while the other children turn cartwheels or play tag.[35]

Pilgrims are usually considerably less interested in Padre Cícero's
innate powers than in the relationship between him and his fellow
schoolmates. Unlike residents, who often underscore the astonishment
or admiration of the other children, they describe the youngsters' taunts
and jibes. In contrast to local storytellers' descriptions of the child Cícero
as *todo diferente,* "completely different from others," they frequently char-
acterize him as *sofredor,* "one who suffers." The children in the following
visitor's story treat the future priest with the same injustice that will be
his lot as an adult. The concluding assertion, "and that was the beginning
of my Padrinho's persecutions," sets up this incident as the first in an
extended narrative progression.

39. When my Padrinho was a little boy he liked to pray beneath an
    orange tree. So then the other children decided to go tattling to the
    teacher. "Oh Dona, Cícero goes and stands beneath that orange
    tree every day on the way to school."
    "Don't you worry about Cícero," she said. "He is a good student.
    You just let him be."
    So then the children got very angry. "Let's really get him in
    trouble," they said. And they went and left him no place to hang
    his hat. When my Padrinho arrived in school, he saw that all
    the hooks were taken. So then he went and tossed his little hat up
    against the wall and there it stayed. The other children practically
    died of envy.

35. For examples of similar activities ascribed to medieval saints see C. Grant Loomis,
White Magic: An Introduction to the Folklore of Christian Legends, pp. 15–26.

"You are going to pay us, Cicinho," they whispered. *And that was the beginning of my Padrinho's persecutions* [my italics].
—Isidoro da Conceição (P). Genipapo, Bahia, 1911. [Marital status unknown]; farmer (own land). 7 pilgrimages. (November 1, 1982.)

Pilgrims may posit not only chronological but also causal links between miraculous episodes. Dona Quinou's initial hostility toward the future priest is echoed in his playmates' desire to get him into trouble with the teacher. Padre Cícero's role in the alleged transformation of a host into the blood of Christ generates false rumors that prompt the pope to summon him to Rome. When the priest proceeds to outshine a number of highly placed church authorities by opening a door that none of them can budge, the bishop of Fortaleza demands that he restore a mute boy's speech. Following the child's revelation that his father is none other than this same bishop, the latter declares war on Juazeiro. Padre Cícero's naming of Dr. Floro as his chief lieutenant in this Revolution of 1913–14 gives the doctor a thirst for power, and this leads him to betray his benefactor. Even the priest's death many years later does not put an end to others' envy. Continuing resentment of Padre Cícero's powers motivates the bishop of Crato to attempt to steal his body.

The theme of unjust persecution reiterated in these incidents invites the listener to see the priest's sufferings in terms of other people's jealousy and fear. This explanation makes considerable sense to people accustomed to watching powerful patrons battle their rivals for hegemony. Moreover, one needs no knowledge of history, politics, or church doctrine to comprehend the basic, if base, emotions that motivate Padre Cícero's opponents in this emerging master legend or latter-day "saint's life."

Not all pilgrims run one or more of these episodes together to form a single tale. Nevertheless, my recordings document a significant number of meaningful associations between incidents that remain autonomous in the case of local storytellers. Furthermore, although only about a quarter of all the pilgrims with whom I spoke posit these sorts of links between individual episodes, this percentage rises to well over a third in the case of persons who, because they are under the age of fifty, could not possibly have known Padre Cícero. Younger persons' greater tendency to associate two or more usually separate stories suggests that we are dealing with a phenomenon likely to grow more marked over time.

TENDENCY TOWARD DEVELOPMENT OF A "LIFE"

On the surface, visitors to Juazeiro appear to have a weaker sense of history than residents of the city, whose stories are more firmly rooted in documentable persons and events. We have seen how the absence of concrete personal memories sometimes disposes pilgrims to embark on flights of fancy.

And yet, despite their stories' tenuous relationship to the facts as scholars know them, visitors have a much more fully developed concept of Padre Cícero as a historical personage. Although they may insert themselves or a relative into a pilgrimage-related story, they consign other tales to a past that is largely the product of a group evaluation. While disagreeing from time to time on the details of individual stories, a significant number of visitors employ a framework that orders and gives meaning to otherwise isolated events. The resulting master tale or "life" is not only a record of significant events but is also an explanation of their causes. As such, it comes to function as a communal myth.

The emergence of a unified narrative progression is a logical result both of pilgrims' decreased proximity to Padre Cícero and of their involvement in the journey to Juazeiro, which involves movement in space and time. Their openness to a more or less standard narrative does not mean that they are inherently more public-spirited than local storytellers, but rather that their needs and wishes are in some ways very different.

For people who are not bombarded daily with reminders of Padre Cícero, a "life" serves as a necessary introduction to the priest. It provides a ready-made answer when a six-year-old child in Rio Grande do Norte or Alagoas asks, "Grandfather, who is that old man with the funny hat in that picture on your wall?"

Then, too, pilgrims do not encounter the sorts of difficulties faced by local storytellers in disentangling their own lives from that of Padre Cícero. The distancing many residents resist with such tenacity has already been imposed on visitors to Juazeiro and is not a matter of choice. Because they usually must draw on a more limited number of stories, pilgrims also have less trouble in selection. For them, talking about the priest is less like talking about a parent, whose name conjures up a flood of powerful, often highly visual memories, than it is like discussing a grandfather who died many years before their birth. Although they have grown up with strong positive feelings about Padre Cícero, he is for many a face to whom a personality has not yet been attached.

Unlike residents, for whom storytelling is an essentially circular process of re-creation, non-residents are likely to adopt a linear approach. Their stories are therefore not a form of repeated circumambulation but an attempt to connect a series of episodes that would otherwise function much as random dots on an experiential page. The goal-directed progression of the "life" suggests the journey, toward a designated destination, upon which as pilgrims they consciously embark. For them, a master legend represents not an impoverishment of experience through fixation and definition, but the construction of a past that would otherwise not exist.

A "life" of Padre Cícero also provides justification for the journey to Juazeiro in the face of the church's continued rejection of the priest. People who might otherwise have little to say to one another can thus unite in the ambitious venture of creation of a "saint." Because pilgrims' ability to transcend personal interests in the name of Padre Cícero is a source of pride as well as pleasure, they are far more apt than residents to accept another's version of a given story.

At the same time that this emerging narrative provides a rallying point for total strangers on their way to Juazeiro, it allows people back home to reaffirm their identity as followers of the priest. We have seen that residents' stories are primarily a means of self-differentiation. Pilgrims, however, may have neighbors who are spiritists or Protestants or simply skeptics. They therefore have a strong incentive to band together with others in meeting outside challenges to a common faith.

Precisely because it is often their peers whose doubts or disbelief visitors feel compelled to counter, they are apt to transform the powerful *coronéis* of residents' stories into people more like themselves. Thus while most local storytellers present the father of the young hunter as a wealthy landowner, many pilgrims describe him as a man like "that foolish Severino, who is always laughing at my Padrinho." The girl whom the priest turns into a dog is less likely to be the daughter of a wealthy rancher than "a Protestant like Dona Rita, who prays out loud like a bleating goat and will surely come to a bad end."

This pressure to respond to doubt, if not ridicule, from non-believers also helps to explain why pilgrims stress the punitive aspects of well-known stories. Because their need to impress others with the consequences of lack of faith is considerably more acute, they often give the impression of being more vindictive. As Padre Cícero represents a vision of the world whose dissolution would result in intense emotional damage, they are far more likely than local storytellers to use their stories as a first line of defense.

Although we are unquestionably dealing with a single narrative corpus, the two groups of storytellers reveal essential differences. Residents' proximity to Padre Cícero leads them to recast even the best-known tales in the form of memories characterized by their concreteness, their concern for Juazeiro, and their random, extremely personal presentation.

Pilgrims not only favor shorter, more abstract versions of these stories but are also more inclined to weave miraculous episodes into a coherent whole whose forward motion suggests their own movement through time and space. The result is a more or less standard "life" or master legend distinguished by its public, as opposed to a tenaciously private, quality.

Josefa André Gonçalves stands at the door of her home before the third station of the cross in the Rua do Horto.

Francisca Rosa dos Santos listens to her stepdaughter, Josefa André Gonçalves. The hat hanging above her head belonged to her husband, Manuel, who has been dead for several years now. It remains on the wall to assure his continued presence.

Olívia Josefa da Conceição listens to her husband, José Ferreira da Silva, reminisce about his encounters, as a young man, with Padre Cícero.

Pedro Ribeiro da Silva recounts the story of the carpenter who fell from the Horto church.

Maria Aparecida da Silva cleans rice in a sieve. The soda bottles to her left are for sale to passersby. Note the rosary about her neck.

Maria Josefa dos Santos tells the story of the enchanted grove.

Maria Angélica de Jesus, a lover of *cordel* stories, and a young friend.

Oreliana Maria da Conceição, known to her neighbors as Maria dos Benditos, in the door of her home in the upper portion of the Rua do Horto. On the right side of the house is a mural of the New Jerusalem. A paper flag of Brazil is pasted over the door.

A pilgrim and her small daughter pause in the doorway of Dona Maria dos Benditos' home to ask for water. Dona Maria offers them as a remembrance the printed text of a hymn she has written.

The owner of a makeshift canteen in the Rua do Horto talks with a passerby on a sunny afternoon.

A woman selling bread toward the top of the Rua do Horto. Part of the Cariri Valley is visible in the distance.

Newcomer in the Promised Land. A man with all his possessions packed into two brightly painted wooden suitcases pauses to rest beneath a tree in the Rua do Horto. The sacks contain rice and beans.

A man rides down the Rua do Horto past a group of neighbors who are setting up a makeshift stall to sell refreshments to pilgrims.

A child weaves a straw hat beside a pile of bricks near the top of the Rua do Horto.

Beggars and vendors sit beneath the twelfth station of the cross.

A vendor offers souvenirs of Juazeiro: dolls, key chains, plastic birds and flowers. Pictures of Padre Cícero and the candidates of two opposing political parties are affixed to his display. (Courtesy Tânia Quaresma.)

A *cordel* vendor offers his wares to
pilgrims in a *rancho*. The woman in
the background is dressed much like
the dancers in an Afro-Brazilian cult
service.

A pilgrim from Alagoas tells the story
of Padre Cícero's birth. She is smoking a clay pipe.

The interior of a *rancho*. The hallway is lined with hammocks and the kitchen is in the background.

Pilgrims raise their hats outside the chapel of Our Lady of Perpetual Help on All Souls' Day. It was cameramen who urged the presiding priests to bless the hats in order to create a striking image for national television, but these same reporters now refer to this innovation as "the traditional blessing of the hats."

An old woman from the backlands of Paraíba smiles while her neighbor from Bahia weeps.

Pilgrim from Rio Grande do Norte in the church of Our Lady of Sorrows.

Pilgrims from Sergipe in the truck that will take them home.

PART THREE

VARIATIONS: THREE TALES

V.

The Revolution of 1913–14

And thanks to my Padrinho's miraculous powers, holy
Juazeiro was triumphant.
                                    Resident of Juazeiro

His enemies would fall away but the pilgrimage would
continue. That is the story of the war of 1914.
                                    Pilgrim from Pernambuco

The division between residents and pilgrims outlined in the last
section is in no way static. It reflects two distinct but equally
dynamic approaches to the creation of a single, personally meaningful
Padre Cícero. This and following chapters offer illustrations of the specific forms these separate approaches may assume.

Each of the three narratives offered for discussion presents a somewhat different set of problems. In the first example, the Revolution of
1913–14, pilgrims' and residents' emphases on opposing aspects of the
same story produce tales much alike in structure but often quite different
in content. In the second instance, the confrontation between Padre Cícero and Dr. Floro, pilgrims' greater distance from the doctor allows
them to employ the standard challenge scheme. Because this framework
poses certain problems for residents, the tales reveal potentially more
serious modifications. The third example, the alleged transformation of
1889, is by far the most dramatic. In this case, differences not only in
content but also in underlying structure become clear.[1]

1. Although most studies of transformations in historical material are diachronic rather
than synchronic, they may be helpful in understanding differences within the Padre Cícero
tale corpus. The work of Américo Paredes is particularly useful: see his *"With His Pistol in
His Hand": A Border Ballad and Its Hero;* his "Folklore e historia. Dos cantares de la frontera
del norte"; and his "José Mosqueda and the Folklorization of Actual Events." Other studies
of interest include Moacyr Flores, "Sepe Tiaraju: Lenda, mito e história"; and Bess Lomax
Hawes, *"El corrido de la inundación de la Presa de San Francisquito:* The Story of a Local

This chapter and the following two begin with a brief description of the event or persons on which the stories are based. I have tried to keep this identification to a minimum. Although it is essential to know what actually happened in order to appreciate the ways storytellers tailor the past to their own specifications, my primary interest remains the stories in and of themselves.

The Revolution of 1913–14

Most of the people who fought in the Revolution or "war" of 1913–14 are no longer alive, but memories of the days when government soldiers marched on Juazeiro have not died.[2] Both residents and pilgrims take pride in the confrontation they see as a single-handed victory for the all-powerful Padre Cícero. The fighting that actually occurred between December of 1913 and January of 1914, however, reflects much broader political developments on both the state and the national level. Since these developments are extremely complicated, I will summarize only the most important.[3]

In 1911 the governor of Ceará was Antonio Pinto Nogueira Accioly, an old-style oligarch. Although Accioly had controlled the state's political machinery since 1888, an increasingly powerful middle class was challenging his hold. In response, the governor sought to garner support among the lower classes by naming Padre Cícero as third vice-president of Ceará. This measure, which did not give the priest any real say in state affairs, pleased the populace but was not enough to prevent Accioly's overthrow in December of 1912. Although the Brazilian chief executive, Marshal Hermes da Fonseca, ordered that the governor be restored to office, neither he nor Senator José Gomes de Pinheiro Machado, the true power behind the presidency, had any intention of enforcing the directive. Instead, they hoped to find someone who could succeed Accioly within the confines of the existing political structure. When the ex-

---

Ballad." See also Clemente Saenz García, "Una excursión bibliográfica: El ángel de Cascajar (leyenda soriana)," in which the author traces the treatment over centuries of a miracle that supposedly occurred in San Esteban de Gormaz during the Reconquest.

2. The Revolution is known as the "Sedition" of 1913–14 by Padre Cícero's opponents: see Rodolfo Teófilo, *A Sedição do Joazeiro*. See also Antônio Gomes de Araújo, "À margem de 'À margem da história do Ceará,'" and José Maria Bello, *A History of Modern Brazil, 1889–1964*, pp. 21–22, for negative comments on Padre Cícero's role in the confrontation.

3. For a more complete discussion of the Revolution, including relevant bibliographical material, see Ralph della Cava, *Miracle at Joaseiro*, pp. 145–189; I am once again heavily indebted to della Cava in my presentation of the facts. Another account worth consulting is Irineu Pinheiro, *O Joaseiro do Padre Cícero e a Revolução de 1914*.

governor's supporters realized that Rio de Janeiro had betrayed them, they threw their support to the opposition candidate, Lt. Col. Marcos Franco Rabelo, who thus won the election.

The alliance that brought Franco Rabelo to power in July of 1913 soon disintegrated, leaving the so-called *rabelistas* on one side and the opposing *marretas* on the other.[4] Conflict between these factions became increasingly evident throughout the state. In Juazeiro the dissident wing of the *marreta* party, presided over by Padre Cícero's political advisor, Dr. Floro Bartolomeu da Costa, supported João Bezerra de Menezes against the *rabelista* candidate for mayor. After Bezerra de Menezes triumphed, he promptly turned on Floro, inviting Franco Rabelo to send his military police into the Cariri. Even though the soldiers' official mission was to control the outlaws known as *cangaceiros*, their presence represented a thinly disguised challenge to Padre Cícero's authority. Franco Rabelo's subsequent participation in an interstate campaign against these outlaws, whom the Cariri's old-style landowners had traditionally recruited and protected, confirmed his hostility.[5]

Never one to waste time, Floro set about convincing the Crato landowner Antonio Luis Alves Pequeno III, a cousin of Accioly and the son of Padre Cícero's godfather, to join him in a counterattack on the governor. Rio de Janeiro readily endorsed Floro's plan to depose Franco Rabelo because the latter had defeated Pinheiro Machado's candidate in 1912. The first step was to be the election of Floro as president of the state legislative assembly in a special rump session held in Juazeiro, but fighting broke out before this plan could be put into effect. As early as September of 1913, the *rabelista* mayor of Crato threatened to invade Juazeiro. The ensuing arrival of fresh troops from Fortaleza made armed confrontation certain.

Padre Cícero, who had been elected mayor of Juazeiro in 1911, initially refused to take any action against the troops. As the government's hostile intentions became clearer, however, Floro succeeded in getting the priest to order his followers to build a wall of earth and stone encircling

4. *Marreta*, a stonemason's hammer, was the name originally adopted by Accioly's supporters.

5. The term *cangaceiro* comes from *canga*, "yoke," and refers to the way rural bandits slung their rifles across their backs. There is a lengthy bibliography on *cangaceiros* both as a group and as individuals. For an introduction see Amaury de Souza, "The Cangaço and the Politics of Violence in Northeast Brazil." A portrait of the single most famous *cangaceiro* is provided by Billy Jaynes Chandler in *The Bandit King: Lampião of Brazil*. For a study of Lampião in folk literature see Ronald Daus, *Der Epische Zyklus der Cangaceiros in der Volkspoesie Nordost-Brasiliens*. Further works are listed under *cangaceiro* in Robert M. Levine, *Brazil: An Annotated Bibliography for Social Historians*.

the city. On December 20, the day after completion of the six-foot-high wall, the state forces quartered in Crato invaded. They were repulsed some fifteen hours later, but because Padre Cícero would not authorize a counteroffensive, the siege dragged on for over a month. Only when heavy reinforcements from Fortaleza began arriving in Crato in preparation for a second assault on Juazeiro did the priest agree to attack. Crato fell on January 24; Barbalha, three days later. Despite the priest's express orders against looting, considerable theft and destruction of property occurred. Floro's military aides then began their march on Fortaleza, entering the capital on March 19. Once under fire, the *rabelista* regime fell with little bloodshed. Some two months later, Benjamin Liberato Barroso, an army officer acceptable to Marshal Hermes and Pinheiro Machado, assumed the post of governor.[6]

The Revolution of 1913–14 was important to Juazeiro because it confirmed the city's independence from Crato, nominally achieved in 1911. Padre Cícero's victory signaled the emergence of the Cariri Valley as a power in state politics. Also, although the "war" worsened already bad relations between Padre Cícero and those church officials who thought priests should restrict themselves to purely religious functions, it confirmed his followers' faith in him as a miracle worker. Who else, they asked each other with triumphant certainty, could ever have defended them from such powerful attackers?

Residents' Accounts of the Revolution of 1913–14

In their high degree of personal involvement, tales of the Revolution resemble other residents' stories. If anything, they are more idiosyncratic and therefore more varied than other tales, which deal with isolated occurrences involving a limited cast of characters. The resuscitation of the man from São Pedro, for instance, occurs in a single day and features a maximum of a half-dozen actors. The birth story, which unfolds in the space of an hour, focuses on three or four persons. Because the actual Revolution of 1913–14 spanned at least a month, affecting the entire population of the Cariri Valley, accounts of this event necessarily differ.

A number of older individuals have vivid childhood recollections— which may, of course, be mixed with fantasy—of the government attack. "I remember," says one woman now in her seventies, "how a bullet sliced the cord that held my uncle's hammock. He was sleeping but woke up with a start when he hit the floor. I was only six years old but I can

6. For a description of the effects of the Revolution on state politics see della Cava, *Miracle at Joaseiro*, pp. 157–161.

Figure 4. Double Challenge in Revolution of 1913–14 Tale

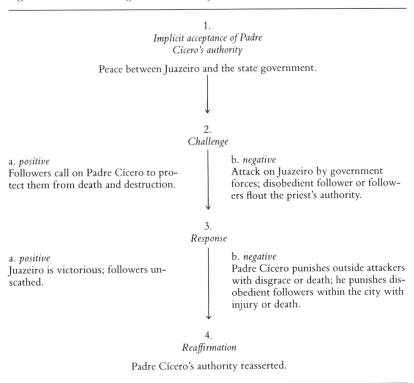

1.
*Implicit acceptance of Padre
Cícero's authority*
Peace between Juazeiro and the state government.

2.
Challenge

a. *positive*
Followers call on Padre Cícero to protect them from death and destruction.

b. *negative*
Attack on Juazeiro by government
forces; disobedient follower or followers flout the priest's authority.

3.
Response

a. *positive*
Juazeiro is victorious; followers un-
scathed.

b. *negative*
Padre Cícero punishes outside attackers
with disgrace or death; he punishes disobedient followers within the city with
injury or death.

4.
Reaffirmation
Padre Cícero's authority reasserted.

remember the zing-zing-zing of the soldiers' bullets as if it were yesterday."[7] Storytellers who are themselves too young to recall the event often
incorporate relatives' descriptions of the defense of Juazeiro into an otherwise conventional account.

The larger than usual amount of personal material at many residents'
disposal does not preclude the existence of a basic story line. Tales of the
Revolution customarily begin with an affront to the priest's authority by
soldiers either from Fortaleza or from neighboring Crato. Padre Cícero
meets this threat by directing his followers to construct a protective wall
of stone around Juazeiro. The soldiers' bullets then bounce off all but one
or two followers who ignore the priest's instructions. The defenders'
triumph and the attackers' defeat make the tale a standard double challenge, which can be diagrammed as in Figure 4.

7. Ana Rosa da Conceição (R). Salgueiro, Pernambuco, 1907. Arrived Juazeiro as child.
Widow; retired. (August 2, 1981.)

Like other residents' tales, most versions of the Revolution of 1913–14 place Padre Cícero squarely at the center of the action. The tellers are apt, however, to be as interested in the particulars of the fighting as in the priest's climactic victory. It is usual for residents to rely on concrete details, but the number of these in their accounts of the confrontation is exceptionally high.

Some people, for instance, will go on for twenty minutes about the political situation that prompted the "war." Although their explanations are seldom strictly accurate, these individuals often know the names of the key figures in the conflict and the parties they represented. They may speak at length about the deal between Dr. Floro and Pinheiro Machado or describe the goals and membership of a particular interest group.

These persons are also often very definite about the specifics of the attack. They may, for instance, give the exact dimensions of the wall that men, women, and children succeeded in erecting around the city in a mere four days. A few insisted that I not just listen to their description of the bulwark but also accompany them to gaze at the remnants, offering me a crumbling stone as proof of the fighting. An occasional storyteller would rummage through a trunk in search of a rusty rifle carried by a father or grandfather in the "war" or would produce a tattered photograph of some of the defenders.

Because of residents' general familiarity with the incident, their accounts often have an authoritative ring. In the following example, the speaker, whose family lived in Pernambuco until the 1960s and thus could not have participated in the fighting, mistakenly dates the invasion as December of 1914 instead of 1913, introduces an anachronistic airplane, and calls the governor Rabeira (a colloquial term for "rear end") instead of Rabelo. His relative restraint nonetheless succeeds in giving the story an almost documentary quality. There are two, not twenty, cannons; one, instead of a hundred, airplanes. "Many," not all 2,500, of the attackers die.

40. Franco Rabeira was a governor of the state of Ceará. He did not like my Padrinho Cícero because he himself wanted to be the most important person in all of Ceará. He wanted to be the master [literally, "owner"] of the state, understand? That is why he sent his troops to destroy Juazeiro in December of 1914. He sent 2,500 fully armed soldiers, two cannons, and an airplane. When my Padrinho learned that the soldiers were coming to Juazeiro, he ordered Dr. Floro to build a wall of stone around the city. Then he gave a rosary and a rifle to each of his followers. The soldiers

fired until all their bullets were gone but it did no good. Almost no one on my Padrinho's side died. The only ones to die were those who disobeyed him. But the soldiers were not so lucky; many soldiers died.

—Geniflides da Silva (R). Garanhuns, Pernambuco, 1961. Arrived
Juazeiro as child. Single, *cordel* vendor. (November 20, 1982.)

Even when local storytellers veer toward fantasy, they are usually careful not to go too far. A given tale may contain a greater than usual number of clearly fictive elements but the speaker will seek to root these in the here and now. The following woman, who describes the miraculous medals Padre Cícero distributed to the city's defenders, attributes this information to "three old men, Seu Zé Romeiro, Seu Cazuza, and Seu Capistrano." Although the *beato's* insouciant dance across the newly erected wall is hardly the stuff of history books, the storyteller does not picture saints or angels descending from the sky. Because the dancer is a human being who successfully taunts the soldiers, whose uniforms earn them the nickname of "monkeys" or *macacos,* the event remains within the limits of possibility. Likewise, the little donkey who leaps over the wall adds an appealing down-to-earth touch.

41. During the war of 1914 there were many proofs of my Padrinho's powers. I know because there were three old men—Seu Zé Romeiro, Seu Cazuza, and Seu Capistrano—who always used to talk about the old-timers who fought against the government soldiers. When the day arrived for my Padrinho's followers to face the enemy, he called everyone together. He blessed them and gave each a medal of Saint Benedict for protection. And he said, "Go, drink nothing, touch nothing that doesn't belong to you, and no bullet will harm you." So then his followers went to fight with the soldiers and many soldiers died. But the only one who died on his side was a boy who drank sugar rum. There was even a *beato* who danced upon the city wall. The "monkeys" [soldiers] shot at him again and again but he didn't fall. That medal around his neck made the bullets slide away like water. So then he kept on dancing on top of that wall until they almost went mad.

—Rosa Vieira da Silva (R). Baixa D'Anta, Ceará, 1924. Arrived
Juazeiro as child. Married; makes hats. (July 8, 1981.)

Storytellers whose families participated in the Revolution in some way are likely to treat this borrowed experience as if it were their own. One teller, for instance, describes how his grandparents flee the soldiers who kill "even the beggar lice" they encounter in their path. He goes on to speak of his relatives' arrival in a city in which "everyone down to the smallest child" is busy gathering stones for the protective wall. In his account, the disobedient follower is a young man who flaunts the priest's order by trying to seduce a young woman. "My grandfather," the speaker explains, "saw the bullets streak by him and thought that his end was near, but no, only that man who would not listen to my Padrinho fell." The recalcitrant defender's unhappy end contrasts with the good fortune that is the lot of the teller's family when they return to their home in the hills. "The soldiers had taken everything," he says, "but with my Padrinho's help the manioc harvest was twice as big as usual and the beans grew big as small potatoes."[8]

Although storytellers will generally use a relative's experience to supplement a well-known story, on occasion it becomes the tale itself. We have seen in the preceding chapter how a speaker who had no intention of digressing may become so caught up in a personal memory as to forget all else. The following account begins in the usual manner with a reference to the wall that rises around Juazeiro. As the woman speaks, however, her eye alights on the mortar and pestle she uses to grind coffee. Accordingly, her thoughts turn to her father-in-law and his brush with death during the Revolution. While recounting his experience, she walks over to the mortar. Running a finger over the well-worn bowl, stained and scented with the oil of countless beans, she seems to see the leafy tree from which it was carved.

42. During the war of 1914 my Padrinho promised that none of his followers would suffer any harm. So then he made a wall entirely of stone around Juazeiro in order to protect the city from the soldiers. And no one who obeyed him died. Look—that mortar and pestle there in the corner, do you see them?—they were once an enormous green pequi tree, very pretty, which stood in front of my mother-in-law's house. Well then, in 1914 there was a war and my Padrinho Cícero ordered everyone who was living outside Juazeiro to come into the city. Because the fighting was about to begin, don't you see? So then the people living outside the city left their homes and all their possessions. They only returned from time to time, to get a little food when my Padrinho let them. So then one day Seu Vicente [the speaker's father-in-law] asked permission to return home by the Logradouro road. He crossed the

8. Joaquim Ferreira de Lima (R). Surubim, Pernambuco, 1901. Arrived Juazeiro 1938. Married; rendeiro. (November 23, 1981.)

river and picked up the Santo Antonio road on the Crato side. When he arrived, poor thing, he grabbed whatever food he could before the soldiers could get close. Well then, on this last trip before the shooting started, the tree, the pequi tree, was still there, all green and lovely.

Well then, four or five days after the war was over, my Padrinho Cícero sent everyone home. He told them they should leave the city, they should get back to work. So then when Seu Vicente arrived home, he found the pequi tree lying on the ground. The bandits [soldiers] had cut it down. So then Seu Vicente was very sad, because that tree had always given a lot of fruit and also a lot of shade. So then he decided to make that mortar and pestle. You can see that today it [the speaker points to the bowl of the mortar] is very worn, but it serves as a remembrance of the war of 1914. And for this reason I cannot bring myself to exchange [leave] it for another.

—Josefa André Gonçalves (R). Limoeiro de Anadias, Alagoas, 1916.
Arrived Juazeiro 1923. Widow; makes hats and does ironing.
(July 3, 1981.)

Our general discussion of local storytellers has shown that some people's attachment to a particular personal reminiscence may be so strong as to cause them to contradict or explicitly question some element of the standard narrative. In this way, one woman's emotional involvement in her grandmother's narrow escape from enemy soldiers during the time of the Revolution leads her to summarily reject the possibility of any follower's death. Asked if there was not an individual who challenged Padre Cícero's authority, the speaker shakes her head. "No," she says, "not one, *not one* of the defenders died."

This story begins with a lengthy, highly detailed description of a pilgrimage undertaken by the speaker's grandmother and two small children in 1913. When the little group asks for shelter on a farm not far from Juazeiro, the owner warns the woman that the soldiers are on their way, then asks her to take "a litle ram with curly hair as white as cotton" to the priest as a present.

Although the grandmother is reluctant to burden herself any further, she accepts the animal because it is intended for Padre Cícero. Minutes later, she and her children are hurrying along the dark trail, pausing only to give the ram a handful of corn when it begins to bleat. When they finally reach the city, the grandmother knocks on the gate. Then, the speaker explains:

43. The guard said, "I am not going to open this gate because the
shooting is about to start. The gate has closed; no one can enter or
leave."
   So then my grandmother said, "No, you have to open up because
I am here with a ram meant for my Padrinho Cícero."
   The guard looked at the ram and he felt sorry for those two
defenseless children. "You can come in," he said, "but hurry."
   Well, no sooner had the three of them entered with the little ram
than the shooting started. The bullets whined through the air in
all directions but did not strike a single follower. No, not one, *not
one* of his followers died.

   —Marina Alves da Costa (R). Chã Morena, Pernambuco, 1923.
   Arrived Juazeiro 1975. Married; nurse's aide. (July 21, 1981.)

Although the grandmother's situation has an obvious influence on
the story, Padre Cícero is the focus of the tale. The speaker takes pride
in the woman's courage but sees her experience first and foremost as a
confirmation of the priest's ability to protect Juazeiro. Like the father-in-
law who loses his pequi tree or the grandparents who return home after
the fighting to raise beans big as potatoes, she is not only an individual
but also a representative of a larger community.

The tellers' close, positive association with a number of the participants in the fighting, coupled with Northeast Brazilians' general enthusiasm for public displays of courage, would under other circumstances
almost certainly result in stories about an uncle who faced a hundred
soldiers single-handedly or a grandfather who leapt over the city wall to
engage in hand-to-hand combat with an enemy general. This sort of
glorification of individual defenders is conspicuously absent from these
tales. The one storyteller who claims to have taken part in the fighting
speaks of his own fear. "I am not going to tell you that I was not scared
because I was," he says. "Who but my Padrinho would not have been
afraid? Why me, I wanted to run!"[9]

The purpose of residents' stories is thus always twofold: they serve
to celebrate a victory in which many people have, or would like to have,
a personal involvement, and at the same time they affirm Padre Cícero's
special pact with Juazeiro, which the tellers see as a guarantee of his
continuing protection.

Because the defenders' victory would be impossible without the soldiers' defeat, accounts of the Revolution are always a double challenge,

9. João Luís da Silva (R). Salgueiro, Pernambuco, 1897. Moved to Sítio Carnaúba (Palmei-
rinha) as young man. Widowed; *morador.* (July 26, 1981.)

and few storytellers omit the punishment that complements the reward. Most, however, are clearly less interested in the soldiers or the disobedient follower than they are in the victorious defenders. As a result, the percentage of the total narrative dedicated to the invaders' losses is usually very small. A single sentence at the end of the story is often all one will find. "And so many soldiers died," a storyteller may assert, or "There was an old man who did not heed my Padrinho's word and so a bullet hit him." Sometimes the disobedient follower is omitted altogether. Only if one asks, "And did anyone in Juazeiro die?" will the teller say, "Oh yes . . . ," and go on to identify the person or persons.

This apparent aversion to gory particulars in tales about the Revolution should not be taken as a reflection of local storytellers' pacific natures. Under other circumstances the same individuals would undoubtedly devote considerably more time and energy to the punishment of the disobedient follower or the defeat of the enemy. It is because their attention is riveted on Padre Cícero's ability to help residents of Juazeiro that they play down the story's punitive aspects.

Their own close association with the city explains this somewhat skewed perspective on the event. A look over the preceding accounts confirms the close connection between Padre Cícero and Juazeiro. In most cases the two names are interchangeable. Just as an attack on the priest is an attack on his city, so Padre Cícero's triumph is also Juazeiro's. The stories are thus celebrations not only of a moment in time but also of a carefully defined geographic space. "The powers of my Padrinho are very great," asserts one man who lives in the Rua do Horto. "It was he himself who said, 'Juazeiro will be attacked but it will never be defeated. The whole world will end but Juazeiro will survive.' That is why Juazeiro is my Padrinho's city and why we are so proud to be its sons and daughters."[10]

Pilgrims' Tales About the Revolution of 1913–14

In line with what one would expect from the overview in Chapter IV, pilgrims' versions of the Revolution tend to be briefer and more abstract than those of residents. They also reveal a growing fondness for fantastic details, an emphasis on the negative aspects of the double challenge that provides the underpinnings for the story, and the suggestion of causal links to other "historical" incidents. Unlike residents, for whom Padre

10. Brás Ibiapina de Farias (R). Souza, Paraíba, 1920. Arrived Juazeiro 1949. Married; construction worker. (October 24, 1982.)

Cícero and Juazeiro are all but synonymous, visitors tend to see the "war" as an attack on the institution of the pilgrimage as distinguished from the city proper. And because they are primarily interested in the priest, pilgrims often minimize his followers' role in the city's defense.

The small minority of non-residents with friends or relatives who took part in the Revolution of 1913–14 tell stories much like those that appear in the preceding pages. Most, however, cannot draw on this sort of direct experience, so their stories are often shorter and less anecdotal than those we have just seen. Even when they credit their tales to "a man in Pedro Segundo who went with his brother to fight in Juazeiro" or to "a pilgrim from Lajes who got so close to the soldiers that he could see the whites of their eyes," they usually have only a limited amount of information at their disposal.

The following stories are typical of the majority of visitors' accounts both in their brevity and in their lack of specificity. Neither of the speakers makes any reference to time, place, or individual participants in the action. Note that in both cases the soldiers fire directly on the priest instead of attacking the city or the priest's followers.

44. Everyone liked my Padrinho. The only person who didn't like him was a general—I don't remember his name—but he was a very important person. He didn't like my Padrinho because of the pilgrimage, because there were always so many pilgrims coming here. So then he wanted to be greater than my Padrinho. For this reason he sent his soldiers against my Padrinho and my Padrinho laid down a pebble which grew into a great wall. The soldiers came to fire on him but the bullets turned to water. They fired and fired but they could do nothing because of his miraculous powers.
—Joana Gomes (P). Currais Novos, Rio Grande do Norte, 1952. Married; seamstress. 3 pilgrimages. (October 8, 1982.)

45. Crato wanted to end the pilgrimage to Juazeiro. So then my Padrinho Cícero and Our Lady dug a ditch. They surrounded the city with a wall of cactus overnight. The soldiers kept on firing on my Padrinho but their bullets didn't hit him. They bounced back at the soldiers and killed them but not a single follower died. Only one who had robbed his neighbor's goat died. He did not pay attention to my Padrinho, so a bullet struck him in the heart.
—Josefa Maria da Conceição (P). Queimadas, Paraíba, 1947. Married; moradora. 2 pilgrimages. (October 13, 1982.)

Although residents' accounts of the Revolution of 1913–14 reveal numerous minor inaccuracies, most local storytellers have a fairly good idea of the incident's basic outlines. They can, for instance, identify Franco Rabelo as the governor who sent his troops to the Cariri and are usually aware that soldiers from both Fortaleza and neighboring Crato marched on Juazeiro in December of 1913. By and large, they are much closer to the facts than pilgrims, many of whom give the wrong date for the Revolution (1889, 1918, 1930, etc.) or confuse it with other, unrelated military campaigns. Some pilgrim storytellers simply forget the name of the commander of the enemy soldiers. (See the first of the two preceding accounts.) Others confuse Franco Rabelo with Moreira César (the general who died leading an expedition against the messianic community of Canudos), Dantas Barreto (a governor of the neighboring state of Pernambuco), or even "the bishop of Fortaleza." They may go so far as to claim that the soldiers come from Paraíba, Alagoas, Rio de Janeiro, or even France or Germany.

Their diminished sense of the "war" as a specific confrontation involving readily identifiable participants leads to a high incidence of contamination, or mingling of elements from two normally separate incidents, that is not at all characteristic of residents' accounts. For most pilgrims, the Revolution is one more instance of Padre Cícero's miraculous powers, with no particular relevance for them as individuals. Residents' incorporation of even larger than usual amounts of personal material often blurs the story's outline. Partly as a result, pilgrims may seek to reclarify the standard challenge pattern by grafting the incident onto another well-known tale in which the challenge sequence is more readily apparent.[11]

Among the stories that pilgrims are most apt to fuse with that of the Revolution are those of the war in Germany, the man who asks Padre Cícero for a protective weapon, and the would-be assassin in a hammock.[12] Tales in which the priest descends from a cloud to halt an enemy attack on Juazeiro are therefore not unusual. In another version of the

11. This sort of contamination is particularly evident in the Hispanic ballad tradition, where it has been duly commented on by scholars. For an excellent discussion of the sort of artistic elaboration, abbreviation, transformation, and re-creation characteristic of the *romance* but applicable to other folk forms, see Diego Catalán, "Los modos de producción y 'reproducción' del texto literario y la noción de apertura."

12. Even though neither the story of the man from São Pedro nor that of Manuel Correia is particularly popular among pilgrims, a number of tales about the Revolution focus on the priest's resurrection of one of the city's defenders. Not infrequently, this individual's name is either Pedro or Manuel.

Revolution fairly common among pilgrims, a man may ask the priest for a weapon to protect himself against invading soldiers instead of the more customary bandits.

In still other cases, the would-be assassin becomes one of Franco Rabelo's henchmen. When the governor of Ceará fails to vanquish Padre Cícero after "ninety days and ninety nights of war," he resorts to trickery. Dressing one of his soldiers as a sick pilgrim, the enemy leader directs him to plunge a dagger into the priest's heart in the hour of confession. The soldier, however, dies long before he can harm Padre Cícero. "After this," the storyteller explains:

46. Franco Rabelo said, "In order to kill this Padre Cícero we are going to have to destroy Juazeiro with a bomb." So then the soldiers dragged the cannon up the Araripe Mountains. But when the hour came for the cannon to fire, instead of firing on Juazeiro it fired on the troops. It killed all of them. Franco Rabelo's soldiers were blown to little pieces, and so he had no way to do away with my Padrinho.
   —Manuel Capitolino da Silva (P). Ibimirim, Pernambuco, 1921.
   Married; carpenter. 7 pilgrimages. (November 2, 1982.)

Pilgrims' diminished sense of the Revolution as an actual occurrence sometimes leads them to produce a series of narrative hybrids, but it more frequently results in a proliferation of fantastic detail. Whereas local storytellers refer in concrete terms to the wall that hundreds of defenders erect around the city, pilgrims speak of a towering barricade of cacti that springs up spontaneously from a single thorn. Residents sometimes claim that enemy bullets bounce off the city's defenders, but pilgrims go several steps further by claiming that they turn into water or fly into the soldiers' pockets. They may also insist that the attackers' rifles turn to sticks or suddenly sprout leaves.[13]

In one popular pilgrims' version of the story, a pilot sent to wipe out Juazeiro finds to his amazement that the city has disappeared. Each time he drops a bomb, it explodes without effect in the woods. He is finally so impressed by the priest's miraculous powers that he places himself and his plane at the service of the defenders.

47. A pilot came to bomb Juazeiro. But my Padrinho ordered everyone to pray. The city became enchanted and where there had been houses, now there were only woods. The pilot could not see

13. See C. Grant Loomis, "Legend and Folklore," for other examples of the use of folk material in legends.

anything, so bombing became useless. Finally he said, "Do you know something, I am going over to my Padrinho's side, which is the side of good." And in that moment Juazeiro suddenly reappeared.

—Simeão Araújo Magalhães (P). Altos, Piauí, 1940. Married;
  morador. 3 pilgrimages. (October 3, 1982.)

Local storytellers may envision a Padre Cícero whose steady gaze causes the soldiers to quail before him, but the white-haired priest is unlikely to turn into a young man before their astonished eyes. Although the Virgin Mary sometimes aids the defenders in residents' stories, she usually does no more than send down a dark cloud that envelops the attackers. Pilgrims, however, often cast her as a leading figure in their narratives. The following account begins with the sort of detailed description of the protective wall one would expect of a resident, but the teller then shifts to another plane of action by introducing the devil and the Virgin as direct participants in the conflict.

48. Have you see that remnant of a wall up there in the Horto? Well, it is from the time of the war in which the governor sent his soldiers to chop off my Padrinho's head. He was very jealous of my Padrinho and so he decided to declare war on him. So then my Padrinho ordered everyone to surround the city with a wall ten hands thick. No sooner had they finished than the war began. The soldiers fired but they did not even come close to hitting my Padrinho. So then they got to feeling so desperate that they called upon the devil. The devil came and told them he would like to help them, but he couldn't because there was a woman on top of the wall against whom he had no power whatsoever. That woman kept walking back and forth, back and forth, so that he could not pass. He was sorry, he would have liked to help them, but that woman was enough to drive him crazy. And so there was nothing he could do.

—José Severino de Sena (P). Itaíba, Pernambuco, 1931. Married;
  peddler in open-air market. 18 pilgrimages. (October 23, 1982.)

The relative restraint that is a hallmark of local storytellers is notably lacking in most visitors' accounts. In the version of the "war" that follows, the battle is no longer between flesh-and-blood attackers and defenders of the city but between the age-old forces of good and evil. The priest's followers are reduced to a symbolic sixty men with sixty rifles and sixty rosaries who successfully confront no fewer than "a hundred thousand troops."

49. In that war Franco Rabelo sent a hundred thousand troops to put an
    end to the pilgrimage. The soldiers arrived with their guns already
    hot. But when they went to fire on Juazeiro they could not believe
    their eyes. Sixty men with sixty rifles and sixty rosaries came to
    meet them. So then the ditch that my Padrinho's followers had dug
    became full of soldiers' bodies. Rivulets of blood flowed. For my
    Padrinho had told everyone that he would not let the soldiers pass.
    But they paid no attention to him and so they had to suffer. It was a
    terrible sight.
    —Pedro Santos da Silva (P). Bom Jardim, Pernambuco, 1944.
    Married; *rendeiro*. 6 pilgrimages. (November 20, 1982.)

The same sort of apocalyptic flavor characterizes a version of the
story in which the teller condenses the fighting that dragged on for over
a month into a mere three days. One can practically hear the heavens
boom as the standard-bearers of virtue march out to face the enemy. In
this quasi-mythic universe, blood "flows like water." Once again the Virgin Mary plays an active role.

50. There was a terrible war here once. Blood flowed like water for
    three days without stopping. The light went out in the church.
    There was smoke and fire everywhere. In the end, Our Lady
    descended in a cloud. There was a clap of thunder so loud that the
    world almost ended in that moment. So then the soldiers knew that
    they were going to lose. Many of them died but no one on my
    Padrinho's side was hurt. There were only two people who dis-
    obeyed. They laid hands on others' property, and so there was no
    other way; they died.
    —Juarez José dos Santos (P). Poço Redondo, Sergipe, 1942. Married;
    rendeiro. 11 pilgrimages. (October 25, 1982.)

This largely atemporal battle between good and evil appears in the
cordel accounts still popular throughout the Northeast. The following
verses, which a pilgrim from Paraíba recited to me, emphasize the universal dimensions of the confrontation. Although the *folheto* proper contains considerable information about the Revolution, few visitors bother
to memorize this portion of the narrative. ("I only learn the really good
parts," the storyteller explained.)[14]

14. These verses represent a slightly altered form of lines 169–182 in Antonio Batista, "A
Guerra do Juazeiro em 1914," p. 350.

Padrinho Cícero venceu	Padrinho Cícero won
a guerra sanguinolenta.	the bloody war.
Os rabelista correram	The *rabelistas* ran
dessa cidade benta.	from this holy city.
Foi arte do Satanás,	[Their attack] was Satan's doing,
deixaram pra nunca mais	but they were forced to abandon forever
essa campanha nojenta.	that disgusting campaign [against Juazeiro].
Meu Padrinho sempre dizia	My Padrinho always said
se acabou a grande guerra.	that the great war was over.
Foi pela inveja do diabo	It was the devil's envy [of him]
o sangue ensopou a terra.	that had caused blood to drench the earth.
Amanhã o mundo geme	"The world will groan tomorrow
e depois a terra treme,	and the earth will tremble," he said
mas meu romeiro não erra.	"but my pilgrim will not go astray."

In line with their stress on the larger battle between light and darkness, pilgrims tend to downplay the role of individual human combatants. As a result, Padre Cícero often seems to vanquish the enemy without any help from his followers. Although local storytellers agree that the priest is responsible for the city's stunning victory, they are far less likely to insist on the solitary splendor in which he appears in this and other visitors' accounts.

51. A whole army came to wage war on my Padrinho. And my Padrinho said, "Let them come. I am not afraid." So then when the soldiers arrived, their weapons fell to the ground. There were shotguns, there were knives, there were fish knives there in the middle of the street. Because my Padrinho had a lot of power, he had more power than anyone. When the soldiers came to kill him he raised his hand and said, "There will come a day in which the biggest castle in the world will be transformed into a church." He raised his hand like this—are you watching, friends?—and the soldiers let their weapons fall.

—Maria Valeriano (P). Surubim, Pernambuco, 1916. Widow;
   moradora. 28 pilgrimages. (September 24, 1982.)

The same challenge pattern we were able to distinguish in residents' stories lies beneath the smoking surface of many pilgrims' tales. Because non-residents are more willing to stress the punitive aspects of the Revolution, however, their versions of the incident may at first glance look quite different.

For a local storyteller, the story of the Revolution is often that of

Uncle Pedro's encounter with the enemy troops. Visitors, however, lack this direct emotional bond. Moreover, as their homes are usually far from the Cariri Valley, most make a distinction, ordinarily lost on residents, between the locus of power, which is Juazeiro, and their own access to this power, which is the pilgrimage.

Because of their status as non-residents, almost all the visitors who told me stories were less interested in the priest's willingness to defend his adopted home than in his continuing accessibility to them. Unlike local storytellers, who see the Revolution as a pact between the priest and his adopted city, these individuals are disposed to view it as a defense and thus an affirmation of the journey to Juazeiro. "My Padrinho," explains one man, "told the pope that this pilgrimage was never going to end. Well now, that pope is dead and gone, but the pilgrimage lives on. It lives on and it will continue until the end of the world."[15] Some visitors' accounts end with Franco Rabelo signing a paper that guarantees the state will not interfere with "the pilgrimage or any pilgrim until the end of time." Those persons who claim to have a relative who participated in the fighting often present this individual as a witness to the signing of this (fictional) accord.

Pilgrims' willingness to set their tales of the "war" outside the city limits further underscores essential differences in narrative perspective. No resident would ever conceive of the Revolution as something apart from Juazeiro, but a significant minority of visitors describe the fighting's effect on people in other states. One quite common story concerns an unbeliever who decides to join Franco Rabelo's forces. Each time he tries to leave home, however, something happens: his horse dies, his burro sickens, and then he breaks a leg. Finally he realizes that opposition to the priest is hopeless, and he sets out for Juazeiro to fight on Padre Cícero's side. Thus even though the story ends in the usual manner with the defeat of the attacking forces, the transformation of the unbelieving non-resident into a believer is its real subject.

Pilgrims' decreased emphasis on Juazeiro's victory is also a result of their interest in that larger pattern associated with a "life." Because of their ability to see the confrontation as one more illustration of unjust persecution, visitors are quicker than residents to stress its punitive aspects.

Some individuals are content to note that Franco Rabelo "did not like" Padre Cícero. Others are considerably more explicit. We have seen

15. Geraldo Vital Duarte (P). Lagoa de Roça, Paraíba, 1928. Married; farmer (own land). 5 pilgrimages. (September 25, 1982.)

that in one of the preceding accounts the unnamed general opposes the priest because "so many pilgrims always came to see him." Another storyteller explains that Franco Rabelo wants to destroy Padre Cícero in order to put an end to the pilgrimage, which detracts from his own prestige. Still another points out the governor "was jealous" of the priest. Although the educated observer may dismiss these claims as sheer invention, they provide persons largely unfamiliar with the history of Juazeiro with a motivation for an otherwise incomprehensible attack on its virtuous leader.

Yet other pilgrims' tales present the Revolution as a direct result or cause of another well-known event. In these stories, which account for a small but significant percentage of the versions I recorded (a little over 15 percent), the bishop replaces the governor as the priest's arch-enemy. The "war" is thus no longer the product of political differences but rather a vindictive response to Padre Cícero's miraculous opening of a church door or the restoration of a mute boy's speech. Sometimes the ninety-nine clerics who have failed to accomplish what the priest does band together to attack Juazeiro. In other instances Padre Cícero's identification of the bishop as the mute boy's father leads the latter to send his soldiers against the city.

52. There was a bishop who became the lover of a nun. And they had a child whom they put in an orphanage. This child was born dumb; he never said a word to anyone. So then the bishop summoned my Padrinho Cícero to Rome—it was either Rome or Fortaleza— because everyone said that he worked a lot of miracles. He summoned my Padrinho Cícero and my Padrinho came. So then the bishop said that he wanted him to make this child speak. And the child opened his mouth and said, "My father is the bishop and my mother is the nun Fulana de Tal ['So-and-So']." So then this was the cause of the revolution that followed. There were ninety days of fighting, in which many soldiers died. No one in Juazeiro died because my Padrinho turned the soldiers' bullets to water. But many soldiers died. Anyone who was against him died.
—João Antônio Gonçalves Neto (P). Águas Belas, Pernambuco, 1915. Widowed; carpenter and construction worker. 6 pilgrimages. (October 28, 1982.)

Visitors may also associate the tale of the Revolution with that of a Dr. Floro whom some identify as "Padre Cícero's rifle" or "the head of my Padrinho's forces during the war of 1914." In these stories Floro usually tries to wrest control of Juazeiro from the priest once victory is sure.

The alleged transformation or the mute boy's revelation triggers the "war," and Juazeiro's victory is responsible for the confrontation between the priest and his once-trusted advisor. Thus the Revolution functions as a double link in an ongoing narrative chain.

Visitors' recasting of the Revolution of 1913–14 as an attack on the pilgrimage instead of on Juazeiro does not alter the basic challenge framework. In visitors' stories, as in those of residents, the priest successfully rebuffs an affront to his authority by punishing both the invading soldiers and a token number of disobedient followers. Local storytellers' propensity to incorporate eyewitness material into their accounts of the "war," however, makes the story a prime example of the drive toward direct personalization that distinguishes their tales. Visitors' attempts to see the confrontation as both a celebration of the pilgrimage and one segment of an emerging life progression lead them to stress different aspects of the same narrative. Thus although the structure of these tales about the Revolution remains more or less constant, they reveal considerable variation in content.

VI.

Padre Cícero and Dr. Floro

Dr. Floro was not like my Padrinho. He was very different.
His law was another law.

Resident of Juazeiro

Dr. Floro made my Padrinho suffer but his own ambition
brought him to an unhappy end.

Pilgrim from Alagoas

B etween his arrival in Juazeiro in 1908 and his death in Rio de
Janeiro in 1926, Floro Bartolomeu da Costa, Padre Cícero's political advisor, was the second most influential individual in the Cariri
Valley. Considering the amount of power he wielded, it is not surprising
that many persons today should have strong feelings about him or that
he should occupy a privileged niche within the miracle corpus. As representative to the state and then the national legislature, Floro acquired a
fame that reached well beyond the Cariri. He is, for this reason, the only
"local" personality important to both groups of storytellers.

The differences between residents' and pilgrims' stories run deeper
in the case of Floro than in that of the Revolution of 1913–14. Whereas
local storytellers' relative proximity to the doctor predisposes them to a
series of extended contrasts, pilgrims favor a conclusive confrontation
that fits more directly into a larger "life." Despite these dissimilarities,
the two sets of narratives are not diametrically opposed. Although each
group reworks the material from its own perspective, pilgrims' stories
often hint at relationships expressed more fully in residents' tales.

The Historical Figure

Floro Bartolomeu da Costa was born in 1876 in Bahia, the southernmost
state of the Northeast. After studying medicine in the capital city of Salvador, he practiced as an itinerant physician in the backlands of Bahia

and Pernambuco. He also worked as a journalist and public notary before branching out into a series of commercial ventures. In 1907, he joined a French mining engineer, Count Adolpho Van den Brule, in a search for diamonds and semiprecious metals. A year later, the two men traveled to the Cariri Valley to visit the disputed Coxá copper deposits, in which a Paris-based firm had demonstrated interest.[1]

Padre Cícero too was concerned about the future of these deposits. He had used money donated to him by supporters to acquire property rights to most of the copper fields, which he apparently hoped might serve as patrimony for a future bishopric of the Cariri centered in Juazeiro.[2] (This hope was dashed in 1914 when Crato was declared the seat of the new diocese.) It was therefore natural that Padre Cícero and Dr. Floro should meet. As a result of this initial encounter, the doctor became the priest's representative in the Coxá matter.

The dispute over the fields catapulted Floro into local politics. After a district court approved Padre Cícero's request to demarcate the properties, Floro and three others came close to losing their lives in a retaliatory ambush. The doctor did not hesitate to strike back at the would-be assassin, who turned out to be employed by a close relative of that same Antonio Luis Alves Pequeno III with whom he was later to join ranks in opposing Governor Franco Rabelo.[3] Therefore while Floro's armed rebuff represented a victory for Padre Cícero, it marked the end of his longstanding political neutrality.

It is not hard to see why the doctor might have chosen to stay in Juazeiro after the resolution of the Coxá affair. Floro was a typical *bacharel*, one of those upwardly mobile urban university graduates who made a career of serving old-style landowners or *coronéis* during the period beween 1894 and 1930 known as the Old Republic.[4] Unable to follow

1. For a more detailed discussion of Floro and his importance to the development of Juazeiro see Ralph della Cava, *Miracle at Joaseiro,* pp. 103–114. Useful information is contained in Floro Bartolomeu da Costa, *Joazeiro e o Padre Cícero: Depoimentos para a história.* On p. 303, della Cava lists various newspaper articles by Floro. See also Rui Facó, *Cangaceiros e fanáticos: Gênese e lutas,* and Nertan Macedo, *O padre e a beata.* For biographical information consult Azarias Sobreira, "Floro Bartolomeu."

2. See della Cava, *Miracle at Joaseiro,* pp. 104–105.

3. Since this Antonio Luis was the son of the man by the same name who served as Padre Cícero's godfather and who financed his seminary education, Floro's retaliatory action must have been somewhat embarrassing to the priest.

4. The classic discussion of the *coronel* remains Victor Nunes Leal, *Coronelism: The Municipality and Representative Government in Brazil.* See also Edgard Carone, "Coronelismo: Definição, história e bibliografia," and Lúcia Maria Gaspar and Fernando José Leite Costa, "Contribuição ao estudo da sociedade tradicional: Bibliografia comentada."

the usual pattern of marrying the *coronel*'s daughter, Floro sought to in-
gratiate himself to the general population, which looked to the priest as
a father, in his role as the city's only resident physician. At the same time,
he carefully cultivated contacts among the elite.

Padre Cícero must have respected Floro's university education as
well as his natural shrewdness. The Coxá mining dispute was just one of
many skirmishes from which the doctor was to emerge apparently un-
scathed. We have already witnessed his elaborate political maneuvers in
regard to the Revolution of 1913–14. A mere six years after arriving in
Juazeiro, Floro assumed the presidency of Ceará's legislative assembly.
Reelected state deputy in 1916, he went on to the lower house of the
national congress as the Cariri representative in 1921. He retained this
seat until his death at the age of fifty, some five years later.

Floro's rapid rise to power earned him many enemies. Some were
disgruntled political opponents; others, who were old friends of the
priest, such as the journalist José Marrocos, felt that the doctor had
usurped their place in Padre Cícero's affections. These individuals denounced him as a ruthless opportunist.

Floro's hostility to a series of popular religious manifestations generated ill will among the lower classes as well. Largely out of a desire to
quell outsiders' jests about the backwardness of the region he represented, the doctor took a strong stand against not only bandits and gam-
blers but also the members of various religious sects. It was he who gave
the order to disband a society of penitential flagellants that had become
a tradition in Juazeiro, as well as a millenarian group called the "Celestial
Courts" or "Celestial Hosts."[5] Floro also ordered the observance of national holidays such as Carnival, the national independence day, and
Juazeiro's anniversary of municipal autonomy. These secularizing measures upset many of the extremely conservative pilgrims who had come
to settle in the city.

Padre Cícero, however, appears to have supported (critics would say
"obeyed") his advisor throughout the course of their almost twenty-year
association. The only documentable confrontation between the priest
and the doctor occurred at that critical moment in 1914 when Floro
broke with Ceará's new governor, Benjamin Liberato Barroso, by pub-

5. The Penitents of Barbalha are one such group that has survived into the present. The
Celestial Courts (a self-contained religious community in which each member represented
a saint) appear to have enjoyed a resurgence after Floro's death. For religious groups that
functioned after Padre Cícero's death see Ann Morton, "Religion in Juazeiro (Ceará, Brazil)
since the Death of Padre Cícero: A Case Study in the Nature of Messianic Religious Activity in the Interior of Brazil."

licly refusing to recognize the latter's candidates for two empty seats in the state legislature.[6] This refusal threatened the survival of a regime already wracked by financial difficulties stemming from the war in Europe. After political leaders in both Fortaleza and Rio de Janeiro urged Padre Cícero to exert his influence to end the dispute, the priest wrote to the doctor, requesting his cooperation.

Recognizing that unwitting intervention could destroy the balance he had so carefully established, Floro took a characteristically large risk. Assuring Padre Cícero that he was working for the good of Juazeiro and the country, he insisted that the priest either reaffirm his trust in him or end their alliance on the spot. Under pressure, Cícero chose to submit to Floro, thereby ensuring the doctor's political future.

Residents' Tales

Accounts of Dr. Floro reveal the multiplicity, concreteness, and attention to detail characteristic of the great majority of residents' tales. And yet, while local storytellers are more personally involved with the doctor than are pilgrims, the nature and the degree of this involvement are quite different than in the case of the Revolution of 1913–14. The latter is a documentable event in which a large number of residents participated, but stories about Dr. Floro turn on an encounter between the priest and the doctor in which the event is less important than the personalities.

Although Floro continued to visit the Cariri after he became a state deputy, then a national deputy, his new duties required extended stays in Fortaleza and then Rio de Janeiro. Both the relatively short time that he passed in Juazeiro and his superior social standing would have made it difficult for most residents to develop a close or extended association with him. As a result, their knowledge of the doctor is usually based on brief, superficial encounters or on a type of hearsay that has grown over the decades into a more or less fixed body of communal lore. Therefore even though it is not difficult to find individuals whose mother or next-door neighbor supposedly knew Floro, accounts of the doctor are usually less directly personal than those concerning the Revolution.

Floro, usually a negative presence in residents' stories, is nevertheless a readily identifiable person. A medical doctor from the state of Bahia, he is short and stocky with a booming voice and an exuberant mustache that twirls up at the ends. He wears on his finger a ring that symbolizes

6. See della Cava, *Miracle at Joaseiro*, pp. 158–161, for more information about the disagreement between the doctor and the priest.

his university training; he tips his hat to ladies and winks at them on the city streets.

Some residents inject their own memories into the Floro stories. Often, recollections of the doctor spur a series of general reminiscences about the past. "I remember," the speaker may say, "how he used to walk down such-and-such a street," going on to describe landmarks that have long since disappeared.

Occasionally, actual contact with the doctor will prompt a storyteller to come to his defense. The individual may go so far as to deny the friction between Padre Cícero and Floro that provides the basis for most stories of the two. "After the war of 1914," one man explains, "Floro started to lose control over his men. They became so disorderly that he finally had to use force to get them to obey him and that is where his reputation for violence started. But he was not a cruel person. He was a friend of my Padrinho until the day of his death."[7] "I knew Dr. Floro," asserts another, "and he was not at all like people say. Those stories about him are the invention of jealous people, and I know for a fact that my Padrinho wept on the day he died."[8]

Most local storytellers, however, appear quite comfortable with the prevailing opinion of Floro as a man who misuses the power delegated to him by the priest. After Padre Cícero then rebukes him in no uncertain terms, the doctor demands to know why, then, the priest ever gave him so much authority. Padre Cícero retorts that the person who makes another great has the ability to make him small. This exchange fits a standard negative challenge framework in which the fourth step—reaffirmation—is missing but implied (Figure 5).

Although the story is easily seen as a conventional negative challenge, the lack of a conclusive ending sets it apart from similar narratives that leave no doubt about the fate of the individual who dares to question Padre Cícero. The rancher who asks for rain loses all his possessions and, often, his life. The girl who asserts that she would sooner wear mourning for her dog than for the leader of Juazeiro assumes canine form. The priest who reneges on his promise never to deny Padre Cícero's miraculous powers immediately goes blind. These direct physical responses contrast with the scolding that ends the Floro tale. Local storytellers almost never indicate whether the doctor repents, grudgingly gives up

7. Manoel Gomes Vieira (R). Panelas, Alagoas, 1897. Arrived Juazeiro as child. Married; *rendeiro*. (July 13, 1981.)
8. Olímpio Praciano de França (R). Palmeira dos Índios, Alagoas, 1901. Arrived Juazeiro 1922. Widowed; still works as farmer. (July 30, 1981.)

Figure 5. Negative Challenge in Dr. Floro Tale

1.
*Implicit acceptance of Padre
Cícero's authority*
Floro functions as the priest's most trusted aide.

↓

2.
Challenge
Heady with newfound power, Floro rebels against Padre Cícero by publicly pitting his authority against that of the priest.

↓

3.
Response
Padre Cícero rebukes Floro, affirming his own power to
diminish him.

↓

4.
Reaffirmation
Floro is presumably humiliated by the priest's sharp words.

---

trying to outmaneuver Padre Cícero, or persists in his errant ways. The absence of a climax is thus no mere detail but a conspicuous anomaly.

Residents' relative proximity to the doctor helps to explain why this story is different from others. Because the real Floro remained such an important and at least sporadically visible fact of political life for almost two decades, most persons would have difficulty in insisting on an untimely end. A more drastic conclusion would also deny Padre Cícero's well-known positive feelings for Floro, forcing storytellers to make an unmitigated villain of a man known to have been the priest's personal friend. Finally, and undoubtedly most important for citizens of Juazeiro, Floro's early death would severely limit his potential as a scapegoat since he could not easily be blamed for events occurring in his absence.

The ability to blame the doctor for a whole series of specific wrongs is of great importance to local storytellers. By holding Floro responsible for actions that adversely affected them or others like them, they absolve the priest of error. Likewise, in portraying Padre Cícero as a victim of his supposed ally, these individuals dispel the painful, if not threatening, suggestion that the man they regard as a saint could willfully enforce measures of which they disapprove.[9]

Because a strong conclusion to the Floro tale is not plausible for residents, they adopt other courses of action. The great majority transfer the time and energy they would normally devote to the confrontation to an initial sequence that illustrates the differences between the priest and doctor while providing a motivation for the ensuing rebuke.

These initial episodes reveal the sort of variation we have come to expect of resident storytellers. Although virtually everyone agrees that Floro does something wrong, individual storytellers ascribe different offenses to the doctor. He may, for instance, insist on staging a Carnival celebration against Padre Cícero's wishes. Or he may kill a pet ox belonging to Padre Cícero, jail one of his *beatos,* or execute an individual for a petty offense.

Although none of these incidents is related with strict accuracy, each has a number of bases in fact. At the same time, all these specific actions point to a larger division between spiritual and temporal power. Often found in tales of Christian holy figures, these more general qualities can be broken down as follows:

Padre Cícero (spiritual power)	*Dr. Floro* (temporal authority)
Special relationship to the sacred.	Irreverent, earthbound.
Omniscient.	Knowledge limited to the tangible.
Uninterested in earthly power.	Greedy for glory and therefore proud and rebellious.
Controls through moral force.	Lacking in moral authority and therefore dependent on physical force.

9. It is worth noting that the majority of Brazilian spiritual leaders have had right-hand men—or, occasionally, women—who have not only aided them in an administrative capacity but who have also traditionally borne the brunt of followers' dissatisfaction when things went wrong. Although one cannot assert that Padre Cícero chose Dr. Floro as an advisor because he consciously desired an administrator who could function as scapegoat, the Cícero/Floro partnership follows a common pattern.

| Respects time-honored rules that grant even the humblest individual access to power on this earth. | Interested only in self-aggrandizement, which denies the individual access to power and thus all hope of temporal justice. |

The overwhelming majority of residents' accounts of Floro hinge on one or another of these fundamental oppositions. Padre Cícero's special relationship to the sacred, for example, finds expression in stories stressing the doctor's attachment to physical pleasures. In the following account the speaker, who had gone to the priest's house to seek his advice, recalls the doctor's appearance during the course of his visit. On the surface the tale is nothing more than an eyewitness description of the doctor's fondness for food, but it serves to call attention to a corporeal nature at odds with Padre Cícero's lack of interest in material concerns. According to the storyteller, the priest simply watches while the doctor wolfs down plate after plate of food. The "pei, pei, pei" here is meant to suggest the sound of Floro's greedy swallows.

53.   There was a knock on the door and when my Padrinho Cícero went to open it I saw Dr. Floro. He was short and fat with a mustache that curled up at the ends like this [gesture], and he talked in a loud voice. "Padre Cícero," he almost shouted, "I am starving. Shall we eat?"
      "Of course, eat, Dr. Floro," my Padrinho said. "Lunch is on the table. Serve yourself."
      "No, Padre Cícero," he said, "I will only eat if you do too."
      "I don't want anything," my Padrinho said. "Thank you anyway, but you serve yourself."
      "All right, Padre Cícero, then excuse me while I have a bite to eat." Pei, pei, pei, he ate and ate and ate so much I could not believe it. When he finished eating he took a cigar from his pocket and began to smoke. Then he left. They say there was a woman with whom he was involved but I couldn't say for sure.
      —Pedro Ribeiro da Silva (R). Paulo Jacinto, Alagoas, 1900. Arrived
      Juazeiro 1971. Widowed; guard and farmer. (October 10, 1982.)

Another good example of a story with an immediate as well as a more universal significance is that of Floro's jailing of the *beato* José Lourenço, who went on to become the leader of the Caldeirão settlement.[10] This tale may well reflect residents' concern over the doctor's imprison-

10. See pp. 51–52, above.

ment of the *beato* following action in 1918 against the Celestial Courts. In this instance, Dr. Floro, with Padre Cícero's full knowledge, decided to disband one group after the husband of a woman who refused to return home complained. When the priest sent two soldiers with a message for the leaders, the frightened group pelted them with stones. In response, Floro ordered these individuals arrested and had their heads shaved. José Lourenço, who played the role of Saint Joseph of Egypt in the Courts, was one of the persons detained.

The priest's rebuke of the doctor in the following account has the effect of denying Padre Cícero's documentable participation in the affair. His explanation that the *beato* is really not in Floro's jail speaks to followers' doubts about how the priest could allow the doctor to imprison José Lourenço. Realizing that the supposed captive is a mere semblance of the flesh-and-blood person, who is elsewhere, Padre Cícero feels no compulsion to come to his aid.

54. The *beato* Zé Lourenço remained a prisoner in Dr. Floro's jail for
     seventeen days. He didn't eat, he didn't drink, he didn't sleep a
     wink. So then Dr. Floro got upset and went to see my Padrinho.
     "Padre Cícero, what kind of man is this who doesn't eat, who
     doesn't drink, and who doesn't sleep? He has been in my jail for
     seventeen days now and he just remains there without giving any
     sign of life."
         So then my Padrinho said, "Floro, you are thinking that José is in
     your jail when he is really with his followers, working, eating
     lunch and dinner, and praying his rosary. You don't realize that it is
     only a semblance of José that you have there in your jail." So then
     the doctor left in a rage. He was furious because my Padrinho
     knew things that he could not even imagine.
         "Floro," my Padrinho told him, "be careful, because he who
     made you great can also make you very tiny."
     —Enrique Ferreira da Silva (R). Serra de Lisgomé, Rio Grande do Norte, 1900.
       Arrived Juazeiro 1946. Married; repairs furniture. (August 2, 1981.)

This story addresses an issue of great concern to some residents of Juazeiro, and it also underscores the general theme of Padre Cícero's omniscience versus Floro's dependence on his own five senses. As such it appeals to persons who have forgotten or who never knew about José Lourenço or the Celestial Courts. Because the doctor lives in a world of outward appearances, he must depend on Padre Cícero to interpret inner meanings. The priest's confirmation of the *beato*'s bilocality causes Floro to fly into a rage not only because his prisoner has escaped him but also because the doctor is forced to recognize the limits of his own power.

Stories that deal with Floro's killing of a prize ox known as the Boi Mansinho ("Gentle Little Ox") further document residents' ability to fit an incident of local significance into a broader frame in which it achieves a metaphoric force. Once again, this episode has some basis in fact.[11] When rumors reached the doctor's ears that members of José Lourenço's following in a place called the Baixa D'Anta were worshipping the animal, he reacted against this alleged display of fanaticism by ordering its slaughter. As Padre Cícero had given the ox to the community for safekeeping, the doctor's action struck many people as both cruel and insulting to the priest. Their shock and disapproval are obvious in stories such as the following, in which Padre Cícero expressly condemns Floro's actions.

55. It was an ox so tame that it was a pleasure to see. And as it belonged to my Padrinho, everyone treated it with great affection. But Dr. Floro wanted to be more important than my Padrinho. And so he arrived in the Baixa D'Anta and set fire to everything because he said that the people there were praying to the ox. Then after the soldiers had burnt down the houses, they paraded around with the ox. My Padrinho Cícero sent a message that they were not to kill the ox, but they killed it anyway. The ox fell, it let out a roar, the tears streamed from its eyes. So then the soldiers roasted the meat and forced everyone to eat.

—Luzia Maria das Neves (R). Lagoa de Baixo, Paraíba, date unknown. Arrived Juazeiro 1946. Married; *rezadeira*. (August 2, 1981.)

Storytellers who belonged to the *beato*'s community or whose parents were followers of José Lourenço insist that the ox was no more than a pet whom people enjoyed pampering and adorning with ribbons.[12] Whatever the truth, the killing of the animal generated a hostility toward Floro obvious in their accounts. This storyteller's insistence that Padre Cícero punishes the soldiers by making their tongues bleed is intended to suggest that the priest does not accept passively this alleged affront to

11. There are varying accounts of what actually happened. For a summary of the more or less official version of the event see Maria Isaura Pereira de Queiroz, *O messianismo no Brasil e no mundo*, p. 261. For an alternative view see Rosemberg Cariry, "O beato José Lourenço e o Caldeirão da Santa Cruz."

12. Most insist that because of its association with Padre Cícero the ox was treated as a sort of mascot. To this day some of the individuals forced to consume the animal's flesh refuse to eat beef.

his authority. The men's willingness to flout the former church injunction against eating meat on Friday simply exacerbates the punishment they have courted by defying the orders of the priest concerning the ox.

56. My Padrinho Cícero said that no one should kill that ox. Still Dr. Floro paid no attention. He ordered his soldiers to kill it. So then everyone who ate the meat got sick. For it was a Friday and my Padrinho Cícero had said that no one should touch the ox. Still they murdered it anyway, they defied his word. They ate that meat on a Friday and their tongues grew and grew until they reached the ground. So then their tongues began to itch and turned all red and bloody. Finally Dr. Floro went to tell my Padrinho that his soldiers' tongues were bleeding. "Be careful," my Padrinho told him, "because he who made you great can make you very small."
—Antonio Ferreira (R). Bom Jardim, Pernambuco, 1920. Arrived Juazeiro 1940. Marital status unknown; *rendeiro*. (July 23, 1981.)

In disassociating Padre Cícero from disruptive memories, these stories reaffirm the tension between temporal and spiritual power. Although Floro owes his elevated position to the priest, he is proud and rebellious. Unlike his benefactor, who defers to secular and religious authorities so long as they do not attempt to make him act against his conscience, Floro flaunts his delegated power. Even worse, he attempts to impose his will on others.

Sometimes, as in the following version of the Carnival story, his use of force acquires a comic air. After Floro decides that he and his soldiers are going to parade against Padre Cícero's wishes, a rare cloudburst drenches them. The doctor refuses to cancel the celebration, forcing the scowling men to go plodding through the puddles in full costume rather than admit defeat. This tale almost certainly has roots in the real Floro's insistence on Juazeiro's observance of a number of secular holidays. (Although Carnival is linked to Lent, it does not entail any formal religious observance.) The ludicrous portrait the story creates makes it a favorite of the tellers, who often laugh as they shake their heads at the doctor's stubborn pride.

57. My Padrinho Cícero told Floro that he didn't want Carnival celebrations in Juazeiro because he didn't like them. But Floro never listened to my Padrinho. He always thought he knew better. And so when the day came, he ordered his men to get all dressed up in silly outfits and they went out together parading through the streets. They sang and danced and beat their drums and everybody

stared. Well then, all of a sudden the sky opened and a huge wave of water came pouring down over their heads.

"Let's go home!" yelled the soldiers, but Floro wouldn't let them. And so they went on dancing through the puddles for hours, banging on their drums and sneezing a lot.

"Floro," my Padrinho said, "you had better stop this nonsense before he who made you great decides to make you small."

—Severina Maria da Conceição (R). Panelas, Alagoas, 1943. Arrived Juazeiro 1971. Married; sells vegetables. (November 14, 1982.)

Although we have seen that in the miracle stories Padre Cícero does not hesitate to use force when necessary, he is usually able to rely on his powers of persuasion. The Carnival tale therefore provides a light-hearted illustration of the difference between moral authority and physical coercion.

Not all such examples are so amusing. The following account of a woman accused of stealing by a neighbor has a far darker quality. The tale probably reflects residents' memories of that "law and order" period following the Revolution of 1913–14 in which Floro's attempts to eradicate a persistent criminal element from Juazeiro resulted in harsh punishments for even petty offenses. In this disturbing tale of a turkey hen, the same heavy-handed justice that supposedly made it possible for inhabitants of the city to sleep with their doors wide open is responsible for the deaths of two women.[13]

58. There was a woman who lived next door to another. And this woman had a turkey hen that wandered off into the woods. When the turkey hen didn't return, the owner went to Dr. Floro and told him her neighbor had eaten the hen. Dr. Floro said, "Are you sure it was she who ate it?" And she said yes, she was absolutely sure. So then he sent his soldiers to the neighbor's house.

"Was it you who ate your neighbor's turkey hen?" one asked.

"No, it wasn't, sir," she responded. "I wouldn't do a thing like that."

"Well, your neighbor has accused you of eating her hen. So we are going to take you with us." And they went off with that woman and no one ever saw her again.

Well, after a week or so, the turkey hen returned. It had been waiting for its eggs to hatch but now it had returned. When the hen returned, the owner went to see Dr. Floro. "My turkey hen is

13. A verse (cordel) account of this "law and order" period is available in Manuel Caboclo e Silva, História Verdadeira do Juazeiro.

back," she said. "So you can let the woman out of jail because I was mistaken." But Dr. Floro's soldiers had already killed the other woman. So there was no way to free her, see?

"Well," he said, "since I cannot free your neighbor, you are going where she went." And the soldiers took her away too.

So then when my Padrinho learned what had happened, he summoned Dr. Floro. "How can you go around killing innocent people?" he asked.

"Padre Cícero," Dr. Floro said, "wasn't it you who gave me my power?"

"It was I," my Padrinho said, "but don't you forget that he who made you great can also make you small."

—Manuel Barros da Silva (R). Garanhuns, Pernambuco, 1910. Arrived Juazeiro 1965. Married; *rendeiro*. (October 24, 1982.)

The two unwarranted deaths stand as grim proof of the extent to which the Floro of these stories is ruled by personal ambition. The owner of the turkey hen errs by accusing her neighbor too hastily, but her own sense of right and wrong leads her to admit her mistake. Because the doctor is only concerned about protecting his own position, however, he flaunts the moral code on which traditional Northeast Brazilian notions of justice are based. He is thus guilty not only of murder but also of a more generalized disregard for time-honored mores.

This last story suggests the degree to which all the preceding tales about the priest and the doctor reflect a culturally specific concept of authority. The priest is not only a symbol of spiritual power but also the idealization of a landowning system in which the patron is supposed to embody the ethical force known in Portuguese as *moral*.[14] Floro, in this context, stands for a secular, modernizing state in which interpersonal obligation is perceived to yield to physical force. The fact that the historical doctor cast his lot with the old-style oligarchy by representing Padre Cícero's interests in the state and national assemblies does not prevent storytellers from seeing the two men as opposing entities. Storytellers' biggest problem with Floro is not that he is cruel but that he is capricious. His lack of commitment to the vision of the world that Padre Cícero consistently affirms through concrete actions in the miracle corpus makes it impossible for the less privileged to predict how he will act toward them. Moreover, his lack of respect for the rules casts unwelcome doubt on their validity, adding to the insecurity of the dispossessed.

14. For a fuller consideration of *moral* and its behavioral implications see Allen Johnson, *Sharecroppers of the Sertão*, pp. 125–127.

In sum, most residents' tales of Padre Cícero and Dr. Floro operate on not one but three separate, if related, levels. Virtually all grow out of memories, many by now half-forgotten, of incidents that troubled residents of Juazeiro. They illustrate a general opposition between spiritual and temporal power at the same time that they serve to ratify a particular social contract. The priest is not simply an incarnation of some vague celestial authority but is a recognizably Northeast Brazilian patron. Floro, for his part, exemplifies a new order that storytellers find alien because it negates the long-established view of power as a personal relationship binding two individuals of unequal social status.

Pilgrims' Stories About Floro

The initially most striking feature of visitors' accounts of Floro is their relative brevity. Unlike residents' stories, which usually concentrate on an introductory episode that both locates and explains the ensuing exchange between the priest and the doctor, the great majority of pilgrims' tales focus exclusively on the confrontation. As a result many, such as the following, are only a few sentences long. In this instance, Floro's insistence that he is much older than the priest should be interpreted as a bid for the deference Northeast Brazilians traditionally grant to age. Because the doctor does not command respect in his own right, he seeks here to exact it through deceitful means.

59. Dr. Floro was a governor, a governor of Ceará. My Padrinho raised him up but Dr. Floro showed him no respect. "Look here, Padre Cícero," he always said, "I am greater than you. I was born before the time of Noah's Ark. And so I am much older than you who were born yesterday."

   "Stop this nonsense, Dr. Floro," my Padrinho told him. "He who made you great can make you small." But Dr. Floro paid no attention to anything he said and went and killed a lot of people. My Padrinho did everything to get him to stop but he wouldn't abandon that life as an assassin. So then my Padrinho had to do away with him.

   —Anísio da Mata Oliveira (P). Teresina, Piauí, 1926. Married; *rendeiro*. First pilgrimage. (October 2, 1982.)

Pilgrims' accounts are not only shorter but are also considerably less detailed than residents' stories. Their Floro does not sport an irrepressible mustache, tip his hat and wink at women, or gulp down enough food for a small army. The stories are no longer extended contrasts but rather are brief, decisive clashes between good and evil, on the order of those we saw in the case of the "war" of 1913–14.

The lack of detail in these stories is largely a function of decreased proximity to the subject. None of the visitors with whom I spoke had any personal memory of Floro, and only two or three mentioned friends or relatives who had supposedly known him. Unlike residents, most of whom are aware of the doctor's historical significance, pilgrims often refer to him as *um grandão* ("a big-shot"), *um capitão* ("a captain"), or *um amigo de Satanás* ("a friend of the devil"). Others mistakenly identify him as *um governador do Ceará* ("a governor of the state of Ceará"), *o ministro da guerra* ("national war minister"), *um amigo do bispo* ("a friend of the bishop"), or *um dos rabelos* ("one of Franco Rabelo's soldiers"). The real Floro might well have grabbed at the post of governor or minister. Considering the fury that he directed at the ecclesiastical establishment and other enemies in a well-known speech before the national legislature in 1923, however, the doctor might actually have preferred the devil to the bishop.[15] It is likewise ironic to find him described as a soldier of the same Franco Rabelo whose downfall he largely engineered.

Less aware of the facts than local storytellers, pilgrims also lack residents' access to a more or less communal store of anecdotal material. Because they have little, if any, sense of Floro as an individual, they find it far more difficult to illustrate his bad behavior. Although they often insist more vehemently than residents on his negative features, their denunciations seldom exhibit as much specificity as residents' tales. Questioning confirms that most visitors have never heard of incidents such as those involving the turkey hen, the *beato* José Lourenço, or the slaughtered ox.

This inability to draw on a body of local lore inclines many pilgrim storytellers toward allegory. The first speaker below portrays Floro as an insignificant mustard seed (no reference to the biblical grain symbolizing faith). The second sees him as an emblematic black bone that rises out of the depths of the earth to torment Padre Cícero.

60. One day my Padrinho summoned Dr. Floro. "Dr. Floro," he said, "you have become too great."

So then Dr. Floro asked him, "Well then, why did you make me this way?"

15. See Floro Bartolomeu da Costa, *Joazeiro e o Padre Cícero: Depoimentos para a história*, for the text of the speech. Floro also used this opportunity to attack enemies such as [Antonio] Xavier de Oliveira, who had suggested in his *Beatos e cangaceiros* that the doctor was directly responsible for the continued banditry and disorder in the Cariri.

My Padrinho Cícero said, "Be careful. He who made you great can make you even smaller than a little mustard seed."

So then Floro asked again, "Why did you make me great?"

"You are going to end up just like a little mustard seed," my Padrinho said. "A very little seed that the wind carries off without anyone noticing." And that is exactly what happened. Shortly afterward Dr. Floro went to Rio de Janeiro and there he died. He wanted to be great but the wind carried off his greatness. And nobody noticed. Nobody even cared.

—Raimundo Nascimento da Silva (P). Santa Cruz, Pernambuco, 1922. Married; itinerant peddler. 11 pilgrimages. (October 26, 1982.)

61. It was Dr. Floro who made my Padrinho Cícero suffer. The Sacred Heart of Jesus gave Juazeiro to my Padrinho. The Sacred Heart told my Padrinho that he was to take charge of everything. And suddenly, from deep within the earth a black bone rose up to make my Padrinho suffer. I say that the black bone was this Dr. Floro. It was he who was responsible for all of my Padrinho's persecutions.

—Maria José da Conceição (P). Surubim, Pernambuco, 1905. Widow; *moradora*. 8 pilgrimages. (November 24, 1982.)

Visitors' distance from Floro also means that they lack any incentive to keep him alive in their tales. Not only are they unaware of the historical doctor's close relationship to Padre Cícero; they also lack any need for a scapegoat for local problems. As a result, their accounts almost always end with Floro's death. In one pilgrim's version of the Carnival incident, for example, the rain no longer simply causes the marchers to sneeze. Instead, it triggers a fatal illness that the storyteller regards as punishment for the doctor's defiance of the priest. Stripped of the amusing details characteristic of residents' versions of the story, the tale becomes a stark confrontation between Padre Cícero and Floro.

62. In the past, there was no Carnival celebration in Juazeiro, and there is still no Carnival today. But there was a big-shot by the name of Dr. Floro. He was like a king but he wanted to be still more powerful than my Padrinho—ha, ha, ha! So then my Padrinho said, "Floro, he who made you great can also make you small." But Dr. Floro only laughed and told his soldiers to stage a big parade. Well then, it started raining and Dr. Floro came down with a fever and chills. He became so sick that he ended up dying in Rio de

Janeiro. He wanted to be greater than my Padrinho, so how else could things have turned out for him?

—Luzia Marques de Souza (P). Altos, Piauí, 1923. Widow; *rendeira*.
2 pilgrimages. (October 6, 1982.)

In an attempt to make Floro responsible for his own unhappy end, storytellers may have him explicitly dismiss an opportunity to mend his ways. These rejections serve to dispel any lingering sympathy for the doctor, who is seen to court the sort of direct, physical punishment customarily meted out to villains in negative challenge tales.

63. He was a big-shot, Dr. Floro. Padrinho Cícero liked him but he did many cruel things. He killed a lot of people and in the end he too died. My Padrinho warned him that he could not go on in this way but he didn't listen, no. So then he got sick and not long afterward he died. My Padrinho gave him a medicine that would have cured him. But he didn't want my Padrinho's medicine and so he died on the spot. Because he was very stubborn, don't you know?

—José Ribeiro Nunes (P). Flores, Pernambuco, 1914. Widowed;
rendeiro. 6 pilgrimages. (October 15, 1982.)

Pilgrims' conception of Floro as an unrepentant rebel makes the story more like others such as that of the would-be assassin or that of the rancher who asked for rain. It also brings the incident into line with others to suggest an incipient master legend or "life." Seen in this context, the doctor's ingratitude is yet another cause of Padre Cícero's unjust suffering.

In order to emphasize this larger pattern, pilgrims may link the tale of Floro to accounts of the Revolution of 1913–14 or the alleged transformation of 1889. In the first case, Padre Cícero makes Floro his lieutenant during the "war." In the second, an example of which appears below, the doctor's callous treatment of Maria de Araújo prompts the usual verbal showdown between him and the priest. Although Floro actually arrived in Juazeiro almost two decades after the supposed miracle of the communion wafer, pilgrims' interest in constructing a single coherent narrative leads them to associate the doctor with this event.

64. Dr. Floro was a big boss here. So then one day he heard that my Padrinho had placed the host in the mouth of the *beata* Maria de Araújo. And that it had turned to blood. So then when he heard the news, he ran to see the *beata*. He stuck his big old finger in her mouth. Because this Floro didn't believe in my Padrinho's powers.

He even scratched the *beata*'s throat. So then my Padrinho Cícero
got angry.
"Dr. Floro," he said, "show me some respect!"
"Why?" Floro said. "I am more powerful than you."
"That is what you think," my Padrinho said, "but you had better
be careful because he who has raised you up can surely make you
fall." Well, a little while later Dr. Floro left for Rio de Janeiro. But
he never got there because he died along the way.

—Pedro Gomes de Oliveira (P). Queimadas, Paraíba, 1941. Married;
rendeiro. 4 pilgrimages. (October 15, 1982.)

The teller's willingness to let Floro perish, as in many other pilgrims'
stories, suggests the extent of the differences between the two groups of
storytellers. Yet despite their insistence on a dramatic climax, many visitors' stories are ultimately condensed expressions of relationships more
fully described in residents' tales. The following pilgrims' account, for
instance, looks at first glance quite different from residents' highly detailed versions of the tale. Nevertheless, close examination of the texts,
shown here in both Portuguese and English, confirms the presence of
oppositions much like those associated with local storytellers.

65. Tinha um dotô por nomi di Dotô Fulori, um grandão daqui. Meu
    Padim gustava deli, dava muntu pudê a eli. Era baixinhu i gordu,
    arvu di cabelu ruim. Era estrangeru, bichão, crenti. Falava grossu i
    enroladu, ninguém entendia, não. Aí a justiça deli era di matá u
    povu. Matava munta genti. Aí meu Padim dixi, "Vem cá, Fulori.
    Acaba cum essa vida di matá u povu, viu? Você não tá sabenu quem
    mireci essi castigu."
        Aí eli dixi, "Óia, Padi Ciçu, foi u sinhô quem mi feiz grandi.
    Antão porqui mi feiz ansim?"
        Eli dixi, "Cuidadu, Fulori, qui quem ti feiz grandi podi ti fazê
    piqueninu du pé da pueira." Antão eli adueceu. Foi pru Riu di
    Janeiru i logu dipois murreu. Qui u corpu deli ficô lá qui não pudia
    si enterrá aqui im terra santa.

65. There was a doctor named Dr. Floro, a big-shot here. My Padrinho
    liked him; he gave him a lot of power. He was short and fat, white-
    skinned with wiry hair. He was a foreigner, a bully, a Protestant.
    He talked loudly and in a garbled manner so that no one understood
    him. His brand of justice was to go around killing people. He
    killed a lot of people. So my Padrinho said, "Come here, Floro.
    Stop killing people, understand? You have no way of knowing who
    deserves this punishment."

So then he said, "Look, Padre Cícero, it was you who made me great. Why, then, did you make me this way?" He said, "Be careful, Floro, because he who made you great can make you small as dust." Then he got sick. He went to Rio de Janeiro and shortly afterward he died. And his body remained there because it could not be buried here in holy soil.
—Pedro Rolim dos Santos (P). Maceió, Alagoas, 1896. Widowed; sells saddle equipment in open-air market. 28 pilgrimages. (October 23, 1982.)

The storyteller's initial reference to Floro as a *doutor* ("dotô"), or "doctor," sets up an implicit contrast between him and the priest. The title *doutor*, which refers to any powerful person (a physician is a *médico*), connotes deference but has none of the overtones of intimacy and affection accruing to a *padrinho* or godfather. Thus at the same time that Floro commands respect because of his superior social status, he does not inspire that deep loyalty people feel toward Padre Cícero.

The description of Floro as "short and fat, white-skinned with wiry hair" (*baixinhu i gordu, arvu di cabelu ruim*) corresponds in very general terms to photographs of the doctor. In fact, at first glance the description appears to be uncharacteristically concrete. Each component of the phrase, however, has another, more symbolic dimension that helps to explain its presence in the story. Although the primary meaning of *baixo* is "short," it has moral connotations. A person *de baixo caráter* lacks scruples. He or she is a "low" person.

By coupling this term with *gordo*, "fat," the speaker emphasizes those corporeal aspects of Floro's personality on which local storytellers are disposed to expand. *Cabelu ruim* literally means "bad hair." It refers specifically to the coarse, very curly texture indicating the African blood that most speakers—who often have this sort of hair themselves—equate with social inferiority. The miscegenation that has occurred over centuries has resulted in a goodly number of fair-skinned Brazilians with "African" hair. In this case, however, the pairing of "white-skinned" with "wiry-haired" is an effective way of calling Floro a wolf in sheep's clothing. The doctor's refusal to live up to the obligations of his elevated rank within the social order leads the speaker to suggest that he is not what he initially appears.

The storyteller also refers to Floro as "a foreigner, a bully, a Protestant" (*estrangeru, bichão, crenti*). *Bichão*, which means "bully," is literally a big *bicho* or animal. The term thus reemphasizes Floro's bestial or earthbound nature. *Crenti* or *crente* applies not only to Protestants but to any non-Catholic as well. It is a derogatory synonym for "unbeliever." Floro is "foreign" not only because he comes from the relatively distant state of Bahia but also because his moral behavior is so different from that which people have been taught to expect.

In a similar manner, the doctor's habit of speaking "in a garbled manner so that no one understood him" may be seen initially as a reference to Floro's university education as well as to his regional provenance. The doctor's difficulties in interpersonal communication, however, go beyond vocabulary and pronunciation. Storytellers do not understand him, because he represents an alien way of thinking; metaphorically at least, he speaks another language. His habit of speaking loudly makes him the opposite of the soft-spoken Padre Cícero who gets what he wants without raising his voice.

The assertion that the doctor's "brand of justice is to go around killing people" serves as an ironic restatement of a point made by local storytellers. Floro is spiritually dead—that is, incapable of any sort of constructive action—because of his conscious divorce from a traditional moral code.

Padre Cícero's way of addressing his advisor emphasizes his own superiority. *Vem cá* ("Come here") is a summons employed for a child or a servant. The priest's use of the familiar *tu* form (*Quem ti feiz grandi podi ti fazê piqueninu*) contrasts with Floro's use of the polite *o senhor* form in addressing the priest. The doctor sets out to insult the priest by calling him "Padre Cícero" instead of the more deferential "my Padrinho." He lapses again into formal usage when acknowledging that it was indeed the priest (*"foi o sinhô"*) who is the source of his power.

Padre Cícero's threat to reduce Floro to "dust" prompts visions of death and decay. The ground is also a symbol of social inferiority and as such suggests a loss of temporal standing. In Christian literature, physical ailments are often an outward manifestation of spiritual disease, so the allegorical significance of the doctor's illness is difficult to overlook. Floro ostensibly leaves for Rio de Janeiro because he is a federal deputy, but as the seat at that time of the national government Rio is meant to stand in contrast to Juazeiro, which the storytellers regard as the spiritual capital of Brazil. Floro's body remains in Rio because his legislative post demands an official state burial. On a deeper level, however, he has chosen permanent exile. The *terra santa* to which the speaker refers is thus at once the consecrated earth of any cemetery and the "holy city" of Juazeiro. The doctor's corpse must remain in Rio not only because the body would decompose during the long journey by boat and then horseback, but also because he has willfully forfeited his place at "the center of the world."

At the same time that this extended metaphorical "translation" points to the complexity of many seemingly simple narratives, it confirms the continuing bond between the two groups of storytellers. If the relationships hinted at in pilgrims' stories were not spelled out at length by residents, this sort of decoding would be considerably more difficult.

And yet although oppositions normally associated with local storytellers may remain beneath the surface of pilgrims' tales, there is no denying growing dissimilarities. Unlike descriptions of the Revolution of 1913–14, in which residents and pilgrims stress different elements of the same double challenge pattern, accounts of Padre Cícero and Dr. Floro suggest nascent structural modifications. Although pilgrims' willingness to supply the fourth step missing in most residents' stories does not constitute a radical departure, it heralds a more profound division than that which we observed in the preceding chapter.

VII.

Maria de Araújo and the "Miracle" of 1889

Maria de Araújo was just like Our Lady. The wafer turned to
blood in her holy mouth.

Resident of Juazeiro

Was it a punishment? Of course it was a punishment. My
Padrinho punished that woman because she doubted his
miraculous powers.

Pilgrim, Rio Grande do Norte

The single most critical occurrence in the history of Juazeiro is the
so-called transformation of 1889. We have seen that after Padre
Cícero administered communion to the *beata* Maria de Araújo, the wafer
allegedly grew red with the blood of Christ. This "miracle" triggered
the pilgrimage to Juazeiro and resulted in the bishop's partial suspension
of Padre Cícero's holy orders some three years later. Partly because of its
importance, the event poses problems of a kind not associated with either
the Revolution of 1913–14 or the confrontation between the priest and
Dr. Floro. Residents' and pilgrims' accounts of the supposed transformation vary not only in content but also in underlying structure.
Whereas local storytellers tend to see the bleeding host as a positive occurrence, pilgrims are more prone to view it as a punishment of the *beata*
fitting the larger framework of a "life." Their stories therefore constitute
a contradiction of what earlier visitors to Juazeiro considered to be an
immutable fact.

Maria de Araújo and the "Miracle" of 1889

The problem of the blood's origin and the mechanics of its appearance
have never been convincingly explained.[1] The alleged miracle raises a

---

1. For a detailed description of the event and its immediate consequences see della Cava,
Miracle at Joaseiro, pp. 31–51. The author does not attempt to explain the bleeding.

number of perplexing questions impossible to resolve today for want of scientific evidence. Despite the existence of various written accounts by the priest's contemporaries, it is not always easy to say exactly what happened, let alone how and why. The miracle stories that follow must therefore be seen as interpretations of an event that has long been clouded by debate.[2]

Most people of the period saw only two possible explanations for the blood's appearance: either it was a divine sign, or it was a hoax. Because doctors a hundred years ago in the Brazilian backlands had little sense of the close relationship between mind and body, they restricted themselves to detailed examinations of Maria de Araújo's mouth.[3] When they found no sign of wounds, and strict surveillance of the *beata* seemed to rule out the possibility of deceptive action on her part, many people concluded that a supernatural force must be at work. When the urn containing the hosts and stained cloths disappeared from the Crato altar—a theft precluding any sort of later laboratory identification—some of these same individuals reversed their initial opinion and now denounced the incident as a malicious fraud.

The anxiety engendered by both the threat of drought and the impending dissolution of a social order in effect for some four centuries makes this apparent rush to judgment more comprehensible. It is worth reemphasizing that Padre Cícero appears initially to have entertained doubts about the nature of the event and that it was not he but other clerics who first labeled it a miracle. Moreover, the priest suggests that the *beata* shared these early misgivings. "I am a witness," he says in an undated personal letter, "that when the host turned to blood, she [Maria de Araújo] demonstrated great affliction, fearing that it was a punishment and an indignity."[4]

2. Portions of the documents regarding the alleged transformation are available in J. Soares Pimentel, ed., *Os Milagres do Joazeiro ou Grande Colecção de documentos que attestam a veracidade da transformação da Sagrada Hóstia em sangue . . .* , and in "Documentos sobre a questão religiosa do Juazeiro." The report of the First Commission of Inquiry, composed of Padre Clycério da Costa Lobo and Padre Francisco Ferreira Antero, is entitled "Cópia Authéntica do Processo do Inquérito Instruído pelo Excmo. e Revdmo. Dr. Dom Joaquim José Vieira sobre os factos extraordinários occurridos em Joazeiro, 1891." I have not seen the text.

3. It is worth noting that Maria de Araújo is said to have been infirm since childhood. Some writers suggest that she suffered from epilepsy. She is also said to have been a stigmatic. Some recent scholarship on the religious experiences of women in the Middle Ages is useful in considering possible explanations for the alleged transformation. I am indebted to Caroline Walker Bynum for allowing me to read a draft of her "Women Mystics and Eucharistic Devotion in the Thirteenth Century." See also Elizabeth Petroff, *Consolation of the Blessed,* a study of four medieval Italian women saints that includes a useful bibliographical section on pp. 179–203. A broader context for the events in Juazeiro is provided by George Tavard, *Women in Christian Tradition.*

4. Letter 8, in Packet 36, Salesian Archives.

One can just as readily understand how the bishop of Fortaleza, Dom Joaquim Vieira, might have come to see the *beata* as the instigator of a malicious deception. First, her testimony would have been disturbing to anyone with a background in theology. Unlike Padre Cícero, who carefully phrased his version of the events in a language familiar to persons with a seminary education, Maria de Araújo did not hesitate to speak of a "new mystery" with which church officials had not yet dealt.[5] Her claims, which struck many persons of the epoch as extravagant if not heretical, were particularly distressing to a bishop from progressive São Paulo charged with safeguarding the doctrinal purity of the Catholic faith.

The visitors who began pouring into the Cariri after the "miracle" became public knowledge insisted on venerating not only the cloths supposedly stained with Christ's blood but often Maria de Araújo herself as well. Their adulation apparently prompted a number of other *beatas* to emulate the new "saint." These women ran through the streets of Juazeiro with crucifixes, inviting the growing crowds of pilgrims to share in their supposed visions. Under threat of excommunication, the self-styled prophetesses later repudiated any claim to extraordinary experience.[6] Although Maria de Araújo staunchly refused to follow suit, the recantations of her imitators must have struck the bishop as indirect proof of her own guilt.

Then too, the disappearance of the urn containing the stained cloths could not fail to suggest that someone had something to hide. Despite his anger at Padre Cícero, Dom Joaquim seems to have dismissed him as a suspect. He was more disposed to blame José Marrocos, among whose personal effects the urn resurfaced many years later, and the *beata,* who he assumed must be working with the journalist to deceive the priest.[7]

Dom Joaquim's reluctance to point an accusatory finger at Padre Cícero may stem in part from their personal acquaintance. Then too, as the bishop had publicly commended Padre Cícero's sincerity and zeal only a short time earlier, it would have been somewhat awkward suddenly to brand him as a thief.[8] Furthermore, laying aside the problems the events

5. Della Cava, *Miracle at Joaseiro,* p. 45.

6. For a description of these women see Renato Dantas, *As beatas do Cariri e de Juazeiro.*

7. What happened to the urn after its reappearance is not clear. After its discovery among Marrocos' belongings, it was handed over to church officials, who presumably destroyed the contents. The urn, however, has become part of local lore. Numerous individuals claim to have seen it, or one of the stained cloths, in the recent past, and there is a whole body of tales about these objects.

8. Dom Joaquim publicly praised Padre Cícero in 1884 in the course of a visit to the Cariri to consecrate the altar of the chapel of Our Lady of Sorrows, which the priest had succeeded

of 1889 had caused the bishop, the two men had much in common in terms of goals and education. The same cannot be said for Dom Joaquim and Maria de Araújo, the latter the representation of an institution—the *Casa de Caridade*—that the bishop would almost certainly have disbanded if he had not had to worry about the reaction of the local elite.

After the second commission's report the bishop ordered the *beata* to retire to the Charity House in neighboring Barbalha. When her family refused to let her leave Juazeiro, he ordered Padre Cícero never to speak about the alleged transformation or Maria de Araújo again.[9]

The *beata* lived on, well out of the public eye, until 1914. Following her death during the Revolution, Padre Cícero had the corpse entombed in the as-yet-unconsecrated chapel of Our Lady of Perpetual Help. His action angered episcopal authorities, who saw both his choice of site and his continuing consideration for Maria de Araújo as gestures of rebellion. Although the *beata*'s body remained in the chapel during the priest's lifetime, after his death it was removed to an unmarked grave in the surrounding cemetery.[10]

Residents' Accounts of the Events of 1889

Medieval miracle literature—not necessarily familiar to local storytellers—is full of transformations of the communion bread and wine.[11] Sometimes the metamorphosis is a wholly positive occurrence; the host may, for instance, suddenly become a baby. Frequently it turns into milk or honey which nourishes the devout recipient.

In those cases in which the transformation has negative connotations, the host usually turns to blood. The wafer may stain the hands of

---

in rebuilding. See Amália Xavier de Oliveira, *Dados que marcam a vida do Padre Cícero Romão Batista*, p. 6.

9. Padre Cícero obeyed the bishop's order, going so far as to refute the alleged transformation publicly in the church square in 1916. From the letters preserved in the Salesian Archives, however, it is clear that he continued to believe in the "miracle" until his death. In a letter addressed to Padre Constantino Augusto and dated October 23, 1914, he asserts that the bishop asked more of him than of the other priests whom he ordered to abjure the event. "He asked," says Padre Cícero, "that I commit perjury . . . and that I slander the poor innocent Maria de Araújo by saying that she had deceived me and committed other irregular acts which she never did." (My translation.)

10. Some residents of Juazeiro recount a story about the *beata* much like the well-known tale of the slipper in the tomb. According to these individuals, when church authorities went to remove her body from the chapel they found nothing except a single rose.

11. See Peter Browe, *Die Eucharistischen Wunder des Mittelalters*. A number of eucharistic miracles are related by Caesarius of Heisterbach in the *Dialogue on Miracles*, 2, pp. 103–170.

a doubting priest or the knife of a non-Christian. A communicant may tuck the host into a corner of his or her mouth, only to discover later that it has begun to bleed.

A good example of this sort of punitive transformation concerns an unnamed priest who finds himself doubting the truth of the doctrine of transubstantiation as he consecrates the host. The wafer immediately begins to weep blood. Watching the altar before him grow crimson, the priest regains his faith. When the pope learns of this apparent miracle he has the bloodstained items sent to a church in the town of Orvieto, where an array of ecclesiastical authorities come to pay them homage. The story is thus intended to provide support for the new emphasis on eucharistic devotion characteristic of the twelfth and thirteenth centuries.[12]

Residents' stories of the "miracle" of 1889 differ from this and other narratives that have come down to us in writing in that they present the wafer's metamorphosis into blood as a wholly positive occurrence. The alleged transformation is not a typical reward. Because the event does not constitute a response to either an unbeliever's insult or a believer's call for help, it is difficult to fit into the four-step challenge pattern. Padre Cícero's peripheral role in most versions of the incident likewise makes it difficult to see the story as an explanation or affirmation of his miraculous powers.

Local storytellers are well aware of the alleged transformation's anomalies. Even more than in the case of the Revolution of 1913–14 or of Dr. Floro, however, they feel bound to abide by what they consider to be fact. This sense of obligation often stems from close association with the *beata*. In addition, the event represents a welcome reassertion of Juazeiro's importance. As the site of a "great miracle," the city takes on a significance it would not assume were the alleged transformation a punitive response.

Maria de Araújo achieved prominence long before Dr. Floro's arrival in the Cariri. In fact, the two overlapped by only six years. Nevertheless, there are understandably many more residents who claim some sort of contact with the lowly *beata* who spent her whole life in Juazeiro than with the rich and powerful doctor who visited the city on occasion. A number of local storytellers cite parents or grandparents who not only knew the *beata* but who were also supposedly present at the transforma-

12. The story appears in Brewer, *Dictionary of Miracles,* p. 489. A summary of eucharistic practice and devotion is available in "Eucharist," *New Catholic Encyclopedia,* 5, pp. 594–620. For a discussion of the symbolic aspects of the Eucharist see Jung's "Transformation Symbolism in the Mass."

tion of the host. The following account is one of many examples in which the storyteller presents the "miracle" through the eyes of a relative. Note that the host in this instance bleeds *before* the priest administers it to Maria de Araújo.

66. That case involving Maria de Araújo is very complicated. My mother—no, it was my grandmother—used to go to church a good deal during that time. Well then, my grandmother—her name was Ana—was at mass one fine day when my Padrinho Cícero elevated the host and a ribbon of blood ran down each arm. So then my Padrinho placed the host in the mouth of Maria de Araújo and the host turned into bright red blood. And that isn't all. The exact same thing happened the next day. When the bishop learned of the event, he summoned the doctors. They examined her to see if there was not some sort of wound in her mouth. But they found nothing. And so it was certain that the host had turned to blood in the *beata*'s mouth.

—Manoel Caboclo e Silva (R). Juazeiro, 1916. Married; *cordel* poet
and horoscope writer. (July 5, 1981.)

In its dependence on detail, this story is characteristic of residents' tales in general. Although the twin ribbons of blood running down the priest's arm are an individualizing feature, the concrete detail here is typical of most accounts by local storytellers. At the same time, stories of Maria de Araújo stand apart from others within their repertoire. By curtailing or omitting the sort of dialogue and movement ordinarily so important to them, the tellers often end up with a series of curiously impersonal tales.

Storytellers' reluctance to talk about the transformation reflects not only the structural difficulties the tale poses but also their own disturbing memories of the event. Most people who live in Juazeiro are aware that the bishop forbade Padre Cícero to talk about the "miracle" or the *beata*. They can remember the sanctions—denial of the sacraments, threat of excommunication—that members of the clergy levied against those who insisted on professing their faith in the alleged transformation. Even though this sort of overt opposition is a thing of the past, painful recollections make it all but impossible for residents to speak of the *beata* with the ease with which they talk of Manuel Correia or the rancher who asked for rain. Some actually tell the story in the guise of a disclaimer. "Oh yes," says one individual, "Maria de Araújo. She was the one in whose mouth the host turned to blood. The doctors came to examine her and said that yes, it was the blood of Our Lord Jesus Christ, but I know nothing about it because it was before my time."[13] "Maria de Araújo?" asks another. "There was a host that started bleeding during the communion, but I couldn't tell you anything about the Precious Blood."[14]

Even when people respond in a more positive manner, they may be almost epigrammatic. A sizable number of residents offer no more than a summary identification of the *beata*. The same persons whose tales of the Revolution of 1913–14 or Dr. Floro rely on numerous supporting details often drastically pare down their accounts of the alleged transformation in an attempt to protect themselves from complications.

67. When my Padrinho Cícero arrived to give communion, he put the host in the *beata*'s mouth. And it turned into blood. This is the story of the Precious Blood. The host turned into blood in the *beata*'s mouth.

    —Cecília de Lima (R). Recife, Pernambuco, 1908. Arrived Juazeiro 1918. Married; makes straw hats. (July 30, 1981.)

Storytellers may seek to fend off problems by creating a sense of narrative distance. To this end, they introduce an unusually high number of qualifiers and roundabout constructions. In the following example, the speaker declares three times that her mother–in–law, not she herself, is responsible for the information regarding the alleged transformation.

68. I cannot say much about the transformation of the host. Because it was before my time, see? But my mother–in–law knew the *beata*. She says that this Maria de Araújo was a very devout Catholic, that she had practically lived in the church ever since she was a child. So then one day my Padrinho Cícero went to give her communion and the host turned into blood. At least that is what my mother–in–law says. I wasn't there to see it but my mother–in–law says that my Padrinho went to give communion to her, to the *beata,* three times. And the host turned into blood each of these three times. So then my Padrinho started crying but no one knows why. Then they took the *beata* to Crato, where she remained a prisoner. When they freed her my Padrinho came to give her communion at midnight so that no one would see.

    —Maria das Dores da Silva (R). Just outside Juazeiro, 1914. Separated; laundress. (July 24, 1981.)

13. Carmina da Conceição (R). Baixio Verde, Ceará, 1911. Arrived Juazeiro as child. Widow; sells charcoal from door to door. (August 3, 1981.)

14. Francisco Campos da Silva (R) Várzea Alegre, Ceará, 1932. Arrived Juazeiro as child. Married; on-the-spot photographer. (July 4, 1981.)

Especially when speaking in the first person, the storyteller will hedge. The unmistakably tentative character of the next account sets it apart from other miracle narratives. The speaker's comments are in no way unconventional, but she is obviously fearful that someone will challenge her.

69. Well, *they say* that the *beata* put the host in her mouth and it turned to blood. *They say* that there were some people who didn't believe what had happened and who set out to stir up doubts. *I don't know* how it was *but they say* that these people went around claiming it was actually ox blood on those cloths. But she [the *beata*] went to Rome and *it appears* that the event was accepted as truth. *It appears so.* Of course *I don't know* because women aren't like men, who can go everywhere they please and who know everything that happens. *But so far as I know,* it was all true [my italics].
    —Maria Vicência da Luz (R). Missão Velha, Ceará, 1902. Arrived
    Juazeiro 1918. Widow; retired. (August 10, 1981.)

The alleged transformation presents another problem for residents in that it is qualitatively different from tales that focus on lack of rain, the sudden hunger of a group of workmen, or a traveler's fear about the journey home. Although Padre Cícero employs supernatural means to reward his followers and punish his detractors in these other narratives, the hat that sticks to the schoolhouse wall or the chicks who manage to find food in an empty house are reassuringly familiar. The communion wafer belongs to another order of experience, which most people would rather not attempt to explain. The transformation is too miraculous, too outside the circle of everyday activity for storytellers to appropriate to their own ends.

The historical significance as well as the profound "otherness" of the event makes many residents wary. "That business of the *beata* is very complicated," asserts one woman. "I don't want to talk about it because I'd be afraid to say something wrong."[15] "I believe that the host turned into blood in the mouth of the *beata*," a man says, "but I am not going to tell you the story because it is much too important for a person to get only half-right."[16]

The "miracle's" abstract "theological" side does not negate its overtly physical dimension. The supernatural occurrence on which the story focuses is intimately associated with not just a human, but a spe-

15. Maria Gurgel da Silva (R). Carnaúba, Rio Grande do Norte, 1916. Arrived Juazeiro 1946. Single; retired. (August 5, 1981.)

16. Ludugero Salviano (R). Viçosa, Alagoas, 1913. Arrived Juazeiro 1942. Married; ren deiro. (October 24, 1982.)

cifically female, body. As such, it suggests deeply rooted menstrual taboos posing, by extension, the broader issue of traditional sex roles in
Northeast Brazil.[17] In a society where "women aren't like men, who can
go everywhere they please and know everything that happens," strong
reaction to a situation in which a woman assumes the leading role normally reserved for Padre Cícero is hardly surprising.

Local storytellers have devised a number of ways of dealing with this
obvious physicality. The great majority either divorce the *beata* from the
transformation proper or concentrate on the effects of the "miracle"
rather than on the event itself. Both these alternatives allow them to side-
step the events of 1889.

Older storytellers in particular often shift their focus from the alleged transformation to the figure of the *beata*. In a particularly lovely
ballad, which I have not heard outside Juazeiro, the devil in the guise of
a handsome young suitor tries to seduce Maria de Araújo. He first dances
and plays his guitar for the *beata,* who is seated in a window making lace.
He then attempts to distract her with a perfumed handkerchief, the perfect symbol of luxury and elevated social status for people too poor to
think of using a special cloth to blow their noses. The devil concludes by
offering Maria de Araújo bread and coffee, but she assures him that the
wine and wafer of communion provide all the nourishment she needs.
Although this final allusion to the Eucharist recalls the alleged transformation, the ballad makes no explicit reference to the *beata*'s role in the
event.

Accounts of Maria de Araújo that do not touch on the events of 1889
often focus on the speaker's own relationship to her. Many residents
credit the *beata* with cures or other personal favors. The following storyteller describes how, when he invokes her aid, "Saint" Maria de Araújo
appears before him to breathe new life into a dead horse.

70. I was riding in the woods alone. During that time there were many
    mountain lions and it was dangerous to spend the night outdoors.
    So then I was hurrying along when suddenly one of these big
    snakes appeared from nowhere. It bit my horse. Poor thing, it gave
    a whinny and then a great shudder before falling to the ground.

17. For a discussion of sex roles in Latin America see Ann Pescatello, ed., *Female and Male
in Latin America;* an extensive bibliography appears on pp. 293–334. See also Meri Knaster,
"Women in Latin America: The State of Research." For a broader perspective see Peggy
Reeves Sanday, *Female Power and Male Dominance;* Sherry B. Ortner and Harriet Whitehead,
eds., *Sexual Meanings: The Cultural Construction of Gender and Sexuality;* and Michelle Rosaldo and Louise Lamphere, eds., *Women, Culture, and Society.* I am grateful to Kay Turner
for bibliographical suggestions and valuable criticisms of an earlier draft of this chapter.

So then, there I was, all alone, without a horse to ride and the night about to fall. Well, in that very instant I called on Saint Maria Araújo for aid. If she would have compassion on me and resuscitate my horse, I would offer a mass in honor of her holy soul. So then suddenly the horse gives another shudder and gets to its feet. So then we go galloping through the brush until we reach a farmhouse where we pass the night.
—José Dantas Filho (R). Juazeiro, 1904. Married; retired. (July 12, 1981.)

In a similar manner an old woman in the Rua do Horto describes how Maria de Araújo helps her to obtain a long-desired house of her own. In appreciation for the *beata*'s apparent intervention, the woman periodically trudges up the steep thoroughfare at noon with an enormous portrait of the "saint" around her neck. The picture shows, not the frail mulatta who appears in history books, but an individual with the white skin, blue eyes, and regular, European features normally associated with Christian iconography.[18]

The approach most common among local storytellers is to employ the alleged transformation as a springboard. Whether the ensuing story focuses on Padre Cícero or on Maria de Araújo depends largely, although not exclusively, on the teller's own sex. Men are prone to see the "miracle" as a motive for Padre Cícero's trip to Rome or for his confrontation with Padre Monteiro. Women are more likely to talk about the *beata*'s unjust sufferings.[19]

Storytellers' willingness to make the transformation part of a larger story does not necessarily imply a direct causal relationship between the events they describe. In the majority of cases, the "miracle" becomes nothing more than a pretext for a largely unrelated narrative. The following speaker, for instance, recounts how Padre Cícero threatens to end the world by knotting the corners of a towel stained by the Precious Blood. Although Maria de Araújo appears at the beginning of this story, she plays no role whatsoever in the ensuing action.

71. My Padrinho was administering communion to the people and the host turned into blood in the mouth of the *beata* Araújo. So then the bishop, the pope, and all the priests there summoned him to Rome. Because he was going to have to account for those blood-

18. The picture many storytellers believe to be of Maria de Araújo is a widely available portrait of the Virgin Mary.
19. See Stanley Brandes, *Metaphors of Masculinity: Sex and Status in Andalusian Folklore,* for a discussion of men's perspectives expressed in folk form.

A picture presumed by many people to be Maria de Araújo, together with an actual photograph of the woman herself. Both pictures are available in the shops and stalls that cater to pilgrims, but the madonna-like *beata* is considerably more popular among those persons who regard her as a saint.

stained towels. Either he was going to account for them or he was going to die.

They made him suffer so much, so much, in Rome that he finally said, "Just a moment!" Then he took one of those bloodstained cloths from his pocket and began to knot each of the four corners.

So then everyone shouted, "Don't do this, Padre Cícero!" Because they knew that if he knotted those four corners, the world would end right then and there. They knew he was telling the truth. They knew that stain was none other than Our Lord's Precious Blood.

—João José da Silva (R). Lagoa de Gato, Pernambuco, 1906. Arrived Juazeiro 1931. Marital status unknown; retired. (October 18, 1982.)

Those residents who make Padre Cícero the focus of their stories often imply that the *beata* somehow wronged the priest. Although descriptions of how her opponents "scraped and pulled out her tongue" seem to suggest that Maria de Araújo is the victim, the speakers may explicitly refer to *Padre Cícero's* sufferings. (Italics added in all cases.)

72. There was a *beata*, Maria de Araújo. She went to take communion and the host turned into blood. *It was because of this beata* that my Padrinho Cícero was suspended from his orders.
   —Manuel Fernandes de Lima (R). Alagoas [city not stated], 1907. Arrived Juazeiro 1935. Married; odd jobs. (July 8, 1981.)

73. Maria de Araújo? Yes, I have heard the story. *It was because of her* that my Padrinho Cícero was called to Rome.
   —José Pedro da Silva (R). Caruaru, Pernambuco, 1929. Arrived Juazeiro 1971. Married; construction worker. (August 1, 1981.)

74. Then after that day when the host turned into blood there were some people who went about saying that Maria de Araújo was a liar, that she was a damned soul. They scraped her tongue and pulled it from her mouth, and *that was the beginning of my Padrinho's sufferings*.
   —Manuel Roberto (R). Lagoa de Gato, Pernambuco, 1919. Arrived Juazeiro as child. Married; *rendeiro* and pequi-nut vendor. (July 13, 1981.)

Restructuring the story in a way that makes Padre Cícero its undisputed focus has obvious advantages for those storytellers who feel uneasy about the transformation proper. By concentrating on the consequences of the "miracle" rather than on the event itself, they can eliminate troublesome details, thereby bending their stories to fit the familiar challenge framework. This increased flexibility does not explain, however, why all the preceding comments should reveal such an undercurrent of resentment. Why, one is forced to ask, should Maria de Araújo be responsible for the priest's suffering, if she did nothing more than accept the communion wafer he offered?

The answer to this question almost certainly lies outside the miracle corpus, in prevailing ideas about male dominance and female subordination. Resident storytellers' discomfort with Maria de Araújo's leading role in an event that would ordinarily demonstrate Padre Cícero's miraculous powers finds expression in veiled associations between the blood that reddens the host and that of menstruation.[20]

20. Useful general discussions of menstruation are Janice Delaney, Mary Jane Lupton, and Emily Toth, eds., *The Curse: A Cultural History of Menstruation,* and Penelope Shuttle and Peter Redgrove, *The Wise Wound: Eve's Curse and Everywoman,* which provides a bibliography on pp. 309–326. I have also found the work of Mary Douglas on purity and pollution useful: see her *Purity and Danger.* See further relevant articles in Nancy Falk and Rita M. Gross, eds., *Unspoken Worlds: Women's Religious Lives in Non-Western Cultures;* Judith

Because of the unavailability or expense of an alternate method of protection, Northeast Brazilian women have traditionally had to rely during their menstrual cycle on nothing more than rags tied about the waist or an extra skirt. As a result, staining is a fairly common occurrence, generating considerable anxiety. The following speaker's reference to the blood on a dress (*vestido*) rather than the usual altar linens (*panos*) is therefore impossible to ignore. The fact that women were formerly prohibited from taking communion during the menstrual period reinforces the suggestion of ritual impurity.[21]

75. My Padrinho Cícero administered communion to Maria de Araújo and the host turned into blood. Not just once but twice. They say that her dress turned bright red, that it turned red the first time and even redder the second. They also say that the bishop took away these dresses because he was not pleased. He was not pleased at all.
   —Francisco Albuquerque (R). Limoeiro, Pernambuco, 1933. Date of
   arrival in Juazeiro uncertain. Married; candy maker. (July 21, 1981.)

Storytellers may expressly deny the possibility of the blood being menstrual bleeding. One woman, who made me promise never to mention her name in connection with the story, weeps in anger when she remembers one priest's alleged references to the blood's origins. The fact that the event still triggers such emphatic reactions underscores its deeper cultural significance.

76. One day the *beata* Maria de Araújo arrived in church and went over to where my Padrinho Cícero usually celebrated mass. Then he offered her communion. And the host turned to blood in her mouth. So then my Padrinho Cícero said it was the Precious Blood of Our Lord Jesus Christ. Then all the other priests began to argue with him, saying it was not true. There was even a priest who

---

Plaskow and Joan Arnold Romero, eds., *Women and Religion;* and Ruth Hubbard, Mary Sue Henifin, and Barbara Fried, eds., *Women Look at Biology Looking at Women.* It is also worth consulting Charles T. Wood, "The Doctor's Dilemma: Sin, Salvation and the Menstrual Cycle in Medieval Thought."

21. Women in the Rua do Horto tell numerous stories about other women who begin menstruating in public. Perhaps the most common tale concerns a bride who stains her wedding dress on her way to church. This and similar stories suggest an association between the blood of menstruation and that which signifies a loss of virginity. Some women still refuse to commune during their menstrual period. They continue to respect a number of other taboos as well, such as refusing to sit beneath a lemon tree during their period. For documentation of similar taboos associated with menstruation in Brazilian folk culture see Luís da Câmara Cascudo, *Dicionário do folclore brasileiro,* 2, pp. 193–195.

said that the blood—God forgive me—was [the speaker lowers her voice] menstrual blood. Ah, that anybody could say such a slanderous thing!
—Woman (R), age 59.

As the suggestion of menstrual bleeding must cast doubt on the divine nature of the alleged transformation, it is initially difficult to see why storytellers should undercut an event on whose miraculous nature they themselves insist. Much of the explanation for this seeming paradox lies once again in the event's anomalous quality. I have already noted that while Padre Cícero normally dominates the miracle stories, the *beata* in this case assumes the leading role. The resentment evident in a number of comments about Maria de Araújo most likely reflects local storytellers' (not necessarily conscious) feeling that she has usurped the priest's rightful place.[22] People would resent any apparent interloper, and the fact that the *beata* is female only intensifies their chagrin.

Since menstrual bleeding is inextricably linked to procreation, the blood's appearance also constitutes an assertion of sexuality in direct opposition to Padre Cícero's vow of celibacy as a priest. From this perspective, the stained host appears to cast suspicions on his, as well as the *beata*'s, virtue. Because the bleeding is expressly associated with Maria de Araújo, it is the *beata* whom storytellers blame for—as one man puts it—"getting my Padrinho Cícero in trouble." "All his problems started in that moment," the man observes.[23] Thus even though I never heard a resident actually accuse Maria de Araújo of wrongdoing, the undercurrent of suspicion, if not of actual hostility, in many residents' accounts is unmistakable.

Many women speak to these half-stated accusations by defending Maria de Araújo. Their stories often, although not always, emphasize a willingness to suffer that most Northeast Brazilians associate specifically with females. By comparing Maria de Araújo to the Virgin Mary or by identifying her as Padre Cícero's sister, these individuals seek to deny any possibility of a sexual attachment between the priest and the *beata*.

22. The sense of hierarchy that pervades the miracle stories thus applies specifically to male and female relationships in tales of the alleged transformation. For useful parallels, see Eleanor Leacock, *Myths of Male Dominance: Collected Articles on Women Cross-Culturally.* Although the people of whom I am speaking are all poor, female subordination is not limited to the lower classes. For a summary of an important murder case in which by invoking "legitimate defense of honor" a husband was exonerated of the charge of killing his wife, see Warren Hoge, "Machismo Murder Case: Women Bitter in Brazil."
23. Antonio Ferreira (R). Bom Jardim, Pernambuco, 1920. Arrived Juazeiro 1940. Married; *rendeiro*. (July 23, 1981.)

In the following tale, Maria de Araújo stands apart from other women in terms of purity. Previously, the communion wine was thought to be the blood of Christ only in the mouth of the priest, who alone had the privilege of drinking it. For the lay person, and especially for a woman, blood was (and often still is) profane and polluting. But because of the purity which the storyteller goes to such lengths to stress, the *beata* transcends the double barrier of her sexual and her non-ecclesiastical identity, to assume a role otherwise reserved for a special class of men.

77. Maria de Araújo was exactly like the Virgin. When my Padrinho Cícero went to give her communion, the Precious Blood appeared, you see. There were three women at the communion table when he arrived but the blood only appeared in her. He gave communion to holy Maria de Araújo and the blood welled up from her mouth. I didn't see it but I believe with all my heart the people who did. They buried her in the Church of Our Lady of Perpetual Help, but her body vanished from the coffin because she went to heaven as a saint.

—Maria Cândida da Conceição (R). Pão de Açucar, Alagoas, 1900.
Arrived Juazeiro 1915. Widow; sells milk door-to-door.
(August 5, 1981).

The exact nature of the suspicions commonly directed at the *beata* is once again apparent in these women's refutations. The speaker may, for instance, deny that the *beata* tries to stage a "miracle" by using the blood of an animal to color the host.

78. They say that Maria de Araújo wanted to become a saint, that she carried a little flask of ox blood and so on. But I don't believe it. A dozen doctors came to examine her. And they said that the blood was neither human nor animal, that it was a kind of blood completely different from any other. And they did not find a scar or anything else in her mouth. So then you can be sure that she was innocent, without sin, and a virgin among virgins.

—Francisca Furtado do Nascimento (R). Juazeiro, 1932. Widow; makes
straw hats and cooks for community school. (August 10, 1981.)

Those resident storytellers who make Maria de Araújo the focus of their stories often evoke the *beata*'s physical sufferings in graphic detail. In some accounts she is obliged to submit to an examination by a team of priests and doctors who proceed to pull out all her teeth or who scrape her tongue until it bleeds. Other individuals provide somewhat more idiosyncratic, though no less gory, descriptions of the various tortures or

"martyrdoms" the *beata* endures.[24] In the following tale the speaker explains how Maria de Araújo's enemies oblige her to grind corn until the
blood from her hands stains the entire house. The fact that the mortar
and pestle are in Northeast Brazil used almost exclusively by women
makes this forced labor an emphatic confirmation of the *beata*'s inferior
role. The blood she sheds in preparing the corn recalls that of the transformation, and the grinding motion of the pestle adds an ironic, phallic
undertone to this enforced exhibition of "women's work."

79. Maria de Araújo's house was all covered with blood: the walls, the
sitting room, everything. The people of Crato had her brought
there—those people who did not like Juazeiro. And when she
arrived in Crato they set her to grinding corn. They say she ground
corn two, three days at a time. She ground so much corn that her
hands became raw flesh. They locked her in a room. Then when
she had finished grinding that whole pile of corn they let her
go. When she got home she drank some [medicinal] tea. So then
her mother said, "But why are you doing this? Tell them that you
are not going back there, that they should get a man to do that
heavy work." But they wanted nothing other than to torment her.
When her hands got better, another message came for her to go
to Barbalha. She arrived there and they locked her in a room where
she had to grind corn. She kept on for two, three days, grinding
and grinding until the skin began coming off her hands. When they
let her go, she went back to Juazeiro. But they summoned her
again to grind still more corn. Pah, pah, pah! They did this many
times.
—Maria das Dores Alves de Albuquerque (R). Serra de Raiz,
    Pernambuco, 1920 (died 1981). Arrived Juazeiro 1953. Married;
    made straw hats. (July 21, 1981.)

Female storytellers offer many other extremely interesting examples
of the *beata*'s sufferings. Sometimes a group of soldiers drags her through
the streets tied to a donkey's tail before the bishop pulls out her tongue.
On other occasions, her success in unlocking a closed church door—
which cannot fail to recall accounts of Padre Cícero's trip to Rome—
prompts a group of men to saddle and "ride" her like a horse until she
bleeds from the mouth. These and other tales reaffirm the degree to

---

24. *Cordel* literature is full of these stories, known as *martírios* or "martyrdoms," in which
the protagonist is inevitably a woman. The best-known of these are probably the tales of
the Empress Porcina and of the hapless Genoveva, both of which were brought from Europe to Brazil.

which stories about the *beata* reflect much broader notions of how men and women ought to act. Because Maria de Araújo is punished in each case for asserting an authority incommensurate with her female identity, the storyteller's defense of the *beata* extends to include all members of her sex.

The specifics of these stories are less important to the purposes of this discussion than the fact that the tales exist. Were the "miracle" itself less troublesome in terms of narrative structure, these feelings would be less likely to impose themselves with such intensity. It is because the incident does not fit any preestablished literary or cultural pattern that people's accounts of it are often ambiguous, if not contradictory. Had their own parents and grandparents not insisted on the event as a resounding confirmation of Juazeiro's importance, they might well ignore or else recast the alleged transformation.

Pilgrims' Versions of the Events of 1889

Most pilgrims have little sense of Maria de Araújo as a person. They regularly confuse her with other well-known *beatas* such as Mocinha (Joana Tertulina de Jesus) and Bichinha (Josefa Maria de Jesus).[25] At the same time, they often posit a special relationship between Maria de Araújo and the pilgrimage. Some claim that she was not a resident of Juazeiro but a visitor who went to take communion upon her arrival in the city. Others refer to her as Our Lady of the Pilgrimage, asserting her willingness to perform special favors for travelers who ask her aid.

About a third of the pilgrims who told me stories had an essentially positive vision of the events of 1889. These persons often draw heavily on pilgrims' hymns about Maria de Araújo. Many of the people who sang or recited verses from these *benditos* had learned them from grandparents, a fact which suggests their relative age.[26] Some pilgrims also recited curative prayers in which the *beata* figures. These, too, had frequently been handed down within the family over several generations.

80. Maria de Araújo was a young woman who went to take communion and the host turned into blood in her mouth. Today she is

25. The term *moça* applies to post-pubescent, unmarried women. *Mocinha* is an affectionate diminutive which literally means "little maiden." *Bichinha* means "little creature." (A *bicho* is an animal; the term *bichinha* is not, however, insulting.) Both the desire of storytellers to assert Maria de Araújo's purity and their doubts about her character find expression in these names.

26. Printed versions of some of the *benditos* still sung by pilgrims date back to the beginning of the century. I am indebted to *cordel* poet Manuel Caboclo e Silva for sharing examples of these with me.

in heaven and we pray to her like this: "Oh, Maria de Araújo, you have your rosary in hand / To lead us to my Padrinho Cícero's promised land." There are other verses too, but I forget them. All I know is that Maria de Araújo is a very powerful saint.
—Severina Francisca do Carmo (P). Nova Cruz, Rio Grande do
Norte, 1917. Separated; farmer (own land). 3 pilgrimages.
(November 15, 1982.)

Short, positive identifications like the preceding contrast sharply with other, usually more detailed accounts that present the *beata* in a far less favorable light. Fully two-thirds of the pilgrims who told me stories about Maria de Araújo perceive the transformation as a negative challenge. In their accounts the bleeding of the host is not a mark of virtue but a shameful punishment. It may be a response to the *beata*'s disbelief, to her lack of respect for Padre Cícero, or to sexual misbehavior. Interestingly enough, female pilgrims are as likely as their male counterparts to offer this sort of negative assessment.

We have seen that direct modification of the transformation story is not an option for most residents. Their memories of the event are still too vivid and their sense of the "miracle's" importance to Juazeiro and to Padre Cícero too strong for them to tamper with "the facts." Pilgrims are once again more distant from the source. Many have no idea that the first pilgrims traveled to Juazeiro expressly to pay homage to the *beata* and "the Precious Blood."[27] Although their own great-grandparents may well have figured among these early visitors, these individuals generally have little, if any, sense of the historical impact of the transformation.

Then too, the church's long campaign against the "miracle" of Juazeiro affected all of the Northeast. People unwilling to believe ill of Padre Cícero were often more disposed to censure a woman with whom they had no personal association and on whom they might then blame his troubles. Because the priest complied with the bishop's order by not speaking of the *beata* or the transformation in public after 1892, later pilgrims would have been unlikely to seek her out. The very fact of Padre Cícero's silence may have confirmed or created doubts about Maria de Araújo.

27. For many present-day pilgrims, the "Precious Blood" refers to an unrelated story in which an enormous *tamboril* tree in the Horto is cut down in order to make way for a television tower. As Padre Cícero had allegedly forbidden anyone to touch the tree, his followers are not surprised when blood (the "Precious Blood") gushes from the earth. The tower subsequently proves useless and has to be torn down. In its place the city erects the enormous statue of the priest that dominates the Serra do Catolé today. Amália Xavier de Oliveira offers one version of the story in *O Padre Cícero que eu conheci: Verdadeira história do Juazeiro do Norte*, pp. 63–64.

As a result, a number of visitors' accounts of the transformation recall those medieval stories in which the bleeding of the host during the act of communion shocks an unbeliever into the realization of Christ's presence in the Eucharist. In tales such as the following, the *beata*'s doubts trigger the appearance of the blood on the wafer.

81. Maria de Araújo was a sinner who did not believe in Jesus. So then when she went to take communion my Padrinho punished her: the host turned into blood. He put the host in her mouth and when the blood began welling up, she asked for pardon.
   —José Cardoso Segundo (P). Machado, Pernambuco, 1919. Married;
      farmer (own land). 10 pilgrimages. (October 5, 1982.)

82. That business of the host was a punishment of the *beata* because she did not believe. The old people where I live often told my mother that when she [the *beata*] went to take communion, she always let the host fall on the floor. So then one day when she let the host fall, blood appeared. She did not believe it was the body of Our Lord Jesus Christ. So then my Padrinho gave her communion and the host turned into fresh blood.
   —Sebastiana Lima (P). Nossa Senhora da Glória, Sergipe, 1943.
      Married; housework. First pilgrimage. (October 31, 1982.)

Although pilgrims' accounts are undeniably closer to early miracle stories than those of residents are, Padre Cícero's role in this narrative still does not really fit the pattern. The numerous accounts in which Maria de Araújo's skepticism focuses not on the host but on the priest diverge even further from the local storytellers' view of the event. Instead of expressing misgivings about the doctrine of transubstantiation, the *beata* may directly challenge Padre Cícero's *personal* authority.

83. Maria de Araújo was one of these people who did not believe in my Padrinho Cícero's powers. She went around telling everyone that he was a priest like any other, that he had never worked a single miracle. So then one day my Padrinho got tired of her insinuations about him. So when he went to give her communion, the host turned into blood. She was punished like that rancher who ordered rain, or that girl whom he told not to go dancing and she went anyway. The person who did not respect him was always punished. So then how could he fail to punish her?
   —Maria Lourdes da Silva (P). Ibimirim, Pernambuco, 1919.
      Widowed; laundress. 3 pilgrimages. (October 25, 1982.)

Stories such as the preceding clearly correspond to the four-step challenge framework also found in visitors' tales of the Revolution of

Figure 6. Negative Challenge in Maria de Araújo Tale

1.
*Implicit acceptance of Padre
Cícero's authority*

Maria de Araújo gives outward appearance of loyalty to the
priest even though she secretly does not believe in his powers.

2.
Challenge

The *beata* affronts the priest's authority, either by voicing
doubts in him or by attempting to hide from him the truth
about herself.

3.
Response

Padre Cícero causes the communion wafer to bleed as a sign
of his own power and as a punishment of the *beata*.

4.
Reaffirmation

Maria de Araújo is discredited by the bleeding, which functions as a proof of the priest's miraculous powers.

1913–14 and of Dr. Floro (Figure 6). By demonstrating her disrespect
for Padre Cícero the *beata* triggers an immediate punitive response that
confirms the priest's omnipotence.

Often the *beata* does more than simply express her disregard for
Padre Cícero. She may, for instance, set out to create the illusion of a
miracle in the hope that a deluded priest will hail her as a saint. In this
case she usually hides a tiny flask of chicken's blood beneath her tongue.
Padre Cícero obliges her to open her mouth, extracts the flask, and then
administers the wafer, which grows red with blood in retribution for her
intended offense.

More often, the *beata* attempts to conceal from the priest not an object but, rather, knowledge about herself. The hints about her sexual impurity that are present but never fully developed in residents' stories thus become a shameful fact in many pilgrims' tales. Accustomed to nothing more than innuendo on the part of local storytellers, I was so unprepared for a visitor's outright assertion that Maria de Araújo was "a bad woman" that my surprise must have showed. "Yes," the man said ruefully, "I was afraid that I might shock you. I too was shocked, you know, the first time that I heard about that shameless creature, but it is true, all true."[28]

In most tales in which the *beata* tries to hide her true identity, she claims to be a virgin when she is or was a man's mistress and, sometimes, the mother of his child. The fact of her sexual activity is, however, considerably less important to most storytellers than her attempt to conceal the truth from Padre Cícero.[29] When the priest informs her that he knows she "is not what she claims to be," the *beata* refuses to acknowledge the truth of his assertions. The priest then proceeds to demonstrate his miraculous powers by turning the host to blood in the *beata*'s mouth.

84. She was a woman [non-virgin], she knew she was a woman and so she no longer wanted to remain in her parents' house. So then she came to work for my Padrinho, saying that she was a young woman [virgin], but my Padrinho knew that she was a woman. So then when he went to give the host to her, it turned to blood. Because she did not want to admit to him what she was. So then the blood dripped, dripped, dripped onto the church floor.

—Severino Barbosa (P). Surubim, Pernambuco, 1924. Married; *rendeiro*. 4 pilgrimages. (October 15, 1982.)

28. The man, a forty-five-year-old *fretante* from Bom Jardim, Pernambuco, had volunteered to give me a guided tour of the Padre Cícero Museum, which he prides himself on knowing "from top to bottom." A photograph of Maria de Araújo in a glass case among other pictures and memorabilia prompted his initial comment. When I inquired about the *beata*, he was hesitant to elaborate. After we left the museum, he told me the story in a carefully lowered voice. Once I realized that pilgrims were telling these sorts of stories about Maria de Araújo, it was not hard to glean other versions of the tales. I should add that the man's attitude toward me changed considerably after he had told the story. He switched from the formal "a senhora" to the intimate "tu," and when we parted he suddenly kissed me on the cheek—not at all characteristic behavior. In retrospect it seems probable that the request for the story struck the teller as unconventional, an impression reinforced by my obvious surprise. My momentary discomfiture caused me to lose the status of a researcher and to become, at least temporarily, a sexual object in his eyes. This sort of reaction did not occur in subsequent storytelling sessions, both because it was clear that I already knew the "secret" and because the tale was elicited in a group context.

29. Although many Northeasterners are extremely conservative in their approach to sexual matters, the real misdeed in these tales is not the *beata*'s lack of virginity but her *falsidade* or

Largely because of their more personal attachment to the alleged transformation, residents of Juazeiro vehemently reject these direct assertions of guilt. When I relayed what visitors had told me about the *beata* to my neighbors in the Rua do Horto in an attempt to gauge their reaction, even those who had identified Maria de Araújo as the cause of Padre Cícero's sufferings were scandalized. "Why do you insist on listening to those crazy pilgrims?" they demanded of me. "Ask someone who lives here if you want to know what happened." Some residents went on to accuse the visitors of deliberate prevarication.

Pilgrims, for their part, often do more than simply whisper about Maria de Araújo's indiscretions. They may identify her lover as the bishop of Fortaleza or of Crato, even though no episcopal seat existed in the latter location at the time of the "miracle." The story thus comes to function as an explanation for all Padre Cícero's ensuing difficulties as well as one more illustration of the larger theme of unjust persecution. Because of the narrative's sexual implications, Maria de Araújo's behavior is more distressing to most storytellers than that of the disobedient follower in tales of the Revolution of 1913–14, or even that of Dr. Floro. While the doctor spurns the priest's friendship in the interest of personal ambition, the *beata*'s betrayal inflicts a deeper wound. Because Padre Cícero is a man and she is a woman, her story evokes unspoken meanings that give it added force.

85. Maria de Araújo said that she was a virgin. She passed for a virgin but she was really the bishop's mistress. It was for this reason that the bishop suspended my Padrinho from his orders. He stopped him from saying mass after he transformed the host to blood in her mouth for everyone to see. The bishop was very frightened. He thought my Padrinho was going to take the bloody cloths to Rome in order to show them to the pope. So then he said that it was my Padrinho who had slept with her, that it was he who had been that woman's lover.
   —Apolinário de Souza Neto (P). Altos, Piauí, 1914. Widowed; farmer (own land). 3 pilgrimages. (October 12, 1982.)

The *beata* in these stories may be not only the bishop's mistress but also the mother of the mute boy whom Padre Cícero cures in a more

---

deceit. For a discussion of *falsidade* and its complement, *firmeza* or unconditional loyalty, in relation to sexual mores, see Candace Slater, *Stories on a String: The Brazilian "Literatura de Cordel,"* pp. 154–158.

often unconnected episode. In this case the mute boy's revelation illumines the bishop's otherwise perplexing reaction to the alleged transformation. His subsequent attempt to silence the priest before he can make the truth known to others becomes further proof of the repeated pattern of injustice which unites an emerging "life." The poison with which the bishop attempts to kill Padre Cícero is an effective symbol of the hostility born of fear and envy.[30]

86. Maria de Araújo was a *beata* who went to take communion and who then began to spit blood. My Padrinho gave her the host, but she was such a sinner that it turned to blood. This Maria de Araújo already had a child, a little mute boy. So then the bishop ordered my Padrinho to make the boy speak. "If you don't make this child speak I am going to suspend your orders," he said. For the bishop was very angry on account of the *beata* and wanted to ruin him. So then he brought the little mute boy, thinking that my Padrinho could do nothing with him. But my Padrinho put his hand on the child's head. He said, "Boy, in the name of God, tell us the name of your father and your mother." So then the child said, "My father is the bishop of Fortaleza and my mother is the *beata* Araújo." The bishop got so angry as a result that he wanted to poison my Padrinho. "Drink this wine," he said to him. My Padrinho made the sign of the cross over the chalice like this [gesture] three times. So then he drank the wine and nothing happened. Nothing!

—Justina Maria de Jesus Lins (P). Maceió, Alagoas, 1930. Separated; runs corner grocery stand. 7 pilgrimages. (November 30, 1982.)

The transformation may provide pilgrims with a motive for Padre Cícero's trip to Rome. In residents' accounts, the priest responds to the pope's summons by defending both the truth of the "miracle" and the honor of Maria de Araújo. Visitors may have the bishop inform the pontiff that the priest has been conducting a liaison with the *beata*. When Padre Cícero responds to this charge by proving that the guilty party is none other than his accuser, the bishop retaliates by initiating the "war" of 1913–14.

87. There was a *beata*, Maria Mocinha, who had been the bishop's mistress. She was the mother of a mute child but nobody knew,

30. Unsuccessful attempts to poison a holy figure are common in saints' literature. For various examples see Brewer, *Dictionary of Miracles*, pp. 82, 408, 438–439. "Saint invulnerable to poison" is found under motif numbers D1840.1.2 and H1573.3.1 in Stith Thompson, *Motif-Index of Folk Literature*.

you see? She still called herself a young woman [virgin] and lived among the other young women as if she were just like them. My Padrinho said, "Daughter, I know your secret." But she refused to confess her sin to him. So then in the hour of communion he gave her the host and it turned to blood. Afterward, she went to complain to the bishop. And then the bishop told the pope that my Padrinho had been that woman's lover. So the pope summoned my Padrinho to Rome. There he had to open a very large door which had never before been opened. And behind that door was the mute child who was the bishop's son. "I want you to make that child speak," the pope said to my Padrinho, "because the bishop says that you are [the boy's] father."

Well then, my Padrinho tapped the boy on the forehead three times. "Boy," he said, "tell his Holiness the name of your father." The child said, "My father is the bishop of Fortaleza and my mother is the *beata* Maria de Araújo." Not long afterward, the bishop sent his troops against Juazeiro. There was a great war in which my Padrinho was the victor.

—Francisca Gomes (P). Campo Maior, Piauí, 1952. Married;
rendeira. First pilgrimage. (September 20, 1982.)

A look at residents' and pilgrims' versions of the transformation story confirms the existence of fundamental differences. The "Precious Blood" that stains the host in residents' accounts of Maria de Araújo has become in many instances *um sangue sem-vergonha* or "a shameless blood." As the *beata* herself initially "demonstrated great affliction" at the event, fearing that it might be "a punishment and an indignity," this trajectory has a certain logic. The changes in the story are nonetheless startling, considering the incident's pivotal role in the history of Juazeiro.

Local storytellers have developed a variety of ways of dealing with the difficulties posed by the tale of the *beata*. They may restrict their accounts to identifications, divorce Maria de Araújo from the "miracle" proper, or create new stories that focus exclusively on the aftermath. Yet, although ambiguities and contradictions regularly creep into their narratives, they insist on the validity of the alleged transformation. These individuals are therefore unlike the many visitors who treat the "miracle" as an explicit negative challenge.

The seeds of doubt are present in a good number of residents' accounts of the *beata,* and not all visitors to Juazeiro regard Maria de Araújo as a fallen woman. All the same, the dissimilarities between the two groups of tellers go far beyond those evident in tales of the Revolution or of Dr. Floro. Pilgrims' lack of personal involvement in the alleged transformation and their desire to see the event as part of a recurring pattern may lead them to introduce radical alterations not only in content but also in underlying structure. The dissimilarities evident in our previous examples thus take on a far more profound dimension.

Conclusion

And like this story which I have just told you
there are at least a million more.

Pilgrim from Maranhão

Chapters V–VII illustrated specific differences between the stories of
residents and pilgrims, ranging from minor dissimilarities in content to
radical oppositions in underlying structure. We have observed storytellers' greater or lesser attention to detail, focus on Juazeiro versus a concern for the pilgrimage, and willingness versus reluctance to link miraculous episodes. These differences point to a more general division
between personal experience and public evaluation evident in the emergence of a master legend or a "life."

People tell the best-known stories over and over because they like
them. These accounts provide a way of reliving memories of the priest
or parents and grandparents, as well as of celebrating the pilgrimage to
Juazeiro. The tales' primary function, however, is neither recollection
nor celebration but the creation of a personally meaningful Padre Cícero
who goes on to function as the protagonist of many other, more idiosyncratic episodes.

The accounts of the priest's lifetime on which this study has focused
represent only one, albeit crucial, part of a much larger narrative totality
within which similarities, not differences, prevail. Picking out a resident's version of the birth story or of the would-be assassin from that of
a pilgrim is usually quite easy. Distinguishing between first-person accounts of how the priest cures a chronic headache or finds a follower a
new job is considerably more difficult, if not impossible. As a result, if

the "life" of Padre Cícero is the culmination of an extended narrative journey, it is also the means by which this journey can continue. To fail to appreciate the best-known stories' double nature is to lose sight of their larger meaning.

The effort both residents and pilgrims pour into their tales is initially puzzling. Why, one wonders, with the plethora of canonized Christian saints at their disposal, should they go to so much trouble to construct yet another holy figure, one whom the church refuses to acknowledge? What aspect or aspects of their own experience do the miracle stories permit their tellers to explain?

The Padre Cícero whom we have met in the preceding pages is a symbol of resistance to oppression. He is also a trusted personal friend. This dual role, which assures his privileged place in the Northeastern pantheon, is clear throughout the best-known stories. In this final chapter I will emphasize its importance to the corpus as a whole.

Their common heritage provides a first level of identification between the storytellers and the priest. "Surely someone who once lived where we live today can understand us," says one resident of Juazeiro.[1] "My Padrinho Cícero is as much a saint as Saint Sebastian," declares a pilgrim. "He was a prophet—and the only prophet—of this century. If people in other centuries had their saints, their prophets, why shouldn't we Brazilians have one of our own?"[2] "My Padrinho Cícero is the shining star of the Northeast," a resident observes, "but he is known throughout the nation. It is he who stands above the Horto holding a chain of gold with which he will encircle Juazeiro on the day of judgment."[3]

And yet, despite the importance of Padre Cícero's regional and national identity, his rejection by an elite to which he as a priest automatically belonged is ultimately more compelling to many followers. As not simply a Northeasterner but a Northeastern martyr, he exerts a unique attraction for those who look to him for guidance.

The word *martyrdom* normally implies bodily suffering that results in death. Anyone who has leafed through the earliest saints' lives is well aware of the intricate variety of tortures these individuals are thought to have endured in the name of the Christian faith. Even the most terrible bodily trial, however, has a limited impact on members of a society in

1. Alzira Bezerra da Silva (R). Juazeiro, 1918. Separated; laundress. (September 25, 1982.)
2. Maria de Araújo Sales (P). Campo Maior, Piauí, 1922. Married; *rendeira*. 7 pilgrimages. (September 20, 1982.)
3. José Ferreira da Silva (R). Santa Cruz de Iguabaribe, Pernambuco, 1944. Arrived Juazeiro 1969. Married; *cordel* and *bendito* writer and vendor. (October 28, 1982.)

which violence has long been a way of life. The individual who has just seen a disgruntled *coronel* knock out all of his neighbor's front teeth with a shovel cannot be expected to be overly impressed by Saint Lucy's loss of sight. Because of their desperate yearning for some semblance of security, Northeastern storytellers are apt to react more strongly to a threat to a person's social standing then to a threat to his or her physical well-being.

The outside observer may see little, if any, comparison between the bishop's curtailment of Padre Cícero's priestly orders and the systematic dismemberment of an early Christian. Many members of this still strongly patriarchal society, however, would argue that the priest's suspension constitutes an affront to his honor far more serious than any more direct attack. Because in Northeast Brazil "a man's wealth is his reputation," a challenge to the latter represents an assault on his very life.

Followers' need for a powerful defender, as well as their dearth of formal religious education, helps explain references to Padre Cícero as one of the persons (most commonly the second) of the Christian Trinity comprising Father, Son, and Holy Spirit. Northeast Brazilians' tendency to speak of one individual as another's "second person" in cases involving the delegation of authority makes this identification somewhat less startling. If the owner of a factory, for instance, has to leave town for a few days, the trusted foreman who temporarily assumes his place is his "second person." The neighbor who agrees to care for a child in the parent's absence is the parent's "second person." When someone says, "All priests are second persons of God," he or she means that they are all representatives of the deity. Storytellers may go a step beyond normal usage by equating the regional "second person" with the second person of the Trinity. In their eyes, Padre Cícero's identity as "*a* Christ" or "one who suffers unjustly" may make him all but identical to *the* historical Christ. "I know I am very ignorant," one storyteller asserts, "but in my view there is little difference between a man who acted like Our Lord and Our Lord himself."[4]

The miracle stories provide a way of reaching out to a self-sacrificing Padre Cícero. The repeated use of diminutives signaling intimacy is just one indication of the tellers' depth of feeling for the priest. The same people who refer to the Christian saints with the formality with which they would address a landowner or a police chief speak freely of Padre Cícero's "little hat" or his "little shoes." The strong-willed protagonist

4. Joaquim Alves dos Santos (P). Imperador, Maranhão, 1952. Single; truck driver. 3 pilgrimages. (September 29, 1982.)

who reduces an enemy to ashes may go on to place a "little hand" upon a believer's head. "My poor Padrinho!" people exclaim with a tenderness usually reserved for children. "He took the cares of the world on his little shoulders." The frilly sheets and hand-stitched coverlet adorning the narrow iron bed that stands in the Padre Cícero Museum are eloquent reminders of the affection which regularly tempers awe.

Storytellers, to be sure, sympathize with the priest of Juazeiro not only because he suffers for them but also because his suffering suggests theirs. "We spend our lives in the fields," a woman says, "where the ant bites us, the sun burns us, and the thorns tear at our fingers. For this reason, it is we who understand my Padrinho's trials. He, like us, knew the meaning of humiliation. For this reason he remains a saint in the hearts of his people."[5]

The challenges to the priest that provide the underpinnings for the great majority of miracle stories thus recall the hardships that are the lot of the Brazilian poor. "Why is it," the storyteller may wonder, "that I, who live up to my obligations, have such trouble surviving? How can it be that I work hard and still do not have the money to buy food? What explains the fact that other people's children grow up healthy while mine die?" Seen from this perspective, the true subject of the Padre Cícero stories is not bilocality or enchanted mangoes but human lives cut to the very bone. "I am going to show you everything I own," one woman in the Rua do Horto assured me with unmistakable enthusiasm. "My birth certificate, the photograph of my marriage, and the picture of my baby in the coffin."[6]

Storytellers' ability to discern parallels between their own and the priest's situation fosters a sense of fellow feeling. "After my Padrinho's death," observes one visitor to Juazeiro, "the bishop wanted to take away the body but his followers would not let him do this because my Padrinho belonged to them."[7] "With my Padrinho and his pilgrims," another comments, "it is like the iron in the fire which grows hotter and hotter until the iron is the fire and the fire is the iron."[8]

His followers' view of Padre Cícero as a victim of injustice makes

5. Francisca Delmira Alves (R). São José do Egito, Pernambuco, 1904. Arrived Juazeiro as infant. Single; *rendeira*. (August 10, 1981.)

6. Maria Antonia de Jesus (R). Garanhuns, Pernambuco, 1910. Arrived Juazeiro 1918. Married; begs for a living. (July 25, 1981.)

7. João Mateus de Abreu (P). Limoeiro, Pernambuco, 1905. Marital status unknown; *rendeiro*. 3 pilgrimages. (September 23, 1982.)

8. José Pedro da Silva (R). Caruaru, Pernambuco, 1929. Arrived Juazeiro 1968. Married; construction worker. (August 1, 1981.)

him a potential ally against a long string of oppressors. These may be hostile soldiers in the Revolution of 1913–14 or a present-day employer who withholds his workers' pay. "The world tried to put an end to my Padrinho Cícero," one storyteller asserts with defiant pride. "The world crushes ordinary people but it could not crush my Padrinho. No, no, my Padrinho was stronger than the world."[9] Although the following story, in which three different hospitals refuse to treat a dying child for lack of money, is an angry denunciation of injustice, it is also an affirmation of self-worth.

88. It was during that time in which there was a great deal of meningitis here in Juazeiro that my son—he was still a boy then—suddenly took ill. So then I rushed to the hospital with him. He remained there on a table for almost five hours. When the doctor finally arrived, he looked at him and said, "Your son has this meningitis business. You are going to have to go with him to Crato."

"Doctor," I said, "it is not likely that the people there are going to help him if we are from Juazeiro."

"I can't do anything more," he said.

So then I packed the boy into a taxi and we rushed off to Crato. So then they put him on another table. But they didn't do anything because one of the attendants said, "Wait just a minute. This boy is from Juazeiro. He should not be here." So then what could I do? I took the boy and went with him to Barbalha because there was no other way.

When we arrived in Barbalha, the boy was kicking his legs as if he were about to die. So I said to the nurse there in the hospital that my son was very sick. But she didn't want to let him enter without paying 300 cruzeiros. So then I said, "Take the boy inside and I will go home to get the money."

"I won't do that," she said, "I will only let the boy enter when you give me the 300-cruzeiro entrance fee."

So then I got angry. I got damn angry. "Well then, you just keep your money and to hell with everything," I said, "because I am leaving with my son."

Well then, when we entered Juazeiro I told the driver to turn there in front of the statue of my Padrinho Cícero. "My Padrinho will be my son's only doctor from this moment on," I said.

When we arrived home the sun was setting. Just at this moment,

9. Enrique Ferreira da Silva (R). Serra de Lisgomé, Rio Grande do Norte, 1900. Arrived Juazeiro 1946. Married; repairs furniture. (October 15, 1982.)

the boy opened his eyes. "My Padrinho Cícero!" he said. "Where was I all this time?"

—Joaquim Bento da Silva (R). Patos, Paraíba, 1923. Arrived Juazeiro 1965. Married; porter. (July 16, 1981.)

Padre Cícero is not only a last resort in times of trouble but is also a source of continuing support. The concern storytellers regularly lavish on him is thus reflected in his role as a friend who counsels and consoles.

Most followers of the priest are quick to ask material favors of a wide variety of official saints. They may call on Saint Francis as readily as on Padre Cícero to rescue a drowning man from a raging ocean, cure a fatal disease, arrange a marriage or a baby, or recover lost or stolen objects.

The person who approaches Saint Francis in regard to a new roof or a safe journey to São Paulo, however, may hesitate to participate in an extended dialogue. Fearful of abusing the "foreign" saint's patience by asking too much too often, many individuals depend on the less distant Padre Cícero for routine comfort or practical advice. Therefore, although they are as likely to seek Saint Francis's intervention in moments of crisis, they turn to the priest for a long list of lesser favors.

We have seen how the Padre Cícero who conquers death by raising a man bitten by a viper may go on to cure a simple stomachache occasioned by gobbling down a forbidden guinea pig. The same all-powerful individual who converses with popes and bishops is fully capable of feeding a pilgrim's hungry chicks. Thanks in part to these stories' ability to convince people of the priest's accessibility, it is Padre Cícero and not another holy figure who dominates their dreams and visions.

Because of their long familiarity with the patriarch of Juazeiro, his followers do not seem overly surprised when he suddenly materializes. Many have had experiences comparable to that of the pilgrimage organizer in an earlier chapter who wept upon remembering the sudden vision of the priest the man experienced upon his first trip to Juazeiro. "I knelt before my Padrinho's bed," this individual says, "and then—he suddenly appeared. Yes, it's absolutely true. He was suddenly there. Speaking to me. And I was speaking to him." [10]

Another man describes how the priest communicates a remedy, intended for an ailing wife, to him in a dream. "'Take such and such a root,' my Padrinho told me, 'and add three drops of oil and a pinch of sweet grass.' 'My Padrinho, she is going to die!' I cried, and he put his arm around my shoulder. 'Go back to sleep,' he told me, 'because she

10. Firmino Afonso da Silva (P). Feira Nova, Pernambuco, 1915. Married; farmer (own land). "Too many trips to count," beginning in 1943. (October 11, 1982.)

will be all right.'"[11] A woman, unsure whether she should wed a persistent suitor, has a similar vision of the priest in which he advises her to marry. Padre Cícero then reappears after her husband's death to reassure her.

89. When I was a young woman there was a man by the name of
Porfírio who wanted me to marry him. But I said no because I
hardly knew him. So then one night I began to dream of my
Padrinho Cícero. It was high noon, in the fields, the sun shining all
about his head.
   My Padrinho looked at me and said, "You can marry Porfírio
because you are going to be happy."
   And I said, "My Padrinho, if you say so, yes, then I will marry
him."
   So then we got married and we were very happy for the fifty
years until he died.
   On the day of his death I thought that I would die of grief. I
cried and cried without stopping. And then I felt my Padrinho's
hand upon my arm. "Didn't I tell you that you would be happy
with Porfírio?" he asked me. "Well then, you can stop crying
because Porfírio is now with me."
   —Célia Ferreira Leite (P). Maceió, Alagoas, 1915. Retired; 29
   pilgrimages. (December 4, 1982.)

If Padre Cícero speaks, he also knows how to listen. A willing confidant, he encourages people to share their deepest secrets. It is impossible to sit for an hour in the church of Our Lady of Sorrows during the pilgrimage season without becoming a party to the most intimate sorts of conversations between followers and the priest. "We talked and talked," explains one visitor, "and I told him everything there is to tell about my life." "My Padrinho is different from the other saints," asserts a woman in the Rua do Horto, "because he talked with us. And we could talk with him too. We could talk with him."[12]

The importance of the miracle stories as a sounding board cannot be overemphasized. Even in a less rigid, more individual-oriented society, speaking about oneself is not necessarily easy. People born into a traditional hierarchy find it particularly hard to put their thoughts and feelings into words.

11. Joaquim Cordeiro Neves (R). Pesqueira, Pernambuco, 1905. Arrived Juazeiro 1923. Widowed; sells plastic handbags. (August 9, 1981.)

12. Josefa André Gonçalves (R). Limoeiro de Anadias, Alagoas, 1916. Arrived Juazeiro 1923. Widowed; irons clothing and makes straw hats. (October 15, 1982.)

Lower-class Northeasterners' chronic lack of self-esteem helps explain this difficulty. Taught from the day of their birth to regard themselves as undeserving of notice, many persons have internalized this sense of their inferiority. "But why would anyone want to remember me?" asked a resident of the Rua do Horto in surprise when I showed up one day with a camera.[13] "I would tell you more stories of my Padrinho but I forget them," says a woman to her neighbors by way of apology. "My brains were fried away before the age of ten from picking cotton in the hot sun, so I remember nothing."[14] "That *rancho* is bad but it is good enough for us," says one pilgrim to another. "After all, the man accustomed to the yoke does not seek a saddle."[15]

Convinced on some level that their lives are "only suffering and suffering is boring," most followers of the priest are hesitant to reminisce about an individual past. "I always wanted to be a *cordel* poet and to wander through the world selling my verses," one man in the Rua do Horto explains to listeners in a storytelling session. "If I had succeeded I would have had many adventures. But my school was the end of a shovel and my teacher was a dry wind, so I have seen little and have little to tell others."[16]

The priest's followers do not fail to speak of their own or others' adventures in vivid detail or to describe persons and places important to their lives. Almost always, however, the focus is on what happened rather than on the individual's response to or perception of the event. If one says, "And so how did you feel then?" the person often looks embarrassed or simply confused. Storytellers seldom speak in terms of motivation. When I asked why a character in a particular tale did something or other, both pilgrims and residents answered in objective rather than subjective terms. "But how would I know why So-and-So did such-and-such?" they would respond if I persisted.

Many persons also fear that others will somehow use their own experiences to the other's advantage.[17] Because their lives are so difficult,

13. Mariano Ferreira da Silva (R). Freixeira, Pernambuco, 1898. Arrived Juazeiro 1950. Married; begs for a living. (September 26, 1982.)

14. Marinalva da Silva Santos (P). Surubim, Pernambuco, 1948. Married; *rendeira.* 12 pilgrimages. (October 21, 1982.)

15. The second part of the quotation is a common saying, *Quem já viveu na canga não procura a sela.*

16. Manuel Roberto (R). Lagoa de Gato, Pernambuco, 1919. Arrived Juazeiro 1922. Married; *rendeiro* and pequi-oil vendor. (November 11, 1982.)

17. These fears are linked to a larger vision of the world which George Foster has labeled the concept of *limited good* in his "Peasant Society and the Image of Limited Good." This

they are wary of all but the closest friends and family members. Convinced that strangers will respond to their triumphs with jealousy and to
their misfortunes with secret pleasure, storytellers hesitate to share their
experiences with the community at large. "Silence is the best way,"
people often told me. "The person who says nothing has nothing to
regret."

Some individuals fear that those in power will punish them for re-
vealing negative thoughts and feelings, and others are certain that nobody would pay attention if they did express themselves. "I would like
to tell the people of the world about the fathers who cannot find even a
handful of manioc flour to feed their families," one woman says. "But I
do not know whom I could get to listen."[18]

At the same time, the priest's followers shy away from areas of experience that are necessarily distressing. "The suffering of people—not
only in this street, because there are many streets just like it," confides
one woman in the Rua do Horto, "—is worse than the suffering of a
prisoner in a jail. The prisoner has a master [literally, "an owner"], he
has someone to care for him, but the people on this street must all fend
for themselves."[19]

The storytellers' feelings of impotence and rage are too strong to
simply disappear. Instead, they keep these feelings bottled up but threatening to explode one day. "I do not speak," one man says, "but sometimes my throat hurts from the urge to shout."[20] "The tears I have not
shed are all inside me," asserts a woman. "Each time I feel them brim-
ming over, I have to fight to contain them."[21]

For many individuals Padre Cícero represents not only a last resort
for seemingly insurmountable problems but also a unique opportunity
to translate pent-up emotions into words. Followers who would not
mention a brother's repeated bouts with madness under other circumstances will often speak at length of how the priest manages to calm the
man. Suicide is normally a forbidden topic of conversation in the Rua do

concept is debated from a Marxist perspective by Michael T. Taussig in *The Devil and Commodity Fetishism in South America*.

18. Severina Rosa do Espírito Santo (P). Mogeiro, Paraíba, 1910. Widowed; *moradora*. 8 pilgrimages. (November 20, 1982.)

19. Maria Antônia da Silva (R). Juazeiro, 1907. Widowed; *rendeira*. (October 19, 1982.)

20. Inácio Ramos da Costa (P). Afogados de Ingazeira, Pernambuco, 1908. Marital status unknown; *rendeiro*. 7 pilgrimages. (September 30, 1982.)

21. Josefa Caetano (P). Pilar, Alagoas, 1953. Widow; *moradora*. 2 pilgrimages. (September 27, 1982.)

Horto, but an individual may describe how Padre Cícero removes a rope he or she had fastened about the neck. ("Would you like to see the scars?") People may also explain how the priest sends home a philandering spouse or marries off a pregnant daughter. So long as the story is ostensibly about Padre Cícero the speaker feels free to touch on a whole range of subjects he or she would customarily avoid.

Although residents in particular seldom utilize any sort of preface in the case of the best-known stories, a formulaic introduction is integral to these more idiosyncratic, first-person tales. "I am going to tell you about one of my Padrinho's examples that I saw with my own eyes," the speaker informs the listeners. This stock phrase signals that the tale is intended as an instance of Padre Cícero's miraculous intervention. As such, it is to be treated with the respect accruing to anything associated with the priest.

If only because they are afraid of the consequences of disrespect, most listeners hesitate to use these tales against the teller. Although there are naturally exceptions to this rule, the priest's followers are generally quick to insist that the individual who recounts "an example" merits consideration. Residents therefore slap the child who giggles, glower at the adult who makes a wisecrack, and perfunctorily refuse to engage in gossip based on these stories ("That is between X and my Padrinho. Can't you find something else to say?"). Those pilgrims who talk out loud to each other or who make unnecessary noise while someone in the group is recounting a story usually incur immediate censure. "Why did you come here if you only wanted to yak-yak-yak?" one traveler may demand of another. "The next time, stay home! You are insulting my Padrinho."

Padre Cícero's intervention in people's lives confers a certain status on them. Just as followers during the priest's lifetime would brag about an admonitory tap as readily as about a gift or blessing, a present-day storyteller may refer with a certain satisfaction to the errant behavior that prompted the priest to punish him or her.[22] An individual whom Padre Cícero has aided is eager to relive the privileged moment. "I am Antônio Luís Ferreira, your servant," one man says resolutely, "and I cannot read. I can barely write my name. But when I open my mouth to speak of my Padrinho, I know every bit as much as the president of this great Brazil."[23]

Above all else, these stories provide their tellers with a way of ex-

---

22. Manoel Dinis mentions the followers who brag about these taps in *Mistérios do Joazeiro*, p. 83.

23. Antônio Luís Ferreira (R). Mata Grande, Alagoas, 1913. Arrived Juazeiro 1966. Married; *rendeiro*. (July 23, 1981.)

pressing gratitude. Too poor to offer Padre Cícero anything of material value, his followers force themselves, by way of a gift to him, to over-come their customary fear of public exposure. The psychic cost of such exposure is a large part of its appeal. The disappointment of a yawn or the lingering sting of a betrayal does not deter most individuals from recounting an apparently miraculous experience. The tales are thus expressions of a larger faith in Padre Cícero that sustains believers in their darkest moments.

A number of the memories people choose to share are extremely painful. One woman, for instance, describes her ex-husband's rape of their teenage daughter and the girl's ensuing pregnancy with a gravity soon reflected in the faces of her listeners.

90. I was thirteen years old when I got married. And once married, I was never happy again until the day my husband left me. Now I have another husband who treats me very well but I am not married to him in the eyes of the church. I am only married in the eyes of the state.

Well then, my first husband left me with a daughter who was very pretty ever since the day of her birth. When she was fourteen years old, her father reappeared. After he left she seemed locked in sadness. So then I asked, "Daughter, what is troubling you?" She said, "Nothing," but I had my doubts. So then I began to note that her stomach was getting bigger. But my Lord, she had never had a boyfriend, so how could she be with child? Well then, I got more and more worried. Finally I took her to the doctor. And so he told me that she was five months pregnant. Then she started to cry and I said, "My love, tell me who the father is." So then she put her hand on my shoulder and said, "Mother, it is my father."

So then I went crazy with such an enormous hatred that I wanted to stick a knife in that man's heart. I went into the woods and I stayed there a long time in such a fury that I could not even see. Well then, shortly afterward—it was on her fifteenth birthday—my daughter took ill and lost the child. I was so full of hatred, of sorrow, that I finally made a promise to my Padrinho Cícero. If he would give me a way to get to Juazeiro, then I would come to ask pardon for my first husband at the feet of Our Lady of Sorrows. I would put an end to this hatred I was feeling. Because I knew that my Padrinho must be grieving to see me in this way. And as he has done so much for me how could I make him sad?

—Raimunda dos Santos Araújo (P). Chapadinha, Rio Grande do Norte, 1945. *Rendeira;* first pilgrimage. (October 16, 1982.)

This example underscores the therapeutic function of the miracle corpus as a whole. The joy, anger, and relief associated with the best-known stories are equally apparent in more idiosyncratic tales. The woman's ability to verbalize and thus release the grief and outrage occasioned by the violation of her young daughter makes her account meaningful to the group at large.

The teller, however, does not use the story to dig out from an avalanche of bitterness or to call attention to her ability to transcend a moment of crisis. Although the woman sees her tale as an example, she is primarily interested in affirming the bond between herself and the priest. Her reluctance to grieve Padre Cícero leads her to forgive the person who has willfully caused her pain. That the priest may ultimately be understood as one part of herself, rather than an exterior intervenor, does not diminish the curative power exhibited in the tale. The woman's words are deeply meaningful because of the price she has paid to speak them. It is this interior force that gives the story its appeal.

Not all the miracle tales share this account's intensity. Many first-person stories are so full of idiosyncratic details that they are of interest primarily to the person to whom the event occurred. Although other people listen politely, they can seldom remember the particulars of the story. Asked later about the tale, they will usually shrug and say something like, "Oh, it was the story of one of my Padrinho's miracles."

The less than universal applicability of some of the Padre Cícero narratives does not diminish the depth of feeling that characterizes the corpus as a whole. Of vital concern to the priest's followers, the tales have much to interest the outside observer as well. In reemphasizing the indirect but nonetheless undeniable association between artistic form and social structure, they affirm the notable resilience of the miracle story as a literary entity. The tales also suggest the degree to which the past is inevitably a creation of the present, born of the interplay between the individual and the group of which he or she is a part.

Although the narratives that we have seen are clearly heirs to a long-standing literary tradition, they reflect a very specific cultural reality. The four-step challenge pattern that underlies the great majority of these accounts suggests the continued, if fragmented, hold on a significant percentage of the Northeastern population of an older social order that perceives power in terms of personal relationships. The miracle tale lives on with such force in Juazeiro not simply because of the tellers' predilection for supernatural solutions but also because of the constraints on them in the here-and-now. Were their lives different, these individuals would almost certainly have discovered or invented another way of talking about Padre Cícero and, thus, about themselves.

In their loyalty to people's everyday experience, the miracle narratives demonstrate the extent to which "timeless folk forms" assume the contours of a specific time and place. Differences among as well as between residents' and pilgrims' stories reaffirm the essential malleability and precision of this—and, by extension, all—symbolic expression. The fact that accounts of the Revolution of 1913–14 are both like and unlike others involving Maria de Araújo or Dr. Floro emphasizes the degree to which even the most highly patterned literary genres adjust or are adjusted to varying needs. Of limited efficacy in ascertaining "what really happened," the tales are nonetheless eloquent expressions of what Northeast Brazilians hold most important.

In this capacity the corpus confirms the extent to which the past is always a construction of the present. Residents treat their tales much like collectors who keep a growing jumble of stamps in a cigar box, less interested in date or place of origin than in the wealth of shapes and colors. Pilgrims, in contrast, organize their stories with the care that other collectors show in pasting their stamps in albums, with carefully lettered headings and with long strips of cellophane to protect them. The disparity in these approaches does not affect either the pleasure both take in the act of collecting or the pride generated by the resulting assemblage. Because the real purpose of the personal experience story as much as the "life" is to create a figure with whom the tellers can go on to interact as individuals, these tales' objective truth or falsity is of secondary importance. As re-presentations whose ultimate focus is not the facts but the speaker's reaction to them, even the best-documented accounts are necessarily fictions.

The tellers themselves may be aware of their participation in the construction process. Although virtually all insist on their stories' veracity, some speak directly of their will to believe. One woman, for instance, tells of a man who crosses the ocean in order to deliver a letter entrusted to him by Padre Cícero. After concluding her description of the mile after mile of white flowers the would-be messenger encounters, she suddenly embarks on a personal declaration of faith.

91. My Padrinho opened the waters of the ocean and this man rode across to the other side. So then he looked about and all he saw was that endless stretch of white and fragrant flowers. He was amazed at the sight. Then when he remembered the letter that my Padrinho had given him to deliver, he could not find it anywhere. So then he got on the little horse again and made the journey back across the sea.

"My Padrinho," he said, "when I went to cross the sea the waters

opened. But when I arrived on the other side there was no water,
no mountains nor trees nor any living soul. There were only
flowers, so many that they tired my eyes. And oh, my Padrinho, I
don't know what happened to your letter. Because when I went
to look for it in my pocket it was no longer there."

So then my Padrinho said, "But you did deliver the letter. You
did just as I wanted. Very good."

. . . Ah, my God, the first time that I heard this story I thought
that it was so beautiful that I *wanted,* oh I really *wanted* to believe it.
Now then, it is only what people say. I myself have never been
there beyond the ocean, understand? I myself have never seen the
sea. And as I am old and going to die soon I think that I never will.
I know that the world is round and has no end. And I know that
there are people who travel from island to island. But I still *want* to
believe that heaven begins there on the other side.
—Maria Vicência da Luz (R). Missão Velha, Ceará, 1902. Arrived
   Juazeiro 1910. Widowed; retired. (September 12, 1982.)

At the same time that the people who tell the Padre Cícero stories
are primarily interested in what the priest can do for them as individuals,
they remain dependent on their listeners' support. The desire not only to
speak but also to be heard accounts in large part for the tales' essential
ambiguity. Confirmations of a status quo in which the teller seeks to
establish an exclusive one-to-one understanding with an omnipotent patron, the stories are also a stubborn affirmation of a whole community.
Not infrequently, the individuals who set out to boast of their personal
relationship with Padre Cícero end up as active spokesmen for the group.

The miracle stories' inherent conservatism is beyond any question.
The absolute authority the priest of Juazeiro wields within them reinforces their tellers' sense of powerlessness. By encouraging people to
abdicate responsibility for their own lives, the tales foster continued dis-
unity and thus exploitation from above.

But if these narratives reflect and thus corroborate a repressive social
order, the passion with which tellers imbue their stories often contradicts
their apparent moral. The neighbors of the man who strives to get his
dying son admitted to not one but three clinics clench their fists as he
describes each new rejection. Men as well as women weep with the
mother as she remembers how her ex-husband raped the couple's daughter. A murmur of approval ripples through the group as a young girl
impulsively flings both arms about the old lady who remembers Padre
Cícero's words to her in a sunlit meadow. In their elation at the triumph

of the Revolution of 1913–14, their indignation at Dr. Floro's betrayal, their wonder at the alleged transformation of the host in the mouth of the *beata*, the priest's followers find themselves as one. Suddenly convinced that "I am no better than she is," a young pilgrim takes his place beside an elderly beggar.

The power of the Padre Cícero stories to inspire those who hear and tell them confirms their identity as art. The priest who dominates these tales is not simply a projection of the individual but is also a full-fledged human being capable of surprising the speaker as well as the listener. Waving his walking stick in a determined manner, the white-haired priest regularly leaps out from the confines of a given story to address the group in his own voice.

The empathy that the miracle stories regularly succeed in generating cannot sustain the everyday reality of interpersonal competition. People's sudden perception of similarities in their situation is forgotten as the battle for survival resumes. Once the story is completed, once the pilgrimage is over, the momentary union fades. The ability of these tales to make people weep or clench their fists or open their arms to each other is not, however, illusory because it is transient. Unable to escape the structures that in large part define them, the stories nevertheless succeed in transforming a regional holy figure into a universal symbol of human dreams and human disappointments.

Because the following tale, in which death crowds around a man who disregards a promise, invites two potentially contradictory interpretations, it is an excellent illustration of the miracle corpus's essential ambiguity. The teller begins by speaking in the third person but concludes in his own voice. The tale is his response to my query about the reason for his presence in Juazeiro. (He had come to fulfill a promise to Padre Cícero contracted on behalf of one of his ten children.) The pilgrim, a forty-three-year-old man, died of a heart attack less than twenty-four hours after recording this story. His unexpected death (he had no previous health problems) gives added meaning to the rancher's assertion, "Ah, there is some mystery here." "But the bad thing is not to die," explains the teller, not realizing that he will not be returning home from Juazeiro, "the bad thing is to die without doing something that we promised we would do."

92. There was a rich rancher—he had many servants, he had a lot of land, he had everything, you see? So then one day he took his shotgun and he said, "I am going hunting." He walked and walked and then suddenly he saw a hummingbird more beautiful and less

timid than any he had ever seen. He remained there at the edge
of the trail watching it for a long time.

Then the bird—who was really a dead soul in the form of a
hummingbird, you see—said, "Will you fulfill a promise for me
which I did not fulfill before I died?"

So then the rancher said, "Ah, there is some mystery here. What
is the promise? What do I have to do?"

The bird said, "You have to walk with a cross on your back to
holy Juazeiro. Afterward, you can leave the cross beneath this tree.
Will you promise to do this for me?"

The rancher said, "Well, I wasn't expecting anything like this.
But I feel sorry for you and yes, I will."

When he arrived home, the rancher told his wife all that had
occurred. When he had finished she said, "Are you out of your
mind? There is no way you can do this. Look, that man made
a promise and he didn't fulfill it. Is it your fault that he died without
fulfilling it? It is his duty to carry that cross to Juazeiro, understand?" So then the rancher did nothing about the promise. And
soon all his animals started dying. One by one they died. There
was no way to save them.

So then the rancher took no more joy in life. He went and said to
his wife, "Do you know something? You convinced me to put
aside my desire to fulfill that promise. But do you know what? I
am going to keep my word." So then he ordered his men to make a
cross and he walked with it to Juazeiro. It took him three whole
years. And at the end of those three years he returned home more
at peace and richer, richer than he had ever been.

But look well at what I am saying. If that rancher had not fulfilled
that promise, his cattle would have disappeared, his children would
have taken sick, and he too would have died. So then, little sister,
why am I telling you this story? I am telling you this story to show
you that death is always nearby and that we might die tomorrow.
But the bad thing is not to die. The bad thing is to die without
doing something that we promised we would do.

—Severino Belarmino (P). Orobó, Pernambuco, 1939. Married;
    rendeiro. 19 trips. (November 12, 1982.)

The rancher in this story enters into a binding agreement on which
he then reneges. As the original promise is to Padre Cícero (the bird had
agreed to carry a cross to Juazeiro), the man indirectly affronts the priest.
The death of his cattle is thus an act of retribution, like so many others

within the miracle corpus. By rectifying his error, moving to fulfill his part of the bargain, he enhances his own standing, returning home "richer, richer than he had ever been." Seen from this perspective, the story is a conventional restatement of the need to honor interpersonal obligations regardless of the cost.

The rancher's willingness to help the bird, however, suggests another possible reading in which an individual chooses to reach out to another in need ("Well," the man says to the hummingbird, "I wasn't expecting anything like this. But I feel sorry for you and yes, I will."). Because the rancher's wife does not share her husband's fellow-feeling, she initially convinces him to brush off an onerous responsibility ("Are you out of your mind? It is his duty to carry that cross to Juazeiro, understand?"). The rancher accordingly experiences a deep inner dissatisfaction symbolized by the loss of the cattle, which represent the cornerstone of a Northeasterner's wealth. Unable to accept his failure to fulfill a promise, he finally decides to leave the comfort and security of home in order to take up the other's cross. The ensuing pilgrimage permits the rancher to return home not just richer but "more at peace."

The concept of voluntary sacrifice of the self for others is a central tenet of Christianity. In the context of a rigidly hierarchical Northeast, however, the story's stress on individual choice rather than obligation is in no way routine. To the extent that the man's promise to the bird reflects a fully conscious desire to help an equal for no ulterior motive, it stands in opposition to other actions dictated by duty. The rancher in this tale does not abdicate responsibility but instead assumes it, thereby ensuring that his own life will never be the same.

The future of the Padre Cícero tales remains open to question. If they follow the same trajectory as other oral traditions, residents' stories should become increasingly similar to those now told by pilgrims.[24] The gradual disappearance of persons who can remember Padre Cícero will make it harder for local storytellers to insist on the sort of direct personal involvement that is currently the hallmark of their tales. They will almost certainly experience a growing pressure to adopt many of the narrative devices presently associated with visitors to the city. Accordingly, although the concern for Juazeiro as a place unlike all others will almost surely continue to distinguish their stories, residents may begin to find themselves more amenable to the notion of a "life." The researcher who

24. See Joseph C. Miller, "Introduction: Listening for the African Past," in *The African Past Speaks: Essays on Oral Tradition and History,* pp. 1–60, for a discussion of changes customary over time.

returns to record stories in ten, let alone twenty or fifty, years may well find a far less marked division between the two groups than exists today.

Because the Padre Cícero tales are certain to keep on changing along with Brazil, other sorts of modifications should also be apparent. Little by little, as additional numbers of subsistence farmers become wage workers in an increasingly industrialized economy, both the city and the countryside are assuming new dimensions. The growth of mass communications, the increasing availability of education, and the ease if not the necessity of travel have brought previously isolated individuals into contact with a larger, though not necessarily easier or more just, world. That the effects of this exposure are not always positive, immediate, or total does not minimize their longterm significance. The future researcher may therefore discover that existing differences between rural and urban, old and young, male and female storytellers have become clearer and more consistent and that new divisions have appeared.

Juazeiro itself is both a repository of traditional values and a modernizing city with new possibilities and problems. The Padre Cícero devotion, grown out of an older agricultural—even "feudal"—way of life, is increasingly an urban phenomenon. A significant minority of pilgrims come not only from the coastal capitals of the Northeast, where farming is only a memory, but also from the manufacturing south. Although most of the individuals who make the journey from Rio de Janeiro, São Paulo, and Brasília were born in the Northeast or are the children of Northeasterners, friends and neighbors born and raised in other parts of the country have begun to accompany them to Juazeiro.

The miracle corpus has registered a number of these changes.[25] There are, for instance, various antiurban stories about a man or woman who insists on moving south against Padre Cícero's orders. Conversely, a growing body of tales deals with miracles supposedly worked by the priest in São Paulo. Most of these are modeled on the conventional challenge pattern, but others reveal incipient structural modifications.[26]

In Chapter I, I noted that Padre Cícero has always meant different things to different people. Although the future will surely make increased demands on his adaptive powers, the stories at this moment give every indication of resilience. Inventions of an empty stomach and a

---

25. I do not mean to imply that change in general or urbanization in particular is necessarily good. The Northeast has come to function as a source of cheap labor for an industrial south whose products are required to pay off a staggering foreign debt, and personal and political freedoms are still decidedly curtailed.

26. For a study of comparable developments in the southern *literatura de cordel* see Candace Slater, "Joe Bumpkin in the Wilds of Rio de Janeiro."

heavy heart, they bear witness to a seemingly inexhaustible imagination and an enduring faith. Not content with the poverty and injustice that confront them, storytellers transform the world before them in accordance with their vision of how things ought to be.

Although the ambiguity that marks the Padre Cícero stories as a body is characteristic of folk forms in general, these tales are distinguished by their urgency. The priest of Juazeiro has become the destination of a pilgrimage not quite like any other in the modern world, because his followers perceive him on some level as a fellow traveler. To the extent that the stories allow their tellers to express emotions they would normally keep bottled up inside them, they represent a first step on a long and tortuous trail. Born of oppression, the narratives hold out a glimmering promise of liberation that is nothing other than concealed desire.

The individuals who leave their homes in the chill of night to journey deep into the backlands are often acting in self-interest, but the midday sun may teach them loyalty and love. Because Padre Cícero's story is the story of their own lives, the tellers do not tire of exchanging tales. Testaments to personal desires, these accounts may succeed in creating a fellowship where there was once "a compaignye of sondry folk."[27]

The forward motion into narrative is often hesitant or angry. Because, however, it is an offering not only to the priest but also to others, it is always an expression of hope. Even the person too poor to afford more than a handful of beans for supper has a story that only he or she can choose to share or to withhold. "Everyone who lives here has at least one tale," a resident of the Rua do Horto once assured me. "Why, if you stay here long enough, you'll probably end up with one of your own." My account concerns the power of words to change as well as to reflect the present. It is about what it means to tell the story of a life.

27. E. T. Donaldson, ed., *Chaucer's Poetry: An Anthology for the Modern Reader* (New York: Ronald Press, 1958), p. 6 line 25. "And pilgrimes were they alle," notes Chaucer at the beginning of his *Canterbury Tales*.

Appendix A.

SOCIAL IDENTITY OF
THE STORYTELLERS

The following table offers an overview of pilgrim and resident storytellers. Age, marital status, place of birth, and occupation are noted for both groups. The table attempts to suggest the degree of proximity to Padre Cícero by providing information on the percentage of individuals who knew, or whose parents and grandparents knew, the priest. This breakdown is based on conversations with 250 residents and twice that number of randomly selected pilgrims. The figures are not intended to be comprehensive from a statistical standpoint but rather to indicate the general characteristics of the persons who told me stories.

In the case of local storytellers I have indicated length of residence in Juazeiro, as well as age on arrival and number of visits prior to relocation for those not born in the city. For pilgrims, I have given the total number of trips to Juazeiro and the type of community (rural or urban) in which they were born and in which they now live. Although the majority of persons continue to reside in the place of their birth, there is a discernible movement to small and, particularly, large cities from the countryside. I have also noted whether the respondents' parents or grandparents were pilgrims, and whether either they or close relatives knew Padre Cícero.

The information reflected in this table is in many cases approximate. Because birth certificates were not the rule in the past, storytellers may have doubts about their age. A number thought that they might be "around fifty" or "perhaps seventy years old but I don't know for sure." Pilgrims who were frequent visitors to Juazeiro had often lost count of their trips. ("It's over thirty, I know, but I don't think it's quite fifty.") I have noted the tellers' primary occupation, but many people work at two or three jobs at the same time. The list of their activities, while in no way exhaustive, is meant to suggest the variety of ways they earn a living.

Residents

Number of respondents

Men	121
Women	129
Total	250

Age

0–10	2%	51–60	14%
11–20	2	61–70	23
21–30	3	71–80	20
31–40	11	Over 80	9
41–50	15	Don't know	1

Marital status

Single	8%
Married	61
Living together	2
Separated	14
Widowed	12
Other	3

Primary occupation

Farming	49%
Handicrafts	26
Retired	12
Other[a]	13

Present residence

Rua do Horto	48%
Elsewhere in Juazeiro	32
Outlying farm community	18
Other	2

State of birth

Alagoas	23%
Bahia	2
Ceará (includes Juazeiro)	32
Maranhão	1
Paraíba	11
Pernambuco	24
Piauí	2
Rio Grande do Norte	4
Sergipe	1

[a]Includes astrologers, bakers, barbers, beggars, blacksmiths, butchers, candy makers, carpenters, construction workers, cooks, *cordel* poets, factory workers, gardeners, guards, laundresses, lottery ticket salesmen, midwives, milk vendors, netmakers, porters, *repentistas, rezadeiras,* saucepan makers.

Birthplace of parents

Alagoas	23%
Ceará (includes Juazeiro)	23
Paraíba	24
Pernambuco	6
Piauí	2
Rio Grande do Norte	9
Don't know	13

Year of arrival in Juazeiro
(persons born outside city)

Before 1910	4%
1911–20	15
1921–30	16
1931–40	13
1941–50	18
1951–60	13
1961–70	10
1971–80	8
1981–	3

Age at arrival in Juazeiro
(persons born outside city)

0–5	9%
6–10	15
11–20	19
21–30	14
31–40	12
41–50	7
51–60	6
61–70	9
71–80	6
Over 80	3

Number of trips before settling in Juazeiro
(persons born outside city)

1	64%
2–5	21
6–10	4
11–20	4
Over 20	2
Don't know	5

Respondent knew Padre Cícero

Yes	49%
No	51

Parents or grandparents knew Padre Cícero

Yes	86%
No	10
Don't know	4

Pilgrims

Number of respondents

Men	253
Women	247
Total	500

Age

0–10	2%	51–60	25%
11–20	3	61–70	22
21–30	7	71–80	11
31–40	11	Over 80	2
41–50	16	Don't know	1

Marital status

Single	6%
Married	69
Living together	4
Separated	1
Widowed	16
Other	4

Primary occupation

Farming	68%
Carpenter	1
Factory	1
Peddler	2
Seamstress	1
Retired	11
Other[b]	16

Type of community of present residence

Countryside	71%
Small city	15
Large city	14

[b]Includes accordion players, barbers, bicycle repairmen, bootblacks, bottle collectors, brickmakers, cake decorators, cane cutters, construction workers, cowmen, electricians, fishermen, fortune-tellers, gold miners, laundresses, mechanics, midwives, plumbers, prostitutes, *rezadeiras,* saddlemakers, shoemakers, and telegraphists, as well as truck, bus, and taxi drivers.

State of residence

Alagoas	19%
Bahia	2
Ceará	1
Maranhão	2
Paraíba	14
Pernambuco	34
Piauí	12
Rio Grande do Norte	9
São Paulo	2
Sergipe	4
Other	1

Type of community where born

Countryside	83%
Small city	13
Large city	4

Number of trips to Juazeiro

1	13%
2–5	40
6–10	18
11–15	6
16–20	3
21–30	7
Over 30	10
Don't know	3

Were parents or grandparents pilgrims?

Yes	64%
No	36

Respondent knew Padre Cícero

Yes	4%
No	96

Parents or grandparents knew Padre Cícero

Yes	51%
No	41
Don't know	8

Appendix B.

PORTUGUESE ORIGINALS OF
ENGLISH STORIES IN TEXT

The transcriptions included in this section are meant to suggest the flavor of the Portuguese originals. Because my tapes are full of background noise and competing voices, these texts are necessarily approximations and are offered in that spirit. The reader should be aware that differences in pronunciation and, sometimes, grammatical usage vary from individual to individual as well as from region to region and that these differences are reflected in the transcriptions.

In the interests both of cost and of accessibility to the general reader, I have chosen to spell the stories in accordance with the rules of standard Portuguese orthography.[1] I have, however, used the "h," which is silent in Portuguese (except in *ch, lh* and *nh,* where the two letters together represent a single sound) as a weak back aspirate similar to that in the English "how," omitting the "h" in cases where it is not pronounced ("hora" thus becomes "ora," and "havia," "avia"). I have also replaced the final "e" in many cases with an "i" ("parece" thus becomes "pareci") without attempting to insert a potentially confusing accent over the penultimate syllable. The reader who knows Portuguese can easily tell from the context whether the verb is meant to be the first person singular preterite or the third person singular present.

I must reemphasize that the texts themselves are only one part of a performance involving gestures, verbal mimicry, and facial expressions. The reader should therefore approach them as part of a larger whole.

1. Antis, sim, eu neguciava na rumaria. Levava coisa pra vendê, trazia coisa pru pessoá di lá ondi moru. Mais eu não façu mais. Oli, uma noiti antis di viajá pra qui eu mi deitei. I quandu foi certas ora da noiti, Nossa Sinhora das Dori apariceu frenti di mim. Dissi, "Você tá cum pocas rumaria im Juazeru."
   Eu dissi, "Não, qui eu tô cum vinti treis."
   Ela dissi, "Você só tem é duas."
   "Cumu podi sê?" eu preguntei.

1. For a summary of the debate about literary dialect, including relevant bibliography, see Elizabeth Fine, "In Defense of Literary Dialect: A Response to Dennis R. Preston," and Dennis R. Preston, "Mowr Bayud Spellin': A Reply to Fine."

"É qui estas duas vezi você vinha só," ela dissi. "As otras vezi levava coisa pra neguciá. I quandu não levava, trazia pra vendê. Ora, cuidadu nessa rumaria qui si uma pessoa pedi pra você comprá uma coisa im Juazeru, você traiz i vendi pelu memu preçu qui pagô. Ansim faiz viagi limpa. Aí faiz cincu anu qui eu façu ansim.

2. Óia, meu Padrim mudô-si quandu eu era criança. Ainda mi lembru du dia. Qui eu istava na roda da Casa di Farinha i chegô um véiu chamadu Du, qui vendia pão, cum a notícia. Aí eu fiquei tristi, tristi, mais dixi para mim, "Ainda qui eli num esteja mais nu Juazeru eu vô lá di tudu jeitu." Bão. Antão passô-si várius anu, mi casei, fui pai di famia. I era memu.
   Qui um dia apariceu um caminhão di romeru na porta. Eu dixi para a muié, "Sabis di uma coisa? Eu vô para Juazeru." I quandu cheguei aqui, fui vê a casa deli, a cama, u retratu. Mi ajoeei frenti da cama deli naquela intenção di fé. Aí eli apresentô-si ansim, di repenti. Sim. É a pura verdadi. Eli istava ali. Falandu cumigu. I eu falandu cum eli. Nóis palestrava, palestrava i eu contei toda a minha vida para eli. Ah, até oji eu num deixu di chorá quandu pensu im cumu meu Padrim oiô para mim.

3. Eu tava lá nu Ortu oji di manhã i tinha uma mocinha qui veiu tirá fotografia, ela di uma brusinha destas bem transparenti qui as minina usa muntu oji im dia. I antonci quandu eu óiei pra ela, num possu negá qui censurei. Pensei, "Cumu é possivi qui essa moça si vesti ansim num lugá tão santu?" I nessi memu momentu eu quasi qui caí. I só num caí mesmu qui uma pessoa pertu di mim segurô. I daí eu tinha a intuição qui issu foi um castigu. Por eu tê pensadu ansim. Qui foi meu Padim quem mi deu aqueli impurrinhu. Qué dizê, eu num tava ofendenu eli muntu mais im pensá dessi jeitu du qui aquela mocinha di brusa transparenti?

4. Aí quanu a genti foi descansá, chegô uma véinha nu ranchu. E ela contava muntu ezemplu di meu Padim qui ela era du ôtru séculu, né? Aí eu achei u qui ela contava bem bunitu. Qui dispois, qui ela dissi, "Vô pra igreja," eu dissi, "Vô mais a sinhora." Aí dei um dinheru pra ela tomá café. Antão quanu cheguemu na igreja, ela entrô pra rezá. Aí eu fui lá ondi tava rezanu. I fiquei a pensá. "Sabi di uma coisa? Eu não sô mais qui ela. Eu sô iguá a ela." Aí mi sentei ao ladu dela. Nu chão. Antão vi qui tudu mundu tava oianu pra mim. Antão pensei, "Mais é possivi? Elis tão achanu qui queru robá ela." I fiquei ansim, tão emocionadu qui nem pudia falá. Qui eu tinha entendidu pela premera veiz na vida qui eu não era mais du qui a criatura mais umidi. I lá aquelis otrus pensanu qui eu tava cum ôiu nu dinherinhu da muié. Foi uma coisa qui não sei ti dizê.

5. Dizi qui Dona Quinô era mãe di meu Padrim mais num foi ela quem deu a luiz a eli, não. Óia, pocu dipois da nascida deli, u maridu dela foi dixi ansim, "Quinô, deixa u nenê durmí na redi i vem mais eu buscá melancia na roça." Pois então a melancia era u qui ela mais gustava. Aí ela foi mais u maridu— u nomi deli era Joaquim Romão—foi pra roça. I ali elis ia tirandu as melancia mais grandi, mais gostosa.
   "Cume mais, Quinô."
   "Não," ela dixi, "ach' qui u mininu já si acordô i istá churandu pra cumê."
Aí us dois vortaru pra casa. Quandu chegaru mais di pertu Quinô viu uma

muié bem bunita tudu de azú saindu da casa cum um embruiu ansim, nus
braçu.

"Quem será essa dona?" ela preguntô pru maridu.

"U qui?" eli dixi. "Eu não vi ninguém."

Aí quandu Quinô foi oiá pra criancinha, deu um gritu ansim. "Essi mininu não é meu! Aquela muié devi tê deixadu u fiu dela nu lugá du meu."

"Deixa di besteira, muié," u maridu dixi. "É qui você cumeu melancia
dimais i istá cum u juizu viradu."

"Deixa eu vê di novu," ela dixi. Mais naqueli mumentu a luiz dus seus
ôiu apagô-si i daí ela nunca tinha memu certeza.

6. Naqueli tempu im qui meu Padinhu Ciçu istudava na Cajazeira, us mininu
custumava deixá u chapéu num pregu na paredi. Mais antão um dia quandu
meu Padinhu chegô, incontrô todus us pregu já ocupadu. Num tinha ondi
deixá u chapéu deli. Aí eli foi botô u chapéu deli na paredi—puf—i ficô ali.
Quandu us otru mininu vieru u qui eli tinha feitu, tentaru fazê a mesma
coisa. A sinhora sabi cumu é criança. Si um delis faiz águ, todus queri fazê
iguá. Pois bom, elis butaru u chapéu delis na paredi mais todus caía nu chão.
Só u chapeuzinhu du meu Padim era qui ficava lá sim pregu nenhum. Aí
mesmu quandu eli era minininhu du tamanhu di Joãozinhu, meu Padinhu
Ciçu já istava obrandu milagui.

7. Tinha um povu qui tava cum tantu ciumi du meu Padim Cíçaru qui quiria
matá eli. Aí resolveru trazê um ômi qui si fazia di duenti a meu Padim drentru duma redi. I aqueli ômi tava cum pexeira na mão qui quandu meu Padim
fossi abri a redi para confessá eli, tava para metê a pexeira nu curação deli.
Antão essi pessoá trazia u ômi à casa du meu Padim. Quandu chegaru lá,
dixeru ansim, "Padim Cíçaru, a genti trôxi um doenti qui qué si confessá
cum sinhô."

"Sintu muntu," meu Padim dissi, "má não possu fazê nada pra difuntu,
não."

"Não, não," elis dixeru. "Eli tá duenti, não mortu."

"Aí voceis podi oiá pra eli," meu Padim dixi, "qui aqueli ômi murreu faiz
tempu." I quandu foru abri a redi viru qui era uma verdadi. U ômi tava
mortu!

Aí meu Padim dixi, "Óia lá u facão cum qui eli pensava mi matá." I lá
aquela pexeira na mão isquerda du ômi.

8. Tinha um fazenderu num lugá por nomi di Fuloris, qui eli num dava valô au
meu Padim Ciçu. Um dia quandu um romeru passô por ondi morava, u
fazenderu falô ansim pra eli. "Tudu aqui tá tão secu, tão secu qui u gadu tá
murrendu im pé. Aí você diz para seu Padi Ciçu qui eu pidi cincu tostão di
chuva a eli." Pois bem, quandu chegô a Juazeru, u romeru tinha vergonha
di dizê aquilu para meu Padim.

"Portadô num mireci pancada," meu Padim dissi pra eli. "Num si acanha
di dizê u qui aqueli fazenderu qué di mim."

"Meu Padim, Fulanu pidiu cincu tostão di chuva au sinhô."

"Qué cincu tostão?" meu Padim preguntô pra eli. "Apois você podi dizê
pra Fulanu qui cincu dava dimais." I deu u trocadu para eli. Plinc-plinc-
plinc-plinc. Quatru tostão na mão. "Agora você vai dizê pru fazenderu qui
si apronti apois a chuva chega já já."

Ansim u romeru foi dá u recadu du meu Padim au fazenderu. "Fica jantá cum a genti," eli dissi.

"Num possu!" u romeru dissi, correu. Apois bem, má eli saiu, a chuva pegô a caí grossu, bem grossu. Mais só na terra deli, du fazenderu, viu? Caiu tanta da chuva qui u ômi i a famia intera ficô até u pescoçu di água. Num ficô nem um pedacinhu di pão doci pra lembrá eli du doci da vida.

9. Tinha uma veiz uma biata por nomi di Maria di Araúju. Eu não vi ela mais a minha tia viu i contô tudu para mim. Meu Padrim foi dá a comunhão a ela i a óstia virô sangui. Quandu eli colocô a óstia na língua dela, ficô feitu um curação. Meu Padrim oiô i dixi, "Essi é u sangui apreciosu di Nossu Sinhô Jesui Cristu." Aí todu mundu qui tava lá na igreja churava di vê tão grandi mistériu.

10. São Pedru era u primeru papa. Um dia eli trancô a porta duma grandi igreja na Roma i jogô a chavi nu matu para qui ninguém pudessi abrí aquela porta di novu. Pois bem, quandu meu Padinhu veiu a Roma u sinhoris Papa foi dissi, "Padi Ciçu, eu sôbi qui você anda obranu milagui. Aí queru qui você mi abra essa porta."

"Sua Santidadi," meu Padim dissi, "Eu sô um simpris padi. Não tenhu comu abrí."

"Si você não abrí aquela porta eu mandu meus sordadu a Juazeru cum u canhão mais grandi qui tenhu."

"Está bem, Sua Santidadi. U sinhô querenu, eu abru, sim."

Aí eli falô pra porta treis vezi. "Eli quem ti fechô ti abra." Ansim treis vezi i nas treiz veiz qui eli falô a porta abriu pra deixá meu Padim subí uma escada da cor di miu verdi.

Aí u Papa arrependeu-si di não tê acreditadu nus puderi deli. "Padi Ciçu," eli dissi, "você vem a Roma morá aqui mais eu."

"Muntu obrigadu, Sua Santidadi," meu Padinhu dissi pra eli. "Agradeçu seu belu conviti. Mais meu curação pertenci a Juazeru i é lá qui vô ficá."

11. U bispu—ach' qui foi u bispu di Fortalcza—si incontrô cum meu Padim Ciçu um dia. "Sô Padi Ciçu, sua Isselência," meu Padim dissi para eli.

"Ah sim," eli arrespondeu. "Num é você quem anda pó essas banda obranu milagui? Apois queru qui você curi um mininu qui nasceu sem fala."

"Eu curu eli sim, qui é u sinhô qui tá mi pidindu," meu Padim dissi, "mais di ôtru jeitu, não."

Aí eli botô a mão na cabeça du mininu i perguntô ansim, "Rapaiz, é fiu di quem?" ansim, treis vezi.

Aí u mininu dissi, "Eu sô fiu du bispu du Ciará i da abadessa du conventu."

"Aí tá, Isselência," meu Padim dissi. I u bispu ficô cum tanta da raiva qui quasi qui pipocô. É uma passagi qui tudu mundu aqui di Juazeru conheci.

12. Logu adipois qui meu Padrim Ciçru mudô-si apariceu uma mocinha di Alagoa qui si negava a botá lutu para eli. Ela dissi qui perferia vistí pretu pra cadela dela du qui pra um ômi qui não era conhecidu seu. Apois antão a cadela murreu nu mermu dia, aí ela foi pra rua di lutu pra tudu mundu vê. Mais tinha um rapaizinhu qui espiô u rabu di cachorru por adibaixu da ropa

dela. Aí eli pegô a gritá i tudu mundu, ansim, di oiá. Antão adipois u rabu ia si aumentandu, si aumentandu até qui a moça virô numa cachorra. Tem pessoas qui dizi qui ela ficô cachorra, cachorra. Eu num vi ela mais u meu irmão conheci quem viu.

13. Deu-si uma guerra aqui i muntu sordadu veiu atacá Juazeru. Aí meu Padim Ciçu arreuniu us romeru deli pra botá elis por fora da cidadi. Eli prantô uma roda di macambira qui arrodeô a cidadi, dois metru di artura, di noiti pru dia. Us sordadu não conseguiru passá. Quandu começaru a tirá, as bala não pegaru im ninguém, só vortavu pra elis. Muntu sordadu murreu mais aqui im Juazeru tinha só dois—um véiu i um mininu—qui feiz pocu da palavra du meu Padim. Essis sim, murreru na ora.

14. Um dia meu Padim taha nu meiu du sermão deli quandu fechô us ôiu comu quem durmi. I antonci as pessoas começaru a fazê assim i di comentá assim baixinhu, "Meu padim tá ficandu tão veinhu qui adurmece assim." Antonci passô meia ora, uma ora, duas, tudu mundu isperandu sem sabê qui fazê.

Aí quandu abriu us ôiu meu Padim falô pra elis. "Eu tava bem longi daqui na Alemanha parandu uma guerra muntu feroiz. Um romeru meu valeu-si di mim i eu fui descê à terra numa nuvi."

Agora aconteci qui tinha lá na Alemanha dois fotógrafu qui bateru uma chapa du meu Padim enquantu descia du céu. Acabada a guerra, elis foru percurá. Percuraru im pelu menu oitenta paisi i nada deli. Por fim um dissi, "Oxenti, ainda não fomu percurá nu Brasil." Aí elis pegaru um avião para u Riu di Janeiru.

I quando mostraru u retratu pru pessuá di lá tudu mundu dizia, "Apois é, essi padi tem qui sê aqueli qui mora nu Ciará."

Antão elis foru para Fortaleza i as pessoas disseru, "Apois bem, essi padi pareci muntu cum aqueli du Juazeiru." Aí chegaru aqui por fim lá pelas treis ora da tardi. Munta genti quem viu sabi contá para você.

15. Um dia quandu meu Padim Ciçu taha celebranu a missa, fechô us ôiu di repenti.

"U qui tá acontecenu cum meu Padim?" tudu mundu preguntô. Eli ficô ansim bem meia ora sem dizê palavra pra ninguém.

Então quanu eli abriu us ôiu por fim dissi, "Tô di vorta agora memu di Cacimbinha. Uma minininha qui caiu num poçu ali si valeu di min. Aí eu fui socorrê mais tô di vorta entri voceis."

Pois bem, pareci qui tinha um ômi qui num confiava na palavra du meu Padim. "Comu é qui uma pessoa podi tá im dois lugá na mesma ora? Ha, ha, ha!" Ficô zombanu dessi jeitu. Mais dipois quandu eli chegô em casa sôbi qui a própria filinha quasi qui tinha si afogadu naqueli instanti. I quandu a muié falô pra eli u qui tinha si dadu, u risu deli ficô naqueli choru mais tristi du mundu.

16. Tinha um ômi qui nem eu, ajuntava u pessuá du lugá ondi morava para ir a Juazeru todu anu. Ma essi ômi tinha u pai qui eli num acreditava nu meu Padrim. "Ba, você é doidu mesmu di perdê tempu nessa bestera di romaria," eli sempri dissi pru fiu.

Apois bem, uma veiz quandu u ômi chegô im Juazeru meu Padrim perguntô para eli, "Cadê seu pai? Gostaria di conhecê eli."

U fiu dissi, "Ficô im casa, meu Padrim. Eli ach' qui eu sô doidu di vir aqui tudu anu."

"É mesmu?" meu Padrim dissi. I falaru di mais ôtras coisa. Má logu na saída du ômi, meu Padrim dissi, "Óia, eu sei qui você é caçadô. Dá pra você trazê a primera caça qui incontrá na vorta pra mim?"

"Dá, sim, eu tragu cum muntu prazê," u ômi dissi.

Antão nu dia dipois du omi chegá im casa, lá vai eli cum us cachorru. Cum pocu um delis começô a ladrá, ladrá por dibaixu dum pé di pau até qui u caçadô foi subí nela. I u qui é qui eli achô ali má u própiu pai? Qui eli tinha subidu pra modi pegá um dessis pássaru qui u pessuá dessis sertõi gosta muntu di comê. Quandu eli viu u pai, eli foi dissi, "Meu pai, agora tô vendu qui é u sinhô essa caça qui u meu Padrim Ciçu tantu quiria. "Vamu para Juazeru?"

Bão, quandu u veinhu oviu a istória num podia deixá di ri. "Pó fim di contas, aqueli padri véiu é muntu sabidu," eli dissi pru fiu. I daí im dianti us dois ia juntus pra vê meu Padrim tudu anu sem faltá.

17. Era um dotô daqui, um tau di Dotô Flori. Era muntu amigu du meu Padrinhu i uma pessoa dessas bem importanti. Mais acabô briganu cum meu Padrinhu poquê quiria sê má qui eli. Essi Dotô Flori era muntu crué i matava munta genti. Por fim meu Padim não pudia mais cum eli.

"Flori, não podi andá mais dessi jeitu," eli dissi.

"Bom, si u sinhô não tá gostanu por quê mi feiz grandi?"

Aí meu Padim dissi ansim, "Flori, quem ti feiz grandi podi ti fazê piquenu." I foi certeza qui cum pocus dia u Dotô Flori murreu.

18. Uma moça saiu para Juazeiru cum mais uns rumeru i quandu chegô a noiti tudus si arrancharu na serra. Mais a moça taha tão cansada da andada, coitada, qui não acordô cum a luiz du sol. Aí us ôtru deixaru ela a durimí lá naquela serra ondi nus tempu antigu tinha munta onça braba, viu?

Uns dia dipoizi, us romeru chegaru nu Juazeiru. "Antão meu Padim Cíçaru perguntô pra elis, "Cadê aquela incomenda qui eu deixei cum voceis?"

"Qui incomenda, meu Padim?"

"Apoizi aquela moça qui voceis deixaru a durimí lá na serra, a onça comeu ela mais a arma dela chegô aqui antis di voceis."

Aí tudus ficaru muntu tristi i na vorta du Juazeru elis fizeru uma cruiz nu caminhu ondi a onça tinha comidu aquela moça. U carru passô por ali ontem quandu a genti ia pela serra i nóis mandô o motorista pará pra tudu mundu vê.

19. Quandu meu Padim Ciçu separô-si u bispu du Cratu dixi, "Eu vô a Juazeru tirá u corpu daquelis miseravi rumeru. Tem tantu du fanatismu, essi pessuá, qui ninguém sabi u qui vão fazê si eu deixá u corpu ficá lá cum elis."

Pois bem, u bispu i us impregadu deli foru pra igreja. Qui u meu Padim Ciçu tinha si interradu lá às treis ora da madrugada. Eli mandô us impregadu tirá u caixão deli mais quandu abriru não incontraru nada fora dum chinelinhu pretu, pontadinhu, ansim. Aí u bispu mandô elis fechá pra ninguém sabê. Mais u vigia qui elis acharu roncanu na porta não istava durminu di verdadi i eli falô tudu, tudu pru povu.

20. Um dia quandu meu Padim Ciçu tava construinu aquela igreja du Ortu, veiu uns trabaiadô pidi comida. Meu Padim dissi para um delis, "Você, Fulanu,

vai lá atraiz da igreja i traiz fruita para tudu mundu cumê." Aí us ômi só óiaru um para ôtru. Pois tudu mundu sabi qui num tem nada lá atraiz. "Vamu comê ispinhu?" si perguntava baixinhu, ansim. Mais u ômi foi fazê u qui meu Padim mandô. I bem, achô aqueli mundu di laranja, di banana, di côcu, di manga—quasi qui tava chovenu manga-rosa daquelas bem grandi. Aí eli tirô toda a fruita qui pudia i tudus comeru até qui num pudia mais. Pois bem, mais tardi quanu foi di noiti veiu aqueli ômi buscá mais fruita só pra eli, viu? Foi lá atraiz da igreja i percurô, percurô, mais num achava coisíssima nenhuma. Só achava era ispinhu. I ninguém nunca mais viu manga lá naqueli lugá.

21. Mané Germanu era um pobrizinhu qui tinha uma casinha aqui na Rua du Ortu. Trabaiava im fogu—fogu festivu, era muntu conhecidu. Só qui um dia estalô tudu i quasi qui morre, viu? Aí eli foi pidí ôtru ramu a meu Padrim Ciçu. Pois tinha quatorzi boca im casa, coitadu.

"Tomi aqui," meu Padrim dissi, "i vai comprá algodão." Aí Mané Germanu ficô compranu algodão. Comprava i vendia algodão até qui tinha um recursu grandi. Antão foi, deu a metadi du qui tinha arrumau a meu Padrim. "Deus ti aumenti sua ismola," meu Padrim dissi. I Deus oviu a palavra du meu Padrim pois Mané Germanu murreu ricu, ricu.

22. Meu Padim Ciçu sempri tava obranu milagui. Aí u Padi Monteiru foi dissi, "Padi Ciçu, u sinhô é muntu milagrosu."

Meu Padim dissi, "Obrigadu, Padi Monteiru, mais u qui você diz oji vai negá amanhã."

"Num, num, eu juru pela luiz dessis ôiu qui nunca vô negá."

"Antão fica ansim memu," meu Padim dissi.

Pocu dispois, lá vem u bispu a Juazeiru. "Padi Monteiru," eli dissi, "u Padi Ciçu obra milagui memu cumu tudu mundu diz?"

"U povu fala mais eu nunca vi nada dissu," u Padi Monteiru arrespondeu. I naqueli memu instanti, iscureceu u só du dia.

23. Um ômi por nomi di Pedru foi trabaiá na roça deli lá na Serra di São Pedru. Veiu uma cobra dessas valenti mordê eli i u ômi chamô a famia. "Vai a Juazeru dizê pru meu Padinhu Ciçu qui eu queru qui eli venha mi confessá," eli dissi pru irmão deli. "Pois um cascavé já mi ofendeu i dissu num escapu, num. Aí u irmão deli correu para meu Padinhu i us dois vortaru pra Serra di São Pedru a toda pressa.

Mais foi naquela época em qui a istrada num servia pra nada i só tavu em meiu caminhu quandu um portadô chegô dizê qui u ômi tava mortu. "Num vali a pena ir mais lá, meu Padim," eli dissi, tudu tristi.

Mais meu Padim dissi, "Vô, sim, meu amiguinhu."

Quandu chegaru na cassa du ômi as muié estavu cortanu u panu da mortáia, todas a chorá. Aí meu Padim foi dissi pru mortu, "Pedru, vim ti confessá." Treis vezi ansim. I na treis veiz u ômi arrespirô fundu ansim, abriu us ôiu.

Dipois du meu Padim confessá eli, preguntô si queria ficá na terra ou ir pru céu. "Queru ir pru céu, meu Padim."

Aí meu Padim dissi, "Bem, eu ti dô licença di continuá a sua viagi." I u ômi fechô us ôiu di veiz.

24. Manué Correia era u mió mestri qui tinha nessi Juazeiru. Mais um dia esca-

puliu da torri da igreja du Ortu i quebrô u pescoçu. Quandu meu Padim sôbi qui u mió mestri di tudus tinha murridu eli foi vê. Manué Correia tava lá num poçu di sangui rodeadu por essi povão, todu mundu a chorá. Aí meu Padim foi dissi, "Manué Correia." I di novu, "Manué Correia." Aí, "MANUÉ CORREIA." Ansim mesmu treis vezi.

I nas treis veiz qui meu Padim falô u ômi abriu us ôiu. "U qui foi, meu Padim?"

"Manué Correia, você qué ir nessi instanti pru céu ou qué vivê?"

"Queru vivê, meu Padim. Queru ficá trabaianu na igreja du Ortu."

"Antonci si levanti," meu Padim falô pra eli. I u ômi subiu a torri di novu, u martelu na mão.

25. Naqueli tempu ainda tinha muntu gatu na Serra du Araripi. Aí um cara foi pidiu uma arma au meu Padim Ciçu para si defendê na viagi di vorta. Meu Padim botô a mão nu bocinhu, tirô um rusáriu. "Tomi, meu amiguinhu," eli dissi. "É essa a arma qui vai protegê você di tudu mal."

U cara pegô nu rusáriu i começô andá mais eli num acreditava na palavra du meu Padim. Aí quandu incontra otru viajanti, cum ispingarda forti, boa, eli pergunta si essi num qué dá trocada, a ispingarda nu rusáriu.

"Tá certu," eli diz. Aí deu u rusáriu para eli, eli ficô cum ispingarda. Bão, num tinha andadu nem cincu braçu quandu apareci uma onça. U cara agarrô na ispingarda mais a onça sartou antis qui pudia dá um tiru nela. I é ansim qui acabô-si um rumeiru dus mais besta.

26. Nu tempu du meu Padinhu tinha muntu mocozinhu incima nu Ortu. Era us mocozinhu du meu Padinhu. Qui us romeru tinha trazidu pra eli i não era para ninguém bulí cum elis, né? Mais tinha um ômi qui si achava mais qui meu Padinhu. Um dia qui tava cum fomi dissi, "Sabi di uma coisa, um mocozinhu dessis ia muntu bem na janta." Aí foi matô um mocó i interrô us ossinhu para ninguém sabê. Então trouxi a carni para a casa, feiz assá. Mmmm, cheirinho bom! Mais dipois deli tê comidu tudu, ficô naquela agonia. Doía tantu a barriga que mandô a mulé pidi um remédiu au meu Padim.

Aí ela foi dissi, "Meu Padim, vim pidí um remédiu para uma dor di barriga qui tem u meu maridu choranu iguá a quaqué um nené."

Aí meu Padim dissi, "Diga pra seu maridu qui é para eli cavá ondi deixô us ossinhu du meu mocozinhu. Devi assá i moê bem. Aí ele faiz um chá i bebi. Ansim vai passá a dor." A mulé vortô i dissi tudu pru maridu. Essi logu dispois di tomá u chá ficô bomzinhu. Só qui nunca mais pudia oiá pra mocozinhu sem sentí aquela dor.

27. Uma romeira veiu pra Juazeiru mais us treis fiinhu dela i quandu chegô a ora da saída si encontrô sem dinheru nenhum. Aí foi pidí uma ajuda au meu Padim Ciçu pra viagi. "Tomi aqui," eli dissi pra ela, deu um vintém.

"Mais meu Padim, comu é qui u sinhô quer qui eu faça essa viagi tão grandi sem nada mais di um vintém?" I pegô a chorá.

"Você não sabi qui um pocu cum Deus é muntu i muntu sem Deus não é nada?" eli dissi.

Aí ela pegô nu vintém i us quatru andava, andava. I ondi elis chegava u povu lis dava u qui precisava.

"Si voceis vêm di Juazeru têm qui comê mais nóis," elis disseru. "Si foi u meu Padim qui mandô a sinhora, tem ondi armá a redi aqui."

Aí quandu a muié chegô por fim em casa, u vintém taha ainda nu bossu. I eu achu qui ela devia tê ficadu cum eli até u fim da vida. Você não acha também?

28. Tinha um ômi qui pidiu um jumentinhu du compadi deli pra fazê a romaria deli a Juazeiru. Aí na vorta quandu ia botá a sela nu jumentinhu encontrô eli mortu. Antão foi vê meu Padim.

"Iscuta bem," meu Padim dissi, "qui você vai fazê u qui eu digu. Quandu você vortá pru ranchu, u jumentinhu vai istá di pé ondi você deixô eli. Aí você bota a sela neli i corri sem pará até chegá em casa. Logu qui você chegá, você intrega u jumentinhu au donu. Viu?"

"Istá certu, meu Padim," u ômi dissi. Aí eli vortô pru ranchu, i u jumentinhu tava mesmu di pé. Aí botô a sela neli comu meu Padim tinha faladu, entendi? I correu qui nem u ventu treis noiti i treis dia. Quandu chegô, foi logu intregá u jumentinhu au compadi deli.

"Muntu obrigadu," eli dissi. "Aqui istá u seu jumentinhu."

"Eu nunca vi aqueli jumentu tão ansim di saudi," u donu dissi para si. "Para mim, eli teria murridu nu caminhu, tão véiu qui era. Será qui u ar di Juazeiru é mesmu milagrosu comu u povu diz?"

Nu ôtru dia quandu u donu foi dá comida au jumentinhu só achava a sela por cima dum monti di ossu. Mais num podia nada apois u compadi romeiru tinha deixadu eli im pé.

29. Uma moça bem pobri quiria fazê visita a meu Padim. Aí um dia qui ela viu passá um grupu di romeru frenti di sua porta ela dissi, "Per'aí qui vô a Juazeru mais voceis."

Aí ela correu arrumá as coisinha dela i foi atraiz. Taha cum tanta pressa qui nim pensava na galinha choca dela, coitadinha. Qui essa ficô im casa sim nada di comê. Só dipois dela chegá im Juazeru é qui si alembrô da galinha. Antão quandu us romeru foru vê meu Padim eli perguntô pra ela, "Por qui essa cara tristi? Quem viaja pru Juazeru devi tá filiz."

"Mi perdoi, meu Padim," a moça dissi. "É qui tenhu pena da galinha choca qui ficô im casa sim nada di comê."

"Num si preocupi," meu Padim dissi. "Que tudu vai dá certu."

Bem, quandu a moça abriu a porta da casa u qui é qui ela achô mais aquela galinha arrodiada di pintinhu? Tinha pelu menu uma dúzia, cada um mais gordinhu, mais contenti du otru. "Piu, piu, piu," qui elis num tinha faltadu nada.

Ora, quem foi qui deu xerém para elis? Quem foi qui deu aquelis pintinhu água a bebê?

30. Meu sogru era muntu amigu dessi Manué Germanu qui ficô ricu. Andavu sempri juntus. Antonci um dia Manué Germanu resolveu trazê um pocu di goma au meu Padim Ciçu. Aí meu sogru dissi, "Eu vô mais você."

Quandu chegaru na casa deli, meu Padim Ciçu botô a mão na cabeça di Manué Germanu. Dissi, "Deus ti aumenti, Manué Germanu," ansim, treis vezi.

Aí meu sogru dissi, "Meu Padim Ciçu, boti uma bença im mim também!"

Aí meu Padim feiz uma cruiz cum dedu bem pesadu na cabeça deli. Qui era pra eli si conformá qui ia morrê pobri, viu? Mais u Manué Germanu, essi, num, logu nu ôtru dia começô a miorá di vida. I daí a pocus tempus ficô ricu, ricu dimais.

31. Nu dia im qui meu Padim mudô-si u sinhô bispu veiu du Cratu cuns impregadu deli pra levá u corpu daqui. Chegaru lá por meia noiti para ninguém
vê. . . . Ainda mi alembru daqueli dia du interru, qui era tão tristi, tão tristi.
Eu só cuns seis anu, né? Pidi pra minha mãe mi levá qui quiria ver eli nu
caixão mais ela dissi qui não, qui não pudia poquê eu não churava i só quem
churava tinha direito di ir. Aí fui nu pé di pimenta, tirei as pimenta i passei
nus ôiu, assim. Aí us ôiu ficaru correnu água, duenu, i eu dissi, "Mãe, já tô
churanu, mi levi." Mais ela falô qui não, qui tinha munta genti, qui eu era
piquena dimais. . . . Pois antão só dipois du interru quandu as pessoas tinha
saídu é qui u sinhô bispu veiu robá u corpu deli. Mais não pudia pois não
tinha nada para eli levá. Quandu eli abriu u caixão só tinha era um monti di
rosa. Qué dizê u povu conta, qui eu não tava lá para vê.

32. Óia, morreu meu pai da bala dum assassinu e duranti muntu tempu fique-
mos muntu tristis. Aí por fim u meu Padinhu Ciçu chamô a minha mãe a
Juazeru. "A sinhora tem qui perdoá u ômi qui matô u seu maridu," eli disse
para ela.

   "Mais meu Padinhu, comu é qui eu possu perduá quem matô u meu maridu i deixô us meus filhu sem pai?"

   "A sinhora podi perduá eli pois si não perduá, u seu maridu vai mais eli
pru infernu."

   I então a minha mãe perduô aqueli ômi. I eu também, eu perduei eli. Por
issu, eu disconfiu desti negóciu du fazenderu. Eu contu u qui ôtrus mi con-
taru mais eu disconfiu di todu jeitu, viu? Qui si eu ovi meu Padim dizê qui
íamu perduá u sujeitu qui tinha matadu meu pai, comu é que meu Padim ia
tirá a vida daquelas criancinha ansim, sem pecadu?

33. Meu Padim foi a Roma e quanu eli chegô foi vê u sinhô papa.
   "Padim Ciçu," eli dissi, "mandei chamá u sinhô pra abrí a porta dessa
igreja qui São Pedro fechô."

   "Eu num possu abrí aquela igreja, Santu Papa," meu Padim Ciçu dissi,
"apois um padi é um sordadu, um simpris empregadu."

   "U sinhô faiz u qui tô mandanu," o papa dissi, "apois meu exércitu já tá
prontu a botá Juazeiru nu chão si num fizê."

   "Bem, apois bem," diz meu Padim. "Eu abru a porta si é u sinhô quem
qué." Aí eli diz ansim, "Qui a mão qui ti fechô ti abri," i bati nela treis vezi.
Aí a porta si abri i meu Padim vai entranu.

34. Um dia meu Padim dixi para ela, "Minha mãe, eu não possu disfazê u qui
Deus já feiz. Mais inda qui a minha mãe queria oiá a igreja lá nu Ortu, comu
é bunita?"

   "Já ovi falá dimais naquela igreja," ela dixi. "Vamu lá oiá."

   Aí meu Padim pegô nu braçu dela. Iu subindu juntus a ladeira du Ortu.
Quandu chegaru na igreja, eli dixi, "Per'aí, minha mãe, qui vô abri." Aí
uma veiz qui tavu drentru, dizi qui us ôiu dela si abriru. Óia aí, minha mãe,"
meu Padim dixi.

   "É tão bunitu comu u povu diz," dixi ela, tudu contenti.

   Pois então passaru muntas ora ali. Qui só por fim quandu a noiti vinha é
qui elis ia saindu.

   "Minha mãe tá satisfeita?" meu Padim preguntô para ela.

   Ela dixi, "Sim, qui já vi tantu di coisa boa."

Aí sairu i eli fechô a porta atraiz cum chavi. I logu qui a última luiz du dia tocô nus ôiu dela, cegô di novu. Aí meu Padim pegava nu braçu dela i desceru rua abaixu. Desceru di braçu dadu, meu Padim mais a sua mãezinha.

35. Ovi u casu qui vô contá di minha avó. Ela vinha a Juazeiru di a pés tudu anu sempri até qui num pudia mais. Eu custumava durmi na casa dela, aí ovi tudu qui ela tinha pra contá. Apois bom, um dus casus qui sempri contava era aqueli da moça qui virô cobra i é ansim. . . .

36. Quandu meu pai era rapaizinhu, ia a Juazeru mais us pais deli nessas romaria grandi. Aí um dessis romeru era irmão daquela moça em qui a onça pegô, não sabi? Eli contô tudu pra meu pai di comu foi que a irmã tinha sidu comidu pela onça. Eli dissi qui. . . .

37. Vô contá uma passagi qui ovi di uma véiinha qui mora vizinha di mim. Ela ficô di morada muntus anu im Juazeru, aí sabi contá munta coisa boa. Antis eu lavava ropa mais ela nu riu. Antão eu sempri dizia, "Ô Dona Ana, conti mais uma coisa du meu Padim Ciçu pra a henti." Aí uma veiz ela contô essa passagi du meu Padim minininhu que vô contá pra voceis agorinha. Iscuti. . . .

38. U povu diz qui a mãe di meu Padim Ciçu deu a luiz a um mininu. I antonci, pocu dipois quandu ela taha durmindu, chegô uma dona tudu di azú. Qui essa quiria vê si ela num trocava u mininu dela pra otru qui levava nu braçu. Aí ainda naquele sonhu, num sabi, Dona Janoca dissi qui num quiria trocá di jeitu nenhum. Antonci quandu ela dispreitô foi oiá pra criancinha. I viu qui eli num era dela. Aí começava gritá qui a criança era um bichu qui ela num quiria nada cum um monstru dessis. I foi naqueli momentu qui pirdeu a luiz dus ôiu.

39. Quandu meu Padim era criança gostava di rezá por dibaixu di uma laranjera. Aí us otru mininu resolveru falá pra professora. "Ô Dona, u Ciçu fica por dibaixu daquela laranjera sempri qui vem pra iscola."
"Não si preocupi cum a vida di Ciçu," ela dissi. "Eli é bom alunu. Voceis deixa eli pra lá."
Aí us meninu ficaru danadus di raiva. "Vamu botá uma boa pedra nu caminhu deli," elis dizia. I foru lá na sala i não deixaru pregu nenhum pru chapéu deli. Quandu meu Padim chegô na aula, viu tudus us pregu ansim ocupadu. Aí foi botô u chapeuzinhu deli na paredi i lá ficô. Us otru mininu quasi qui murreru di inveja.
"Você vai nus pagá, Cicinhu," elis dizia baixinhu pra eli. I foi ansim u começu das perseguiçõi du meu Padim.

40. Francu Rabeira era um guvernadô du istadu du Ciará. Eli num gustava du meu Padim Ciçu porqui eli memu quiria sê a pessoa mais importanti di todu Ciará. Quiria sê donu du estadu, num sabi? É por issu qui eli mandô as suas tropa acabá cum Juazeiru im dizembru di catorzi. Mandô dois mi quinhentu sodadu tudu armadu, dois canhão i um avião. Quandu meu Padim sôbi qui us sodadu vinha para Juazeiru mandô u Dotô Flori construí um muru di pedra au redô da cidadi. Antão deu um rosáriu i um rifi a todu romeiru seu. Us sodadu atiraru até ficá sem bala mais num puderu nada. Quasi num morreu ninguém du ladu deli. Só murreu quem pisava na palavra deli. Mais us sodadu num tinha sorti. Muntu sodadu morreu.

41. Duranti a guerra di catorzi ôvi muntus casu. Eu sei porqui us treis véiinhu—Seu Zé Rumeiru, Seu Cazuza, Seu Capistranu—sempri falavu dessi povu véiu qui guerreô contra us sordadu du guvernu. Quandu u dia chegô prus rumeiru du meu Padrim dá batáia aus inimigu, eli ajuntô todu mundu. Botô uma bença nelis i deu uma medáia di São Bentu a cada um, qui ia sirví di pruteção. I dissi ansim, "Voceis vão, não beba cachaça, não mexi im nada di ninguém i não tem bala qui pegui im voceis." Aí us rumeiru foru guerreá cuns sordadu i muntu sordadu murreu. Mais só murreu du ladu deli era um rapaiz qui bebeu cachaça. Até tinha um biatu qui eli dançava incima du muru. Us macacu dava neli sem pará mais eli não caía. Aquela medáia nu pescoçu deli feiz cum qui as bala correru qui nem água. Aí eli ficô dançanu incima daqueli muru até qui elis quasi ficaru doidu.

42. Duranti a guerra di catorzi meu Padinhu prometeu qui nenhum dus romeiru deli ia sofrê mal nenhum. Aí eli feiz um muru tudu di pedra au redô di Juazeiru pra portegê a cidadi dus sodadu. I ninguém qui respeitava a palavra deli murreu. Óia—aqueli pilão, eli qui istá lá naqueli cantu, istá vendu?—era um pé di piqui bem verdi, bem grandi, bunitu, qui tinha na frenti da casa di minha sogra. Aí im catorzi, veiu uma guerra i u meu Padinhu Ciçu mandô qui tudu mundu qui istivessi fora da rua intrassi pra a rua. Qui a guerra ia começá, né? Aí elis di fora deixaru suas casas i tudu qui tinha. Só vortavu a casa di veiz im quandu pra pegá aquela comidazinha quandu meu Padim deixô. Aí uma veiz Seu Vicenti pidiu licença pra subí pela istrada du Logradoru. Passava u riu i foi pegá a istrada di Santu Antoniu pela banda du Cratu. Quandu chegô, coitadu, tirava quaqué coisa di comida antis di qui us sodadu chegassi di pertu. Bom, nessa última viagi antis du tiruteiu di bala, u pé di pau, u piqui, inda istava. Bem verdi, bem bunitu.

Apois então quandu foi cum uns quatru ô cincu dias qui terminô a guerra, meu Padinhu Ciçu mandô tudus percurá suas casas, qui fossi imbora, fossi trabaiá. Aí quandu Seu Vicenti chegô im casa, incontrô u pé di piqui caídu nu chão. Us bandidu tinhu cortadu eli. Aí Seu Vicenti ficô bem tristi, qui aqueli pé rendia muntu, também dava munta sombra. Aí resolveu fazê aqueli pilão. Podi vê qui eli istá bem gastu mas sirvi di lembrança da guerra di catorzi. Aí eu tenhu pena di deixá eli para ôtru.

43. U empregadu dissi, "Não abru mais essi portão qui u tiroteiu tá prontu a começá. U portão si encerrô, nem entra nem sai."

Aí minha avó dissi, "Não, u sinhô tem qui abrí qui tô aqui cum um carneiru du meu Padim Ciçu."

U empregadu oiô, pru carneiru, então teve pena daquelis dois mininu disprotegidu. "Pode entrá," eli dissi, "mais a sinhora vem cum toda pressa."

Bem, má us treis tinha entradu cum carneirinhu, vem u tiroteiu di bala. As bala zumbavu ansim nu ar por tudu cantu mais não pegavu im romeiru nenhum. Não, nenhum, *nenhum* dus romeiru morreu.

44. Tudu mundu gustava du meu Padim. Só quem num gustava deli era um generá di exércitu—num sei mais u nomi deli—mais era um chefão ansim, dus mais importanti. Eli num gustava du meu Padim por causa da romaria, qui sempri vinha muntu rumeru para qui. Aí ficô querenu sê mais qui meu Padim. Antão mandô us sodadu deli contra meu Padim i meu Padim botô uma pedrinha qui deu um muru muntu grandi. Us sodadu vinha atirá neli

mais as bala si transformaru im água. Elis atiraru, atiraru, mais num podia nada contra eli, pois tinha muntu milagui.

45. U Cratu quiria acabá cum a rumaria daqui. Aí meu Padim Ciçu mais Nossa Sinhora fizeru uma trincheira. Arrodearu a cidadi cum um muru di macambira di noiti pru dia. Us sodadu ficaru atiranu im meu Padim mais a bala não pegô. Vortava prus sodadu i matava elis mais nenhum rumeiru murreu. Só murreu um qui tinha pegadu nu bodi du vizinhu. Aqueli não ligava pra meu Padim, aí uma bala pegô nu curação deli.

46. Francu Rabeu dixi, "Pra matá essi Padi Ciçu vamu tê qui jogá uma bomba, acabá cum Juazeru." Aí us sodadu subiru u canhão pela Serra du Araripi. Mais quandu foi na ora du canhão detoná im veiz deli detoná pru ladu du Juazeru, detonô pru ladu da força. Acabô cum tudu mundu. Us sodadu du Francu Rabeu ficaru feitu pedacinhu di genti, aí eli num tinha comu acabá cum meu Padim.

47. Veiu um pilotu di avião bombeá Juazeru. Mais meu Padrim mandava todu mundu rezá. A cidadi incantô-si i ondi tinha sidu casa ora só tinha matu. U pilotu num podia vê nada, aí num adiantava bombeá. Antão dissi por fim, "Sabi di uma coisa, eu vô passá au ladu du meu Padrim, qui é u ladu di bem." I naquela ora Jauazeru apariceu di novu para eli vê.

48. A dona minina já viu aqueli pedaçu di muru qui tem lá nu Ortu? Pois bem, é du tempu da guerra. Qui u guvernadô mandô us sordadu deli degolá u meu Padim. Tinha muntu ciumi di meu Padim, aí resolveu fazê uma guerra contra eli. Antão meu Padim mandô tudu mundu arrodeá a cidadi por um muru deiz mão di grossura. Tão prontu qui elis acabaru, veiu uma guerra. Us sordadu atiraru mais num atingiru meu Padim di jeitu nenhum. Antão começaru a ficá tão desesperadus qui chamaru pru Cão. Veiu u Cão, falô pra elis qui quiria bem ajudá. Mais num pudia, qui tinha uma muié por cima du muru contra quem eli num tinha força nenhuma. Aquela muié andava pra lá, pra cá, pra lá, pra cá, num deixava eli passá. Eli tinha pena, teria gostadu di ajudá elis. Mais aquela muié era mermu pra endoidecê. Aí num tinha jeitu.

49. Naquela guerra Francu Rabelu mandô cem mi tropas para acabá cum a romaria. Chegaru us sodadu cum us rifi já quenti. Mais quandu elis foru atirá im Juazeru, ficaru sem podê acreditá. Sessenti ômi cum sessenti rifi i sessenti rosáriu veiu au encontru delis. Aí u valadu qui us romeru cavaru ficô cheiu di corpu di sodadu. Corria riachus di sangui. Apois meu Padim tinha ditu para todu mundu qui num ia deixá elis passá. Mais elis num ligavu pra eli, aí só podiu sofrê. Era uma coisa medonha di vê.

50. Deu-si uma guerra das mais terrivi aqui uma veiz. U sangui corria qui nem água por treis dia sem pará. Apagô a luiz da igreja. Era fumaça i fogu por todu ladu. Nu fim, Nossa Sinhora desceu numa nuvi. Então deu-si um estrondu tão grandi qui quasi o mundu si acabô. Aí us sordadu sabia qui iu pirdê. Muntus murreru mais ninguém du ladu du meu Padim tevi nada. Só tinha dois qui disobediceru. Pegaru im coisa dus ôtru i num tevi mais jeitu, murreru.

51. Veiu tudu um exércitu guerreá contra meu Padim. I meu Padim dissi, "Deixa qui elis venha. Eu não tenhu medu, não." Aí quandu us sodadu chegaru, as arma deli cairu nu chão. Era ispingarda, era faca, era pexeira lá pelu meiu da rua. Qui meu Padim tinha muntu podê, tinha mais podê du qui quaqué um ôtru. Quandu us sodadu vinhu matá eli, eli botô a mão pra cima i foi dissi, "Vai vir um dia im qui u maior castelu du mundu tem qui virá igreja." Botô a mão pra cima ansim—tá venu, minha genti!—i us sodadu deixaru as arma caí.

52. Tinha um bispu qui era amanti duma freira. Daí apariceu um mininu qui elis butaru num orfanatu. I essi mininu nasceu sem fala, nunca falô para ninguém. Aí u bispu mandô chamá meu Padrim Ciçu a Roma—ô era Roma ô era Fortaleza—qui todu mundu falava qui fazia muntu milagui. Mandô chamá meu Padim Ciçu i meu Padim veiu. Aí u bispu dissi qui era para eli fazê essi mininu falá. Aí u mininu abriu a boca i dissi, "Meu pai é u sinhô bispu i minha mãe é a freira Fulana di Tá." Antão foi issu qui deu a rivolução. Deu noventi dia di guerra im que muntu sodadu murreu. Ninguém di Juazeru murreu, qui u meu Padim transformô as bala dus sodadu im água. Mais muntu sodadu murreu. Quem era contra eli murreu.

53. Bateu na porta i quandu meu Padrinhu Ciçu foi abrí eu vi u Dotô Flori. Era baixinhu, gordinhu, di bigodi qui fazia ansim nas ponta, i falava bem grossu. "Padri Ciçu," eli quasi qui gritô pra eli, eu tô murrenu di fomi. Vamu comê?"

"Apois coma, Dotô Flori," meu Padrinhu dissi. "U amoçu tá na mesa. Vai si sirvinu."

"Não, Padri Ciçu," eli dissi. "Só comu si u sinhô comê também."

"Eu não quero, não" meu Padim dissi. "Muntu obrigadu, mais você si sirvi."

"Apois bem, Padri Ciçu, dê licença qui vô comê um bocadinhu." Pei, pei, pei, comeu, comeu, comeu qui eu não podia acreditá. Quandu acabô di comê tirô um charutu du boçu i foi fumá. Dipois foi-si embora. Dizi qui tinha uma dona cum quem eli andava mais eu não sei li dizê.

54. U beatu Zé Lorenço ficô presu na cadéia di Dotô Fulori dezineti dias. Num comia, num bebia, num durmia nada. Aí u Dotô Fulori espantô-si, foi vê u meu Padim. "Padi Cíçaru, qui ômi é essi qui num comi, num bebi i num durmi? Faiz dezineti dias qui tá na minha cadeia i fica ansim sem dá siná di vida."

Aí meu Padim dissi, "Fulori, tu estais pensanu qui José istá na tua cadeia. Mais eli istá mais us romeru deli trabaianu, amoçanu, jantanu, rezanu u rosáriu deli. Tu num estais entendenu qui é só a aparença di José qui tu tens ali." Aí u dotô saiu danu fogu. Ficô danadu porqui meu Padim sabia di coisas qui eli nem pudia imaginá.

"Fulori," meu Padim falô pra eli. "Cuidadu qui quem ti feiz grandi podi ti fazê bem miudinhu."

55. Era um boi tão mansinhu qui dava gostu a henti vê. I comu era du meu Padim, tudu mundu tratava eli cum tudu carinhu. Mais u Dotô Fulori quiria sê mais qui meu Padim. Aí eli chegô na Baixa D'Anta, tocô fogu im tudu. Apoiz dizia qui o pessuá tava rezanu pru boi. Antão depoiz dus sodadu

quemá as casinha, fizeru disfili cum boi. Meu Padim Ciçu mandô um portadô dizê qui não era pra matá u boi mais mataru di tudu jeitu. U boi caiu, sortô um grandi gritu, as lágrima caíru dus ôiu. Aí us sodadu assaru a carni i feiz tudu mundu comê.

56. U meu Padrinhu Ciçu dizia qui era pra num matá aqueli boi. Mais u Dotô Flori num ligô. Mandô us sordadu deli matá. Aí todu mundu qui cumia daquela carni ficô aduentadu. Qui era numa sexta-feira i u meu Padim Ciçu tinha faladu qui num era para ninguém tocá neli. Mais elis mataru di todu jeitu, pisaru na palavra deli. Comeru daquela carni na sexta-feira i a língua delis cresceu, cresceu até ficá nu chão. Aí dava aquela coceira i ficava vermeia i correnu sangui. Por fim u Dotô Flori foi dizê au meu Padim qui as língua dus sordadu tava sangranu. "Cuidadu," meu Padim dissi para eli, "qui quem ti feiz grandi podi ti fazê bem piquenu."

57. Meu Padrim Ciçu dissi pru Flori que não queria coisa di Carnavá nu Juazeiru porqui não gustava nada daquilu. Mas u Flori nunca prestô atenção ao meu Padrim. Sempri achava qui sabia mais qui eli. Ansi qui quandu u dia chegô, mandô os sodadu deli vestí aquelas fantasia e saíru pra rua. Cantava i pulava i batia nu tambô delis, todo mundu só oiandu pra elis. Pois bem, di repenti o céu si abri e um mar di água cai encima delis.
"Vamos pra casa!" gritavu os sodadu mais u Flori não deixô ninguém saí. Ansim qui ficava pulandu pelas poça duranti oras, batendu i espirrandu forti.
"Flori," meu Padrim dissi, "deixa esta doidici antis di qui eli quem ti feiz grandi resolva ti fazê piqueninu."

58. Tinha uma mulé qui morava vizinha cum otra. I essa mulé tinha uma pirua qui si pirdeu nu matu. Quandu a pirua não vortô, a dona foi vê u Dotô Fulori. Dissi pra eli qui a vizinha tinha comidu a pirua. U Dotô Fulori dissi, "Tem certeza qui foi ela quem comeu?" I ela falô qui sim, qui tinha toda certeza. Aí eli mandô us sordadu lá na casa da vizinha.
"Foi você quem comeu a pirua da mulé?"
"Comi, não, sinhô," ela arrespondeu. "Eu não ia fazê uma coisa dessas."
"Apois sua vizinha chegô danu queixa qui foi a sinhora, sim. Antão vamu levá." Aí foru imbora mais ela i ninguém nunca viu ela di novu.
Bem, dipois di uma semana, mais ô menu, lá vem a pirua. Qui tinha istadu choca nu ninhu mais agora istava di vorta. Quandu a pirua chegô, a dona foi vê u Dotô Fulori. "A minha pirua já vortô," ela dissi. "Aí u sinhô podi sortá a mulé da cadeia qui eu istava errada." Mais us sordadu di Dotô Fulori já tinha matadu a otra mulé. Aí não tinhu jeitu di sortá ela, viu?
"Bem," eli dissi, "comu não possu sortá a sua vizinha, você vai pra ondi ela foi." I us sordadu levaru essa também.
Aí quandu meu Padim sôbi u qui tinha passadu eli mandô chamá u Dotô Fulori. "Comu podi qui você anda matanu essi povu inocenti?" eli perguntô para eli.
"Padi Ciçu," Dotô Fulori dissi, "não foi u sinhô quem mi deu u podê?"
"Fui eu qui dei," meu Padim dissi, "mais você não isqueça duma coisa. Qui quem ti feiz grandi podi ti fazê também piquenu."

59. Dotô Floru era um guvernadô, um governadô du Ciará. Meu Padim botô eli nas artura mais Dotô Floru feiz pocu deli. "Ora, Padi Ciçu," eli sempri

dizia. "Eu sô mais qui u sinhô. Qui eu nasci antis da Arca di Noé. Ansim sô bem mais véiu qui u sinhô qui só nasceu ontem."

"Deixa di besteira, Dotô Floru," meu Padim dissi. "Quem ti feiz grandi podi ti fazê piquenu." Mais u Dotô Floru num ligava pra nada i foi, matô munta genti. Meu Padim feiz tudu pra qui eli deixassi aquela vida di assassinu mais eli num deixô. Aí meu Padim tevi qui acabá cum eli.

60. Um dia meu Padinhu Ciçu mandô chamá u Dotô Flori. "Dotô Flori," ele dixi, "você tá grandi dimais."

Aí u Dotô Flori perguntô pra eli, "Apois, porqui é qui u sinhô mi feiz dessi jeitu?"

Meu Padinhu dixi, "Cuidadu. Eli quem ti feiz grandi podi ti fazê mais piqueninu qui um grãozinhu di mustarda."

Aí u Flori dixi di novu, "porqui mi feiz grandi?"

"Vai acabá qui nem um grãozinhu di mustarda," dixi meu Padim. "Um grãozinhu piqueninu qui u ventu leva sem ninguém repará." I ansim é qui foi. Pôcu dispois u Dotô Flori foi pru Riu di Janeiru i lá morreu. Eli quiria sê grandi mais u ventu levô a grandeza deli. I ninguém reparô. Ninguém si importô.

61. Era u Dotô Fulori quem feiz meu Padim Ciçu sufrê. U Sagradu Curação di Jesuis deu Juazeiru a meu Padim. Falô para meu Padim qui era para eli tomá conta di tudu. I di repenti, di bem drentru da terra surgiu um ossu pretu para fazê meu Padim sufrê. Eu digu qui u ossu pretu foi essi tá di Dotô Fulori. Era eli u responsavi di todas as perseguiçõi du meu Padim.

62. Nus tempu passadu num tinha Carnavá im Juazeru i num tem Carnavá até oji aqui. Mais tinha um chefão por nomi di Dotô Fuloru. Era comu nem um reis mais inda quiria sê mais qui meu Padim—ha, ha, ha! Aí meu Padim dissi, "Fuloru, quem ti feiz grandi podi ti fazê também piquenu." Mais u Dotô Fuloru só ria. Dizia prus sordadu deli qui era pra fazê um grandi disfili. Pois bem, pegô a chovê i u Dotô Fuloru ficô cum febri i cum friu. Ficô tão duenti qui acabô morrendu nu Riu di Janeiru. Qui quiria sê mais qui meu Padim, aí só podi, né?

63. Era um grandão, u Dotô Fulori. U Padim Ciçaru gostava deli mais eli praticava munta cruedadi. Matava munta genti i por fim eli murreu também. Meu Padim dissi pra eli qui num pudia continuá dessi jeitu mais num ligô pra eli, não. Aí adueceu i pocu dispoiz, murreu. Meu Padim deu um remédiu a eli qui eli teria ficadu bão. Mais eli num quis u remédiu du meu Padim, antão murreu na ora. Di teimosu qui era, num sabi?

64. U Dotô Floru era um chefão daqui. Aí um dia eli oviu dizê qui meu Padim tinha botadu a óstia na boca da beata Maria di Araúju. I si virava im sangui. Então quandu sôbi a notícia, correu pra vê a beata. Botô u dedão deli dentru da boca dela. Pois essi Floru num acreditava memu nus puderi du meu Padim. Até rasgô a guela da beata. Aí meu Padim Ciçu ficô cum raiva.

"Dotô Floru," eli dissi, "você mi arrespeita!"

"Por qui?" u Dotô Floru dissi. "Eu sô mais qui u sinhô."

"Você pensa ansim," meu Padim dissi, "mais cuidadu qui quem ti botô nas artura também ti faiz caí." Bem, pocu dipois u Dotô Floru saiu pru Riu di Janeiru. Mais eli nunca chegô ali qui murreu nu caminhu.

65. *See text page 188.*

66. Aqueli casu di Maria di Araúju é muitu complicadu. Minha mãe—não, era minha avó—frequentava a igreja muitu naquela época. Bom, a minha avó— chamava-si Ana—istava assistindu a missa um dia qui meu Padrinhu Ciçu levantô a óstia pra cima i veiu descê duas fita di sangui num braçu i nu otru. Aí u meu Padrinhu botô a óstia na boca di Maria di Araúju i a óstia transformô-si em sangui vivu. I não era só issu. Qui a coisa arrepitiu-si nu otru dia u mesmu. Quandu u bispu tomô conhecimentu du casu, mandô chamá us médicu. Examinaru ela pra vê si não avia algum ferimentu na boca dela. Mais não acharu nada. I foi assim qui era certeza. Qui a óstia tinha si viradu sangue na boca da beata.

67. Na ora da comunhão quandu meu Padim Ciçu chegô, botô a óstia na boca da biata. Qui transformô-se im sangui. É u casu du Sangui Apreciosu. A hóstia virô sangui na boca da biata.

68. Da transformação da óstia não sei falá muntu. Qui não foi du meu tempu, viu? Mais a minha sogra conhecia a beata. Ela diz qui essa Maria di Araúju era muntíssima católica, qui quasi qui vivia na igreja desdi menina. Aí um dia u meu Padinhu Ciçu foi dá a comunhão a ela i a óstia si manifestô em sangui. Diz ela pelu menus. Eu não tava ali para vê mais a minha sogra diz qui meu Padim ia dá a comunhão a ela, à beata, treis vezi. I aconteceu treis vezi qui a óstia si manifestô em sangui. Aí meu Padim pegô a chorá mais ninguém sabi por quê. Aí levaru a beata a Cratu ondi ela vivia presa. Quandu libertaru ela meu Padim veiu dá a comunhão a ela a meia noiti para qui ninguém viessi.

69. Bem, *dizi* qui a beata botô a óstia na boca dela i virô-si sangui. *Dizi* qui tinha um pessoá qui não acreditava i qui quiria botá tudu na dúvida. *Eu não sei* comu foi *mais dizi* qui essi pessoá andava dizendu qui era até sangui di gadu nus panu. Mais ela foi im Roma i *pareci qui* a coisa ficô aprovada. *Pareci.* Agora *não sei* porqui mulé não é qui nem ômi qui anda por todu cantu i sabi di tudu. *Mais para mim* aquilu foi uma verdadi [my italics].

70. Eu tava andanu a cavalu nu matu sozinhu. Naqueli tempu inda tinha munta onça i era um pirigu passá a noiti lá fora. Aí eu tava andanu cum munta pressa quandu di ripenti apareci uma cobra dessas grandi di num sei ondi. Mordeu u cavalu. Coitadu, deu uma rinchada, tremeu forti antis di caí nu chão. Aí lá tava eu, só, sem cavalu i a noiti prontu a caí. Pois naqueli instanti eu mi valei di Santa Maria Araúju. Qui si ela tivessi pena di mim i risuscitassi meu cavalu, eu ia ofirecê uma missa im intenção da santa arma dela. Aí di ripenti u cavalu tremi di novu i si põi im pé. Aí lá vamu correnu matu adentru até chegá num sítiu ondi passamu a noiti.

71. Meu Padrinhu istava dandu a comunhão au povu i a óstia ficô feitu sangui na boca da biata Araúju. Aí u bispu, u papa i todus us padri di lá mandaru chamá eli a Roma. Qui era pra eli dá conta dessas toáia machada di sangui. Ou eli levava conta ou eli ia morrê.

Fizeru cum qui eli sufreu tantu, tantu im Roma qui por fim eli dissi, "Per'aí." Antão tirô um dessis lençu du boçu, começava amarrá ansim nus quatru cantu.

Aí todu mundu gritô, "Num faça istu, Padri Ciçu!" Qui sabiu qui si eli amarrassi us quatru cantinhu u mundu acabava na ora. Sabiu mesmu qui eli istava dizendu era a verdadi. Sabiu qui aquela mancha era mesmu u Sangui Apreciosu di Nossu Sinhô.

72. Tinha uma biata, a Maria di Araúji. Ela foi comungá i a óstia dismanchô-si im sangui. *Foi por causa dessa biata* qui u meu Padim Ciçu ficô suspensu di ordis.

73. Maria di Araúju? Sim, já ovi falá nu casu. *Foi por causa dela* qui u meu Padrinhu Ciçu foi chamadu a Roma.

74. Entonci dispois daqueli dia im qui a óstia transformô-si im sangui tinha um povu qui andava dizenu qui Maria di Araúju era uma mentirosa, qui era uma arma condenada. Rasparu a língua, arrancaru a língua da boca, *aí era u começu dus sofrimentu du meu Padim.*

75. U meu Padim Cíçaru deu a comunhão a Maria di Araúju i a óstia virô-si im sangui. Num foi só uma veiz, foi duas veizi. Dizi qui u vistidu dela ficô tudu encarnadu di sangui. Na primera veiz ficô ansim. A ôtra veiz foi inda mais. Agora dizi qui u bispu levô essis vistidu porqui num gostô. Num gostô memu.

76. Quandu foi um dia a beata Maria di Araúju chegô na igreja, foi aondi u meu Padrim Ciçu custumava celebrá a missa. Antão eli deu a comunhão a ela. I a óstia si transformô im sangui na boca dela. Aí meu Padrim Ciçu dissi qui era u sangui apreciosu di Nossu Sinhô Jesuis Cristu. Aí todus us padri pegaru a discutí cum eli dizenu qui num era pra acreditá. Até veiu um padri dizê qui u sangui—Deus mi pirdoi—era u sangui da menstruação. Ah qui alguém pudessi falá tamanha calunha!

77. Maria di Araúju era Nossa Sinhora pura. Quandu meu Padim Ciçu foi dá a comunhão a ela, apareceu u sangui apreciosu, viu? Tinha treis mulé na mesa da comunhão quandu eli chegô mais u sangui apareceu foi só nela. Deu a comunhão a santa Maria di Araúju i u sangui minô da boca dela. Eu num vi, num, mais acreditu di todu curação im quem viu. Interraru ela nu Socorru mais u corpu sumiu du caixão qui ela foi pru céu toda santa.

78. Dizi qui a Maria di Araúju quiria si santificá, qui levava vridrinhu di sangui di boi i tal. Mais eu num achu. Veiu uma duzia di médicu examiná ela. Aí elis disseru qui num era sangui umanu nem sangui di bichu, qui era um sangui tudu diferenti. I num notavu cicatriz nem nada na boca dela. Aí podi acreditá qui ela era inocenti, sem pecadu i donzela das mais donzela.

79. A casa di Maria di Araúju ficô toda coberta di sangui, as paredi, a sala, tudu. U pessuá di Cratu mandô chamá ela para Cratu—aquelis qui num gostavu di Juazeru. I quandu chegô im Cratu botaru ela para pilá miu. Dizi qui ela pilava miu dois, treis dia sem pará. Pilava tantu miu qui a mão dela ficô carni viva. Botaru ela num quartu trancadu. Antão quandu terminô di pilá aqueli monti di miu deixaru ela imbora. Chegô im casa, tomô um chá. Aí a mãe dela dissi, "Mais por qui é qui você faiz issu? Você diz para elis qui num vorta, qui mandi chamá um varão fazê aqueli trabaiu pesadu." Mais elis só quiriu judiá cum ela. Quandu miorô das mão vinha otru recadu mandanu chamá ela pra Barbáia. Chegô lá, trancaru ela drentu du quartu ondi tinha

qui pilá miu. Pilava dois, treis dia, pilava, pilava até qui a carni saía das mão. Quandu sortavu ela, vortô pra Juazeru. Mais mandaru chamá ela di novu pra pilá mais otru miu. Pá, pá, pá. Ansim fizeru muntas vezi.

80. Maria di Araúju era uma moça qui foi comungá i a óstia virô sangui na boca dela. Oji istá no céu i a henti reza pra ela desti jeitu: "Ô Maria di Araúju, estais cum rusáriu na mão / Pra nóis levá à terra du Padim Ciçu Rumão." Tem mais otrus versus mais eu istô isquicida. Só sei qui a Maria di Araúju é uma dessas santa forti.

81. Maria di Araúju era uma pecadora, qui num acreditava im Jesuis. Aí quandu foi comungá u meu Padim Ciçu apresentô um castigu pra ela qui a óstia virô sangui. Botô a óstia na boca dela i quandu minô sangui ela pedia perdão.

82. Aqueli negóciu da ostra era um castigu da biata, qui ela duvidava. Essi povu mais véiu ondi eu moru contava muntu para minha mãe qui quandu foi qui recebia a ostra, sempri deixava ela caí nu chão. Aí uma dia quandu deixô a ostra caí apariceu foi sangui. Ela num acreditava qui era u corpu di Nossu Sinhô Jesui Cristu. Aí meu Padim deu a comunhão a ela i a ostra dismanchô-si im sangui vivu.

83. Maria di Araúju era uma dessas pessoa qui não acreditavu nus puderi du meu Padim Cíçaru. Falava pra todu mundu qui era um padi qui nem quaqué um otru, qui nunca tinha obradu milagui nenhum. Aí um dia meu Padim cansô dus iscândalu qui ela levava contra eli. Aí quandu foi dá a comunhão a ela a óstia virô-si im sangui vivu. Ela foi castigada comu aqueli fazendeiru qui mandô comprá chuva. Ou aquela moça qui eli dissi qui não fossi pra rua dançá i ia di todu jeitu. Quem fazia pocu deli arrecebia aqueli castigu. Aí comu é qui eli não ia dá um castigu pra ela?

84. Ela era uma muié, ela sabia qui era uma muié i num quis ficá má na casa dus pai. Aí veiu trabaiá na casa du meu Padim Ciçu. Dizendu qui era uma jovi. Má meu Padim Ciçu sabia qui ela era uma muié. Aí quanu eli foi dá a óstia a ela, virô sangui. Qui ela num quiria dizê u qui era pra eli. Aí u sangui pingô, pingô, pingô ansim nu chão.

85. Maria di Araúju dizia qui era uma moça. Passava por moça mais era a mulé du bispu. Foi por issu qui u bispu suspendeu u meu Padim das ordis deli. Tirô eli di dizê a missa quandu eli transformô a óstia im sangui na boca dela para tudu mundu vê. U bispu tinha muntu medu, achava qui meu Padim ia levá us panu insanguentadu a Roma para mostrá au papa. Aí eli dissi qui era meu Padim qui tinha andadu cum ela, qui era eli u amanti daquela mulé.

86. Maria di Araúju era uma biata qui foi comungá, aí começô a cuspí sangui. Meu Padim deu a óstia pra ela. Mais era tão pecadora qui manifestô-si im sangui. Essa Maria di Araúju já tinha um fiu, um minininhu mudu. Aí u bispu mandô u meu Padim fazê u mininu falá. "Si você num fizê essi mininu falá vô botá a sua batina abaixu," eli dissi. Qui u bispu tinha munta raiva por causa da biata i quiria botá eli nu chão. Aí trouxi u minininhu mudu, achanu qui u meu Padim num pudia sacá cum eli. Mais meu Padim botô a mão na cabeça du mininu. Dissi, "Mininu, im nomi di Deus, diz quem é teu pai i tua mãe." Aí u mininu dissi, "Meu pai é u bispu di Fortaleza i minha mãe é a biata Araúju." U bispu ficô cum tanta da raiva por causa distu qui

quiria invenená meu Padim. "Tomi aqui essi vinhu," eli dissi pru meu Padim. Meu Padim feiz o siná da cruiz pô cima da cálici ansim, treis veizi. Aí
bebeu i num tinha nada. Nada!

87. Foi uma biata, a Maria Mocinha, qui tinha sidu muié du bispu. Era mãe dum
mininu mudu mais ninguém sabia, viu? Inda si dizia uma jovi i ficava intri
as otras jovi comu si fossi iguazinha a elas. Meu Padim dissi, "Fia, eu co-
nheçu teu sigredu." Mais ela si negava a contá u picadu pra eli. Aí na ora da
comunhão eli deu a óstia a ela i transformô-si im sangui. Dipois ela foi dá
queixa au bispu. Aí u bispu contô pru papa qui u meu Padim tinha sidu
amanti daquela muié. Aí u papa mandô chamá meu Padim a Roma. Lá tinha
qui abrí uma porta bem grandi qui nunca tinha sidu aberta. I por detrais
daquela porta tinha u mininu mudu qui era fiu du bispu. "Queru qui você
faça essi mininu falá," u papa dissi pra meu Padim. "Qui u bispu diz qui
você é pai deli."

Pois bem, meu Padim bateu na frenti du mininu treis vezis. "Mininu," eli
dissi, "diz pra Sua Santidadi u nomi du seu pai."

U mininu dissi, "Meu pai é u bispu di Fortaleza i minha mãe é a biata
Maria di Araúju." Pocu dipois, u bispu mandô as tropa deli contra Juazeru.
Deu-si uma grandi guerra im qui meu Padim foi vencedô.

88. Foi nessa época im qui tinha munta miningiti aqui im Juazeiru qui meu fiu—
era inda mininu nessi tempu—adueceu di ripenti. Aí eu corri pru orspitá
cum eli. Ficô deitadu ansim numa mesa por quasi cincu ora. Quanu u médicu chegô por fim, oiô pra eli i dissi, "U seu fiu tá cum essi tá di miningiti.
U sinhô vai tê qui i pru Cratu cum eli."

"Dotô," eu dissi, "é muntu difici elis di lá atendê eli si a gente é di Juazeiru."

"Num possu fazê mais nada," eli dissi.

Aí joguei u mininu drentru dum carru i corremu pra Cratu. Aí butaru eli
incima di otra mesa. Mais num fizeru nada qui um dus impregadu dissi,
"Per'aí. Essi rapaiz é du Juazeiru. Num é pra eli tá aqui." Aí u qui é qui eu
pudia fazê? Peguei u mininu i fui cum eli pra Barbáia qui num tinha otru
jeitu.

Quandu cheguemu im Barbáia u mininu tava ispernianu qui ia murrê. Aí
falei pra infirmeira lá du orspitá qui meu fiu taha muntu má. Mais ela num
quiria deixá eli intrá sem us trezentu contu. Aí eu dissi, "Bota u mininu lá
drentru qui eu vô im casa buscá u dinheru."

"Botu, não," ela dissi. "Eu só aceitu u rapaiz intrá quanu você mi dê us
trezentu contu di intrada."

Aí eu fiquei cum raiva. Fiquei danadu di raiva. "Pois voceis fiqui cum u
dinheiru di voceis i tudu si dani," eu dissi, "qui vô-mi imbora mais meu
fiu."

Pois antão, quanu entramu nu Juazeru eu dissi pru motorista drobrá lá na
frenti da istatua du meu Padim Ciçu. "Meu Padim será u únicu médicu du
meu fiu di ora im adianti," eu dissi.

Quanu cheguemu im casa u só taha a caí. Justu nessi mumentu, u mininu
abriu us ôiu. Dissi, "Meu Padim Ciçu! Ondi é qui eu taha?"

89. Quandu eu era moça tinha um rapaiz por nomi di Profíriu qui quiria qui eu
casassi cum eli. Mais eu dissi qui não, pois quasi não tinha conhecimentu

deli. Aí di noiti peguei a sonhá cum meu Padim Ciçu. Era meiu dia, na roça u só brianu au redô da cabeça deli.

Meu Padim oiô pra mim i foi dissi, "Podi si casá cum Profíriu qui voceis vão sê filiz."

I eu dissi, "Meu Padim, si é por ordi du sinhô, eu mi casu cum eli, sim."

Aí a genti foi, casô-si i era muntu filiz pelus cinquenta anu até a morti deli.

Nu dia im qui eli murreu achei qui eu ia murrê di tristeza. Churava, churava, sem pará. Aí senti a mão du meu Padim nu braçu. "Eu não ti dissi qui ia sê filiz cum Profíriu?" eli dissi. Pois podi deixá di churá qui u Profíriu já istá comigu."

90. Eu tinha trezi anu quandu mi casei. Aí dispois di casada eu nunca mais tivi alegria até u dia im qui meu maridu mi largô. Agora tenhu otru maridu muntu bão pra mim mas num sô casada cum eli pela igreja, só sô casada nu civi.

Antão, meu primeru maridu mi deixô cum uma garota qui desdi qui ela nasceu era muntu bunitinha. Quandu ela tinha quatorzi anu u pai dela reapareci. Dispois foi-si imbora di novu i ela si trancô na tristeza. Aí eu perguntei, "Minha fia, u qui é issu?" Ela dissi, "Nada," mais eu disconfiei. Aí comecei a notá qui a barriga dela ia crescenu. Mais meu Deus, nunca tinha tidu namoru, aí comu é qui ia está cum nené? Aí eu, cada veiz mais preocupada. Até qui por fim levei ela nu médicu. Aí eli mi dissi qui ela tava grávida di cincu mesi. Antão ela pegô a chorá. Eu dissi, "Meu bem, mi diz quem é u pai." Aí ela botô a mão nu meu ombru i foi dissi, "Mãezinha, é meu pai."

Aí eu fiquei doida cum aqueli ódiu tão grandi qui quiria metê uma faca nu curação du ômi. Fui pru matu i lá fiquei dentru muntu tempu cum uma raiva tão grandi qui num via mais. Pois bem, pocu tempu dispois—era nu dia dela fazê us quinzi anu—minha fia adueceu, perdeu a criança. Eu fiquei tão cheia di ódiu, di mágua, qui acabei fazenu uma premessa cum u meu Padim Ciçu. Qui si eli mi dessi um meiu di eu ir a Juazeiru eu vinha pidi perdão pru meu primeiru maridu nus pés di Nossa Sinhora das Dori. Eu ia acabá cum essi ódiu. Qui eu sabia qui meu Padim devi tá amaguadu di mi vê desti jeitu. I comu elí já feiz tantu para mim comu é qui eu pudia deixá eli ansim tristi?

91. Meu Padim abriu as água du má i essi ômi caminhô até u otru ladu. Aí eli oiô qui só tinha aqueli mundu di fulô toda branca, cheirosa. Ficô pasmadu di vê. Então quandu lembrô-si da carta qui u meu Padim tinha dadu a eli para intregá não achava ela im cantu nenhum. Aí montô nu cavalinhu di novu i feiz a viagi di vorta, atravessanu u mar.

"Meu Padim," eli dissi, "quandu eu fui atravessá u mar as água abriru. Mais quandu cheguei nu otru ladu não avia água, nem avia serra, nem avia mata, nem avia arma nenhuma. Só avia fulô para cansá a vista. I ô, meu Padim, não sei dizê qui aconteceu cum sua carta. Qui quandu fui procurá nu boçu não istava mais."

Aí meu Padim dissi, "Mais você intregô a carta. Feiz comu eu quiria. Muntu bem."

. . . Ah meu Deus, a primeira veiz qui ovi essi casu eu achei eli tão bunitu qui eu quiria mesmu, ô eu quiria mesmu acreditá. Agora é u qui dizi, qui eu nunca fui lá au otru ladu du mar, viu? Eu mesmu nunca vi u mar. I comu já sô velinha i istô para murrê eu ach' qui nunca vô vê. Eu sei qui u mundu é feitu uma bola qui não acaba mais. Sei qui tem genti qui vai di ia im ia. Mais ainda *quiru* acreditá qui u céu começa lá nu otru ladu du mar.

92. Era um fazendeiru ricu, tinha muntus impregadu, tinha as terra deli, eli tinha di tudu, num sabi? Aí um dia eli pegô a ispingarda, dissi, "Vô caçá." Andô, andô, andô, andô, aí di repenti viu um beijafulô mais bunitu, mais mansu du qui quaqué um otru. Ficô na beira da vareda oianu pra eli ansim duranti muntu tempu.

Aí u pássaru—qui era uma arma im forma di beijafulô, num sabi?—dissi, "Tu mi paga uma premessa qui fiquei devenu?"

Aí u fazendeiru foi dissi, "Ah, tem algúm mistériu aqui. Comu é a premessa? U qui é qui tenhu qui fazê?"

Eli dissi, "Você anda cum cruiz nas costa para santu Juazeiru. Dipois você deixa a cruiz dibaixu desti pé di pau. Você prometi fazê issu pra mim?"

U fazendeiru dissi, "Bom, eu num istava isperanu uma coisa dessas. Mais tenhu pena di você e eu faço, sim."

Quandu chegô im casa u fazendeiru falô tudu pra muié. Terminô, ela dissi, "Você tá doidu? Num tem jeitu, não. Óia, aqueli ômi feiz uma premessa, num pagô. É cuipa di você qui eli murreu devenu? É pra eli carregá aquela cruiz a a Juazeiru, viu?" Aí u fazendeiru num feiz mais nada. I tudu quantu foi criação deli pegô logu a murrê. Murria um por um, num tinha jeitu cum elis.

Aí u fazendeiru num tinha mais prazê. Foi dissi pra muié, "Sabi di uma coisa? Você me deu um conseiu qui eu disvaneci da disposição di pagá aquela premessa. Mais qué sabê di uma coisa? Eu vô cumprí cum minha palavra."

Aí eli mandô us impregadu deli fazê a cruiz, andô cum ela até Juazeiru. Dimorava ansim treis anu im totá. I au cabu daquelis treis anu votô a casa mais tranquiu i ricu, mais ricu qui nunca.

Mais óia só. Si aqueli fazendeiru num tivessi pagadu, u gadu deli ia-si imbora, us fiu deli aduecia i eli murria também. Aí, irmãzinha, por qui istô contanu essi casu pra você? Istô contanu u casu pra você vê qui a morti sempri istá di pertu. Qui a genti podi murrê amanhã. Mais u má num é murrê. U má é murrê sem fazê aquela coisa qui a genti dissi qui ia fazê.

References Cited

I have followed standard alphabetizing procedures for English and for the various foreign languages represented. In Spanish, for instance, the first surname is listed before the second.

For the Portuguese, where alphabetization is often erratic, I have consistently used the last element of the surname except in cases of compound names connected by an "e" (e.g., Manuel Caboclo e Silva). "Filho," which is the equivalent of the English "Jr.," is not alphabetized. The reader should be aware that the spelling and accentuation of Portuguese proper names still varies considerably. He or she should therefore not be surprised to find "Manuel" and "Manoel"; "Luis," "Luís," and "Luiz"; "Antônio" and "Antonio"; "Therezinha" and "Teresinha," both in this list of references and in the body of the book.

Aarne, Antti, and Stith Thompson. *The Types of the Folktale.* 2nd rev. ed. Folklore Fellows Communications 184. Helsinki: Suomalainen Tiedakatemia, 1961.

Acta Sanctorum quotquot toto orbe. New ed., 67 vols. Paris: V. Palmé, 1863–1940.

Aigrain, René. *L'Hagiographie: Ses sources, ses méthodes, son histoire.* Paris: Bloud et Gay, 1953.

Altman, Charles F. "Two Types of Opposition in the Structure of Latin Saints' Lives." In *Medieval Hagiography and Romance* (*Medievalia and Humanistica* n.s. 6), ed. Paul Maurice Clogan, pp. 1–11. Cambridge: Cambridge University Press, 1975.

Alves, Isidoro Maria da Silva. "*O carnaval devoto*": *Um estudo sobre a Festa de Nazaré em Belém.* Coleção Antropologia 13. Petrópolis: Editora Vozes, 1980.

Alves, Joaquim. "O Vale do Cariri." *Revista do Instituto do Ceará* 59 (1945), pp. 94–133.

Amado, Janaína. *Conflito social no Brasil: A revolta dos Mucker.* São Paulo: Símbolo, 1978.

Analecta Bollandiana 17. Brussels: Société des Bollandistes, 1898.

Anderson, James Charnel. "The Caldeirão Movement: A Case Study in Brazilian Messianism, 1926–1938." Ph.D. diss., George Washington University, Washington, D.C., 1971.

Andrade, Carlos Drummond de. "Retrato de Família." In his *Poesia e prosa,* pp. 205–207. Rio de Janeiro: Editora Nova Aguilar, 1979.

Andrade, Manuel Correia de. *A terra e o homem no nordeste.* 3rd ed. São Paulo: Editora Brasiliense, 1973.

Anselmo e Silva, Otacílio. *Padre Cícero—Mito e realidade.* Rio de Janeiro: Civilização Brasileira, 1968.

Araújo, Antônio Gomes de. "À margem de 'À margem da história do Ceará.'" *Itaytera* 8 (1962), pp. 5–19.

―――. "Apostolado do Embuste." *Itaytera* 2 (1956), pp. 3–63.

Attwater, Donald. *The Penguin Dictionary of Saints.* Baltimore: Penguin Books, 1965.

Azevedo, João Lúcio de. *A evolução do sebastianismo.* 2nd ed. rev. Lisbon: A. M. Teixeira, 1947.

Azevedo, Thales de. *O catolicismo no Brasil.* Rio de Janeiro: Ministério de Educação e Cultura, 1955.

Azzi, Riolando. *O catolicismo popular no Brasil: Aspectos históricos.* Cadernos de Teologia e Pastoral 11. Petrópolis: Vozes, 1978.

Baring-Gould, Sabine. *Lives of the Saints.* Rev. ed., 16 vols. Edinburgh: John Grant, 1914.

Barroso, Gustavo. *Ao som da viola.* Rio de Janeiro: Livraria Editora Leite Ribeiro, 1923.

Bastide, Roger. "Religion and the Church in Brazil." In *Brazil: Portrait of Half a Continent,* ed. T. Lynn Smith and Alexander Marchant, pp. 334–355. New York: Dryden Press, 1951.

Batista, Antonio. "A Guerra do Juazeiro em 1914." In *Literatura popular em verso: Antologia* 1, pp. 347–451. Rio de Janeiro: Ministério de Educação e Cultura/ Casa de Rui Barbosa, 1964.

Batista, Francisco das Chagas. *Cantadores e poetas populares.* João Pessoa: Editora F. C. Batista Irmão, 1929.

Bauman, Richard, and Joel Sherzer, eds. *Explorations in the Ethnography of Speaking.* Cambridge: Cambridge University Press, 1974.

Bausinger, Hermann. "Exemplum und Beispiel." *Hessiche Blätter für Volkskunde* 59 (1958), pp. 31–43.

Bello, José Maria. *A History of Modern Brazil, 1889–1964,* trans. James L. Taylor. Stanford: Stanford University Press, 1966.

Ben-Ami, Issachar. "Folk Veneration of Saints among the Moroccan Jews (Tradition: Continuity and Change. The Case of the Holy Man, Rabbi David u-Moshe)." In *Studies in Judaism and Islam,* ed. Shelomo Morag, Issachar

Ben-Ami, and Norman A. Stillman, pp. 283–344. Jerusalem: Magnes Press, Hebrew University, 1981.

Ben-Amos, Dan. "Analytical Categories and Ethnic Genres." In *Folklore Genres,* ed. Dan Ben-Amos. American Folklore Society 26, pp. 215–241. Austin: University of Texas Press, 1976.

———. "The Concept of Motif in Folklore." In *Folklore Studies in the Twentieth Century: Proceedings of the Centenary Conference of the Folklore Society,* ed. Venetia Newall, pp. 17–36. Suffolk and Totowa, N.J.: D. S. Brewer/Rowman and Littlefield, 1980.

Ben-Amos, Dan, and Kenneth Goldstein, eds. *Folklore: Performance and Communication.* The Hague: Mouton, 1975.

Berger, Peter. *The Sacred Canopy.* New York: Doubleday, 1967.

Bhardwaj, S. H. *Hindu Places of Pilgrimage in India.* Berkeley and Los Angeles: University of California Press, 1973.

Blau, Peter. *Exchange and Power in Social Life.* New York: John Wiley and Sons, 1964.

Bloch, R. Howard. *Etymologies and Genealogies: A Literary Anthropology of the French Middle Ages.* Chicago: University of Chicago Press, 1983.

Boehrer, George. "The Church and the Overthrow of the Brazilian Monarchy." *Hispanic American Historical Review* 48 (1968), pp. 380–401.

Boesch Gajano, Sofia, ed. *Agiografia altomedioevale.* Bologna: Il Mulino, 1976.

Boggs, Ralph S. *Index of Spanish Folktales.* Folklore Fellows Communications 90. Helsinki: Suomalainen Tiedakatemia, 1930.

Boon, James A. *Other Tribes, Other Scribes: Symbolic Anthropology in the Comparative Study of Cultures.* New York: Cambridge University Press, 1982.

Booth, Wayne C. *The Rhetoric of Fiction.* Chicago: University of Chicago Press, 1961.

Borges, José. *A vida do Padre Cícero.* Recife: Universidade Federal de Pernambuco, 1972.

Boyer, Régis. "An Attempt to Define the Typology of Medieval Hagiography." In *Hagiography and Medieval Literature: A Symposium,* ed. Hans Bekker-Nielsen et al., pp. 27–36. Odense: Odense University Press, 1981.

Brandes, Stanley. *Metaphors of Masculinity: Sex and Status in Andalusian Folklore.* American Folklore Society n.s. 1. Philadelphia: University of Pennsylvania Press, 1980.

Brewer, E. Cobham. *A Dictionary of Miracles.* Philadelphia: J. B. Lippincott, 1884.

Browe, Peter. *Die Eucharistischen Wunder des Mittelalters.* Breslauer Studien zur historischen Theologie n.f. 4. Breslau, 1938.

Brown, Peter. *The Cult of the Saints: Its Rise and Function in Latin Christianity.* The Haskell Lectures on History of Religions n.s. 2. Chicago: University of Chicago Press, 1981.

————. "The Saint as Exemplar in Late Antiquity." *Representations* 1, 2 (1983), pp. 1–26.

————. *Society and the Holy in Late Antiquity.* London: Faber and Faber, 1982.

Bruneau, Thomas C. *The Church in Brazil: The Politics of Religion.* Austin: University of Texas Press, 1982.

————. *The Political Transformation of the Brazilian Catholic Church.* New York: Cambridge University Press, 1974.

Burns, E. Bradford. *A History of Brazil.* New York: Columbia University Press, 1970.

Butler, Alban. *Lives of the Saints,* ed. Herbert Thurston and Donald Attwater. Rev. ed., 4 vols. New York: P. J. Kenedy and Sons, 1956.

Bynum, Caroline Walker. "Women Mystics and Eucharistic Devotion in the Thirteenth Century." In *Medieval Women,* ed. Hope Weisman. Special issue, *Women's Studies* (1984), pp. 179–214.

Caboclo e Silva, Manuel. *Os Tempos do Passado.* Juazeiro do Norte: Folhetaria Casa dos Horóscopos, 1981.

Cabral, João de Pina. "A Peasant Worldview in Its Context: Cultural Uniformity and Differentiation in Northwestern Portugal." Ph.D. diss., Oxford University, 1981.

Cabral, Oswaldo R. *João Maria: Interpretação da campanha do Contestado.* São Paulo: Cia. Editora Nacional, 1960.

Caesarius of Heisterbach. *Dialogue on Miracles,* trans. H. von E. Scott and C. C. Swinton Bland. 2 vols. New York: Harcourt, Brace, 1929.

Calasans, José. *O ciclo folclórico do Bom Jesus.* Bahia: Tipografia Beneditina, 1950.

Cariry, Rosemberg. "O beato José Lourenço e o Caldeirão da Santa Cruz." *Nação Cariri* 1, 5 (1981–82), pp. 12–15.

Carone, Edgard. "Coronelismo: Definição, história e bibliografia." *Revista de Administração de Empresas* 11 (1971), pp. 85–92.

Carroll, Malachy, and Pol de Leon Albaret. *Three Studies in Simplicity: Padre Pio, Martin de Porres, Benedict the Black.* Chicago: Franciscan Herald Press, 1974.

Carvalho, José Rodrigues. *Cancioneiro do norte.* 3rd ed. Rio de Janeiro: Ministério de Educação e Cultura, 1967.

Cascudo, Luís da Câmara. *Dicionário do folclore brasileiro,* 2 vols. Rpt. Edições de Ouro. Rio de Janeiro: Tecnoprint Gráfica, 1969.

————. *Rede de dormir: Uma pesquisa etnográfica.* Rio de Janeiro: Serviço de Documentação, Ministério da Educação e Cultura, 1959.

Castro, Nei Leandro de. *Universo e vocabulário do 'Grande sertão.'* Coleção Documentos Brasileiros 144. Rio de Janeiro: José Olympio, 1970.

Catalán, Diego. "Los modos de producción y 'reproducción' del texto literario y la noción de apertura." In *Homenaje a Julio Caro Baroja,* ed. Antonio Carreira et al., pp. 245–270. Madrid: Centro de Investigaciones Sociológicas, 1978.

Cavalcante, Rodolfo Coelho. "O sonho do Padre Cícero Romão Batista." In *Literatura popular em verso: Antologia* 1, pp. 353–362. Rio de Janeiro: Ministério de Educação e Cultura/Casa de Rui Barbosa, 1964.

Caxton, William. *The Golden Legend.* London: J. M. Dent, 1900.

Chagas, Benício das. "História dos acontecimentos da Pedra do Rodeador." *Revista do Instituto Archeologico e Geographico Pernambucano* 37 (1890), pp. 79–82.

Chandler, Billy Jaynes. *The Bandit King: Lampião of Brazil.* College Station: Texas A & M Press, 1978.

———. *The Feitosas and the Sertão of Inhamuns: The History of a Family and a Community in Northeast Brazil, 1700–1930.* Gainesville: University of Florida Press, 1972.

Christian, William A., Jr. *Apparitions in Late Medieval and Renaissance Spain.* Princeton: Princeton University Press, 1981.

———. "La religiosidad popular hoy." In *Galicia, realidad económica y conflicto social*, pp. 551–569. La Coruña: La Voz de Galicia, 1978.

Christiansen, Reidar Th. *The Migratory Legend, A Proposed List of Types with a Systematic Catalogue of the Norwegian Variants.* Folklore Fellows Communications 71. Helsinki: Suomalainen Tiedakatemia, 1958.

Clifford, James. "On Ethnographic Authority." *Representations* 1, 2 (1983), pp. 118–146.

Cohn, Norman. *The Pursuit of the Millennium.* New York: Oxford University Press, 1961.

Costa, Floro Bartolomeu da. *Joazeiro e o Padre Cícero: Depoimentos para a história.* Rio de Janeiro: n.p., 1923.

Costa, Francisco Augusto Pereira da. "Folklore Pernambucano." *Revista do Instituto Histórico e Geográfico Brasileiro* 12 (1908), pp. 33–44.

Costa, J. Augusto da. "Expedição do Rodeador, 1–2." *Revista Brasileira* 4 (1880), pp. 341–352.

———. "Expedição do Rodeador, 3." *Revista Brasileira* 7 (1881), pp. 243–251.

Crapanzano, Vincent. "On the Writing of Ethnography." *Dialectical Anthropology* 2 (1977), pp. 69–73.

Cunha, Euclides da. *Os sertões,* trans. into English by Samuel Putman as *Revolt in the Backlands.* 2nd ed. Chicago: University of Chicago Press, 1970.

Cunniff, Roger Lee. "The Great Drought: Northeastern Brazil, 1877–1880." Ph.D. diss., University of Texas, Austin, 1971.

Dantas, Renato. *As beatas do Cariri e de Juazeiro.* Coleção Juazeiro 6. Juazeiro do Norte: Instituto Cultural do Vale Caririense, 1982.

Daus, Ronald. *Der Epische Zyklus der Cangaceiros in der Volkspoesie Nordost-Brasiliens.* Biblioteca Ibero-Americana 12, Berlin: Colloquium, 1969. (Portuguese edition is *O ciclo épico dos cangaceiros na poesia popular do nordeste,* trans. Rachel Teixeira Valença. Rio de Janeiro: Fundação Casa de Rui Barbosa, 1982.)

Dégh, Linda. *Folktales and Society: Story-Telling in a Hungarian Peasant Community*, trans. Emily M. Schlossberger. Bloomington: Indiana University Press, 1969.

Dégh, Linda, and Andrew Vázsonyi. *The Dialectics of the Legend.* Folklore Preprint Series 1, no. 6. Bloomington: Folklore Institute Publications Group, 1973.

———. "Legend and Belief." In *Folklore Genres,* ed. Dan Ben-Amos. American Folklore Society 26, pp. 119–223. Austin: University of Texas Press, 1976.

———. "The Memorate and the Proto-Memorate." *Journal of American Folklore* 87 (1974), pp. 225–239.

Delaney, Janice, Mary Jane Lupton, and Emily Toth, eds. *The Curse: A Cultural History of Menstruation.* New York: E. P. Dutton, 1976.

Delehaye, Hippolyte. *The Legends of the Saints,* trans. Donald Attwater. New York: Fordham University Press, 1962.

Della Cava, Ralph. "Brazilian Messianism and National Institutions: A Reappraisal of Canudos and Joaseiro." *Hispanic American Historical Review* 48 (1968), pp. 402–420.

———. "Catholicism and Society in Twentieth-Century Brazil." *Latin American Research Review* 11 (1976), pp. 7–50.

———. *Miracle at Joaseiro.* New York: Columbia University Press, 1970.

Diégues Júnior, Manuel. *População e propriedade da terra no Brasil.* Washington, D.C.: Pan American Union, 1959.

Dinis, Manoel. *Mistérios do Joazeiro: História completa de Pe. Cícero Romão Batista do Joazeiro do Ceará.* Juazeiro do Norte: Tipografia de 'O Joazeiro,' 1935.

"Documentos sobre a Questão Religiosa do Juazeiro (Do arquivo particular do consócio Hugo Catunda)." *Revista do Instituto do Ceará* 80 (1961), pp. 266–297.

Donaldson, E. T., ed. *Chaucer's Poetry: An Anthology for the Modern Reader.* New York: Ronald Press, 1958.

Douglas, Mary. *Implicit Meanings: Essays in Anthropology.* London: Routledge and Kegan Paul, 1975.

———. *Purity and Danger.* Rpt. London: Routledge and Kegan Paul, 1978.

Droulers, Paul. "Roman Catholicism," trans. Daphne Woodward. In *The Nineteenth Century World,* ed. Guy S. Métraux and François Couzet, pp. 282–315. New York: Mentor Books, 1963.

Dunaway, David K., and Willa K. Baum, eds. *Oral History: An Interdisciplinary Anthology.* Nashville, Tenn.: American Association for State and Local History, 1984.

Dundes, Alan. "From Etic to Emic Units in the Structural Study of Folklore." *Journal of American Folklore* 75 (1972), pp. 95–105.

Dupront, Alphonse. "Pèlerinages et lieux sacrés." In *Mélanges en l'honneur de Fernand Braudel* 2, pp. 190–207. Toulouse: Privat, 1973.

Eggan, Fred. "From History to Myth: A Hopi Example." In his *Essays in Social Anthropology and Ethnology,* pp. 295–315. Chicago: University of Chicago, Department of Anthropology, 1975.

Evangelização no presente e no futuro da América Latina. Conclusões da III^a Conferência Geral do Episcopado Latino-Americano, Puebla de los Angeles, México 7–1 a 13–2 de 1979. São Paulo: Edições Paulinas, 1979.

Facó, Rui. *Cangaceiros e fanáticos: Gênese e lutas.* 6th ed. Retratos do Brasil 15. Rio de Janeiro: Civilização Brasileira, 1980.

Falk, Nancy, and Rita M. Gross, eds. *Unspoken Worlds: Women's Religious Lives in Non-Western Cultures.* San Francisco: Harper and Row, 1980.

Farmer, David Hugh. *Oxford Dictionary of Saints.* Oxford: Clarendon Press, 1978.

Feitosa, Neri. *Eu defendo o Padre Cícero.* 2nd ed. Quixadá: n.p., 1982.

Fernandes, Rubém César. *Os cavaleiros do Bom Jesus: Uma introdução às religiões populares.* Primeiros Vôos 7. São Paulo: Editora Brasiliense, 1982.

Fine, Elizabeth. "In Defense of Literary Dialect: A Response to Dennis R. Preston." *Journal of American Folklore* 96 (1983), pp. 323–330.

Finucane, Ronald C. *Miracles and Pilgrims: Popular Beliefs in Medieval England.* Totowa, N.J.: Rowman and Littlefield, 1977.

Flores, Moacyr. "Sepe Tiaraju: Lenda, mito e história." *Veritas* 21 (1975), pp. 108–115.

Forman, Shepard. *The Brazilian Peasantry.* New York: Columbia University Press, 1975.

Foster, George M. "The Dyadic Contract: A Model for the Social Structure of a Mexican Peasant Village." *American Anthropologist* 63 (1961), pp. 1173–1192.

———. "Peasant Society and the Image of Limited Good." *American Anthropologist* 67 (1965), pp. 293–315.

França, Maria Cecília. *Pequenos centros de devoção paulistas de função religiosa.* São Paulo: Universidade de São Paulo, 1976.

Fukui, Lia Freitas Garcia. *Sertão e bairro rural.* Ensaios 58. São Paulo: Editora Ática, 1979.

Gaspar, Lúcia Maria, and Fernando José Leite Costa. "Contribuição ao estudo da sociedade tradicional: Bibliografia comentada." *Dados* 5 (1968), pp. 167–180.

Gayangos, Pascual, ed. *Escritores en prosa anteriores al siglo XV.* Biblioteca de autores españoles 51. Madrid: M. Rivadeneyra, 1860.

Geertz, Clifford. *The Interpretation of Culture: Selected Essays.* New York: Basic Books, 1973.

Georges, Robert A. "The General Concept of Legend: Some Assumptions to be Reexamined and Reassessed." In *American Folk Legend,* ed. Wayland D. Hand, pp. 1–19. Berkeley and Los Angeles: University of California Press, 1971.

Gesta Romanorum, trans. Charles Swan. London: George Bell and Sons, 1906.

Glassie, Henry. *Passing the Time in Ballymenone: Culture and History of an Ulster Community*. Publications of the American Folklore Society n.s. 4. Philadelphia: University of Pennsylvania Press, 1982.

Groenen, Hendricus Stephanus Maria. "Schisma zwischen Kirche und Volk: Eine praktisch-theologische Fallstudie des Volkskatholizismus in Nordostbrasilien." Ph.D. diss., Katholieke Universitet te Nijmegen, Netherlands, 1978.

Groetelaars, Martien Maria. *Milagre e religiosidade popular: Reflexões sobre pastoral missionária*. Petrópolis: Vozes, 1981.

Gross, Daniel. "Ritual and Conformity: A Religious Pilgrimage to Northeastern Brazil." *Ethnology* 10 (1971), pp. 132–139.

Guérin, Paul. *Les petits Bollandistes: Vies des saints*. 17 vols. Paris: Bloud et Barral, 1880.

Guimarães, Alba Zaluar. "Milagre e castigo divino." *Religião e Sociedade* 5 (1980), pp. 161–187.

―――. "Os movimentos 'messiânicos' brasileiros: Uma leitura." *Dados* 20 (1979), pp. 9–21.

Guimarães, Therezinha Stella. "Etude psychologique de la fonction d'un Saint dans le catholicisme populaire." Diss., Université Catholique de Louvain: Louvain, Belgium, 1983.

―――. "Os jovens de Juazeiro do Norte e sua devoção ao Padre Cícero." *Revista Eclesiástica Brasileira* 39 (1979), pp. 275–283.

Guimarães, Therezinha Stella, and Anne Dumoulin. *Padre Cícero por ele mesmo*. Petrópolis: Vozes, 1983.

Gutman, Judith Mara. *Through Indian Eyes*. New York: Oxford University Press/International Center of Photography, 1982.

Hall, Anthony. *Drought and Irrigation in Northeast Brazil*. New York: Cambridge University Press, 1978.

Hallinan, Tim. "Bom Jesus da Lapa: A Sertão Shrine." *Proceedings of the Pacific Coast Council on Latin American Studies* 2 (1973), pp. 75–89.

Halpert, Herbert. "Supernatural Sanctions and the Legend." In *Folklore Studies in the Twentieth Century: Proceedings of the Centenary Conference of the Folklore Society*, ed. Venetia Newall, pp. 226–233. Suffolk and Totowa, N.J.: D. S. Brewer/Rowman and Littlefield, 1980.

Hand, Wayland D. "Deformity, Disease and Physical Ailment as Divine Retribution." In *Festschrift Matthias Zender: Studien zur Volkskultur, Sprache und Landesgeschichte*, ed. Edith Ennen and Gunter Wiegelmann, pp. 519–525. Bonn: L. Rohrscheid, 1972.

―――. "Status of European and American Legend Study." *Current Anthropology* 6 (1965), pp. 439–446.

Hansen, Terence L. *The Types of the Folktale in Cuba, Puerto Rico, the Dominican Republic and Spanish South America*. Folklore Studies 8. Berkeley and Los Angeles: University of California Press, 1957.

Hawes, Bess Lomax. "*El corrido de la inundación de la Presa de San Francisquito:* The Story of a Local Ballad." *Western Folklore* 33 (1974), pp. 219–230.

Hoffmann-Krayer, Eduard, and Hanns Bächtold-Stäubli, eds. *Handwörterbuch des deutschen Aberglaubens* 1. Berlin: De Gruyter, 1927.

Hoge, Warren. "Machismo Murder Case: Women Bitter in Brazil." *New York Times,* May 23, 1983, p. 2.

Hølbek, Bengt. *Formal and Structural Studies of Oral Narrative: A Bibliography.* Copenhagen: Institut for Folkemindevidenskab, Kobenshavns Universitet, 1978.

Horstmann, Carl. *The Lives of Women Saints.* Early English Text Society, Original Series 86. London: N. Trübner and Co., 1886.

Hubbard, Ruth, Mary Sue Henifin, and Barbara Fried, eds. *Women Look at Biology Looking at Women.* Boston: G. K. Hall, 1979.

Hulet, Claude L., ed. *Encruzilhadas/Crossroads: First Symposium on Portuguese Traditions, June 1–2, 1978.* Los Angeles: University of California, 1980.

Hutchinson, Bertram. "The Patron-Dependent Relationship in Brazil: A Preliminary Examination." *Sociologia Ruralis* 6 (1966), pp. 3–30.

Johnson, Allen. *Sharecroppers of the Sertão.* Stanford: Stanford University Press, 1972.

Jones, Charles W. *Saint Nicholas of Myra, Bari and Manhattan: Biography of a Legend.* Chicago: University of Chicago Press, 1978.

Journal of the Folklore Institute 14, 1–2 (1977).

Jung, C. G. "Transformation Symbolism in the Mass." In *The Collected Works of C. G. Jung,* ed. Sir Herbert Read, Michael Fordham, and Gerhard Adler, trans. R. F. C. Hull, 2, pp. 296–448. Bollingen Series 20. New York: Pantheon Books, 1958.

Keller, John Esten. *Motif-Index of Mediaeval Spanish Exempla.* Knoxville: University of Tennessee Press, 1949.

Kipple, May Augusta. "African Folktales with Foreign Analogues." 2 vols. Ph.D. diss., Indiana University, Bloomington, 1938.

Knaster, Meri. "Women in Latin America: The State of Research." *Latin American Research Review* 11 (1976), pp. 3–74.

Labov, William. "The Transformation of Experience in Narrative Syntax." In his *Language in the Inner City: Studies in the Black English Vernacular,* pp. 354–375. Philadelphia: University of Pennsylvania Press, 1972.

Labov, William, and Joshua Waletzky. "Narrative Analysis: Oral Versions of Personal Experience." In *Essays on the Visual and Verbal Arts,* ed. June Heller, pp. 12–44. Seattle: University of Washington Press, 1967.

Leacock, Eleanor. *Myths of Male Dominance: Collected Articles on Women Cross-Culturally.* New York: Monthly Review Press, 1981.

Leal, Victor Nunes. *Coronelism: The Municipality and Representative Government in Brazil,* trans. June Henfrey. Cambridge: Cambridge University Press, 1977.

Leers, Bernardino. *Catolicismo popular e mundo rural: Um ensaio pastoral.* Petrópolis: Vozes, 1977.

Leite, Antônio Attico de Souza. "Memória sobre a Pedra Bonita ou Reino Encantado." *Revista do Instituto Archeologico e Geographico Pernambucano* 11 (1904), pp. 217–272.

———. *Memória sobre o Reino Encantado na comarca de Vila Bela: Fanatismo religioso.* Juiz de Fora: n.p., 1898.

Leite, (Pe.) Serafim. *Summa Histórica da Companhia de Jesus no Brasil.* Lisbon: Junta de Investigações do Ultramar, 1965.

León, Angel de. *Mendigo por Dios: Vida de Fray Leopoldo de Alpandeire.* 3rd ed. Granada: Litografía Anel, 1974.

Lévi-Strauss, Claude. *Structural Anthropology.* 2nd ed., trans. Claire Jacobson and Brooke Grundfest Schoepf. New York: Basic Books, 1963.

Levine, Robert M. *Brazil: An Annotated Bibliography for Social Historians.* Garland Reference Library of Social Science 59. New York: Garland Publishing, 1980.

Lima, J. I. de Abreu. "Combate do Rodeador ou da Pedra (1820)." *Revista do Instituto Archeologico e Geographico Pernambucano* 10, (1903), pp. 250–257.

Loomis, C. Grant. "Legend and Folklore." *California Folklore Quarterly* 4 (1945), pp. 109–128.

———. *White Magic: An Introduction to the Folklore of Christian Legend.* Publication 52. Cambridge, Mass.: The Mediaeval Academy of America, 1948.

Lourenço Filho, Manuel Bergström. *Joaseiro do Padre Cícero (Scenas e quadros do fanatismo do nordeste.* 2nd ed. São Paulo: Edições Melhoramentos, 1926.

Lüthi, Max. *Volksmärchen und Volkssage: Zwei Grundformen erzählender Dichtung.* Bern: Francke, 1961.

McDonnell, Ernest W. *The Beguines and Beghards in Medieval Culture.* New Brunswick: Rutgers University Press, 1954.

Macedo, Manuel. *Joazeiro em foco.* Fortaleza: n.p., 1925.

Macedo, Nertan. *O padre e a beata.* Rio de Janeiro: Leitura, 1961.

Maia, Helvídio Martins. *Pretensos milagres em Juazeiro.* Petrópolis: Vozes, 1974.

Marcus, George, and Dick Cushman. "Ethnographies as Texts." *Annual Review of Anthropology* 11 (1982), pp. 25–69.

Mariz, Celso. *Ibiapina, um apóstolo do nordeste.* João Pessoa: n.p., 1942.

Martins, Mário. *Peregrinações e livros de milagre na nossa Idade Média.* Lisbon: Broteria, 1957.

Mecham, J. Lloyd. *Church and State in Latin America: A History of Politico-Ecclesiastical Relations.* Chapel Hill: University of North Carolina Press, 1934.

Medina, Carlos A., et al. "Bom Jesus da Lapa: Uma análise sócio-religiosa." Mimeographed. Rio de Janeiro: Centro de Estatística Religiosa e Investigações Sociais, 1972.

Miller, Joseph C., ed. *The African Past Speaks: Essays on Oral Tradition and History.* Folkestone: Wm. Dawson and Sons, 1980.

Mitchell, Simon, ed. *The Logic of Poverty: The Stagnation of North East Brazil.* London: Routledge and Kegan Paul, 1977.

Monteiro, Duglas Teixeira. "Confronto entre Juazeiro, Canudos e Contestado." *História geral da civilização brasileira* 3, 2, pp. 39–92. Rio de Janeiro/São Paulo: Difel, 1977.

————. *Os errantes do novo século.* São Paulo: Livraria Duas Cidades, 1974.

Montell, William Lynwood. *The Saga of Coe Ridge: A Study in Oral History.* Knoxville: University of Tennessee Press, 1970.

Morel, Edmar. *Padre Cícero, o santo do Juazeiro.* 2nd ed. Rio de Janeiro: Empresa Gráfica 'O Cruzeiro,' 1946.

Morse, Richard. "Some Themes of Brazilian History." *South Atlantic Quarterly* 61 (1962), pp. 159–182.

Morton, Ann. "Religion in Juazeiro (Ceará, Brazil) since the Death of Padre Cícero: A Case Study in the Nature of Messianic Religious Activity in the Interior of Brazil." Master's thesis, Columbia University, New York, 1966.

Mosher, Joseph Albert. *The Exemplum in the Early Religious and Didactic Literature of England.* New York: Columbia University Press, 1911.

Moule, C. F. D., ed. *Miracles: Cambridge Studies in Their Philosophy and History.* London: A. R. Mowbray, 1965.

Moura, Abdalaziz de. *Frei Damião e os impasses da religião popular.* Petrópolis: Vozes, 1978.

Narayan, S. *Sacred Complexes of Deoghar and Rajgir.* New Delhi: Concept Publishing, 1983.

New Catholic Encyclopedia. 17 vols. New York: McGraw-Hill, 1967.

Nogueira, Ataliba. *Antônio Conselheiro e Canudos: Revisão histórica.* São Paulo: Editora Nacional, 1974.

Nordeste brasileiro: Catálogo da exposição. Rio de Janeiro: Biblioteca Nacional, 1970.

Oliveira, Amália Xavier de. *Dados que marcam a vida do Padre Cícero Romão Batista.* 3rd ed. Juazeiro do Norte: Gráfica Mascote, 1980.

————. *O Padre Cícero que eu conheci: Verdadeira história de Juazeiro do Norte.* 3rd ed. Recife: Fundação Joaquim Nabuco/Massangana, 1982.

Oliveira, Antônio Xavier de. *Beatos e cangaceiros.* Rio de Janeiro: n.p., 1920.

Oliveira, Pedro A. Ribeiro de. "Expressões religiosas populares e liturgia." Mimeographed. Rio de Janeiro: Centro de Estatística Religiosa e Investigações Sociais, 1980.

Olsen, Alexandra Hennessey. "'De Historiis Sanctorum': A Generic Study of Hagiography." *Genre* 13 (1980), pp. 407–429.

Ortner, Sherry B., and Harriet Whitehead, eds. *Sexual Meanings: The Cultural Construction of Gender and Sexuality.* Cambridge: Cambridge University Press, 1981.

Paredes, Américo. "Folklore e historia. Dos cantares de la frontera del norte." In *25 estudios de folklore: Homenaje a Vicente T. Mendoza y Virginia Rodríguez Rivera,* ed. Fernando Anaya Montoya and Luz Gorráez Arcaute, pp. 209–222. Mexico City: Universidad Nacional Autónoma de México, 1971.

———. "José Mosqueda and the Folklorization of Actual Events." *Aztlán* 4, 1 (1973), pp. 1–30.

———. *"With His Pistol in His Hand": A Border Ballad and Its Hero.* Austin: University of Texas Press, 1958.

Pentikäinen, Juha. "Belief, Memorate and Legend," trans. J. Lombardo and W. K. McNeil. *Folklore Forum* 6 (1973), pp. 217–241.

Pescatello, Ann, ed. *Female and Male in Latin America.* Pittsburgh: University of Pittsburgh Press, 1972.

Pessar, Patricia. "Unmasking the Politics of Religion: The Case of Brazilian Millenarianism." *Journal of Latin American Lore* 7 (1981), pp. 255–278.

Petroff, Elizabeth. *Consolation of the Blessed.* New York: Alta Gaia Society, 1979.

Petry, Leopoldo. *O episódio do Ferrabrás (os Mucker).* Rio Grande do Sul: Editora Rotermund, 1957.

Petzoldt, Leander, ed. *Vergleichende Sagenforschung.* Darmstadt: Wissenschaftliche Buchgesellschaft, 1969.

Pimentel, J. Soares. *Os Milagres do Joazeiro ou Grande Colecção de documentos que attestam a veracidade da transformação da Sagrada Hóstia em sangue.* Caicó, Rio Grande do Norte: n.p., 1982.

Pinheiro, Irineu. *Efemérides do Cariri.* Fortaleza: Imprensa Universitária do Ceará, 1963.

———. *O Joaseiro do Padre Cícero e a Revolução de 1914.* Rio de Janeiro: Irmãos Pongetti Editores, 1938.

Plaskow, Judith, and Joan Arnold Romero, eds. *Women and Religion.* Rev. ed. Chambersburg, Pa.: American Academy of Religion, dist. Scholar's Press: Missoula, Mont., 1974.

Plummer, Charles. *Miscellanea hagiographica hibernica.* Subsidia Hagiographica 15. Brussels: Société des Bollandistes, 1925.

Poppino, Rollie E. *Brazil: The Land and the People.* 2nd ed. New York: Oxford University Press, 1973.

Porter, Dorothy B. *Afro-Braziliana: A Working Bibliography.* Boston: G. K. Hall, 1978.

Powell, John Duncan. "Peasant Society and Clientelist Politics." *American Political Science Review* 64 (1970), pp. 411–425.

Preston, Dennis. "Mowr Bayud Spellin': A Reply to Fine." *Journal of American Folklore* 96 (1983), pp. 330–339.

Queiroz, Maria Isaura Pereira de. *A dança de São Gonçalo num povoado bahiano.* Salvador: Livraria Progresso, 1958.

———. *La guerre sainte au Brésil: Le mouvement messianique du "Contestado."* São Paulo: Faculdade de Filosofia, Ciências e Letras da Universidade de São Paulo, 1957.

―――. "Messiahs in Brazil." *Past and Present* 31 (1965), pp. 62–86.

―――. *O messianismo no Brasil e no mundo.* São Paulo: Dominus/Editora da Universidade de São Paulo, 1965.

Queiroz, Maurício Vinhas de. *Messianismo e conflito social.* Rio de Janeiro: Editora Civilização Brasileira, 1966.

Rego, José Lins do. *Pedra Bonita.* 7th ed. Coleção Sagarana, 53. Rio de Janeiro: José Olympio, 1968.

Ribeiro, René. "Brazilian Messianic Movements." In *Millennial Dreams in Action,* ed. Sylvia L. Thrupp, pp. 55–79. The Hague: Mouton, 1962.

―――. "O episódio da Serra do Rodeador (1817–1820): Um movimento milenar e sebastianista." *Revista de Antropologia* 8, 2 (1960), pp. 133–144.

Robe, Stanley. *Mexican Tales and Legends from Los Altos.* Folklore Studies 20. Berkeley and Los Angeles: University of California Press, 1970.

Robinson, John A. "Personal Narratives Reconsidered." *Journal of American Folklore* 94 (1981), pp. 58–85.

Rohrich, Lutz. *Sage und Märchen: Erzählforschung heute.* Freiburg: Herder, 1976.

Romano V., Octavio Ignacio. "Charismatic Medicine, Folk-Healing, and Folk-Sainthood." *American Anthropologist* 67 (1965), pp. 1151–1173.

Romão, Antonio Batista. "A Igreja Brasileira canonizou em Brasília o Padre Cícero Romão." Rpt. in Paulo Machado, *O Padre Cícero e a literatura de cordel: Fenomenologia da devoção ao Padre Cícero,* pp. 38–41. Juazeiro: Editora Mascote, 1982.

Romero, Tristão. *Vida completa do Padre Cícero Romão Batista (Anchieta do século XX).* Juazeiro do Norte: n.p., 1950.

Rosa, João Guimarães. *Grande sertão: Veredas,* 10th ed. Rio de Janeiro: José Olympio, 1976. (Trans. into English as *The Devil to Pay in the Backlands* by James L. Taylor and Harriet de Onís. New York: Knopf, 1963.)

Rosaldo, Michelle, and Louise Lamphere, eds. *Women, Culture, and Society.* Stanford: Stanford University Press, 1974.

Rosenfeld, Helmut. *Legende.* Stuttgart: J. B. Metzlersche Verlagsbuchhandlung, 1961.

Saenz García, Clemente. "Una excursión bibliográfica: El ángel de Cascajar (leyenda soriana)." *Celtiberia* 19, 37 (1969), pp. 7–43.

Sanchis, Pierre. *Arraial: A festa de um povo.* Lisbon: Dom Quixote, 1983.

―――. "Arraial—la fête d'un peuple. (Les pèlerinages populaires au Portugal)." Diss., Ecole des Hautes Etudes en Sciences Sociales, Paris, 1976.

―――. "Festa e religião popular: As romarias de Portugal." *Revista de Cultura Vozes* 73 (1979), pp. 245–258.

Sanday, Peggy Reeves. *Female Power and Male Dominance.* Cambridge: Cambridge University Press, 1981.

Schaden, Egon. *A mitologia heróica de tribos indígenas do Brasil.* Rio de Janeiro: Ministério de Educação e Cultura, 1959.

Schiffrin, Deborah. "Tense Variation in Narrative." *Language* 57 (1981), pp. 45–62.

Schmitt, Jean-Claude. *Le saint lévrier: Guinefort, guérisseur d'enfants depuis le XIIIᵉ siècle*. Paris: Flammarion, 1979.

Schupp, Ambrósio. *Os Muckers*. Rio Grande do Sul: Selbach and Mayer, n.d.

Scott, James C. "The Erosion of Patron-Client Bonds and Social Change in Rural Southeast Asia." *Journal of Asian Studies* 32 (1972), pp. 5–37.

———. "Patron-Client Politics and Political Change in Southeast Asia." *American Political Science Review* 66 (1972), pp. 91–113.

Shuttle, Penelope, and Peter Redgrove. *The Wise Wound: Eve's Curse and Everywoman*. New York: Richard Marek, 1978.

Siegel, Bernard. "The Contestado Rebellion, 1912–1916: A Case Study in Brazilian Messianism and Regional Dynamics." *Journal of Anthropological Research* 33, 2 (1977), pp. 202–213.

Silva, Antenor de Andrade. *Os arquivos do Padre Cícero*. Juazeiro do Norte: n.p., 1977.

Silva, José Bernardo da. *Santa Cruz do Deserto, Beato José Lourenço*. Juazeiro do Norte: Tipografia São Francisco, 1935.

Silveira, Ildefonso. "Estado atual da pesquisa sobre o Padre Cícero." *Revista Eclesiástica Brasileira* 36 (1976), pp. 226–260.

Slater, Candace. "Joe Bumpkin in the Wilds of Rio de Janeiro." *Journal of Latin American Lore* 6 (1980), pp. 5–53.

———. "Oral and Written Pilgrim Tales from Northeast Brazil." *Journal of Latin American Lore* 9 (1983), pp. 191–230.

———. *Stories on a String: The Brazilian "Literatura de Cordel."* Berkeley and Los Angeles: University of California Press, 1982.

Smith, Hilary Dansey. *Preaching in the Spanish Golden Age*. Oxford: Oxford University Press, 1978.

Sobreira, Azarias. "Floro Bartolomeu." *Revista do Instituto do Ceará* 64 (1950), pp. 193–202.

———. *O patriarca do Juazeiro*. 2nd ed. Juazeiro do Norte: n.p., 1969.

Souza, Amaury de. "The Cangaço and the Politics of Violence in Northeast Brazil." In *Protest and Resistance in Angola and Brazil: Comparative Studies*, ed. Ronald H. Chilcote, pp. 109–131. Berkeley and Los Angeles: University of California Press, 1972.

Stahl, Sandra K. D. "The Oral Personal Narrative in Its Generic Context." *Fabula* 18, 1–2 (1977).

Stanula, Ceslau. "Um lugar de romaria." *A Vida* 8, 47 (1981), pp. 13–17.

Suassuna, Ariano. *A pedra do reino*. 2nd ed. Rio de Janeiro: José Olympio, 1972.

Sumption, Jonathan. *Pilgrimage: An Image of Mediaeval Religion*. London: Faber and Faber, 1975.

Sydow, Carl Wilhelm von. "Kategorien der Prosa-Volksdichtung." *Selected Papers on Folklore*, pp. 60–88. Copenhagen: Ed. L. Bødker, 1948.

Szmrecsányi, Tamás, and Oriowaldo Queda, eds. *Vida rural e mudança*. 3rd ed. São Paulo: Cia. Editora Nacional, 1979.

Taussig, Michael T. *The Devil and Commodity Fetishism in South America*. Chapel Hill: University of North Carolina Press, 1980.

Tavard, George. *Women in Christian Tradition*. Notre Dame: University of Notre Dame Press, 1973.

Teófilo, Rodolfo. *A Sedição do Joazeiro*. São Paulo: n.p., 1922.

Thompson, Stith. *Motif-Index of Folk Literature: A Classification of Narrative Elements in Folk-tales, Ballads, Myths, Fables, Medieval Romances, Exempla, Fabliaux, Jest-books, and Local Legends*. Rev. ed. 6 vols. Bloomington: Indiana University Press, 1955–58.

Thornton, (S.) Mary Crescentia. *The Church and Freemasonry in Brazil, 1872–1875*. Washington, D.C.: Catholic University of America Press, 1948.

Tiede, David Lenz. *The Charismatic Figure as Miracle Worker*. Dissertation Series 1. Missoula, Mont.: Society of Biblical Literature for the Seminar on the Gospels, 1973.

Tillhagen, Carl-Herman. "Was ist eine Sage? Eine Definition und ein Vorschlag für ein europäisches Sagensystem." *Acta Ethnographica* 13 (1964), pp. 9–17.

Titon, Jeff Todd. "The Life Story." *Journal of American Folklore* 93 (1980), pp. 276–292.

"A Tortura da Seca." *Veja* 780 (August 17, 1983), pp. 56–66.

Trancoso, Gonçalo Fernandes. *Contos e histórias de proveito e exemplo*. Paris: Aillaud et Bertrand, 1921.

Tubach, Frederic C. *Index Exemplorum: A Handbook of Medieval Religious Tales*. Folklore Fellows Communications 204. Helsinki: Suomalainen Tiedakatemia, 1969.

———. "Strukturanalytische Probleme: Das mittelalterliche Exemplum." *Hessiche Blätter für Volkskunde* 59 (1958), pp. 25–29.

Turner, Victor, and Edith Turner. *Image and Pilgrimage in Christian Culture*. New York: Columbia University Press, 1978.

Uspenskiĭ, Boris. *A Poetics of Composition*, trans. Valentina Zavarin and Susan Witting. Berkeley and Los Angeles: University of California Press, 1973.

Vansina, Jan. "Memory and Oral Tradition." In *The African Past Speaks*, ed. Joseph C. Miller, pp. 262–279. Folkestone: Wm. Dawson and Sons, 1980.

———. *Oral Tradition: A Study in Historical Methodology*, trans. H. M. Wright. Chicago: Aldine, 1965.

"Volta por cima." *Veja* 636 (November 12, 1980), p. 71.

Voragine, Jacobus de. *The Golden Legend*, trans. Granger Ryan and Helmut Ripperger. New York: Longmans, Green, 1969.

Wallace, Anthony F. C. "Revitalization Movements." *American Anthropologist* 58 (1956), pp. 264–281.

Ward, Benedicta. *Miracles and the Medieval Mind: Theory, Record and Event, 1000–1215*. Philadelphia: University of Pennsylvania Press, 1982.

Ward, Teresinha Souto. *O discurso oral em "Grande sertão: Veredas."* São Paulo and Brasília: Livraria Duas Cidades/Instituto Nacional do Livro, Fundação Nacional Pró-Memória, 1984.

Webb, Kempton E. *The Changing Face of Northeast Brazil.* New York: Columbia University Press, 1974.

Welter, J. Th. *L'exemplum dans la littérature religieuse et didactique du Moyen Age.* Paris: Occitania, 1927.

Wilson, Bryan. *Magic and the Millennium.* New York: Harper and Row, 1973.

Wilson, Stephen, ed. *Saints and Their Cults: Studies in Religious Sociology, Folklore and History.* Cambridge: Cambridge University Press, 1983.

Wolf, Eric R. "Kinship, Friendship and Patron-Client Relationships in Complex Societies." In *The Social Anthropology of Complex Societies,* ed. Michael Banton. pp. 1–22. London: Tavistock, 1966.

Wolfson, Nessa. "A Feature of Performed Narrative: The Conversational Historical Present." *Language in Society* 7 (1978), pp. 215–237.

Wood, Charles T. "The Doctor's Dilemma: Sin, Salvation and the Menstrual Cycle in Medieval Thought." *Speculum* 56 (1981), pp. 710–727.

Worsley, Peter. *The Trumpet Shall Sound.* London: MacGibbon and Kee, 1957.

Xidieh, Osvaldo Elias. *Narrativas pias populares.* São Paulo: Instituto de Estudos Brasileiros, 1967.

General Index

Index of Story Texts (English)

Titles used for stories in this volume are informal and are based on the words of the tellers. Thus the stories are listed here by number, rather than alphabetically, in order of their appearance in the text. Additional listings for the same story are given in parentheses. (Portuguese originals may be found in Appendix B, 241–262.)

1. A pilgrimage leader on the purpose of the trips, 64
2. A man's decision to make a pilgrimage, 79–80
3. Criticism of a young girl offset by awareness of Padre Cícero's disapproval, 80
4. A young man's sudden realization of the worth of an old woman, 81
5. Padre Cícero's birth, 88–89 (143–144)
6. The hat that stuck to the wall, 89 (144–145)
7. The would-be assassin, 89–90
8. The rancher who asked for rain, 90–91 (122)
9. The transformation of the host, 91 (197, 198, 199)
10. Padre Cícero opens a church door in Rome, 91–92 (124)
11. Padre Cícero makes a mute boy speak, 92
12. The girl who turned into a dog, 92–93
13. Padre Cícero's protection of Juazeiro, 93 (156–157, 162)
14. Padre Cícero stops a war in Germany, 93–94
15. Padre Cícero rescues a child from drowning, 94
16. The hunter's first catch, 95–96
17. Padre Cícero and Doctor Floro in conflict, 96 (184)
18. The girl eaten by a mountain lion, 96–97 (138, introduction)
19. The empty tomb, 97 (121)
20. The enchanted grove, 97–98
21. Manuel Germano, 98 (120)
22. Padre Monteiro, 98–99
23. The man from São Pedro, 99
24. Manuel Correia, 99–100
25. The man who exchanged his rosary, 100
26. The man who ate the guinea pig, 100–101
27. Padre Cícero gives a pilgrim a penny, 101
28. Padre Cícero resuscitates a pilgrim's donkey, 102
29. Padre Cícero feeds a hen and its chicks, 102–103
30. Manuel Germano, 120 (98)

Designer:	Laurie Anderson
Compositor:	Graphic Composition, Inc.
Text:	10/12 Bembo
Display:	Albertus Roman
Printer:	Braun-Brumfield, Inc.
Binder:	Braun-Brumfield, Inc.